AMERICA'S FAMILY SUPPORT PROGRAMS

AMERICA'S FAMILY SUPPORT PROGRAMS

PERSPECTIVES AND PROSPECTS

Edited by
Sharon L. Kagan
Douglas R. Powell
Bernice Weissbourd
Edward F. Zigler

Yale University Press
New Haven and London

Designed by Nancy Ovedovitz and set in Baskerville type by Eastern Graphics. Printed in the United States of America by Murray Printing Company, Westford, Mass.

Library of Congress Cataloging-in-Publication Data

America's family support programs.
  Bibliography: p.
  Includes index.
  1. Family social work—United States.
2. Family policy—United States. I. Kagan,
Sharon Lynn. II. Title.
HV699.A63   1987   362.8′28′0973   87-8305
ISBN 0-300-03857-7 (cloth)
ISBN 0-300-05785-7 (pbk.)

A catalogue record for this book is available from the British Library.

The paper in this book meets the guidelines for permanence and durability of the Committee on Production Guidelines for Book Longevity of the Council on Library Resources.

10 9 8 7 6 5 4 3 2

To Irving B. Harris
whose vision and generosity
gave the family support movement its impetus
and
To Our Families
whose love and support
gave us the opportunity to write of its growth

CONTENTS

FOREWORD
FAMILY SUPPORT:
THE QUIET REVOLUTION

Urie Bronfenbrenner

The publication of this volume marks the first substantial recognition of a major contemporary grassroots movement in the United States—the emergence of locally based, informal systems of support for families and family members. It is noteworthy that, despite the subject's scope and significance, no systematic study has as yet been conducted of the origins and course of this still ongoing social change. One can with some confidence, however, identify a number of factors that have contributed to its development.

In general, the growth of informal family supports represents a response to the changing conditions of life for American families and their children. Although occurring in other modern nations as well, in the United States these changes have taken place at an exceptionally rapid rate and have included special features not present in other so-called post-industrial societies (Bronfenbrenner 1984, 1985). For example, in addition to mounting rates of maternal employment and divorce, the United States has experienced an extraordinary increase in teenage pregnancy and, especially since 1980, in the poverty rate for families with young children. Thus, over this period, the proportion of the nation's children under six years of age living in families below the poverty line rose from one-fifth to one-fourth. At the same time, federal funding for family programs has been sharply reduced, shifting the weight of social responsibility primarily to the state and local level.

Concurrent with, and in part contributing to, these demographic, socioeconomic, and political changes has been a growing disillusion-

I wish to express my appreciation and gratitude to Alexandra Shelley for the editor's art at its best—improving not just the technicalities but the thoughts.

ment—among both professionals and the general public—with the social-welfare policies introduced and expanded on a massive scale during the 1960s and 1970s. These policies and the programs in which they were embodied were the products of an era of optimism in society and in social science. President Johnson's promise of an early victory in a massive "war against poverty" evoked broadly supportive responses not only from the general public but also from the scientific consultants who were called in to help plan the winning strategy. Their enthusiasm and the programs they designed drew heavily on a new line of investigation, based mainly on laboratory studies of animals and demonstrating the power of a stimulating environment in releasing the capacity of living organisms to contribute actively to their own development (Hunt, 1961). It was found, for example, that enriching the perceptual environment of rats, dogs, or monkeys increased their exploratory behavior, which, in turn, led to improved ability in problem-solving. These "hard science" findings from laboratory experiments brought new legitimacy to earlier field studies demonstrating the effects of environmental enrichment on children from deprived backgrounds (Kirk, 1958; Skeels & Dye, 1939; Skeels, Updegraff, Wellman, & Williams, 1938) and stimulated a new wave of research on what came to be called early intervention (Bronfenbrenner, 1974a).

In the social and political climate of the 1960s and 1970s, this more optimistic view of both organism and environment was so rapidly and widely adopted by policymakers and practitioners that practice soon outdistanced the scientific knowledge on which it was presumably based. With some noticeable—but, until recently, unnoticed—exceptions (for example, Head Start), the results of new programs failed to meet the original expectations. Overall, the problems in cognitive and social development experienced by children of families living under stressful conditions did not appear to be abating. Instead, the number of such families was increasing as a function of worsening economic and social conditions. The consequent escalation in program costs coincided with, and clearly contributed to, a changing political and public mood. The turning point came after Reagan's election in 1980, when the existing federal policies and programs serving families in need became prime targets for severe fiscal cutbacks and administrative dismantling.

It is in this economic and political climate that informal, locally based programs of family support began to burgeon. And once again, the basic concepts underlying the programs and some of the programs themselves had their (typically unrecognized) origins in slower paced advances in developmental research. In the 1970s, when investigators began to transplant their careful methods of observation and inquiry from the laboratory into real-life settings (Bronfenbrenner, 1974b), they began to discover that the forces operating in the latter environments were both more complex and, in certain respects, more powerful than had previously been suspected.

These discoveries were of two kinds.[1] The first had to do with the operation of families as systems involving interdependent relationships between family members. For example, the new investigations revealed that fathers were no less important for the development of children than were mothers. Moreover, the father's importance lay not only in his direct effect on the child but also in his indirect influence through his effect on the mother-child relationship. A similar pattern was observed with respect to the impact of the mother on the father's relationships with his children. I have referred to this phenomenon as the "third-party principle" (Bronfenbrenner, 1984).

In addition, study after study suggested that the quality of the marital relationships was a major factor in determining the capacity of either spouse to function effectively in a parental role. Findings of this kind were soon translated into practice as both individual professionals and the agencies in which they worked began to shift from "client-centered" to "family centered" approaches.

Finally, at a broader level, the new research yielded a general pattern of findings indicating that the family, to a greater extent than any other context, influenced the capacity of individuals at all ages to learn and to succeed in other settings—in preschool and school, in the peer group, in higher education, and in the workplace, the community, and the nation as a whole.

A second set of findings was perhaps even more significant in terms of its implications for both theory and practice. As investigators expanded their research designs to incorporate more and broader segments of the environment, their studies revealed that, along with impressive strengths, families also had some vulnerabilities. To a greater degree than had previously been recognized, the viability of family processes, including successful child rearing, could be markedly affected by conditions and events taking place in the other main contexts of life mentioned above. One of the most powerful of these external forces represented an extension of the "third party principle" first observed operating within the family: namely, the capacity of families to function effectively, particularly under stress, depended to a significant degree on the availability and provision of social support from persons outside the immediate family, such as kin, friends, neighbors, and co-workers.

Practitioners in the field have been quick to recognize the implications of such research findings for policy and action. Moreover, as the chapters in this volume testify, they have done so with considerable imagination and energy. Local initiatives, building on local resources, have

arisen in all sections of the country and have forged new linkages between families and other community institutions, notably schools, social
agencies, neighborhood organizations, business and industry, and units
of local government. This array also reflects another new departure in
American family programs—some joint funding and even joint planning by the public and private sectors, albeit only at the local level.

But along with offering innovation and hope, the chapters in this
book sound some sobering notes. Compared with essays on similar topics written two decades ago, today's pieces are more guarded in their optimism, and with good reason. Whereas the new policies introduced in
the 1960s had broad public support, in the 1980s there are strong divi-
sions of opinion. The proponents of community-oriented family support systems, while active and energetic, are still a minority. The majority of the public, perhaps taking the cue from national policy, have
become increasingly apathetic with regard to the needs of the poor. As a
result, even the far more modest funding requirements of the newly
emerging strategies are achievable only with great effort. Moreover, the
outstanding commitment of the "pro-family-support" minority is often
matched, if not surpassed, by the dedication of other, opposing minorities, such as the pro-life and pro-family movements, which condemn
their opponents' ideas and programs for "secular humanism."

The guarded optimism found in this volume also has a scientific basis,
for research on development in context has identified unsuspected debilitating power of even greater magnitude in certain broader environmental forces affecting families and family members. Chief among these
is poverty, with its destructive effects on family functioning and,
thereby, on the development of children. For example, Elder, after his
first report on *Children of the Great Depression* more than a decade ago
(1974), has found in a series of follow-up studies of his original sample
that the consequences of parental unemployment during the economic
collapse of the 1930s can be detected in adult and child behavior, now
across four generations (Elder, Caspi, & Downey, 1986; Elder, Caspi,
& van Nguyen, 1986). The authors' analyses reveal that loss of income
through the father's unemployment increased the likelihood of family
conflict, with resulting ill effects on the development of the children,
who were then more likely to become difficult personalities as adults.
This characteristic, in turn, increased the risk of conflict in their own
marriages, thus perpetuating the vicious cycle into the next generation.

The relevance of such findings for the contemporary scene is indicated in recent studies of the short-term effects of parental unemployment in the 1980s. For example, a thirty-month study of 8,000 unemployed families in California (Steinberg, Catalano, and Dooley, 1981)
revealed that increases in child abuse are preceded by periods of high

job loss, thus confirming the authors' hypothesis that "undesirable economic change leads to increased child maltreatment" (p. 975).

A longitudinal study conducted in Finland highlighted a second disruptive influence on human development in modern societies. Pulkkinen (1982) examined the effect of environmental stability and change on psychological development from 8 through 20 years of age. Specifically, the "steadiness"/"unsteadiness" of family living conditions was measured by such factors as the number of family moves, changes in day-care or school arrangements, frequency and duration of parental absences, and altered conditions of parental employment. Greater instability of the family environment was associated with greater insecurity in later childhood, with a higher incidence of such behaviors as extremes of submissiveness or aggression, early sexual activity, excessive smoking and drinking, and delinquency in adolescence and youth, a pattern similar to that reported by both Jessor (1986) and Kandel (1986) for the United States. In Pulkkinen's research, the effect of environmental stability was appreciably stronger than that of social class. The latter finding may not hold for this country, however, since the effects of social class appear to be stronger in the United States than in other modern, postindustrial nations, perhaps because of the lesser availability of either formal or informal family-support systems in this society compared to all other technologically advanced nations (Bronfenbrenner, 1984, 1985).

The relevance of such findings for programs that rely on the creation and strengthening of social support systems for families under stress is indicated by Crockenberg's finding that, for mothers living under highly stressful environmental conditions, social networks not only cease to exert a positive influence but became a source of stress (Crockenberg, 1985). A similar result is reported in a recent paper by Riley and Eckenrode (1986). In a study of stresses and supports in mothers' lives, the investigators found that the influence of social networks on psychological well-being shifted from positive to negative as a function of three kinds of factors: (1) reduced socioeconomic status; (2) the occurrence of misfortune in the lives of significant others (for example, a close relative suffers an accident); and (3) low levels of belief either in one's capacity to influence one's own life (so-called locus of control) or in the probable success of one's own help-seeking efforts.

Finally, another and equally powerful factor plays a significant role in this regard. There are indications from more general studies of socialization processes (summarized in Bronfenbrenner, 1983, 1986a, 1986b), as well as from materials presented in this volume, that, especially in periods of rapid social change, the provision of family support systems may not be sufficient to activate constructive behavior and development. Structures of opportunity and challenge that encourage, and even insist upon, standards of effective performance may also be needed. The task is to create and strengthen formal systems of challenge and support that will, in turn, create and strengthen *informal* systems that can grow beyond their formal roots.

It is the special strength of this volume that, in presenting family support systems as promising strategies for American society, it does not dodge the difficulties that such strategies must confront. The picture is one of guarded optimism, but optimism nevertheless.

NOTE

1. For a more detailed account of research findings summarized in this chapter, see Bronfenbrenner, 1986a/1986b, and Bronfenbrenner & Crouter, 1983.

REFERENCES

Bronfenbrenner, U. (1974a). *Is early intervention effective? A report on longitudinal evaluations of preschool programs* (Vol. 2). Washington, DC: Department of Health, Education and Welfare, Office of Child Development.

Bronfenbrenner, U. (1974b). Developmental research, public policy, and the ecology of childhood. *Child Development, 45*, 1–5.

Bronfenbrenner, U. (1984, September). Families and education in the U.S. and other countries. *Innovator, 16* 1, 3–6(1) Ann Arbor, MI: University of Michigan School of Education.

Bronfenbrenner, U. (1985). The three worlds of childhood. *Principal, 64* (5), 6–11.

Bronfenbrenner, U. (1986a). The ecology of the family as a context for human development. *Developmental Psychology, 22* (6), 723–742.

Bronfenbrenner, U. (1986b). Recent advances in research on the ecology of human development. In R. K. Silbereisen, K. Eyferth, & G. Rudinger (Eds.), *Development as action in context: Problem behavior and normal youth development* (pp. 287–309). Heidelberg & New York: Springer-Verlag.

Bronfenbrenner, U., & Crouter, A. C. (1983). The evolution of environmental models in developmental research. In W. Kessen (Ed.), *History, theories, and methods* (pp. 358–414), Volume 1 of P. H. Mussen (Ed.), *Handbook of child psychology* (4th ed.). New York: Wiley.

Crockenberg, S. B. (1985). Professional support and care of infants by adolescent mothers in England and the United States. *Journal of Pediatric Psychology, 10*, 413–428.

Elder, G. H., Jr. (1974). *Children of the Great Depression*. Chicago: University of Chicago Press.

Elder, G. H., Jr., Caspi, A., & Downey, G. (1986). Problem behavior and family relationships: A multigenerational analysis. In A. Sorensen, F. Weinert, & L. Sherrod (Eds.), *Human development: Interdisciplinary perspectives* (pp. 293–340). Hillsdale, NJ: Erlbaum.

Elder, G. H., Jr., Caspi, A., & van Nguyen, T. (1986). Resourceful and vulnerable children: Family influences in stressful times. In R. K. Silbereisen & K. Eyferth (Eds.), *Development in context: Integrative perspectives on youth development*. New York: Springer.

Hunt, J. M. (1961). *Intelligence and experience*. New York: Ronald Press.

Jessor, R. (1986). The stability of change: Psychosocial development from adolescence to young adulthood. In D. Magnusson & V. Allen (Eds.), *Human development: An interactional perspective* (pp. 321–341). New York: Academic Press.

Kandel, D. B. (1986). On processes of peer influence in adolescence. In R. K. Silbereisen, K. Eyferth, & G. Rudinger (Eds.), *Development as action in context: Problem behavior and normal youth development* (pp. 203–228). Heidelberg & New York: Springer-Verlag.

Kirk, S. A. (1958). *Early education of the mentally retarded*. Urbana: University of Illinois Press.

Pulkkinen, L. (1982). Self-control and continuity from childhood to late adolescence. In P. Baltes & O. Brim (Eds.), *Life-span development and behavior* (Vol. IV) (pp. 64–102). New York: Academic Press.

Riley, D., & Eckenrode, J. (1986). Social ties, costs, and benefits within differing subgroups. *Journal of Personality and Social Psychology, 51*, 770–778.

Skeels, H. M., & Dye, H. B. (1939). A study of the effects of differential stimulation on mentally retarded children. *Proceedings and Addresses of the American Association on Mental Deficiency, 11*, 114–136.

Skeels, H. M., Updegraff, R., Wellmann, B. L., & Williams, H. M. A study of environmental stimulation: An orphanage preschool project. *University of Iowa Studies in child welfare, 15*, No. 4.

Steinberg, L., Catalano, R., & Dooley, D. (1981). Economic antecedents of child abuse and neglect. *Child Development, 52*, 975–985.

ACKNOWLEDGMENTS

We would like to acknowledge The Bush Foundation, whose financial support made this book possible. We express our gratitude to Alexandra Shelley for her expert and tireless editing of the manuscript and to Gwen Mood, Leslie Branden, and Barbara Emmel for their assistance in its preparation. We also acknowledge the support of our editor, Gladys Topkis.

We would like to thank Heather Weiss for her work in conceptualizing the volume and in developing the family support program typology.

PART I/INTRODUCTION

1 THE PROMISE AND PROBLEMS OF FAMILY SUPPORT PROGRAMS

Sharon L. Kagan and
Alexandra Shelley

Family support programs are as yet an undefined phenomenon. Although thousands of such efforts have grown up across the country in the past fifteen years, we are only beginning to enumerate their characteristics, assess their impact, pinpoint their place in the social service structure, and understand the deeper trends they reflect. Indeed, the authors of this volume are among the first to imply that seemingly disparate programs can be amassed under one rubric—that a parent cooperative day-care center, a comprehensive educational and health program for teenage mothers, a national information clearinghouse for parents of handicapped children, and a children's museum space where parents can mingle and talk to staff members about child development all constitute "family support."

The purpose of this volume is to examine the growth and collective impact of these diverse efforts. It addresses the origins of such programs: What are family support programs? Where did they come from? How are they different from historical efforts to support families? It explores practical issues: How are the programs planned, organized, staffed, funded, and evaluated? Finally, the volume attempts to predict the impact these efforts will have on the structure of bureaucratic social services, the evaluation of preventive programs, and the nature of American social policies for children and families.

Yet this volume may raise more questions than it answers as it considers programs that are novel, diverse, and interdisciplinary in nature. In many ways, the chapters should be considered works in progress. They represent the best thinking of scholars, evaluators, practitioners, and policymakers who have contributed to the book—but are by no means the last word. The volume explores the phenomenon of family support with all its promise, all its problems.

This introductory chapter provides a conceptual and an organizational guide to the book. It introduces the key issues and principles that underpin family support programs and discusses characteristics therein. In doing so, this chapter seeks to define the meaning of the broadly used term "family support programs." It presents ideas about each of the key words—family, support, and programs—distinguishing what each is and what changes there have been in each over time. With these issues in mind, the chapter concludes with an overview of the organization of the volume and brief chapter synopses.

THE NATURE OF THE FAMILY: THEN AS NOW?

The 1980s have been a troubled time for the American family. Caught in the midst of a social revolution, we witness fundamental changes in its structure and function, in ideas about what it is and what it should be. Demographics tell us that the norm of the two-parent, two-child family has all but been swept away by the surge of single-parent, single-child, remarried, and two-worker families. Yet amid this social change, there is a growing call for a return to the "traditional" family structure, with its traditional roles. Our reality, then, is a fragmented one, characterized by a diversity of beliefs about what family structure is and what it should be. Debate also brews regarding the function of the American family. Is the family an inviolable unit responsible for socializing youth to accepted norms? Or is the family a vehicle for social reform?

The debate is not new. Throughout American history, there have been multipronged definitions of family structure and functioning, reflecting both actual demographics and idealized visions of what the family represents to our society. Traditionally, though, Americans have more easily accepted variety in family structure than we have accepted variety in family function. In essence, the family has almost been an ideological tabula rasa throughout our history on which each age writes anew its expectations of family structure and dynamics, but with little actual change tolerated in its underlying, basic function. Individually and collectively, we fortify the concept of the family, at a minimum, as nurturer and protector of the next generation. We provide services to children and their families partly so that the next generation will "redeem our own personal disappointments and will thus help realize our collective vision of a more just society" (Keniston et al., p. 42).

Kenneth Keniston and the Carnegie Council on Children (1977) confirm this social function of the family in their discussion of late nine-teenth-century Americans. Thus, when our predecessors noticed the extremes of wealth and poverty that seemed to belie their "ideal of equality," rather than "strengthening" families by forcing them to con-form to an ideal, the early Americans "postponed it" for the next gener-ation by constructing a free public school system to foster equal opportu-nity. In the social action programs of the 1960s, and in today's family support programs, we, too, idealistically put our hopes in children as the "repositories of the dream."

Yet when policies aim to strengthen families by making them conform structurally to an idealized vision of the family, the policies do not take root. What makes the recent family support efforts unique is their incor-poration of this ideological tabula rasa with a realistic acknowledgment of diversity in family structure. With no single structural model of the family except its well-functioning in society, support programs are ac-cepting of varying life styles and values. In settings that are value neu-tral, families are encouraged to set their own goals and carry them out. Thus a first part of a definition of family support is that it seeks to em-power the family as its own unit, responsive both to its own functioning as well as to that of the larger community in which it exists. In this sense, authors in this volume suggest that family support today is innovative and its programs are a distinct product of the late twentieth century in that they respond to flaws in the traditional social service system (the at-tempt to structure families according to a norm) while recognizing that contemporary families need support (the attempt to help families func-tion, no matter what their structure).

The emergence of these unique family support efforts at this time may suggest that families in the 1980s are faced with stresses unique to contemporary society. But just which of these stresses is really unique to the 1980s? Moroney (chap. 2) poses the question broadly: "But has the family become *more* stressed in the modern era?" Warning us to avoid in answer to this question "the world we have lost syndrome," he suggests that a reasonable case can be made that the family continually trades old stressors for new stressors as social conditions change.

For example, many observers suggest that high mobility is one social condition that helped spur the development of family support efforts. Weissbourd (chap. 3) points out that "families don't stay in one place long enough to develop the intricate neighborhood and community con-nections that were once the mainstay of mutual support." A related fact is that young families spend much time isolated from other family mem-bers and from familiar friends. Therefore, practical parenting skills and support by extended family members are not always around the corner. Yet, the belief that these stressors are uniquely endemic to modern society is refuted by some analysts who cite historical studies indicating that frequent family moves to new regions have always been the norm and that having grandparents, aunts, and uncles under one roof has long been the exception to the rule (Keniston et al., 1977).

A second common perception is that today's families are less able to care for dependent members or to maintain their own economic integrity. One interpretation is that the welfare state hastened this instability and dependency. However, Moroney (chap. 2) points out that as early as the mid-nineteenth century, laws had to be established to ensure that families cared for their infirm. Such observations suggest that the notion of a past society made up of buoyant extended families and mutually supportive communities may say more about what we long for today than about what actually existed in American history. They also suggest that ambiguity about the appropriate role of government in family life persists (Grubb & Lazerson, 1982).

Yet it would be erroneous to conclude that then equals now, for there are significant differences in the family and in society—differences that beg us to look beyond demographics to more subtle characteristics. For example, in the family unit, there are differences in the roles family members play and in the stresses they are challenged to endure. Today, change is likely to characterize the nature of family interactions. Belsky, Lerner, and Spanier (1984) suggest that family members will have to meet one another's needs better to "perform more adequately the familial function—emotional support—that has become dominant in recent decades" (p. 34).

Moving beyond the individual family, we see striking differences in poverty in the 1980s. Although poverty has always existed in our nation, it now afflicts more families and afflicts each more pervasively. More families with young children exist in poverty, and the likelihood of their escaping it seems distant, particularly in families headed by young single mothers. Further, in many "pockets," poverty that has long been present has intensified, placing tremendous burdens on already tenuous informal support systems.

In addition to the increased need for support among some populations, need itself has become more widespread. Family support practitioners and analysts note that in the 1980s *all* families face stresses with which they may need assistance. Garbarino (1982) points out that as society has stripped the family of its productive and educational responsibilities, the family has become the emotional and developmental center. These demands are new and often compounded by other responsibilities. Moreover, they touch a broader range of families, families from all ethnic backgrounds and economic strata, thus extending the types of support needed. This growing need leads us to ask: What is the nature of "support" and what might a definition of that word be if we put the emphasis on the support part of "family support programs"?

THE NATURE OF "SUPPORT": THEN AS NOW?

Just as families today continue to grapple with some of the same difficulties faced by their predecessors, many of the solutions adopted by today's family support programs have their analogues in historical methods and organizations. For instance, Weissbourd (chap. 3) convincingly traces the community service and advocacy characteristics of family support programs to the settlement houses established in the late nineteenth century, which were intended to improve the environment and living conditions of the community and to help people become better informed citizens. Zigler and Freedman (chap. 4) point out that more recently Head Start expanded the tradition by building community control and family support into its earliest design. Other antecedents of the current forms of support emerge from the self-help movement (Weissbourd, chap. 3, and Pizzo, chap. 12) and from parenting education (Weiss, chap. 8; Wandersman, chap. 11; and Powell, chap. 7).

By and large, what distinguishes family "support" from those efforts of the past relates to a 1980s perception of helping institutions and helping professions. Many authors in this volume note that such intimate and value-laden functions as child care and education were transferred in the late twentieth century from the family to institutions, thus diminishing family control and, some argue, family self-esteem. At the same time, scientific and other advances generated increased expectations about an acceptable quality of life, which in turn spawned more "specialists" and more dependency on extrafamilial institutions. Common sense was simply not enough; one needed "expert" advice. As institutions became more important in the social fabric of family life, they grew in size and scope, often becoming more bureaucratic and impersonal. Issues of turf arose among institutions, between clients and professionals, and between professionals and other members of the helping corps. Procedures, rules, and guidelines so proliferated that individuals often felt entwined in a bureaucratic web with which they felt neither comfortable nor conversant: "One of the most debilitating results of modernization is the feeling of powerlessness in the face of institutions controlled by those whom we do not know and whose values we often do not share" (Berger & Newhouse, 1977, p. 7). At times, "support" could hardly be so called, as its effect seemed to diminish family functioning rather than increase it.

By the end of World War II, many institutional reform movements had emerged, with some succeeding in changing institutions as bureaucratized as hospitals and public schools (Shonkoff, chap. 5; Kagan, chap. 9). This legacy of institutional reform is one important antecedent of today's family support efforts. Currently, family support efforts are directed at reforming existing policies and practices so that major institutions will improve family functioning by their support.

Thus the definition of family support gains another dimension as we examine what form support takes today and what actually works to make a family cohesive and whole. The chapters of this book reveal that support can involve a variety of approaches, with a diversity of goals, ranging from home visitation to peer support groups and from health care to parent education. In this context, support can be defined as those activities, either formalized through programs or occurring naturally in community interaction, that empower the individual to act for both his own good and the good of his immediate community.

Examples of support addressed in this volume include modifications of policies in institutions as diverse as schools (Kagan, chap. 9; Wiegerink & Comfort, chap. 10), social service agencies (Jenkins, chap. 15; Williams, chap. 16), child care agencies (Powell, chap. 7), corporations (Muenchow, chap. 14), and hospitals (Shonkoff, chap. 5). These modifications suggest the pervasiveness of family support efforts while simultaneously signaling that a new concept of support may be in the offing, one that is reforming institutional "business as usual." While current institutional modifications reflect the fundamental ideology and character of family support, they are less pervasive than the quasi-autonomous efforts, the programs, that have been designed, in many cases, as alternatives to institutions, to meet family needs. It is in these programs that the characteristics, richness, and diversity of today's family support efforts are most directly evidenced.

FAMILY SUPPORT PROGRAMS: WHAT'S IN A NAME?

Almost all the authors in this volume cite their interpretation of historical antecedents of family support efforts, including such movements as the settlement house, self-help, parenting education, grassroots advocacy, and broader social reforms, suggesting that the *species* is rather old. Yet, they also suggest that a new *breed* of effort is emerging, one that is conceptually and organizationally different from past efforts. To evolve an understanding of these programs—and to hazard predictions as to their continuing survival—we need to examine in what ways the programs resemble and differ from their predecessors.

At first blush, what seems to distinguish today's family support programs from efforts of the past is that while they acknowledge and cull lessons from their heritage, they incorporate more sophisticated conceptualizations of the family based on recent empirical evidence. Thus many of today's family support programs use an ecological approach and embody a belief in universal access. What these phrases mean conceptually, how they translate to program structure, and the dilemmas they pose for these programs are all worth considering.

Family support programs are at the vanguard of the movement away from conventional methods of working with either the child or the parent (generally the mother) separately. In his foreword to this book, Bronfenbrenner, whose work has informed much of today's thinking about the family in its context, enumerates the key research findings to which family support practitioners have responded. These include a recognition of the interdependence of family members, the influence of the family on the individual, the importance of social support from people outside the immediate family, and the powerful effect of wider environmental factors, such as poverty, on the family (Bronfenbrenner, 1979). Together these forces constitute the ecology of human development.

The most basic application of this broad view of development is to design programs involving first the entire family and second an entire community—programs that help family members to understand their role in family life, and that help set the stage for the negotiating and supporting that is so necessary among family members in both their family and community life. Taking the ecological approach a step beyond the family, a commonality of many family support programs is the incorporation of peer support. This entails providing situations in which families can share common concerns, either on an informal basis or in discussion groups with trained facilitators. Reflecting on her program's informality, one director characterized her drop-in center as "an indoor park bench."

While many programs may initially appeal to families because of the tangible services offered (such as job training or respite child care), the opportunity to meet and share with other families, and thus the larger community, is frequently cited as an enduring benefit. Zigler and Weiss (1985) suggest that in addition to allowing parents to realize that they are not alone in having certain problems, peer support provides opportunities for them to give as well as receive assistance. This opportunity for reciprocity, so often missing from formal, bureaucratized social systems, is a wellspring for self-esteem.

The ecological approach to family support further implies that effective programs cannot function in isolation from the communities in which they are embedded. Garbarino (chap. 6) draws the analogy that as the family nurtures and supports the child, so must the community nurture and support the family—the community is parent to the family. Extending the analogy, he points out the reciprocity inherent in both relationships: in child rearing, reciprocity implies parents' shouldering responsibility until their children become capable of doing so; within the community, reciprocity means that the community is responsible for providing nurturance and support to families, particularly high-risk families, until they are capable of being independent, nurturing themselves, and ultimately contributing to the community. Support programs foster reciprocity in several important ways: they provide an opportunity for individuals and families to engage in a natural give and take with others; through services like information and referral, family support programs serve and are served by the community; and through their public information efforts, the programs help make the community more aware of and receptive to the needs of families.

Finally, family support programs reflect the ecological orientation in that they mediate between the family and more remote and bureaucratized institutions, such as corporations and government agencies. In some cases, programs help families navigate complex systems to obtain basic services. In other cases, via support programs, families may mobilize to advocate for improved services or for changes in bureaucratic policies. This may take the form of establishing a child-abuse-prevention trust fund, conducting seminars for employers on the effects of workplace policy on working parents, or training parents to advocate for improved bilingual education in the schools. Pizzo (chap. 12) points out that by restoring parents' sense of self-worth and shared commitment, family support and self-help programs ultimately help them respond to stress with advocacy for social change.

Along with an ecological approach, the commitment to universal access guides the architects of family support programs. The basis for this commitment is empirical evidence from the fields of psychology, sociology, and health, suggesting that all families undergo various transitions and that—extrapolating from a solid body of research on social support as a buffer against the deleterious effects of various life stresses—family support programs can help people adapt to these transitions, thereby preventing serious dysfunctions. Because life transitions are not unique to any social, economic, or racial group, the need for support transcends these traditional human-service demarcations. For example, Dokecki and Moroney (1983) indicate that neither effective parenting nor the desire for parent education is related to socioeconomic status. In addition to coping with transitions, the literature indicates that maintaining family integrity has become more difficult, so that many families, mainstream and others, feel the need for ongoing support.

Hand in hand with data that suggest universal need is the widely touted belief in prevention rather than treatment as a pragmatic, cost-effective approach to human-service delivery. Intervening before a problem emerges is becoming a cornerstone of current health and educational programming and also of the new family support programs.

Translation of the ideology of universal access into practice results in a number of program characteristics. Above all, each program tends to provide a smorgasbord of services so that the needs of a variety of families can be met. The challenge is to match services to diverse families rather than, as in traditional agencies, to fit families into the available services. It is not unusual to see a program fielding formal and informal services or modifying its services frequently, which suggests that flexibility is another important characteristic of these new programs.

Another feature of family support programs is the attempt to build on each family's strengths rather than simply to remedy its weaknesses. This nondeficit orientation is particularly important in working with culturally diverse families. Parenting education, an integral component of most family support programs, is the intervention perhaps most likely to impose the norms of the dominant culture on a family. Yet, as Laosa (1983) points out: "Different groups value different patterns of family interaction; . . . they also differ in their views of what constitutes desirable behavior on the part of children; they differ, moreover, in the conceptions of the attributes that define 'optimal development'" (p. 337). Both Jenkins (chap. 15) and Williams (chap. 16) indicate the liabilities of engaging in human-service efforts without maintaining a culturally sensitive approach. Service providers must construct programs that help culturally diverse families maintain their ethnic identity while offering support that will enable minorities to use their skills to enter the mainstream cultural and economic system, should they so choose (Gray and Wandersman, 1980).

The potential of a nondeficit approach to social services cannot be fully realized, however, until our ideas about the role of professionals are revamped. Family support programs are making headway in this area. New relationships based on equity are cited frequently throughout the volume. Weissbourd (chap. 13) notes that the modified relationship between parents and professionals in family support programs is frequently called a "partnership," a rather facile statement describing a goal difficult to achieve (p. 31). Weiss (chap. 8) delineates a continuum of parent-program relations, suggesting that the *unilateral* relationship in which parents are considered empty vessels "waiting to be filled with professional expertise" has given way in family support to the *bilateral* relationship of parents and professionals as partners. In many programs *multilateral* relationships, in which parents glean information and support from professionals, peers, and nonprogram resources while simultaneously serving as resources themselves, are common.

So we see that family support programs are more than a new name for an old concept. Instead, they represent fundamentally new ways of dealing with social support. Their emphasis on an ecological orientation, coupled with a commitment to universal access and the programmatic manifestations of these orientations, puts them at the frontier of social-service delivery. Functioning at the frontier is never easy, and it remains to be seen whether these unique efforts will be able to maintain their intended goals while sustaining their financial viability.

SUSTAINING FAMILY SUPPORT PROGRAMS: RHETORIC VS. REALITY

The characteristics that unite diverse programs under the rubric of "family support" may indeed provide more conceptual than practical unity. Questions regarding family support programs abound, perhaps because the programs are both symptoms of and solutions to flaws in the current social-service structure, or perhaps because they are a seemingly new yet deeply rooted effort. We now address long-term questions regarding the survival and the impact of these programs.

Some authors in this volume indicate that family support programs are having an impact beyond the families they serve. Williams (chap. 16) presents evidence that the social-service bureaucracy is gradually adopting a family support ideology, which stresses the prevention of family dissolution rather than its remediation. Other authors, in their concern about institutional responses, question whether local family support programs, which at their finest represent families helping themselves and others, might stave off more fundamental reform. Is family support a mere palliative that will allow society-wide illnesses such as the poverty of children to worsen? Are family support programs an alternative to the existing social infrastructure? While we encourage readers to arrive at their own conclusions, our sense is that family support programs will not obviate the need for government programs such as Aid to Families with Dependent Children (AFDC) and subsidized housing. Rather, as Moroney (chap. 2) maintains, government efforts such as these form the necessary infrastructure upon which informal support systems are able to operate. As such, family support programs are not alternatives to government programs but vehicles for humanizing them and making them more efficient. They may accomplish this not only as mediators between families and bureaucracies that have grown too fragmented, large, and complicated to serve effectively but also as testing grounds and models for change.

The extent to which these programs will have impact beyond the immediate families they serve seems to rest on three conditions: the degree to which the programs can sustain themselves economically, the degree to which effective evaluations can support the search for funds and be used to improve programs, and the degree to which these disparate programs will be fortified into a whole, a movement.

It is well known in the family support field that sustaining a program is difficult indeed, particularly if it has a commitment to universal access. Many of the programs, despite public acclaim, are poorly funded and barely manage to survive. In fact, at a conference on family support programs held in 1983, providers identified financial instability as their gravest concern. Weissbourd (chap. 13) and Muenchow (chap. 14) provide insight into the complexities of the financial burdens these programs carry and also suggest some possible solutions. Nonetheless, with diminished federal monies and increased demands on the private sector, family support programs, committed to keeping fees low, find themselves in a competitive race for financial support. Programs must be able to demonstrate their efficacy and their value. Therefore, effective evaluation is critical to their very existence.

Conducting evaluations on family support programs is a challenge because the qualities that make the programs unique—their preventive orientation, their flexibility, and their highly idiosyncratic nature—also make them difficult to evaluate. As a consequence, the programs raise rich and intriguing research questions concerning internal as opposed to external evaluations; the best combination of qualitative and quantitative data; and appropriate outcome measures for evaluating programs that aim to serve the child, the family, and the community as interrelated systems. Seitz (chap. 18) points out the dilemma that although selection bias is "the patron devil of evaluation research," random assignment of families to treatment or no-treatment groups raises ethical considerations for family support programs.

Zigler and Freedman (chap. 20) agree that evaluation must measure more than IQ and more than outcome variables; it must also develop findings that will be useful to program operators. Powell (chap. 17) has taken significant steps in this direction by suggesting that beyond gross differences such as socioeconomic status, social network ties, and child-rearing values, levels of stress and other characteristics that a family brings to a program influence the way the family members participate and what they gain from their participation. Campbell (chap. 19) is also concerned with meeting the needs of practitioners and suggests an evaluation paradigm that entails cross-validating programs through replication, which would allow us to determine which programs have components that will "travel" successfully to other settings.

Campbell's suggestions have special appeal because if the disparate family support programs are to have broad-scale impact, they will need not only to demonstrate positive effects but to band together, to communicate with one another so that the wheel is not reinvented in every setting. In that this public dialogue has only recently begun, even though its subject has existed for at least two decades, family support has indeed been an untold story.

Slowly, the untold story is gaining recognition. The 1980s have witnessed efforts to increase public awareness of family support programs, to bring them together to exchange information, and to facilitate new efforts that incorporate features of existing programs. One such effort, a conference sponsored by Family Focus in 1981, led to the formation of the Family Resource Coalition by the 300 participants representing various programs. Two years later, an invited conference, sponsored by the Yale Bush Center in Child Development and Social Policy with funds from the Bush Foundation and the Administration for Children, Youth and Families, drew more than 400 practitioners, scholars, policymakers, business people, and media representatives. A majority of the chapters in this volume were adapted from presentations made at this conference. The first national conference sponsored by the Family Resource Coalition in Chicago in September of 1986 attracted over 800 participants. So family support is clearly gaining momentum.

With this analytical treatment of family support, we hope to present accumulated wisdom in a way that will serve not only architects of family support programs but also the scholarly and policy communities at a time when economic and political factors are propelling us to rethink conventional social service arrangements. At this juncture the most basic question seems to be "Are family support programs a trend or are they here to stay?" Unfortunately, in an era of programmatic Darwinism, program effectiveness is not the sole factor ensuring survival. The political clout of the populations served, the appeal of a particular program to the media, and the correct contacts for funding all are influential. Some of the exemplary programs discussed in this volume have already folded. Yet others, even in the face of budget cuts, have been able to survive and expand. Programs have formed the basis of federal legislation on such issues as adolescent pregnancy. More and more, family support efforts are building public education components into their programs. In this sense, they contain the seeds of their own survival because they instill parents with the confidence and tools to advocate for the programs that best serve them.

Nevertheless, in the long run, family support may prove the source of its own obsolescence. In the foreword, Bronfenbrenner suggests that our task today is to create formal systems of support that will, in turn, engender informal systems. The solidification of these informal systems will obviate the need for support programs. What if, in fact, family support programs succeeded in their goals of tieing families into peer support networks; changing the fabric of the community so that it becomes a healthier place to raise families; and modifying the public infrastructure, the workplace, the schools, so that they are more able to serve every type of family without creating dependence? Indirectly, we may be rooting for the eventual demise of the family support movement. For the time being, however, we think it is a phenomenon worth fostering.

FAMILY SUPPORT PROGRAMS: THE STATE OF THE ART

The purpose of this volume is to provide an overview of the current state of family support programs as they exist in the United States. To do so, we have divided the volume into six major sections.

Following the introductory chapter, part II provides a philosophical and historical orientation to family support. *Moroney*, in chapter 2, tackles some of the philosophical issues suggested by family support as a whole. He examines support systems in the context of the welfare state, addresses the sensitive balance of responsibility between the family and extrafamilial institutions, and sets forth an innovative formulation for government involvement in family support. In chapter 3, *Weissbourd* traces some of the components of today's programs to efforts of the past, yet also shows how the social climate of the 1970s and 1980s affected the establishment and development of family support programs. *Zigler and Freedman*, in chapter 4, look specifically at Head Start and related federally sponsored demonstration projects as both a model and a national laboratory for family support.

Part III moves to a discussion of various types of family support, providing concrete examples of current programs. Because of diversity on every measurable variable, codifying these programs into an organizational scheme was a challenge, initially undertaken in conjunction with the Yale Family Support Conference. After grappling with the considerable overlap among programs in terms of goals, service-delivery mechanisms, auspices, types of families served, and community settings, conference organizers decided on eight program "types" to categorize the bulk of family support programs that serve families with children under twelve. Some programs fit into more than one category, and, no doubt, some family support efforts may not be captured by any of the eight types. Nonetheless, at this early point it seemed worthwhile to put forth an initial categorization scheme that might help solidify our understanding of family support. It is our hope that this typology will become more precise as our knowledge of family support increases. The program types, each of which is discussed in an individual chapter in this section, include prenatal and infant; child abuse and neglect prevention; early childhood intervention; parent education and support; home-school linkage; assistance to families with handicapped children; family-oriented day care; and neighborhood-based, mutual-help, and informal support.

The part begins with chapter 5, in which *Shonkoff* analyzes the forces that led to family support in the prenatal/early infancy period, including changing views of childbirth and of the infant. He presents three models of such programs and the results of research evaluating their effectiveness with families of varying degrees of vulnerability. *Garbarino*, in chapter 6, considers programs to prevent child maltreatment. Such efforts, he suggests, are tied to both nurturance and control of the family. He explores the ramifications of this fact, the role of the community in providing such support, and research strategies for evaluating abuse-prevention efforts.

Powell, in chapter 7, suggests that day care, a traditionally child-centered service, needs to incorporate a family support orientation and offers concrete suggestions for bringing this about. He stresses the importance of facilitating a good match between the needs of the entire family and the day-care program and underscores the value of enhancing communication between parents and day-care providers.

Weiss, in chapter 8, examines the evolution of early childhood intervention programs that include family support. She suggests that as the goals of federal social policy for the poor have shifted from the provision of equal opportunity to the prevention of dependence, evidence of the long-term effectiveness of family-focused early childhood interventions is attracting notice.

Kagan, in chapter 9, looks at the historical legacies and current models of programs that link the home and school. These programs illuminate forms of family support that function as mediators between the family and bureaucratized institutions. The evolution of home-school relations —from alienation, to mandated parent participation, to the current beginnings of collaboration and reciprocity—indicates the reforming influence family support may have on the social infrastructure. In chapter 10, *Weigerink and Comfort* address the rationale for and criticisms of programs that involve the parents of special-needs children. Because these programs federally mandate parent involvement, they provide an interesting case study, raising questions about the effects of different kinds of parent participation under various circumstances.

Wandersman, in chapter 11, considers programs that primarily educate and support parents. This chapter sets forth more realistic expectations for parent education than have been touted in the past, briefly reviews empirical evidence of the ways in which parent education modifies parents' understanding and behavior, and suggests directions for the improvement of parent education as one element in family support.

In discussing the self-help movement, *Pizzo*, in chapter 12, traces its origins and relates its development to family support. She emphasizes the vital role self-help efforts have played in propelling society-wide change.

Part IV considers issues that arise as family support programs are implemented. *Weissbourd*, in chapter 13, discusses the design, staffing, and funding of family support programs and delineates the ways in which a program's philosophy, goals, populations, and resources affect its structure. The chapter clearly demonstrates both the commonalities and the differences among family support programs. In chapter 14, *Muenchow* also discusses funding issues but focuses on innovative partnerships that support these programs. She provides concrete examples and strategies that may help alleviate the financial instability that besets many programs.

Jenkins, in chapter 15, discusses the importance of recognizing cultural differences in the delivery of social services and provides stunning examples of the consequences of tailoring programs to the unique ethnic and linguistic backgrounds of those involved. In chapter 16, which focuses on black families, *Williams* points out the insensitivity of traditional social services to the styles, needs, and strengths of this minority. He cites ways in which a family support philosophy has been and could be applied in reforming bureaucracies to become more culturally sensitive.

In part V, scientists known for their methodological rigor look at research and evaluation in family support programs. *Powell*, in chapter 17, presents a comprehensive picture of the challenges facing the evaluator of these innovative programs. He discusses the realities of the field setting that militate against "classic" research design and suggests four areas that need to be strengthened to improve evaluation research. In chapter 18, *Seitz* concurs about the need for new research designs and analyzes two quasi-experimental methods for use when random assignment is not possible: treatment partitioning and a time-lag strategy. Looking at evaluation in terms of its role in society, *Campbell*, in chapter 19, presents ideas that question the most basic assumptions of program evaluation. He suggests that evaluation be used primarily to inform program improvement rather than funding decisions, that it be conducted only when a program is "proud," and that staff judgments about a program be given as much credence as an outsider's quantitative data. In chapter 20, *Zigler and Freedman* discuss the scientific and policy issues inherent in social program evaluation, delineating who should be evaluated, and when, how, and by whom. They stress the need to learn systematically from the experience of both the program practitioner and the evaluator.

In the final section of the volume, issues are synthesized and policy considerations raised. The editors present their analyses of the impact of family support efforts on children, families, and institutions. The editors conjecture about the future of family support, its durability and vulnerability, and conclude with specific recommendations for practitioners, researchers, and policymakers.

REFERENCES

Belsky, J., Lerner, R. M., & Spanier, G. B. (1984). *The child in the family.* Reading, MA: Addison-Wesley.

Berger, P. L., & Newhouse, R. J. (1977). *To empower people: The role of mediating structures in public policy.* Washington, DC: The American Enterprise Institute for Public Policy Research.

Bronfenbrenner, U. (1979). *The ecology of human development: Experiments by nature and design.* Cambridge: Harvard University Press.

Dokecki, P. R., & Moroney, R. M. (1983). To strengthen all families: A human development and community value framework. In R. Haskins & D. Adams (Eds.), *Parent education and public policy* (pp. 40–64). Norwood, NJ: Ablex.

Garbarino, J. (1982). *Children and families in the social environment.* Hawthorne, NY: Aldine.

Gray, S. W., & Wandersman, L. P. (1980). The methodology of home-based intervention studies: Problems and promising strategies. *Child Development, 51,* 993–1009.

Grubb, W. N., & Lazerson, M. (1982). *Broken promises: How Americans fail their children.* New York: Basic Books.

Keniston, K., and the Carnegie Council on Children. (1977). *All our children: The American family under pressure.* New York: Harcourt, Brace Jovanovich.

Laosa, L. M. (1983). Parent education, cultural pluralism, and public policy: The uncertain connection. In R. Haskins & D. Adams (Eds.), *Parent education and public policy* (pp. 331–334). Norwood, NJ: Ablex.

Zigler, E., & Weiss, H. (1985). Family support programs: An ecological approach to child development. In R. N. Rapoport (Ed.), *Children, youth, and families: The action research relationship* (pp. 166–205). New York: Cambridge University Press.

**PART II/THE CONTEXT
FOR FAMILY SUPPORT**

2 SOCIAL SUPPORT SYSTEMS: FAMILIES AND SOCIAL POLICY

Robert M. Moroney

From whatever perspective we approach the situation of the modern family—as a result of modernization, liberalism, industrialization, urbanization, capitalism, secularization—the community and with it the traditional family are perceived to have gradually deteriorated. But has the world of the family in fact become *more* stressful? It is probably the case that the modern family is adapting to its context with no more or less difficulty than the family has always had in adapting (Bane, 1976; Hareven, 1974). Although there have been historical transformations of conditions that cause stress for the family, a reasonable case can be made that the family continually trades old stressors for new ones as social conditions change. In this regard, it is important for policy development that we avoid nostalgia for the "world we have lost" (Laslett, 1965) and its highly problematic policy counterpart, the inappropriate use of "loss as a theme in social policy."

The current administration and President Reagan in particular argue that many of our problems will be solved if we return to older values. We are told, and we want to believe, that in an earlier era life was less complex, appropriate values were respected, youth accepted adult authority, and gender roles were not blurred. In general, it was a better time to live. But this picture of the past is highly selective, with certain aspects emphasized and others ignored. If life then was "better," it was also shorter and harder. Life expectancy at the beginning of the nineteenth century is estimated to have been 35 years, and even at the beginning of the twentieth century it was only 47 years. Infant mortality rates were 80 percent higher just 60 years ago, and maternal mortality rates were 100 percent higher. Moreover, the extent of rural and urban poverty in the nineteenth century was staggering.

As society at large has expanded its learning and communication capabilities, we have become more aware of problematic social conditions. Undoubtedly spurred by our personal motivation as family members experiencing family-related stress, our consciousness about the family has been raised. To some extent, we have been led to place the family and the local community on the agenda for public policy.

Support systems, especially natural support systems, are looked upon today as the solution to many of the problems facing America's families. As a movement, family support is offered as an alternative to the welfare state, and as a movement it is not only gaining greater currency but is also attracting proponents from the political left and right.[1]

The concept *support system* has a nice ring to it. It creates images of people helping people, a system that is "natural" compared to the artificial welfare state; a system that is not only superior but will reduce the need for large-scale social welfare expenditures. But the issue of social support needs to be analyzed more systematically. Are the promises more than rhetoric and longing? Are there agendas being played out in the arena of public policy that might be stimulating support networks for hidden political and economic purposes? What kinds of social supports are being proposed and for what purposes? What is feasible and what is myth?

IDEOLOGICAL DISAGREEMENTS

In the best tradition of the modern welfare state, this country has repeatedly expressed its commitment to meeting the basic needs of its people. Yet this same tradition has produced a series of policies, programs, and services that are often contradictory and counterproductive when assessed as a whole. This does not mean that specific policies, taken individually, have not been of value; rather, it means that intervention has often created new problems in other areas or operated at cross-purposes to other policies. More often than not, the secondary effects were neither intended nor anticipated.

For example, Aid to Families with Dependent Children is a program intended to provide financial support to needy families, but as designed it penalizes two-parent families and encourages fathers to desert. Housing policies have been successful in providing adequate shelter to many of those who had been living in substandard housing, but they have also had an unintended negative effect on local neighborhoods and informal support networks (Hearings before the Subcommittee on Executive Reorganization, 1966; Young and Wilmott, 1975). Finally, recent efforts to deinstitutionalize the mentally ill and the mentally retarded, defensible on both therapeutic and financial grounds, have created increased pressure on families in that the discharges have not been accompanied by a comparable expansion of community-based services (Moroney, 1976).

The secondary effects of these and other social policies have, in turn, generated continuous and often bitter debates. The disagreement can be reduced to a number of fundamental questions. Should services be provided as a right or made available only when individuals and families demonstrate their inability, usually financial, to meet their basic needs? Should benefits be provided to the total population or restricted to specific target groups, usually defined as "at risk"? Should government develop mechanisms to continuously improve and promote the quality of life, or should it restrict its activity to guaranteeing some agreed-upon minimum level of welfare, a floor below which no one is allowed to fall?[2] Should it actively seek to prevent or minimize stressful situations, both environmental and personal, or should it merely react to problems and crises as they arise?

Despite ambivalence and disagreement, there seems to be a general consensus that when policies are proposed, the family should be considered in all deliberations. Whether for moral or political reasons, legislators argue that the family should be protected and strengthened as a basic social institution. Even a cursory review of the past forty years shows that social legislation has been promoted on the premise that it would benefit family life and thereby benefit the country. Opponents of such action counter with the argument that it would weaken the family.

The latter position has gained considerable currency over the past ten years. Sir Keith Joseph, a leading theorist for the Conservative party in the United Kingdom and a major policy adviser to Prime Minister Thatcher, has argued that the family and civilized values:

> are the foundation on which the nation is built; they are being undermined. If we cannot restore them to health, our nation can be utterly ruined, whatever economic policies we might try to follow. . . . The socialist method would try to take away from the family and its members the responsibilities which give it cohesion. Parents are being divested of their duty to provide for their family economically, of their responsibility for education, health, upbringing, morality, advice and guidance, of saving for old age, for housing. When you take responsibility away from people, you make them irresponsible. (Joseph, 1974, p. 5)

In this country, similar charges, in strikingly similar language, have been leveled at the social policies formulated by the New Deal in the 1930s and expanded in the Great Society of the 1960s. Both the Carter and the Reagan administrations have charged that the social welfare system has harmed rather than helped families. During the earlier period (1932–

1970) the federal government assumed a proactive stance, exemplified by the Social Security Act (for example, retirement benefits, unemployment insurance), various housing programs (for example, public housing, subsidized housing) and education programs (for example, the GI Bill, guaranteed educational loans, education for the handicapped), to minimize risk and enhance social functioning. Today, this role and function are being redefined, and the federal government is more and more assuming a reactive stance, intervening only when it is absolutely necessary to do so. Many of the New Deal programs are being cut back, dismantled, or passed on to the states through block grants.

Proponents of both positions argue that their formulation of the welfare state provides the most effective guideline for strengthening the family. This tension can be reduced to one fundamental question: What is the most desirable, effective, and feasible division of responsibility between the family and extrafamilial institutions in meeting the needs of individuals, and in what ways can these institutions relate to each other so as to maximize benefits to families?

HISTORICAL INTERPRETATIONS

How is it that one group can argue that proactive social welfare measures are the solution while another can argue that the solution is to dismantle that same social welfare system? In part, each is concerned with a different problem and, in part, each interprets events of the past through a different set of lenses.

Although the two groups agree that social change is the key to the puzzle, they disagree about the nature of the desired change. Those arguing for a proactive state believe that social welfare measures are needed to buffer changes in societal structures and institutions that are harmful to families. They accept the inevitability of these changes (for example, those caused by industrialization and modernization) and attempt to build a new institution to help families function so as to maximize their human potential. Those arguing for a reactive and minimalist government see the need to cut back on social welfare measures because they believe that these have weakened the family. If the cause of the change, the welfare state, is removed, they contend, families will return to their earlier position of strength.

These perspectives are tied to the notion of community—the community today and previous community life. Before modernization and urbanization, the family was the basic institution of social life. As Demos (1983) suggests:

> Families were the building blocks from which all larger units of social organizations could be fashioned. A family was itself a little society. . . . The family

performed a multitude of functions, both for the individual and for the aggregate to which it belonged. Thus, most of what children received by way of formal education was centered around the home hearth; likewise their training in particular vocations, in religious worship, and in what we would call good citizenship. Illness was also a matter of home care. (p. 164)

Similarly, Warren (1978) describes premodern communities as self-sufficient. Families produced their own food, made their own clothing, socialized their own children, and provided necessary social and physical care for dependent members. These earlier communities tended to be homogeneous; that is, the families had similar religious, ethnic, and other characteristics, and held similar values. There was a strong belief in mutual support and community responsibility. If any family experienced a problem, other families stepped in. All of us can relate to the classic example of the barn raising, where the total community comes together to build a home or barn for a new family or for an established family after theirs has burned down. Families willingly gave of their time and resources to help others with the understanding that if they need help, they too will receive it.

Is this what the critics of the welfare state have in mind when they speak of the family reassuming its functions? Is self-sufficiency synonymous with strong families? How realistic is this scenario?

First, this form of community was not the norm for all communities. When communities based on mutual support existed, they were agrarian. Family life in urban areas was quite different. As far back as seventeenth-century England we find the state establishing in law, with its accompanying sanctions, the principle of filial and parental responsibility. The common belief was that families were divesting themselves of their "natural responsibility" to care for their dependent members. Later, in the nineteenth century, the state decided that even harsher measures were necessary to coerce the family to care for its vulnerable members. We find the following statement in the Report of the Royal Commission of 1832:

> It appears from the whole Evidence that the clause of the 43rd Eliz., which directs the parents and children of the impotent to be assessed for their support, is very seldom enforced. In any ordinary state of society, we much doubt the wisdom of such enactment. The duty of supporting parents and children in old age or infirmity is so strongly enforced by our natural feelings, that it is well performed, even among savages, and almost always so in a nation deserving the name of civilized. We believe that England is the only European country in which it is neglected. (*Report of the Poor Law Commission of 1832*, 1905, p. 43)

But England was not the only country experiencing this "deterioration" of the family. The American colonies adopted the Elizabethan

Poor Law, including the family-responsibility clauses. By 1836, all states on the Atlantic seaboard with the exception of New York and the southern states, expanded this notion to include the legal responsibility of grandchildren to provide for their grandparents. Later many states added stipulations extending beyond the consanguinal to the collateral line, making brothers and sisters liable (Coll, 1973).

The first colonial almshouses and workhouses were established during the mid-eighteenth century in urban areas such as Boston, New York, and Philadelphia. By the mid-nineteenth century, all major seaboard cities had almshouses. And yet, even with the proliferation of these institutions, it has been estimated that only 9% percent of the families unable to care for themselves were in the almshouses or workhouses. The majority were either contracted out to another family for a lump sum fixed as low as possible, auctioned or sold to another family, or in some instances provided with "outdoor relief" in their homes.

The picture of the self-sufficient family living in a supportive community had disappeared from the urban areas of the eastern seaboard by the eighteenth century and in all urbanized areas by the mid-nineteenth century. We now return to the question raised earlier: How realistic is the Reagan administration's proposal that families should become more self-sufficient and that the care of dependents should be an intrafamily or, if necessary, an interfamily responsibility? Finally, how accurate is the charge that the welfare state brought about changes in family responsibility and in the willingness of families to develop and maintain supportive networks?

The weight of historical evidence runs counter to this charge. Deteriorating or weakened families existed long before the introduction of the modern welfare state. The situation was endemic during the Poor Law era of the eighteenth and nineteenth centuries—an era that attempted, through repressive social policies, to coerce family responsibility. Even then, the pattern that emerged appears to have been a cycle of major and minor economic depressions followed by more families seeking help, followed by greater expenditures for social welfare, and not the reverse.

If the welfare state did not cause the family to change or "deteriorate," how reasonable is it to think of a return to family self-sufficiency? Is this notion of community feasible or is it an anachronism—a form of social life viable during an agrarian era but impossible in an industrialized and urbanized era? If the answers to these questions point toward a continual need for balance, and the evidence appears to support this, self-sufficiency and community, defined as a clustering of supportive families, would require a radical transformation of society and not a return to an earlier way of life. Unfortunately, nostalgia and, to some extent, myth have become the basis for current policy formulation.

Those who support continued government intervention argue that most western European countries have had some form of public social welfare since the Reformation. While the specific system may have contracted and expanded over time, and while the form and level of services may have changed, governments have made some provisions to meet basic human needs. This does not necessarily mean that these governments have been generous or proactive, or that they always operate with the recipients of services foremost in mind. The welfare state was a necessary creation as we moved from a simple agrarian to a more complex industrial society founded on the belief in a free market economy. As this system matured, the market economy gave way to a form of capitalism called state capitalism or welfare capitalism, in which the government has two responsibilities: to support the economic system and to humanize it (to develop a mechanism that will protect individuals and families from the inevitable negative aspects of the economic system). The first function falls under the term *political economy*; the second falls under the term *social welfare*.

The modern welfare state, unlike the welfare state of the Poor Law, is based on the premise that as a result of significant social change, families experience considerable stress. However, there is no acceptance of the notion that the family has deteriorated and that in its weakened state it is unable to carry out those functions that have traditionally been viewed as falling in its domain—especially as they relate to the care of dependent members. That family structure, family size, and role relationships have changed is not questioned. The argument that these changes are indications of family deterioration has little empirical support. In fact, the evidence suggests that during any period of rapid social change, families have borne the brunt of the transition process by adapting their structure and functions. Bane (1978), for example, questions whether divorce and the work status of women are inherently problematic. "The assumption behind this categorization (i.e., non-problems) is that the ways in which men and women choose to marry, split, have children, or work, are not in themselves problems. There are, of course, circumstances under which their choices cause problems for others, especially for children" (p. 15).

So much for the rationale. If the purpose of the modern welfare state is to buffer these stresses, how successful has it been? More important, how is success to be measured? Wills (1979) offers a reasoned defense of bureaucrats and professionals as necessary agents for dealing with a maddeningly complex world. Featherstone (1979) expands the argument by the following suggestion:

> The problematic, sometimes sinister, and often tragic role that professionals play in dispensing services in a multiethnic and profoundly unequal society is one thing. The assumption that we can water down and dispense with those

services we now have is something else. . . . There are two things generally missing from current policy perspectives. One is that many people do in fact need help. The second point is that public policy ought to be about helping to provide contexts in which people could help each other. . . . The challenge is to frame contexts which offer families more choices about the kinds of help they receive. Help should augment family life rather than diminish it. (pp. 46–47)

This position is an interesting one. As discussed above, the Reagan administration argues that families should reassume their traditional responsibilities. Featherstone appears to be in agreement, at least in terms of the desired end. He questions the thrust and emphasis of current social policies but rejects the notion that a drastic retrenchment of the welfare state is the solution.

The fundamental issue is to "provide contexts in which people can help each other." Is it possible to establish artificial means (in the sense that the social services are artifacts of the welfare state) to augment natural social arrangements? To what extent, then, can family members interact with providers of social services in complementary roles? Can parents, for example, interact as equals with teachers, physicians, and social workers? Even though professionals, by definition, bring expertise that family members do not have, is the idea of partnership in the sharing of vital family functions viable?

To address these questions, the nature of these social relationships needs to be explored in some detail and at a level beyond the somewhat simplistic and nostalgic descriptions that have shaped the position of those opposing the welfare state. One key to understanding these relationships is the notion of reciprocity.

RECIPROCITY, DEPENDENCY AND SOCIAL EXCHANGE

Pinker (1973) has provided a systematic and extremely useful analysis of this issue. He begins with the position that "all social services are systems of social exchange" in which it is possible to distinguish a "category of givers" from a "category of receivers." This exchange, however, tends to be unequal. In general, if someone gives us something, we can never make up for it completely, even if we return the equivalent. Why? While the giver gave voluntarily, the receiver returns under some form of moral or psychological duress or coercion. The initial giver experiences a sense of generosity, the receiver a sense of gratitude accompanied by a sense of obligation. Thus, the "relationship between a giver and a receiver is always unstable and unequal" (p. 153).

Pinker extends the argument by distinguishing between nonsocial service and social service transactions. Using the example of borrowing money, he suggests that the borrower experiences dependency toward the lender, but that this dependency is temporary and ends with the re-payment of the loan plus interest. But when one receives social services, he argues, the dependency is permanent in that it cannot be repaid with interest. Furthermore, he suggests that "the idea of paying through taxes or holding authentic claims through citizenship remains largely an intellectual concept of the social scientist" (p. 142). With the exception of our Social Security retirement system (the elderly have been socialized over a fifty-year period to believe that these benefits are theirs since they have "paid" for them), recipients of entitlement programs are still made to feel stigmatized.

Moreover, the attempt to be responsive to individual family differ-ences and needs by providing highly personalized social services risks making the receiver "acutely aware of his dependency." While more generalized and anonymous services might reduce this feeling of depen-dency, they do so at the price of not being responsive to need.

Pinker reviews the works of anthropologists such as Mauss, Radcliffe-Brown, and Levi-Strauss to see whether they offer examples of prein-dustrial or "simple" societies where other forms of social exchanges or transactions were the norm. His conclusion—yes and no. A sense of ob-ligation and reciprocity along kinship lines appears to permeate these relationships also. However, the issue of dependency does not seem to be as critical in these societies in that interdependency is or was a total way of life. In fact, Pinker concludes that in these relatively simple socie-ties, "systems of exchange are more likely to be based on norms of reci-procity between equals."

Where, then, does Pinker's thesis take us? First, as indicated, the is-sue does not seem to be one of dependency. Dependency exists in all so-cieties, preindustrial and industrial, simple and complex. Within the former, family members are dependent upon one another and families are dependent upon other families, either kin or neighbors. In more complex societies, families no longer function within extensive kinship networks and mutual aid among neighbors is limited.

If the issue is not dependency, what is it? Pinker suggests that it is the nature of the dependency—the extent to which the exchange is among people who perceive themselves to be equal or unequal and the degree to which receivers are able to reciprocate. In simple societies, in which resources tend to be more equally distributed, receivers are more likely to believe that they will be able to reciprocate and givers give with this understanding. The bond is a moral bond grounded in a sense of trust.

In complex societies, this reciprocity appears to be more elusive. While neighbors continue to be willing to help one another (as docu-mented by researchers such as Litwak [1965]), they do not have the requisite resources—including goods, services, specialized knowledge and time—that most families require. Given this, modern societies created social institutions (for example, the school to share with the family the education of children; the hospital to share in the care of the sick; the social services to share in meeting the social and economic needs of family members). In this context, dependency still exists. No longer is it only within and between families; it is also within and among other social institutions. Is it possible for these new social arrangements to be based on the notion of reciprocity—that is, a sense of perceived equality between the giver and the receiver? Do the new givers, the professionals, operate on the assumption of mutual aid, and do the receivers believe that they can eventually meet the obligations they have incurred?

SUPPORT SYSTEMS: FORMAL AND INFORMAL

To explore the issue of reciprocity and mutual aid, we now turn to the issue of social support. The kinship- and neighbor-driven exchanges can best be understood within the notion of "informal" support systems whereas social transactions involving social welfare institutions can be thought of as "formal" support systems.

Bronfenbrenner (1977) discusses support systems as the immediate ecology or environment within which an individual or family lives. This ecology incorporates people who influence and sometimes determine what happens to the individual or family. In general, the support system is made up of extended family members, friends, and neighbors; it may also include persons affiliated with more formal agencies, such as churches, schools, and social welfare agencies.

More than by its membership, however, the support system is identified by what it does for the individual or family (Cobb, 1976; Kaplan, Cassel, and Gore, 1977). At the most basic level, the informal support system is the primary source of love, care, affection, concern, and emotional support for its members. The support system also serves as a primary source of esteem and identity for its membrs; the person is valued as a unique and uniquely important individual. The support system is also the locus where people make commitments to one another and experience a shared history, a sharing of goods and material assistance, a sharing of responsibility and security. Thus, while support systems frequently provide material and task-oriented assistance, they often extend beyond such specific forms of help. This distinction is important, for whereas help in the form of goods and services may foster dependency in the individual, informal support tends to encourage independence and growth (Cobb, 1976).

A major function of support systems is to help the family or individual deal with stress. At a most basic level, individuals without adequate support from their environments have been found to experience "psychologic and physiologic strain" (Kaplan et al., 1977) at some point in time. Weak or inadequate support systems, in conjunction with stress, have been associated with a higher incidence of depression, neurosis, and various other psychiatric disorders (Cobb, 1976). Individuals who have inadequate support systems experience more frequent occurrence and more rapid onset of some diseases; conversely, those with better support systems frequently recover more quickly. A similar pattern has been reported when women attempt to adjust to the death of a spouse (Raphael, 1977). Moreover, Nuckolls, Cassel, and Kaplan (1972) found that pregnant women who experienced high levels of stress in combination with low levels of support from family, friends, neighbors, and community were three times more likely to develop complications during pregnancy than women with low levels of stress or women with high levels of stress and high levels of social support. Finally, in a study of men who had been terminated from their jobs, Gore (1973) found that those who perceived that they had little emotional support from their wives, friends, relatives, and neighbors experienced significantly more psychological and physiological strain than their better supported counterparts. They also saw themselves as economically deprived, were more likely to engage in self-blame, and complained more frequently of illness. The support system acts as a buffer to protect the individual from the most deleterious consequences of stress and stimulates the individual's development of strategies for coping with stress (Dean and Lin, 1977).

Bronfenbrenner (1977) discusses support systems in the context of a person's environment; another major function of support systems is to improve the fit between the person and that environment and to help the individual adapt to change in the environment (Cobb, 1979; Kaplan et al., 1977). The specific activities that persons in the support system carry out may involve the transfer of money or goods and active helping with tasks and responsibilities. The support system also sets out and communicates expectations for the individual, rewards or improves appropriate performance, and may impose negative sanctions as well as comforting the individual when expectations are not met. Underlying these specific activities is the constant transmission of information to the individual that he or she is a valued and respected person.

What role, if any, does the welfare state play in creating or enhancing informal support systems? Can formal support systems intermesh with informal support systems in such a way that the latter are not weakened?

SOCIAL SERVICES AND SOCIAL SUPPORT: THE THEORY

One school of thought would argue that providing social support not only is possible but should be the primary purpose of the social services in a modern welfare state. Kamermann and Kahn (1976) suggest that social services can be thought of as services that attempt to "facilitate or enhance daily living, to enable individuals, families and other groups to develop, to cope, to function, to contribute. . . . Still others offer substitute or safe or protected living arrangements." Within this framework, social services, in theory, have two primary functions: social development/nurturance and social control. These activities are concerned with improving the social skills of individuals who may or may not be living in a family setting, enlarging the resource base of each individual's social network, and linking the individual and family to community institutions (Moroney, 1986).

The social development/nurturance function closely mirrors the activities of the informal support system and can also be related to the family life cycle. First, social services should help families master developmental tasks. Families can be viewed as moving through developmental phases from childless married couples, through several phases defined by the presence of children of varying ages, and finally to aging families. Each phase requires the mastery of family tasks such as physical maintenance, protection, socialization, and the development of independent behavior.

Second, social services should support families by minimizing potentially harmful stresses, thus improving the quality of intrafamily systems and family relations with external systems. Families can be viewed as small systems operating in relationship to other societal institutions such as the extended family, the neigborhood, schools and other service bureaucracies, the community, the world of work, and the marketplace.

Third, social services can be instrumental in improving liaison or linkage to social resources and supports needed by families. Research has underscored the importance of linkages between families in need of help and available social supports. Supporting families, therefore, requires the development of liaison functions to identify and mobilize these resources.

SOCIAL SERVICES AND SOCIAL SUPPORT: THE REALITY

Both the social development/nurturance and social control functions are covered therefore by the term *social services*. However, although we have made the conceptual argument that social services can support families or substitute for families, we are not suggesting that in actuality, social welfare systems manage to balance these differing purposes. In fact, we would argue that current services emphasize a residual and reactive model of social welfare, providing services to families after they have become dependent and can no longer carry out family functions (Moroney, 1976, 1980, 1986). In terms of this approach, the purpose of the services is to provide a remedial or social-control function.

While the social welfare system does not create dependent families, it does foster continued dependency once the family begins receiving services. For example, the use of a means test assumes by definition that a family that is declared eligible is dependent. There is no reciprocity among equals—the receivers are dependent on the givers. In Pinker's (1973) formulation, the interaction between the family and government through its services providers is based on the principle of "unilateral exchange," resulting in a "profound sense of stigma." With such "unilateral exchanges," government reverts to an earlier conceptualization of the welfare state—that of the nineteenth-century Poor Law. The issue is not the prevention of dependency; government waits until dependency occurs. Although the provision of social services may not be as dehumanizing today as it was a century ago, it still requires the family to admit that it cannot meet its own needs. Within this context, government assumes certain family functions.

This "unilateral exchange" goes beyond the practice of selecting recipients of social services. It is also reflected in the attitudes of the service providers interacting with the families. In reviewing literature covering the disciplines of medicine, psychiatry, psychology, and social work, Moroney (1980) found that most professionals tended to view families as less than capable caregivers. Even those who accepted family members as part of the helping team viewed them only as ancillary to the professionals. He concluded that this perspective is shaped in part by the socialization that the professional experienced during his or her training, with its emphasis on the pathology-oriented medical model, and in part by the orientation of the organizations or institutions in which he or she practices.

SOCIAL SERVICES AND SOCIAL SUPPORT: THE POSSIBILITY

Will families be strengthened and not weakened if more broadly defined social services are made available? Kamerman and Kahn's formulation of the purposes of social services, discussed above in relation to the family life cycle, emphasizes the stress that most, if not all, families experience in carrying out family functions and the positive contribution informal support systems can make to family well-being. The key policy issue for the future is likely to be the extent to which the state can strengthen these informal support systems.

Over the past decade, families have joined other families to form support networks, and the evidence suggests that these networks will continue to grow. Such groups tend to have a number of common concerns.

First, the members sense a loss of community, the feeling of belonging to others who are concerned with their well-being on a personal level. Second, they believe that most social institutions are inflexible and highly bureaucratized and that individual needs are shaped to fit existing services rather than vice versa. Finally, these groups are concerned with self-control rather than being controlled by others.

Titmuss (1968), in an insightful discussion of this issue, argues that industrialization and modernization, with their emphasis on economic values and individualization, have brought about community breakdown and alienation through the development of a welfare state that produced a "we-they" society. "We," the nonpoor, provide for a residual proportion of society because "they" are incapable of providing for themselves. In Titmuss' view, social policy is concerned with different types of moral transactions embodying notions of exchange or reciprocal obligations necessary to bring about and maintain social and community relationships.

The issue of dependency as opposed to self-sufficiency, then, has to be seen as a symbolic rather than real argument. It is symbolic in that dependency is labeled a problem to be eradicated, a "dependent" person is projected to be a weak person, and a strong person is still the "rugged individualist of the frontier." If we believe that social services create dependency, it follows that we should stop providing them. This dichotomy, however, is spurious. In reality we are dependent on others just as others are dependent upon us. Furthermore, certain forms of interdependency are highly valued. But if we are not to create stigma, we must believe that we exist in mutually supportive networks in which some individuals are not made to feel inferior and others superior.

Pinker (1973) suggests that a number of factors affect the nature of dependency. Two of these are related to government involvement. First, he points out that stigmatization and deep psychological dependency occur when the receiver is made to feel inferior; and second, this dependency is exacerbated when services are provided continuously and over long periods of time. We dealt with the first issue to some extent when we discussed professional attitudes toward families. A reorientation of professional attitudes is a prerequisite if government and professionals are to interact positively with families and natural support networks. Reducing the length of the dependency is more subtle and perhaps more difficult to achieve. In practice, it would mean that government would intervene to stimulate the growth of support networks (this might entail financial support, information, or expertise) but that the role of government would not be intrusive and would be time-limited. It would mean that families would initially share with professionals the design of the support networks and would eventually control these networks. This strategy can be reduced to a moral and ethical rationale. If we support families in their caring for dependent members, and if we do so in such a way that they are better equipped to carry out family functions, government has made an investment in society's future. This has to be the basis for the intervention since it assumes reciprocity—the family receives support knowing that it will be able to give in return over the long run.

If social policies were to stimulate the development of natural support networks and provide these networks with assistance when necessary, would this result in more self-sufficient families? Undoubtedly. Would it result in a gradual shrinking of the welfare state? No. There will be dependent families for the foreseeable future, whether the dependency is financial, physical, or psychological. This requires government to intervene directly with programs such as Aid to Families with Dependent Children, Foster Care, and Child Protective Services. More important, the social welfare measures that tend to prevent economic dependency (for example, social insurance, health insurance, and subsidized housing for the elderly) must continue. These programs provide the infrastructure enabling informal support systems to operate. Support systems cannot now or in the future provide income support, housing, and jobs on a continuous basis.

Furthermore, an analysis of a sample of support programs whose objective was to strengthen families has found that 19.4 percent were supported only by the private sector; 19.4 percent were supported only by the public sector; and 61.2 percent were supported by some combination of private and public funds (*Programs to Strengthen Families*, 1983). It is clear that most of these programs could not exist without the assistance of the state. It is also clear that the dominant model is a partnership model.

If families are to be strengthened, if family members are to be more capable caregivers, the state should not consider retrenchment of its social welfare systems, thereby suggesting that families can care for themselves by means of informal support groups. Government needs to enter into a partnership with families—a relationship characterized by reciprocity. Otherwise, more and more families will become dependent.

NOTES

1. The phrase *welfare state* is used more in an ideological sense than as a description of a specific set of policies and programs that could be used to differentiate a welfare state from a non-welfare state or to locate individual societies on a welfare state continuum. It refers to the gradual evolution of societies from periods characterized by laissez-faire and little or minimal government intervention to periods where the state (government) accepts increased responsibility for meeting basic human needs. The term

social welfare as used in this chapter refers to the particular set of instrumentalities that a particular society develops to fulfill the goals of the welfare state, and social services are seen as the specific programs.

2. The word *government* as used in this chapter includes all three levels (federal, state, and local) although it is intended to mean a specific level at different times. Furthermore, given our evolving notion of federalism, government involvement is meant to cover almost all forms of social service provision since even private, nonprofit agencies are financially dependent on government funds and purchase-of-service contracts.

REFERENCES

Bane, M. J. (1976). *Here to stay: American families in the twentieth century.* New York: Basic Books.

Bane, M. J. (1978). *Discussion paper: HEW policy toward children, youth and families.* Prepared for the Assistant Secretary for Planning and Evaluation. Washington, DC: Department of Health, Education and Welfare.

Bronfenbrenner, U. (1977). Toward an experimental ecology of human development. *American Psychologist, 32,* 513–531.

Cobb, S. (1976). Social support as a moderator of life stress. *Psychomatic Medicine, 38,* 300–314.

Coll, B. (1973). *Perspectives in public welfare: A history.* Washington, DC: U.S. Department of Health, Education and Welfare.

Dean, A., & Lin, A. (1977). The stress buffering role of social support. *Journal of Nervous and Mental Disease, 165,* 403–417.

Demos, J. (1983). Family home care: Historical notes and reflections. In R. Perlman (Ed.), *Family home care: Critical issues for services and policies* (pp. 161–175). New York: Haworth Press.

Featherstone, J. (1979). Family matters. *Harvard Educational Review, 49,* 20–52.

Gore, S. (1973). The influence of social support and related variables in ameliorating the consequences of job loss. Unpublished dissertation, University of Pennsylvania.

Hareven, T. (1974). The family as process: The historical study of the family cycle. *Journal of Social History, 7,* 322–329.

Hearings before the Subcommittee on Executive Reorganization. (1966). *Federal role in urban affairs.* Senate Committee on Government Operations. 89th Congress, Second Session.

Joseph, Sir K. (1974, October 21). Britain: A decadent new utopia. *The Guardian.*

Kamerman, S., & Kahn, A. (1976). *Social services in the United States.* Philadelphia: Temple University Press.

Kaplan, B., Cassell, J., & Gore, S. (1977). Social support and health. *Medical Care, 15,* 47–58.

Laslett, P. (1965). *The world we have lost.* London: Methuen.

Litwak, E. (1965). Extended relations in an industrial democratic society. In E. Shanas & G. Streib (Eds.), *Social structure and the family.* Englewood Cliffs, NJ: Prentice-Hall.

Moroney, R. (1976). *The family and the state: Considerations for social policy.* London: Longmans.

Moroney, R. (1980). *Families, social services and social policy.* Washington, DC: U.S. Government Printing Office.

Moroney, R. (1986). *Shared responsibility: Families and social policy.* New York: Aldine.

Nuckolls, K., Cassell, J., & Kaplan, B. (1972). Psychosocial aspects, life crisis, and prognosis of pregnancy. *American Journal of Epidemiology, 95,* 431–441.

Pinker, R. (1973). *Social theory and social policy.* London: Heinemann.

Programs to Strengthen families: A resource guide. (1983). New Haven, CT: Yale University Bush Center in Child Development and Social Policy (available from The Family Resource Coalition, 230 North Michigan Ave., Suite 1625, Chicago, IL 60601).

Raphael, B. (1977). Preventive intervention with the recently bereaved. *Archives of General Psychiatry, 34,* 1450–1454.

Report of the Poor Law Commission of 1832. (1905). London: HMSO, Cd. 2728.

Titmuss, R. (1968). *Commitment to welfare.* London: Allen & Unwin.

Titmuss, R. (1971). *The gift relationship.* London: Allen & Unwin.

Warren, R. (1978). *The community in America.* Boston: Houghton Mifflin.

Wills, G. (1978). *Inventing America: Jefferson's Declaration of Independence.* New York: Doubleday.

Young, M., & Wilmott, P. (1975). *Family and kinship in East London.* London: Routledge & Kegan Paul.

3

A BRIEF HISTORY OF
FAMILY SUPPORT
PROGRAMS

Bernice Weissbourd

Writing a definitive history of the family support movement is like writing a biography of a ten-year-old. While a few concrete facts and some clear inclinations have been established, there is still significant development to come. Much of what we can report at this point is conjecture, an attempt to affirm that what exists is derived from some familiar programmatic roots and from some particular aspects of our recent cultural past. The vast differences that exist among family support programs are the best evidence that they are meeting diverse needs expressed at every economic and educational level of our society for stronger, healthier families. Likewise, the emergence of the strength of the family as a political and social issue that cuts across traditional barriers of political parties, economic status, and ethnic origin has increased interest in the programs that have grown out of grassroots efforts to support families as they negotiate realities of life in the late twentieth century.

The rich mosaic of variations on the theme of family support offers insight into the roots of the programs themselves and the cultural climate of the 1960s and 1970s that gave rise to the movement as a whole. Some of the roots of family support are embedded in the informational focus of traditional parent education programs, others can be found in the community orientation of the settlement house movement, and still others in the peer support concepts that are the basis of self-help groups. In the early 1960s, Head Start gave many parents new opportunities to be advocates for their families and gain access to information and resources not previously available to them. In so doing, it added a significant dimension to the concept of family support. Examining these

earlier programs as they relate to family support offers a better understanding of how the family resource efforts emerged and how they currently operate.

ROOTS OF FAMILY SUPPORT PROGRAMS

Parent Education

From the beginning of civilization, parents have been "educated" in one
way or another to accept certain principles of child rearing. Every period of history has had its beliefs about children and how parents should
train, discipline, and prepare them for good citizenship in the society in
which they live. The history of parent education reflects the political and
economic state of the country, the conditions and mood of its people,
and the prevailing attitude toward women and the family.

In the earliest days of our country, child-rearing principles were
based on the moral rectitude of religious beliefs, with the church acting
as a major source of parent education, as did the time-honored daily
contacts among relatives, friends, and even know-it-all neighbors.
Among the earliest efforts to which we can anchor formal parent education were the study groups called "Maternal Associations," which began
meeting regularly in 1815 (Schlossman, 1978a) in Portland, Maine, with
the purpose of discovering the most effective method of "breaking the
will of the child." Their guidelines were prayer and the Bible.

In 1897, the National Conference of Mothers was established. It later
became the Parent-Teacher Association, the first national organization
of women with a primary focus on the role of mothers. The PTA soon
became a popular source of information on child development and in
subsequent years expanded its concerns for child rearing into broader
social reform, a logical step that stemmed from the prevailing inclusive
views of women's moral responsibilities as mothers: the care of all children and the alleviation of social obstacles to the healthy growth of all
children. Social and legal restrictions on women, including the absence
of the right to vote, left only the expanded realm of motherhood as an
acceptable arena for women's influence, and the middle-class mothers
who comprised the bulk of the PTA membership were strongly motivated to extend the benefits of their knowledge of child psychology and
health care to the less advantaged and less educated poor (Schlossman,
1978a).

The rapid changes brought by industrialization and urbanization in
the 1900s saw a shift from a stress on the moral training of children to a
concern with their general well-being. Children required protection
from the effects of a newly industrialized society. Family stress, child la-

bor, and high rates of infant and child death were seen as contributing to a climate in need of reform in medicine, education, and social programs. In the public domain, the move toward reform occasioned the first White House Conference on Children and the establishment of the federal Children's Bureau in 1909 (Grotberg, 1976).

Parent education in the early twentieth century was marked by the prevailing view that, as science and technology would be a panacea for economic and social problems, so they could become a cornerstone for child-rearing practices. Older theories gave way to the behavioral approach of John Watson, and scientifically determined schedules with strict principles of habit formation became the norm in child rearing. This approach was expressed in a flourishing parent education movement generously supported by private foundations (Schlossman, 1978b). Publications from the Children's Bureau were eagerly read and passed along. Information from research institutes were appearing in journals, *Parents* magazine was founded (1925), and parent education classes were offered in colleges, high schools, even grade schools—since few mothers graduated from high school.

It was in the years following the depression that parent education was recognized as of interest and importance to the educationally and financially underprivileged. Programs instituted by the government in the depression years to improve child health, and the nursery schools and play schools run by WPA workers, led the way for expanded discussions of child rearing among parents in poor economic situations (Dowley, 1971).

Concern with the traumatic effects of World War II on children as families were dislocated, fathers lost, and mothers in large numbers joined the workforce characterized parent education in the middle of the twentieth century (Borstelman, 1977). Child-rearing practices focused on children's security and emotional well-being. On the basis of psychoanalytic thinking, promoted by the Child Study Association (established in 1880), parents were encouraged to seek the meaning of a child's behavior, not merely to train the behavior, and were cautioned to respond sensitively to children's needs, to understand the stages of their development, and to allow for the expression of their feelings (American Council on Education, 1945; Hartley, Frank, & Goldenson, 1952; Weber, 1984).

The sense of opportunity, affluence, and confidence in a good future that typified the 1950s, except for those cut out of the mainstream by poverty and racism, was reflected in the prevailing images of family contentment and togetherness that dominated parent education in that decade. Organized parent education was again limited primarily to the middle-class community of parents who were meeting in voluntary associations. In the wake of a new prosperity, the support that government had given to parents beginning in the 1930s and continuing during the war years was virtually eliminated except for the provision of necessary heatlh care to children who could not otherwise get it.

The complacency and blind allegiance to middle-class concepts of family and national life ended abruptly in the early 1960s, and the impact on parent education was swift and direct. As attention focused on ways to redress past discrimination against minorities, education was singled out as the vehicle of choice to increase opportunity and create equality (Schlossman, 1978b). As new research (Bloom, 1964; Gordon, 1966; Hunt, 1961) appeared pointing to the critical importance of the early years of life, there was increasing pressure on the federal government to take an unprecedented role in child welfare: Head Start was established to provide intervention in the early years for "disadvantaged" children, to improve their chances for success in school and therefore for success in American life. The same research that provided the impetus for government programs to enhance the chances for disadvantaged children provided middle-class parents with a new perspective on child development that created possibilities for giving their own children a head start. In the wake of these events, parent education's emphasis on personality development shifted toward an emphasis on cognitive growth. Information for parents on how to teach their children the basic skills of reading and mathematics at an early age was eagerly received by parents, and for many, concern with personality development took a back seat as the rush to "teach" children predominated (Bronfenbrenner, 1961; Dowley, 1971).

Through Head Start, parents who had limited access to formal child-development information and who had not felt any measure of control over the institutions that served their children were able to exert some power over the content and direction of early childhood programs. This involvement of parents spread to other realms, and school and community programs also began to respond to parental concerns. Parents formed supporting networks and began to make demands for their own education as well as the education of their children. Head Start gave parents an awareness of the need for information and support that remains a significant motivation for participation in family resource programs.

Even a limited review of the course of parent education in this country points up its continuing threads in the family support movement. Parent education evolved from an informal process of sharing child-rearing information to an organized association of parents seeking understanding of the best ways to raise their children and ultimately expressing concerns for the general welfare of all children. Over the years, parent education moved from the boundaries of middle-class society to encompass those with fewer advantages. The content of parent education was determined in every period by the prevailing ideas of the leading thinkers in child psychology and development, who themselves were influenced by the tenor of the times. Government involvement and assistance in parent education gradually became available, but only at particular times when the political and economic situation demanded government support. Family support programs reflect the parent education movement in their dedication to informing parents on principles of child development based upon the best thinking of the time, in their recognition that all families benefit from parent education, and in their increasing involvement in the policy issues affecting children and families.

It would be a mistake to describe family support programs without recognizing that they reflect both our times and our state of knowledge in much the same way as the varied forms of parent education in previous decades reflected the conditions in which they emerged. For that very reason, the boundaries of family support extend beyond parent education, as we shall see in the following pages, but its historical link to parent education remains a significant one.

Self-Help

While family support programs have some elements that distinguish them from traditional self-help groups, there is no question that they follow closely in the footsteps of the self-help movement that came into its own during the 1960s. The idea of voluntary associations for mutual aid is not new.

Self-help as we know it has its origins in the Friendly Societies that grew up in nineteenth-century England after the Industrial Revolution. These early mutual-aid groups, like consumer cooperatives, guilds, trade unions, and ethnic-based clubs, were a response to the advent of machines replacing human labor and the subsequent feelings of loss related to major changes in community structure. Like later movements, including family support, mutual-aid societies recreated a sense of community, gave their members valuable information useful in improving their lives, and gave direct help to members experiencing crisis (Evans, 1979).

In the United States, the founding of Alcoholics Anonymous in 1935 marked the beginning of a more structured, problem-specific kind of self-help. AA remains the classic example of the strength of individuals banded together to help one another. Today it boasts 30,000 chapters in 92 countries. AA was followed in the 1930s by the American Association of Retarded Children, the United Cerebral Palsy Foundation, and the Mothers' March of Dimes, which added a new dimension to self-help.

Whereas AA focused on solving individual problems through group support, these later groups extended their activities into advocating changes in society's attitudes or policies that negatively affected members of the group.

The hallmarks of self-help groups have remained remarkably consistent as the number and variety grew to enormous proportions during the 1960s. Groups began with people who shared a common condition or experience and agreed to band together for mutual help. Usually, the common problem was not being addressed by more traditional helping agencies such as hospitals, schools, and churches. Intense loyalty to the group and a high level of commitment to other members fostered a strong sense of belonging. Early self-help groups minimized referrals to professionals or other agencies since in many cases appropriate professional help for their special concern was not accessible. Face-to-face or phone contact and assistance among group members is almost always available without charge. Self-help groups began outside traditional institutions or agencies and relied on donations from members or friends rather than grants or fees of any kind (Borman, 1975; Leiberman, 1979)

The advent of hundreds of thousands of self-help groups in the 1960s, for every imaginable purpose, created a new public awareness that membership in such groups could be rewarding and helpful in reaching personal goals. Belonging to a group of people who shared a similar interest or problem became an acceptable way of acknowledging interdependence, an important antecedent for family resource programs.

Family support programs share some of the characteristics of self-help groups. Parents share a common status, regardless of their economic or ethnic background, and a common concern for the welfare of their children. The motivations that propel parents into resource programs are similar to those for membership in a self-help group: a lack of services for the problems and concerns parents have; barriers such as expense, logistics, or red tape that make existing services hard to utilize; and the simple need to belong to a group of people with similar concerns. As with self-help, the cost for intensive, personal services through family resource programs is usually little or nothing, and groups are open to anyone who wants to participate.

Settlement Houses

While parent education and self-help are prominent threads in the fabric of family resource history, there is another major thread that comes from a very different model of social service: the settlement house. Salient aspects of family resource programs can be traced directly to the principles and ideas that nourished the growth of settlement houses and to the special role played by settlement houses in their communities.

American settlement houses developed at a time of great concern over the stress on individuals and society as new streams of populations moved into urban areas, thereby changing the structure of cities and often bringing about cultural and racial conflict (Hillman, 1960). The settlement houses were described as an "experimental effort to aid in the solution of the social and industrial problems which are engendered by the modern conditions of life in a great city" (Addams, 1910/1972).

Though settlement houses were deeply rooted in the community and differed from one another as communities differ, they also shared common characteristics. They were based in geographical neighborhoods and aimed to understand and develop the services of the neighborhood. Concerned with the family and its life in the community and larger society, they strengthened the capacity of the family for self-direction and growth. Their methods were flexible: developing programs to meet the specific needs of the family in the community and creating a "sense of neighborhood" that provided channels for expressing and acting on community concerns (Hillman, 1960). They did not duplicate the services of other family agencies but rather helped people to utilize them. Settlement houses sought to develop stable and harmonious communities that would establish a common ground for the joining of people of different races and cultures bound together by the living conditions of their community.

The first settlement house opened in New York in 1886, to be followed a few years later in Chicago by the famous Hull House (Addams, 1935). These early settlement houses were staffed by the college-educated, who were inbued with a commitment to community service and determined to be advocates for the poor. Young professionals moved into settlement houses, as Jane Addams said, "not to uplift the masses, but to be neighbors to the poor and restore communications between various parts of society."

Basic to the success of any settlement house was the relevance of its program to the people living in the community (Brueckner, 1963). Program providers were cautioned to design services that came from an understanding of the community, especially its culture and traditions, and a knowledge of the neighborhood itself. Social ills manifested in the community became the targets for action, and settlement houses were host centers for advocacy efforts. Members of settlement houses were encouraged to take action themselves toward improving their living conditions and bettering the environment for families rather than build dependence on the settlement house and its advocacy for them.

Strengthening neighborhood and family life, the clarion call of settlement houses, is echoed in the stated goals of many family support programs. The settlement house view that the family and its fortunes are interrelated with the life of the community and the social policies of the nation is intimately connected with the ecological approach of many family support programs. Just as settlement house staff assisted people to become informed citizens able to act together on their own behalf, so family support programs serve as centers for advocacy efforts. Finally, the commitment of settlement houses to creating a spirit of community and belonging is strongly reflected in the family support programs, where the isolation of contemporary families is alleviated and parents speak of programs as "extended families."

EMERGENCE OF FAMILY SUPPORT PROGRAMS

Although much can be learned from looking at the programmatic roots of today's family resource programs, there is no doubt that they would not have emerged as they did without the influence of the social climate that existed in the mid 1970s. The political and social turbulence of the 1960s initiated a series of rapid changes in our social fabric that confronted parents in the 1970s with an entirely new backdrop for family life. The social values, economic realities, and personal needs that families faced then and continue to face today are qualitatively different from those that confronted past generations, and they help to explain why family resource programs took the particular shape they did.

The current debate over whether the family is in serious and permanent decline began in the 1960s, as other institutions—schools, churches, parental and governmental rights of power—were battered with sometimes violent discontent. The civil rights movement opened a national soul-searching that continued through the Vietnam War and involved every social and economic group and challenged every long-held belief. Much of the challenging came directly back home into the family itself, the traditional seat of social authority (Glasser, 1975). The rampant rebellion against old ideas often took the tangible form of conflict between parents and children, which led both generations to question the content and method of child rearing that had produced such an impasse (Featherstone, 1979). The assault on traditional ideas did not end there. In the wake of the civil rights and Vietnam War protests, the women's movement emerged, fed by simmering resentments of the rigid stereotypes of the 1950s. It began with full force in the early 1970s and continues into the present, bringing with it profound changes in family life and child-rearing patterns (Harris, 1973).

Economics has played a significant role in changing patterns of family life in the past twenty years. The increasing number of families living in poverty, which includes almost 20 percent of all American children, presents a tragic dimension of economic stress on families. For a growing number of middle-class families, in which mothers traditionally stayed home, there is no alternative to two paychecks if they expect to maintain a middle-class standard of living. This generation of parents is the first to face the reality that the standard of living is not necessarily getting better as the cost of staying in place increases (Samuelson, 1985).

In view of the economic realities and the new opportunities opened up by the women's movement, many mothers have gone to work. More than two-thirds of mothers with children under 18 have joined the labor force. Fifty-two percent of all mothers with children under age six and almost 45 percent of mothers with children under age one are employed outside the home—and the figures are rising monthly. Such an exodus of women from traditional homemaking has far-reaching implications for child rearing, employment patterns, family responsibilities, attitudes toward women, and the roles of husbands and fathers (Calhoun et al., 1980; Masnick & Bane, 1980; Smith, 1979).

The notion of fathers as not being responsive to infants and of being less nurturing than mothers has been contradicted by research and rejected by fathers who take an increasing role in child rearing. Research also indicates that fathers provide a different kind of nurturing, which contributes to their children's capacities for social, emotional, and cognitive development (Clarke-Stewart, 1980; Lamb, 1981; Parke, 1981). In direct contrast to earlier ideas about fathers, fathers are now becoming intensely involved in child rearing, beginning with their assistance in the birth of their children.

Another dramatic change in family lifestyle is the frequency with which families move. An increasing number of families do not stay in one place long enough to develop the intricate neighborhood and community connections that were once the mainstay of mutual support. The average family that buys a home sells it within three years, leaving little time for parents or children to develop lasting relationships with neighbors or strong ties to a school. Twenty percent of the American population moves each year, and the average individual will move a total of 14 times in his or her life span (Frishman, 1984). Adjusting to a new community, new friends, a new job, and building a network for support are major tasks, often not completed before the process has to start over again.

Traditional family structures are also changing as the number of single parents rises. Twenty-five percent of all American children will live in a single-parent home before they are aged eighteen. Half of all marriages now end in divorce, and more than 80 percent of those who divorce remarry, usually within two years of divorce. The institution of marriage, and of family, is not declining, although marital partners and members of a family may change. A child is increasingly likely to have two sets of parents instead of one, four sets of grandparents, and two different sets of siblings (Frishman, 1984). The adaptations that these changes require—adjustments to loss and building new relationships with new family members—can be enormously stressful to both children and adults. The support systems left to families undergoing radical change are few and far between, even though the need for them is obvious.

Today's family, as it has emerged from the cauldron of the 1960s, is decidedly different from the idealized image of family that "Leave It to Beaver" portrayed in the 1950s. For most families, there are no clear-cut paths through the maze that life presents to them. The traditional ways in which many of today's parents were brought up simply do not fit the current situation: the family has taken on different forms, experiences different problems, and bases child rearing on different principles (Douvan et al., 1980). The older version of family life, for all its inequities, had clearly defined areas of responsibility for each family member, while today's idea of shared responsibility requires continuous negotiation and cooperation to meet the demands of each new situation (Bernard, 1980).

Nevertheless, families remain central to American culture and the major way in which children are raised. Ninety-eight percent of all children still live in families. Families struggle with isolation, the absence of community feeling, and the demands of social and economic circumstances but are surviving and growing in strength (Bane, 1976). It is against this backdrop of rapid social change combined with a strong desire for the continuity of family life that family support programs have emerged (Pizzo, 1983) The climate was right for the emergence of an entirely new kind of program, based in part on the older form of parent education but also on a community orientation similar to the settlement house model and on the strong desire for peer support popularized by numerous self-help groups that sprang up in the 1960s. The need for a sense of belonging to a community of people with similar concerns was acute, and parents were increasingly eager for support in their roles.

DISTINCTIVE CHARACTERISTICS OF FAMILY SUPPORT PROGRAMS

While the roots of family support are clear, the programs that emerged in the mid-1970s have unique characteristics. The parents' role in "becoming educated" is different. Parents are no longer viewed as vessels to be filled with appropriate information about child development. Being a parent is an integrated, specific stage of adulthood reflecting childhood experiences but also having its own developmental stages. Parenthood is seen as a creative, self-growth period that requires sensitivity and responsiveness to the next generation while at the same time permitting, even necessitating, the expansion of one's own competence, emotional attachments, and coping skills (Anthony & Benedek, 1970). Evidence that parental behavior is a primary influence on the development of the child and that parents who are stimulating and express confidence in child rearing enhance their child's social and cognitive growth (Clarke-Stewart & Apfel, 1978) reinforces the focus of family support programs on the parent as a total person.

Concurrent with the view of parenthood as a developmental stage is an emphasis on the family as a whole. It is through the family, regardless of its structure, that the child receives the care, attention, and love that will enable him to become a healthy, productive member of society. Programs working with children and parents have been assessed as being more effective than programs working with the child alone (Bronfenbrenner, 1974). Furthermore, it has become apparent that concern for children necessitates considering the child in the context of the family, and the family in the larger context of community life, social institutions, and government policies (Bronfenbrenner, 1979). Family resource programs often take an ecological approach, responding to the cultural and social environment of the families they serve as an integral part of improving the families' ability to function.

New knowledge about the capacities of infants and the crucial development that takes place in the first weeks and months of life (Escalona, 1968; Greenspan, 1981; Stone et al., 1973; Osofsky, 1979) has prompted parents to seek educational information and has prompted programs to emphasize the significance of parent-child interaction early on. The evidence on infant and toddler development has stimulated the growth of programs specifically oriented toward parents of newborns. Typically, there have been no services for parents of children of this age group except those with special needs.

Closely allied to the recognition of the importance of the early years is an emphasis on prevention, a key ingredient of family support programs. "Getting the right start" is no insurance against future problems, but it does lay the groundwork for good development, which alleviates the necessity for early remedial measures.

Another dimension of family support that contrasts significantly with earlier models of social service is the movement from a sickness to a health model. Using a nondeficit model in approaching the goal of nurturing families to function more effectively challenges program designers to think in terms of building on the strengths, not only managing the deficits, of the families they serve. Since support for parents is associated with more positive and responsive interaction with children (Colletta,

1981; Crnic et al., 1983; Crockenberg, 1981; Wandersman et al., 1980), the availability of support programs represents a preventive, health-oriented approach to serving families.

Related to acceptance of a health model is the strong emphasis on interdependence that characterizes family resource programs. The notion of self-reliance and independence no longer means that people are expected to function in a vacuum, apart from others. The time is long past when any family could be a self-sufficient unit, producing its own food, educating its own children, relying solely on its own resources. In *All Our Children* (1977), Kenneth Keniston states: "Recognizing that family self-sufficiency is a false myth, we also need to acknowledge that all today's families need help in raising children" (p. 23). Family support programs exist because families recognize a need for interaction and support and understand that the ability to relate to others is a prerequisite for functioning independently.

The community-based nature of family support programs is a direct link to their settlement-house roots. Many of today's parents are immigrants of a different kind, the newly mobile population that stays in the same place for a short time before moving on. The feeling of uprootedness, of the loss of traditional support systems, of the lack of cohesive community is somewhat similar to the experience of the first generation of immigrants trying to make their way in a new country. The importance of supporting networks in alleviating these feelings, reducing stress, and maximizing the family's ability to function has been documented in a growing body of research (Colletta, 1981; Unger, 1979; Wandersman et al., 1980) and adopted as a central focus in family support programs.

The definition of support as "a range of interpersonal exchanges that provide an individual with information, emotional reassurance, physical or material assistance, and a sense of self as an object of concern" describes one of the basic components of family resource programs (Pilisuk & Parks, 1980, p. 158). In these programs this definition has been expanded to include the concept that a growth of self-confidence in response to support enables parents to become advocates in their own behalf and for the family of which they are members. Thus, a social support network provides for individual and family relationships that are nurturing, that build on the family's capacities to cope with daily living, and that help families to become involved in shaping the environment in which their future lies. Support for families can range from informal social interactions to participation in a structured peer group to intensive, long-term management of severe family problems (Gottlieb, 1981; Henderson, 1977; LaRocco et al., 1980; Telleen, 1983).

One thing that distinguishes family support from all other social programs of this century is the overwhelming response of all kinds of families to programs that emerged spontaneously in settings all over the country. For example, Family Tree Parenting Center in Lafayette, Louisiana, reaches 27,000 parents annually through its workshops, support groups, and parenting classes. PIPS (Pre-school and Infant Parenting Services) Warmline in Los Angeles responds to 5,000 calls a year on a five-day-a-week basis. Over 2,000 new parents a year are reached by PACES (Parent and Childbirth Education Society), which operates a network of services in ten Chicago suburbs. In each of these situations, response far exceeded expectations, an experience typical of programs throughout the country and one that should command the attention of policymakers. It is a clear indication of the support that parents desire. Grassroots family resource programs, regardless of their origin or central method of service, have been remarkably sensitive to the immediate needs and the traditional social context of the groups they serve. This sensitivity is not "designed into" programs. It comes from the direct, spontaneous participation of parents who organize the programs, families who have poured through the open doors of family support programs before the paint on the walls was dry.

MILESTONES FOR FAMILY SUPPORT PROGRAMS

There was a virtual explosion of parent support and education programs in the 1970s. Organizations interested in the burgeoning area of parenting education, such as the Junior League, joined forces with professionals working in social service agencies and parents themselves to become actively involved in planning and funding programs. Program initiators used the available resources around them and patched together a web of mutual aid, information, and linkages to other resources to begin meeting the needs they saw. Hospitals and other medical facilities in some communities added family resource components, some networks and agencies developed independently, and in some areas the school districts responded to the demand for family support. The Minnesota Department of Education initiated a statewide program of parent support through the public schools, as did the State of Missouri, and individual districts created parent resource centers in their schools. Recognizing that providing support to families before a child is old enough for Head Start significantly enhanced opportunities for the child to succeed, the federal Head Start program expanded services to families with children up to age three through a nationwide system of Parent-Child Development Centers.

It is not possible to describe the many programs established in the 1970s, so we are limited to mentioning a few of the first programs, diverse in origin, and representative of others. Among the early programs was Parents' Place in San Francisco, California, which began in 1974 as a result of discussions among two mothers, a social worker, and a child development specialist on the stresses experienced by parents. Starting with a small support group, the program is now affiliated with Jewish Family and Children's Services in San Francisco and includes education, support groups, workshops, and a multitude of services to families.

In the same year, a cooperative venture between a women's service organization, Junior Sorosis, and Valencia Community College in Orlando, Florida, began providing parent support programs. Today it offers a broad range of services for parents and children through the Parents Resource Center, which is affiliated with Valencia Community College.

In Houston, Texas, in 1976, five mothers of premature babies and a social worker founded a support group which grew to become Parents of Prematures, a national resource for information on prematures and their families and on ways to establish similar groups for parents of prematures. It has even convinced a local manufacturer to design clothes expressly for premature babies.

In Evanston, Illinois, Family Focus opened its doors in 1976 after a year of planning by early childhood educators, social workers, and community leaders. Its intent was to enhance parent/child interaction in the first three years of life by developing support programs based on the cultural, ethnic, and economic characteristics of the parents in the communities served. Today Family Focus operates centers in seven Chicago communities, which serve parents with a broad spectrum of needs, including teenage parents.

Impetus for the Family Support Center in Yeadon, Pennsylvania, which also started in 1976, came from volunteers from the Junior League of Philadelphia assisted by professionals from child service agencies. The program targeted a population of families at high risk for abuse and neglect and today has grown to include home-based services, a family school, and peer support groups.

Avance, founded in 1973 by a graduate student at Cornell University as a parent education program in a primarily Hispanic community, has developed into a large program dealing with the complex economic and social needs of families in San Antonio, Texas.

Concord Parents and Children was created in 1977 in response to a survey on parents' interest in education and peer support by a childbirth educator. The interest, confirmed by the response, started what today is a large center in Concord, New Hampshire, offering a multitude of activities for parents and children and for families with special needs.

As these programs illustrate, throughout the 1970s the concept of parent support evolved in a variety of programs around the country, independently of one another. Each began with a need perceived by the initiators and grew at a rate far beyond expectations. The response to programs clearly indicated that they were filling a void for parents, and the fact that they developed spontaneously in separate communities indicated that family support was an idea whose "time had come." When the decade of the 1980s was ushered in, parent support programs dotted the whole map of the United States.

In the early 1980s, there was a growing demand from family support programs around the country to share information, make connections, and discover the extent of the movement that encompassed so many different kinds of programs. In May 1981, representatives from family support programs all over the United States and Canada met in Evanston, Illinois, at the invitation of Family Focus. The Administration for Children, Youth and Families provided minimal funding ($2,000) to help set up the conference, which was planned for 100 people. Three hundred people came to Evanston and were accommodated with free rooms and breakfast from local families. Imbued with the spirit of a new movement, participants decided to form an organization to be a supporting network for the variety of programs they represented. The official name for the network became the Family Resource Coalition.

Two years later, in May 1983, the Administration for Children, Youth and Families, in conjunction with the Bush Foundation of St. Paul, Minnesota, funded a second conference, decidedly different from the first but indicative of the increasing attention focused on family support. This conference, held at Yale University, included 300 invited guests: practitioners from representative family support programs, academicians interested in studying the process of developing and implementing programs, researchers interested in what these programs were doing for families, and media representatives interested in reporting about the new movement.

The Yale Conference has been followed by statewide conferences in Florida, Texas, California, New York, Illinois, Colorado, Oklahoma, and Pennsylvania. In addition to the Family Resource Coalition, sponsoring groups have included statewide organizations, colleges and universities, regional offices of Human Development Services, and state agencies. These statewide conferences, and the eagerly sought participation of family resource professionals in a wide variety of other conferences on child abuse, mental health, child development, social policy, and social service, have quickly moved family resource from a collection of independently established programs to a full-fledged movement with the potential to exert tremendous influence on American life.

Within a remarkably short time, program leaders, participants, policymakers, and academicians from a wide variety of fields are beginning to perceive family support programs as an institution that provides an essential service to children and families. The Family Resource Coalition, representing thousands of program providers and participants, publishes a quarterly *Report*, disseminates materials, and serves as a national clearinghouse for family support programs. Family support programs mushroom in ever increasing variety around the country, some stressing the value of parent education, others focusing on the interaction characteristic of self-help, still others emphasizing the sense of community, and most sharing elements of each approach.

From its early beginnings in support in our country's history, family support programs have evolved into a system both recognizable and acknowledged. Only recently have we given this thread of support a name —family support system—and come to understand its definable characteristics. Both as they emerged and today, family support programs share some basic assumptions even as they reflect a wide variety of approaches and methods. These assumptions are as follows.

• All families need support, regardless of economic status or specific concerns. Most parents want to be good parents no matter what their resources are. The varying kinds of support provided by family resource programs are determined by the needs of the parents and are responsive to the cultural and social characteristics of the communities in which the families live.
• The availability of social networks, mutual aid and peer groups, is essential to the family's ability to enhance the child's development.
• Information on child development, obtained both formally and informally, assists families in their child rearing role.
• Support programs increase the family's ability to cope rather than provide a system on which families become dependent. Support should build on the strengths that whole families and individual family members already have. The confidence that family support helps parents build enables families to manage their own lives and participate in shaping the environment in which they live.
• Providing support during the first years of a child's life serves a preventive function. Early and continuing support is aimed at strengthening the family unit and preventing family dysfunction.
• Since families are part of a community, their needs cannot be met in isolation from it. Support is provided in the context of community life and through links with community resources. (Family Resource Coalition, Fall 1981)

In many ways, family support programs are a modern illustration of the ongoing process of human response to change. Using the best information they had and the resources at hand, people through the ages have created their own innovative responses to social and economic circumstances that threatened to diminish the quality of their lives and their capacities to raise their children in the way they chose. The resilience of the family through all the changes marks it as the fundamental unit in which children grow and learn to understand the society in which they live. The conditions of contemporary life have given rise to family support programs as this generation's way of assuring the family's continuing strength.

REFERENCES

Addams, J. (1935). *Forty years at Hull House.* New York: MacMillan.

Addams, J. (1972). *The spirit of youth and the city streets.* Urbana, IL: University of Illinois Press. (Original work published in 1910).

American Council on Education. (1945). *Helping teachers understand children.* Washington, DC: American Council on Education.

Anthony, J. E., & Benedek, T. (Eds.). (1970). *Parenthood: Its psychology and psychopathology.* Boston: Little, Brown.

Bane, M. J. (1976). *Here to stay: American families in the 20th century.* New York: Basic Books.

Bernard, J. (1980). Changing family lifestyle: One role, two roles, shared roles. In E. Douvan et al. (Eds.), *American families* (p. 18). Dubuque, IA: Kendall/ Hunt.

Bloom, B. S. (1964). *Stability and change in human characteristics.* New York: Wiley.

Borman, L. (1975). *Exploration in self-help and mutual aid.* Evanston, IL: Center for Urban Affairs, Northwestern University.

Borstelman, L. J. (1977, April). Public and professional child-rearing concepts: Spock and beyond. Paper delivered at American Orthopsychiatric Association, New York.

Bronfenbrenner, U. (1961). The changing American child: A speculative analysis. *Merrill-Palmer Quarterly,* No. 7, 73–84.

Bronfenbrenner, U. (1974). *Is early intervention effective? A report on longitudial evaluations of preschool programs.* Washington, DC: Department of Health, Education and Welfare, U.S. Children's Bureau.

Bronfenbrenner, U. (1979). *Ecology of human development.* Cambridge: Harvard University Press.

Brueckner, W. H. (1963, October 23–25). Human problems in the core city—Current thinking on the role of the settlement. Proceedings of a conference, The Mental Health Role of Settlement and Community Centers, Swampscott, MA.

Calhoun, J. A., Grotberg, E. H., & Rackley, W. R. (1980). *The status of children, youth, and families, 1979* (DDHS Publication No. OHDS 80-30274). Washington, DC: U.S. Department of Health and Human Services.

Clarke-Stewart, K. A. 1980. The father's contribution to children's cognitive and social development in early childhood. In F. A. Pederson (Ed.), *The father-infant relationship: Observational studies in the family setting.* New York: Praeger.

Clarke-Stewart, K. A., & Apfel, N. (1978). Evaluating parental effects on child development. In L. Schulman (Ed.), *Review of research education*, Vol. 6. Itasca, IL: F. E. Peacock.

Colletta, N. D. (1981). Social support and the risk of maternal rejection by adolescent mothers. *Journal of Psychology, 109*, 191–197.

Crnic, K. A., Greenburg, M. T., Ragozin, A. S., Robinson, N. M., & Basham, R. B. (1983). Effects of stress and social support on mothers and premature and full-term infants. *Child Development, 54*, 209–217.

Crockenberg, S. B. (1981). Infant irritability, mother responsiveness and social support influences on the security of infant-mother attachment. *Child Development, 54*, 857–865.

Douvan, E., Weingarten, H., & Scheiber, J. L. (Eds.), (1980). *American Families.* Dubuque, IA: Kendall/Hunt.

Dowley, E. (1971). Perspectives on early childhood education. In R. H. Anderson & H. G. Shane (Eds.), *As the twig is bent.* Boston: Houghton Mifflin.

Escalona, S. (1968). *The roots of individuality: Normal patterns of development in infancy.* Chicago: Aldine.

Evans, G. (1979). *Family Circle guide to self-help.* New York: Ballantine.

Family Resource Coalition. (1981, Fall). *Statement of philosophy, goals, and structure.* Chicago: Family Resource Coalition.

Featherstone, J. (1979). Family matters. *Harvard Education Review, 49* (1), 20–52.

Frishman, B. (1984). *American families.* Washington, DC: People for the American Way.

Glasser, W. (1975). *The identity society.* New York: Harper & Row.

Gordon, I. J. (1966). New conceptions of children's learning and development. In W. B. Waltjen (Ed.), *Learning and mental health in the schools* (pp. 49–73). Washington, DC: Association for Supervision and Curriculum Development.

Gottlieb, B. H. (Ed.). (1981). *Social networks and social support.* Beverly Hills, CA: Sage.

Greenspan, S. (1981). *Psychopathology and adaptation in infancy and early childhood: Principles of clinical diagnosis and preventive intervention.* New York: International Universities Press.

Grotberg, E. H. (Ed.). (1976). *Two hundred years of children.* (DHEW Publication No. OHD 77-30103). Washington, DC: U.S. Department of Health, Education and Welfare.

Harris, L. (1973). *The anguish of change.* New York: Norton.

Hartley, R. E., Frank, L. K., & Goldenson, R. M. (1952). *Understanding children's play.* New York: Columbia University Press.

Henderson, S. (1977). The social network, support and neuroses. *British Journal of Psychiatry, 131*, 185–191.

Hillman, A. (1960). *Neighborhood centers today: Action programs for a rapidly changing world. Report of a survey.* New York: National Federation of Settlement and Neighborhood Centers.

Hunt, J. M. (1961). *Intelligence and experience.* New York: Ronald Press.

Keniston, K., & the Carnegie Council on Children. (1977). *All our children.* New York: Harcourt, Brace Jovanovich.

Lamb, M. E. (Ed.). (1981). *The role of the father in child development* (2d ed.). New York: Wiley.

LaRocca, J. M., House, J. S., & French, J. R. (1980). Social support, occupational stress and health. *Journal of Health and Social Behavior, 21*, 202–218.

Lieberman, M., Borman, L., & Associates. (1979). *Self-help groups for coping with crisis.* San Francisco: Jossey-Bass.

Masnick, G., & Bane, M. J. (1980). *The nation's families, 1960–1990.* Cambridge, MA: Joint Center for Urban Studies of MIT and Harvard University.

Miller, P., Ingham, J. G., & Davidson, J. (1976). Life events, symptoms and social support. *Journal of Psychosomatic Research, 20*, 516–522.

Osofsky, J. D. (Ed.). (1979). *Handbook of infant development.* New York: Wiley.

Parke, R. D. (1981). *Fathers.* Cambridge, MA: Harvard University.

Pilisuk, M., & Parks, S. H. (1980). Structural dimensions of social support groups. *Journal of Psychology, 106*, 158.

Pizzo, P. (1983). *Parent to parent.* Boston: Beacon.

Samuelson, R. J. (1985, April 8). Selfishness and sobriety. *Newsweek*, p. 63.

Schlossman, S. L. (1978a). Before Home Start—Notes toward a history of parent education in America, 1897–1929. *Harvard Educational Review, 3*, 436–467.

Schlossman, S. L. (1978b). The parent education game—Politics of child psychology in the 1970's. *Teacher's College Record, 79* (4), 788–808.

Smith, R. E. (Ed.). (1979). *The subtle revolution.* Washington, DC: Urban Institute.

Stone, L. J., Smith, H., & Murphy, L. B. (Eds.). (1973). *The competent infant: Research and commentary.* New York: Basic Books.

Telleen, S. (1983). The role of social networks and problem solving in a family support program: Introduction to child development staff guide. Unpublished manuscript. Available from Family Focus, Evanston, IL.

Unger, D. G. (1979). An ecological approach to the family: The role of social networks, social stress, and mother-child interaction. Unpublished master's thesis, Merrill-Palmer Institute, Detroit, MI.

Wandersman, P. L., Wandersman, A., & Kahn, S. (1980). Social support in the transition to parenthood. *Journal of Community Psychology, 8* (4), 332–342.

Weber, W. (1984). *Ideas influencing early childhood education: A theoretical analysis.* New York: Teacher's College Press.

4 HEAD START: A PIONEER OF FAMILY SUPPORT

Edward F. Zigler and
Johanna Freedman

Preceding chapters have noted that today's family support programs represent an "ecological" approach, based on the principle that while families have the most significant influence on children's development, other institutions also affect both family and child. This ecological understanding of human development, inspired by Urie Bronfenbrenner's analysis of the Head Start program, has changed the focus of many intervention programs from single individuals toward the relations among family members and between the family as a whole and the community at large (Bronfenbrenner, 1974; Zigler & Berman, 1983). Family support programs unite the early precept that a healthy society consists of autonomous families, with a more recent conception that government, corporate, and social service communities have an obligation to facilitate family life. Family support programs are characterized by strong working alliances among families, interdisciplinary professionals, paraprofessionals, volunteers, and members of both the public and private sectors. The programs involve families as a whole, stressing strengths as well as solving problems. They generally consist of self-help networks composed of people with similar concerns and often function as much as information and referral services as direct providers of care.

Concerns over the role of the family are as old as human history. The conceptual underpinnings and programmatic techniques of family support programs date at least from the early sixteenth century, with Martin Luther's conceptual and pragmatic construction of a universal, lifelong education system, with cognitive, religious, emotional, and social aspects (Braun & Edwards, 1972). Yet, despite the fact that family support programs are founded on what are clearly immemorial human concerns, the vast majority of family support programs have appeared in the past twenty years (Weiss, 1983) and seem to have originated in the cauldron of social change that produced Head Start.

The social upheaval that fostered the public-sector creation of Head Start and lay construction of family support programs dates from the massive dislocations and strains imposed by the depression, the Second World War, and their aftermath. During the war, families were divided and uprooted as men went to war and women went to work outside the home. Rural populations moved to the cities in pursuit of work in war industries, and urban poverty increased. Traditional groupings of generations, patterns of rootedness, and the structure of the family all changed. Family size dwindled and families grew less cohesive. Daily stories on welfare mothers, poverty, and hunger in the United States captured the national attention. Political pressure to ameliorate the situation increased, and with the New Deal conception that the republic is responsible for the welfare of its citizens widely accepted, Americans turned to the federal government for relief.

At first it was believed that short-term intervention would be sufficient. As socioeconomic conditions worsened, however, it became clear that many families needed continuing intervention in place of the reliable support once provided by relatives and friends. In time, both professionals and families themselves began to create such programs, and ongoing structural support with a focus on prevention replaced short-term aid.

From its inception in 1965, Head Start has functioned as a national laboratory for such intervention efforts. As a consequence of its action-research cycle, it has simultaneously added to our information concerning the components of successful interventions and has developed increasingly sophisticated and successful ways to supply social, informational, and instrumental assistance to families. Head Start's early development of a program that involved parents and community marks it as one of the pioneers of family support's prevention-focused ecological approach to intervention.

Head Start's initial outcome measures for the most part involved the aspect of the program involving child care, but even from the outset, the program focused on the problems of parents and community as well as children (Cooke, 1965). Parents were involved in many aspects of Head Start from the very beginning, owing to social forces mandating active participation by the economically disadvantaged in poverty programs and progressive developmental theory, which recognized the importance of parental inclusion. The federal government issued policy state-

ments and guidelines instituting parental involvement in Head Start, local governments and school boards sought to determine the appropriate
degrees of parental control over the program, and community action
groups and parents themselves defined and shaped roles for Head Start
parents. Parental roles included participation in program construction,
career-development programs, educational opportunities, and participation in children's classrooms.

Head Start's commitment to parental involvement was part of a larger
framework of self-administered programs for the economically disadvantaged. This focus on self-determination rather than dependence on
omnipotent professionals is one of the hallmarks of today's family support systems. While the 1960s were a time of economic prosperity for
the majority of Americans, social concern focused on the "other America" (Zigler, 1979a)—the one in which a sizable minority were economically and socially deprived. At the same time, the civil rights movement
was burgeoning, having achieved some success with the Civil Rights Act
of 1964. The Economic Opportunity Act, also passed in 1964, provided
programs and funds directly to local communities to redress some of the
social, political, and economic inequities that were becoming increasingly apparent. Reformist sentiment was great, legitimated to a large extent by social science theories about the need for political change to right
social injustice (Valentine & Stark, 1979). The most articulate spokes-
men for the poor saw participation as a first step toward "self-determination," and they considered self-determination—insofar as it implied a
basic shift in the power relations both within service institutions and in
the entire political process—a precondition for the development of effective social services.

As a "national emphasis" program, Head Start was under the aegis of
the Community Action Program, part of the "War on Poverty." This is
one reason for the early inclusion of parents in Head Start, as the Office
of Economic Opportunity (OEO) mandated the "maximum feasible participation" of the economically disadvantaged in the construction of such
programs. But OEO policy left it to local governments, parents, and programs to determine the precise nature of the roles parents were to play,
subject to community demands that "the Establishment" remedy structural racial and economic inequality. In the end, Head Start came to be
distinguished by its broad developmental approach and early commitment to a cooperative relationship among paraprofessionals, lay people,
and professionals from a variety of backgrounds. Thus, in a step unusual for the period, the creators of Head Start included not only educators but physicians, psychiatrists, politicians, and early childhood
specialists.

As a unique aspect of the program's broad developmental emphasis, public health physicians emphasized the need for a health component. Reports had revealed that the incidence of tuberculosis, rheumatic fever, physical and mental handicaps, and untreated chronic disabilities was far higher among economically disadvantaged children than among those from more affluent families. There was evidence that poor health care, coupled with inadequate nutrition, compromised physical, mental, and social development. Physicians on the planning board advised that Head Start not only provide children with a balanced meal each day but teach parents the basics of good nutrition, so that this element of the program could be carried on at home. In short, the planners recommended that the intervention program include not only the usual cognitive component but also parental education, medical attention, and nutritional enrichment. Head Start thus became far more than just a nursery school experience for low-income children. It offered instead comprehensive, family-oriented services that have functioned as a model for the programs that followed.

The initial response to Head Start, however, was overly optimistic concerning the amount of effort required to produce permanent changes in the quality of children's behavior. In response to the pressure for accountability, the outcome measure most often used over the twenty-year history of Head Start has been the IQ score or, more typically, the magnitude of change in the child's IQ score. As a result it became all too easy to avoid the rigors of goal-sensitive outcome evaluation and to conclude that a program was a success if it resulted in higher IQs and a failure if it did not.

Project planners were soon disillusioned by the first national evaluation of Head Start's impact on children, the Westinghouse-Ohio study (Westinghouse Learning Corp., 1969). The study reported that Head Start graduates showed only modest immediate gains on standardized tests of cognitive ability and that even these gains disappeared after a few years in school. Many concluded that the War on Poverty was lost, and no remediation of the damages of poverty was possible. This might have been the end of Head Start, and perhaps slowed the development of family support programs, since such programs would have been assumed to be a waste of funding, but criticism of the Westinghouse report softened, though it did not obviate, the report's destructive power. Bronfenbrenner (1979) commented that the findings of no differences resulting from Head Start could have been predicted because the design left so many variables uncontrolled, comparing "noncomparable groups of children under noncomparable program conditions" (p. 87). Campbell and Erlebacher (1970) also criticized the method and statistical procedures of the Westinghouse study. They argued that regression artifacts produced biases tending to underassess program benefits, a result further guaranteed by the fact that matched control subjects were drawn from populations whose average performance surpassed that of populations from which Head Start groups were drawn. Other critics of the report pointed out that the results testified only to the narrowness of the study's outcome measures and other inadequacies of design (Datta, 1976; Lazar, 1981; Madigson & Borbom, 1980; Smith & Bissell, 1970). Head Start was much more than an attempt to provide compensatory education or cognitive enrichment, these researchers argued; it also enhanced social skills (to which the Westinghouse–Ohio study paid limited attention) and provided food, medical, and dental checkups, and corrective services to children who were badly in need of them (Campbell & Erlebacher, 1970; Datta, 1976, 1983; Lazar, 1981; Smith & Bissell, 1970). Thus its justification lay in part in the provision of immediate benefits to low-income populations, not solely in expected future gains. Furthermore, advocates of Head Start argued, many local programs had mobilized parents and become a focus for community organization and expanded services for economically disadvantaged children. Many of the critics' points were supported empirically by an evaluation carried out by Kirschner Associates (1970). This study documented the impact of Head Start on services provided by the community and showed that it worked as a catalyst for improved services for low-income and minority families (Calhoun & Collins, 1981).

In addition, following the devastating Westinghouse report, Head Start planners sponsored a review of their own, which revealed that it was the relatively brief duration of the program and its discontinuity with children's and family's general experiences that accounted for its limited effect on cognitive behavior and they advocated increasing the program's term and family focus (Bronfenbrenner, 1974). In response, Head Start increased its commitment to a variety of "demonstration programs" intended to address the general needs of the family, thus enhancing its role as the conceptual precursor and model for today's family support movement.

Head Start's viability as a continuing program allowed it to serve as a stable base from which to experiment (Zigler, 1979b). The demonstration programs sponsored by Head Start were geographically diverse, extensively planned, carefully mounted, and throughly evaluated. Some of the programs proved ineffective and were discarded; others were demonstrable successes and spawned further efforts. A short description of some of these neofamily support programs follows.

Education for Parenthood, a national program jointly sponsored by the U.S. Office of Child Development and the Office of Education, played a significant role in Head Start programs for children and families. As part of the program, high school students learned about early childhood experientially through work with children in Head Start centers. In addition, curricula in child development and parenthood were developed to help train adolescents in the multiple responsibilities of parenting. This early program, conceived and implemented in the early 1970s, is a perfect example of how Head Start functioned as a family support program in its own time, and as a model in ours. This family-focused, prevention-oriented program, similar to those only now being instituted in a few "progressive" schools, prepared the parents of the future for the stresses that could otherwise lead to family dysfunction.

Follow Through, established in 1967 and administered by the U.S. Office of Education, was designed to continue and build on the cognitive and social gains made by children in full-year Head Start programs or similar preschool programs for children from low-income families. The program provided nutritional and health care, social and psychological services, and special teaching assistance to children during their early years in elementary school.

This program is especially notable for providing clear, quantitative support for the necessity of ensuring continuity in children's experiences and for the position that home, school, and neighborhood realities are synergistic rather than conflicting—the need for continuity among all these spheres of life being one of the theories that underlies many of the programmatic techniques of the family support movement.

Project Developmental Continuity (PDC) was planned to ensure continuity of services for children making the transition from the Head Start preschool program to elementary school. Head Start staff worked with parents, school administrators, and teachers to plan programs that would provide continuing health, social, and educational services through the third grade. An effort was made to maintain parent involvement during the child's first years in elementary school.

This program was a clear forerunner of the present full-family focus advocated by the family support movement, and it functioned as a major source of information for the ecological orientation of today's early childhood educators. The underlying rationale of the program was the importance of continuity, not only in terms of learning but also in terms of an individualized and personal approach to children and families (PDC, 1974). PDC projects emphasized the development of social competence, and basic skills. PDC was intended to ensure the realization of these goals after children had graduated from Head Start, since the philosophy and curriculum of the schools were often at a variance with the broad developmental emphasis of Head Start.

Parent and Child Centers (PCCs), launched in 1967, were the first Head Start experimental programs designed to serve very young children (0–3) and their families. In thirty-three urban and rural communities, these centers sought to improve services for over 4,000 children. The centers also helped parents learn about the needs of their children and about supportive services available in the community. In 1973, seven selected PCCs were provided with funds to develop a child-advocacy component and to promote services for all children in the community. Thus PCCS were the first program to incorporate family support-like, community-focused, and advocacy components. In addition, in contrast to the center-based Head Start program for three- to five-year-olds, which was considered "remedial," the PCCs were seen as "preventive" because children were reached so young as to ward off the incremental damages of deprivation. This focus on prevention of dependence, so characteristic of family support programs generally, thus found its first (perhaps catalytic) expression in Head Start's PCCs.

Each PCC was designed to fit individual community requirements (Hamilton, 1972), which makes the program more difficult to evaluate as a whole but is an expression of the same sensitivity to local needs that constitutes a major conceptual underpinning of today's national family support programs (for example, Parents Anonymous). Thus, the Vermont PCC program was partly center-based and partly home-based, whereas in the South, where center-based care for infants was prohibited by state law, the PCCs established "Alternate Home Mothers" (Costello & Binstock, 1970). During the day low-income children were brought to the homes of "middle-class" women who provided educational experiences. In short, PCCs demonstrated that prevention was viable and redirected the focus of programs from asking that the victims of structural, societal inequality change to advocating changes in society itself.

In 1970, three PCCs became *Parent and Child Development Centers* (PCDCs), part of an intensive research and demonstration program launched by the Office of Economic Opportunity and later sponsored by the Office of Child Development. The PCDC program investigated the significance of developmental processes in infants and the important role of parents in the development of children. In the three PCDC sites, different models of parent–infant interventions were developed and evaluated.

As a carefully sequenced research strategy to inform social policy, the PCDC suffered from a number of problems. A combination of increasing costs, lack of stable funding, and inconsistent political and social science support undermined the researcher's goal of assessing increasingly complex programs over a long period. In addition, the programs' variability in response to the changing needs of participants and to changes in external circumstances subverted the use of program features as independent variables.

As parent evaluation centers, however, each of the PCDCs developed unique methods of program delivery that continue to affect program construction. Such programs include the Birmingham model, which used a step system of increasing maternal responsibility for program work, culminating in staff positions; community paraprofessional involvement in New Orleans; and a carefully planned developmental program in Houston that began with a year of home visits, followed by a year of center programs for both mother and child. In addition, evaluations of PCDCs using mother–child observations demonstrated that PCDCs positively affected mothers' child-rearing skills. Mothers themselves reported that PCDCs were an invaluable source of peer contact and support as well as a vital source of information and services. Finally, the programs significantly affected children's cognitive functioning. Although the PCDCs were expensive in absolute terms, they were cost effective in that both mother and child were involved and comprehensive services, including programs for siblings, were provided (Andrews et al., 1982).

The PCDCs have clearly taught us much concerning what is and is not possible in family support programs. Sensitive service delivery may conflict with overall evaluation, suggesting that reviews will have to be on a program-by-program basis, while the inconsistency of political support could be remedied by protecting program funding against the whims of changing administrations.

Home Start, a three-year demonstration begun in 1972, also focused on the family. The program provided Head Start's health, social, and educational services to children and parents at home rather than at a center. Evaluations showed that this home-based approach was a viable alternative to providing services at a center, though parental social interaction was lost. Some 300 Head Start programs used a home-based approach, and Home Start training centers were created to provide training and technical assistance to Head Start and other programs to establish home-based programs. Home Start was thus an effort to ensure that there was continuity between the curriculum and actual conditions of life in the home. A second rationale for the construction of Home Start was that a center-based program is not possible in many communities. The final rationale for Home Start was the belief that learning that took place in the home would involve the whole family, not simply one child. Services in Home Start programs included referrals and follow-ups. Such outreach programs have since become an accepted part of many family support groups (for example, the Candlelighters, a program for families of children with cancer; and NetCan, a national computer-based child-abuse prevention network).

The *Child and Family Resource Program* (CFRP) was arguably Head Start's purest example of an early model family support program. The greatest advance of the CFRPs was their sensitivity to the heterogeneous needs of economically disadvantaged families. CFRPs were designed to offer a variety of services to meet the unique wants of each enrolled family. The services offered by each CFRP supplemented rather than replaced existing community resources. As in later family support programs, there were four cornerstones to the CFRP approach: (1) an emphasis on support and education for parents; (2) stress on developmental continuity by beginning services before birth and continuing them into elementary school; (3) an effort to coordinate comprehensive social services by way of direct service provision and referrals; and (4) an attempt to individualize services through needs assessment and goal setting with each family. Many CFRP services were selected on the premise that children's development cannot be optimal in the presence of serious unresolved family problems. Difficulties such as alcoholism, severe marital discord, unemployment, poor health, and substandard housing can easily frustrate efforts made to benefit children. One CFRP service involved health care and nutrition provided from the prenatal period onward. Home visitors helped coordinate services including medical and dental screening and free immunizations against a number of diseases. CFRPs also provided free transportation to families who otherwise had no access to the program.

The early education component of CFRP also built on existing resources as much as possible. Infant programs were conducted at the children's homes and/or at CFRP centers, depending upon the preferences of the parents and staff. Head Start programs were part of the services for three- to five-year-old children. A staff person worked to maximize parents' involvement in their childs' academic progress once the child was in school. One example of school-linkage activities was CFRP-sponsored meetings in which school personnel, Head Start teachers, and parents shared information and concerns. Another form of involvement was exemplified by a school-linkage coordinator in Bismark, North Dakota, who sent a questionnaire to first-grade teachers with CFRP children in their classrooms. The information obtained helped the CFRP staff determine which children needed tutoring or other forms of assistance to resolve early school-adjustment problems.

The parent-involvement component of CFRP not only included parents as fully as possible in all decisions affecting their children but also provided services designed for the parents themselves. Specifically, CFRPs offered courses on parenting, use of community resources, sewing, cooking, nutrition, and exercise. Parents were encouraged to continue their formal education, and many completed high school equivalency programs and/or enrolled in local community colleges. Many CFRPs also provided classes in the prevention, treatment, and identification of child abuse and neglect. Finally, CFRPs scheduled social activities for participating families, including parties, picnics, and outings to popular attractions.

The approximate annual cost per family in 1979 was estimated at $1,900 for the CFRPs directly and $1,150 in costs incurred by referring members to outside agencies. The documented benefits of the program include better preventive health care and nutrition for young children, rapid assistance to families during crises, correction of problems such as inadequate housing, and a general improvement in the family's quality of life (Travers, Beck, & Bissell, 1982).

One of the CFRPs' great advantages seems to be that parental choice determined the course of program development, ensuring that parents maintained and increased their sense of competence and control.

In short, one of the major strengths of the Head Start and related demonstration efforts was their flexibility and adaptability to changing goals. As Head Start developed, the program responded to criticism and was sensitive to theoretical advances. Thus, in the case of Head Start, social policy construction has been responsive to theoretical advances in the field of child development. Because of the application of theoretical developments to policy construction, Head Start has evolved into a program that emphasizes the significance of the family, considers all periods of a child's life as important, recognizes that children and families need multiple kinds of services, and has developed social-emotional measures of program success beyond the merely intellectual (Zigler & Trickett, 1978). These perspectives are apparent in the components of the basic program as well as in its demonstration efforts.

The value of Head Start will be more fully documented and understood when sensitive and systematic strategies are developed that are capable of measuring what the programs do. At present, however, a comparison with a very different intervention program, the Milwaukee Project, may be instructive. In sharp contrast to the family support supplied by Head Start, the Milwaukee Project involved extensive alteration of the families' lifestyle. Relative costs and benefits of this program and the CFRPs may give us some insight as to where Head Start's intervention efforts should be focused in the future.

MILWAUKEE PROJECT: A DIFFERENT KIND OF PROGRAM

The Milwaukee Project (Garber, 1975; Garber & Heber, 1977; Heber & Garber, 1975) involved twenty black children whose families resided in one of the poorest sections of the inner city and whose mothers scored lower than 80 on a standardized IQ test. Twenty similar children were randomly assigned to a control group and received no services. The intervention consisted of a seven-hour-a-day, five-day-a-week program, serving children from approximately 3 months of age until first grade. For the first few months each infant was cared for by a "substitute mother," who dressed, fed, played with, and stimulated her charge. Gradually, infants were phased into small-group care, and by late preschool they were receiving special educational enrichment in groups of four or five. Medical care and nutrition were provided, and the mothers received educational services including vocational training and information about homemaking and parenting skills.

Both intervention and control-group children were tested frequently and on a comparable time schedule. For the first year the two groups performed equivalently on the Gesell intelligence test; at about 18 months of age, the control group's performance began to decline. By age 4½, the difference between mean IQs was dramatic, with intervention-group children averaging approximately 120 and controls approximately 95. Despite declines in both groups, a mean difference of over 20 points has remained. By age 8–9, the average IQ was about 104 in the intervention group and about 80 in the control group. The children who received intervention also demonstrated superior academic achievement.

There has been concern about the original equivalence of the two groups (Page & Grandon, 1981), and the program has been criticized for vagueness in descriptions of the actual everyday procedures. A greater concern, however, may be that although the results do suggest that extensive early intervention of the kind provided by the Milwaukee Project can enable at-risk, disadvantaged children to succeed in performing at national norms on achievement and IQ tests, such increases on test scores are at the expense of any normal family life. Further, such programs would constitute an unrealistic financial burden if offered more generally.

The Milwaukee Project was a serious effort to improve the lot of economically disadvantaged children. Yet the family support approach of the CFRPs is relatively less invasive, while providing greater long-range benefits to entire families. It seems that the family support approach is an impressive improvement over more expensive, more intrusive programs. Also, there are ethical reasons to question the humanity and wisdom of replacing parents for most of a young child's day. Because the Head Start program does not separate a child from parents except for short periods, such a program is in keeping with current values of family integrity.

HEAD START: THE PROGRAM AS A WHOLE

So far we have discussed in detail how Head Start demonstration programs functioned as a forerunner of today's family support programs.

The basic Head Start program has functioned in a similar fashion, as is well illustrated by a large body of research which has demonstrated its effects on children, parents, and communities as a whole.

Head Start's policy of trying to involve families is demonstrated by the National Head Start Parent Involvement study (Stubbs, 1980), which reported that current or former Head Start parents comprised 89 percent of the centers' policymaking councils and committees. Ninety-five percent of the programs provided funds for parent-initiated activities, most of which were Head Start related. Most centers had developed lists of community resources to be used by parents. Eighty-six percent of the teachers reported that parents had been taught activities to use at home with their children. In 77 percent of the programs, parents volunteered in the classrooms, and 32 percent of the Head Start centers employed parents.

Similarly, Kirschner Associates' assessment (1970) of the Child Development Associate project (CDA), a program that provides experiential training in meeting all the needs of very young children, found that over a third of CDA trainees were parents of current or former Head Start children. This program helped parents to do well by doing good, as they were simultaneously trained in improved parenting skills, provided career education and employment, and filled a desperate need for competent child-care givers. Clearly, this program is an early, exemplary form of family support, helping children, parents, and the community as a whole to help themselves.

Head Start reaches out to parents in many ways. In a survey of 32 programs involving 656 children (Abt Associates, 1978), 81 percent of the parents reported that someone from Head Start had visited their home. This is in contrast to parents with children in other preschools, only 43 percent of whom reported home visits. Eighty percent of the programs serving parents provided social services including information and referral, counseling, and transportation—services that the parents felt were generally successful. Center staff in 90 percent of the programs reported that parents used community social services such as mental health clinics, guidance clinics, work and recreation facilities, and family planning clinics as a result of Head Start information and referral services.

A number of reviews (Abt, 1976; Datta, 1976, 1983; Grotberg, 1980; Hertz, 1977; O'Keefe, 1978) examined the effects of Head Start preschool programs on families and reported benefits to both parents and children. These studies indicated that parents gained increased satisfaction with life, improvement of life skills, job training, and employment from involvement in Head Start. These are precisely the sorts of gains aimed at by today's family support programs—gains in general social competence rather than narrowly defined skills.

Midco Educational Associates (1972) investigated the effects of parent involvement in Head Start and compared centers where parental involvement was high with those where it was low. The study found that parents who were highly involved felt more successful, happier, and more satisfied than parents who were less involved. The general life satisfaction of the highly involved parents also increased more than that of the less involved during the time their children were enrolled in Head Start. Parents minimally involved in Head Start felt less control over their own lives and less able to influence the schools or their child's education.

O'Kcefe (1978) cites a number of similar Head Start benefits to parents, including increased social contacts, assistance in assessment of family needs and referral to services, parent education opportunities, and strengthening of parental support for their children's education.

Lamb-Parker (1983) examined the effect of Head Start program participation on 82 mothers in New York City. She compared the mothers' psychological well-being at the beginning of the year and nine months later. The mothers who participated most in the program had higher levels of psychological well-being and lower levels of depression, anxiety, and somatic complaints. With increased participation, the mothers' faith or trust in other people also increased.

Several studies have described economic and educational benefits to parents as a result of their involvement in regular Head Start programs. Adams (1976) found that 11 of the 13 most intensely involved parents in her Wisconsin study had gone off welfare as a result of their involvement in Head Start.

The Head Start Assessment study (HEW, 1977) found many parents who reported "dramatic changes in their life attributable to Head Start involvement. A number of parents who start out as volunteers become aides, cooks, teachers and even program directors. . . . The many personal success stories of parents who became actively involved suggest that it is in reality an area of significant program achievement" (p. 10).

Clearly, while parent involvement and parent support are not isomorphic, Head Start's parental involvement component has functioned as a powerful form of support, increasing parents confidence and competence both as parents and as individuals.

EFFECTS OF PARENTAL INVOLVEMENT ON CHILDREN

An indirect but highly important aspect of parental involvement in Head Start is its potential impact on children. Benefits for parents extend to their children because happier, more self-confident, more informed parents are more capable and competent parents. Several studies in the past decade have reported benefits in academic achievement to children with involved parents. In a followup study of 94 children who had attended Head Start in Georgia in the 1960s, Monroe and McDonald (unpublished manuscript) examined differences between children whose parents had been very involved and those whose parents were less involved. Parents whose children had graduated from high school reported that they had participated in Head Start parent activities or served as volunteers more often than parents of dropouts. In a study of 59 children from three New York Head Start programs, Weld (1973) found parents' involvement in Head Start and their children's gains on several intelligence measures to be positively related. Such family-function variables as the mother's perception of the value of education, her sensitivity to the child's developmental level, and her support for individuality were more closely related to the child's profit from Head Start than was family socioeconomic status. Weld states that the development of these behavioral and individual characteristics is a principal goal of Head Start's parental involvement component; as his findings demonstrate, these goals are achieved. In summary, the basic Head Start program has clearly functioned as a family support program and functioned well. Parents participate in a wide variety of ways and gain benefits commensurate with their efforts. The positive effect on communities has been no less.

IMPACT ON COMMUNITIES' SOCIAL SERVICES

Head Start has worked with communities as a whole, providing services to families and contributing to the local economy. The major study of the impact of Head Start on communities was conducted by Kirschner Associates (1970), which compared 58 Head Start communities to 7 non-Head Start communities. A total of 1,496 changes related to Head Start objectives were counted in the Head Start communities while few were found in the non-Head Start areas. Changes included more health and educational opportunities for the economically disadvantaged and minorities, increased involvement of low-income persons in decision-making, and increased employment of local people in paraprofessional work.

Head Start often plays an intermediary role in linking families to services. In our extremely complex society, the economically disadvantaged often have little or no access to information on how to find the programs that could help them. Head Start's information outreach work thus serves as a guide through bureaucratic complexities and ensures awareness of and access to relevant programs.

Head Start also advocates for families involved. For example, Head Start project personnel serve on advisory boards, testify in legislative hearings, and lobby for improved services. They act as advocates for families with other social service agencies and help parents learn to advocate for themselves (HEW, 1977). Some studies have found that parents increase their involvement and leadership roles in other community activities in addition to the public schools following their Head Start experience. The Service Delivery Assessment report (HEW, 1977) states explicitly that Head Start involvement has helped foster parental confidence and community activism by empowering parents and making them feel more capable of determining the course of events in their lives and their communities.

The success of Head Start enabled nascent family support programs to validate their application for seed money. In addition, the existence of Head Start empowered its participants and made them aware that they could alter an unsatisfying and destructive status quo; thus, when other Office of Equal Opportunity programs were closed down during a period of conservative retrenchment, Head Start parents defeated attempts to terminate the program. The presence of these active, successful advocates within a community could not fail to make it easier for others to voice their opinions and work to gain their ends (Asch, 1951; Malof & Lott, 1962; Morris & Miller, 1975). Increased self-confidence inevitably decreases conformity (Krech, Crutchfield, & Ballachey, 1962). Thus, Head Start's success in empowering parents may well have made them models for, and leaders of, family support programs after Head Start.

FUTURE DIRECTIONS

As a result of a cycle of research and program development initiated by Head Start, combined with recent interest in how children's environments affect their growth and well-being, the conventional wisdom about how to promote early child and family development is shifting from a child-centered approach to one that emphasizes the importance of interrelationships among the child, the family, and society at large (Bronfenbrenner, 1979; Weiss, 1985; Zigler & Berman, 1983). Through practice, much has been learned about how to build and evaluate family support programs. Still, there is much room for refinement.

One criticism of the family support model is that families may become dependent on those providing support (Gray & Wandersman, 1980). This problem has been addressed by the Family Matters Project (Cochren & Woolever, 1983), which unites families in self-help groups and familiarizes them with resources in the community. The project uses a combination of home visits and group meetings to involve families in common activities; once supportive social networks are established, the families function without further dependence on the program organizers. The ultimate goal of the project is to foster a sense of parental empowerment, enabling families to help themselves and their children. An intervention program with the same theme might help parents enhance their interactions with their children and strengthen their feelings of control over the factors that affect their family's well-being.

Another issue of concern is the problem of eligibility. In the past, federal criteria for intervention were almost invariably based on family income level. But income actually reveals little about a family's strengths and needs. Such salient variables as ethnic-group background, geographic location, and family history are entirely lost. In fact, "the poor" are an extremely heterogeneous group on a variety of economic, sociological, and psychological dimensions. Use of the family-income criterion effectively avoids the vital question of which families can profit most from family support programs. The financial resources available for social programs are finite and to date have been insufficient for the magnitude of problems facing American families. If we spread allocations too thin, the promises of many programs will go unfilfilled, resulting in increased alienation among the economically disadvantaged and pessimism about producing change on the part of researchers and policymakers. We must discover more realistic indicators for selecting eligible families, including family incomes, parental education, and intactness of family (Finkelstein et al., 1978; Ramey et al., 1976), without introducing negative "labeling" effects that could work to the detriment of the children and families involved.

Despite these problems, Head Start and other family support programs have already made much progress both in supplying general support and in increasing our knowledge of what works in intervention programs. As an early example of the action-research cycle, Head Start has functioned as a productive, albeit tense, collaboration between researchers and practitioners in an effort to add to scientific knowledge and simultaneously to solve social problems (Rappaport, 1985). The program has provided much of the data suggesting that the most effective way to benefit children is to improve their family and community environment. Yet research on the relation among stress, support, health, and developmental outcomes is still largely correlational, based on quasi-experimental paradigms. The work of Head Start at present and family support programs in general "must do more than the available knowledge permits, by expanding it while putting it to use" (Zigler & Weiss, 1985, p. 4). Thus we can expect a continuing assortment of programs, designed and redesigned to fit the great variety of needs of American families and children.

REFERENCES

Abt, C. (1976). *The evaluation of social programs*. Beverly Hills, CA: Sage.

Abt Associates, Inc. (1980). Day Care Centers in the U.S.: A National Profile, 1976–1977. Final Report of the National Day Care Study, Vol. III. Cambridge, MA.

Adams, D. (1976). *Parent involvement: Parent development*. Berkeley, CA: Center for the Study of Parent Involvement.

Administration for Children, Youth & Families. (1980). The impact of Head Start: An overview. Washington, DC.

Andrews, S., Blumenthal, J., Johnson, D., Kahn, A., Ferguson, C., Lasater, T., Malone, P., & Wallace, D. (1982). The skills of mothering: A study of parent child development centers. *Monographs of the society for research in child development. 47* (6), G.

Asch, S. (1951). Effects of group pressure upon the modification and distortion of judgments. In H. Guetzkow (Ed.), *Groups, leadership and men*. Pittsburgh, PA: Carnegie Press.

Braun, S., & Edwards E. C. (1972). *History and theory of early childhood education*. Belmont, CA: Wadsworth.

Bronfenbrenner, U. (1974). Is early intervention effective? In M. Guttentag & E. L. Struening (Eds.), *Handbook of evaluation research* (Vol. 2). Beverly Hills, CA: Sage.

Bronfenbrenner, U. (1979). *The ecology of human development*. Cambridge, MA: Harvard University Press.

Calhoun, J. A., & Collins, R. C. (1981). From one decade to another: A positive view of early childhood programs. *Theory into Practice. 20*, 135–140.

Campbell, D. T., & Erlebacher, A. (1970). How regression artifacts in quasi-experimental evaluations can mistakenly make compensatory education look harmful. In J. Hellmuth (Ed.), *Compensatory education: A national debate* (Vol. 3). (pp. 185–210). New York: Brunner/Mazel.

Cochran, M., & Woolever, F. (1983). *Beyond the deficit model: The empowerment of parents with information and informal support*. New York: Plenum.

Comptroller General of the United States. (1979). *Report to the Congress: Early childhood and family development programs improve the quality of life for low-income families* (Document No. HRD-79-40). Washington, DC. Government Accounting Office.

Cooke, R. (1965, February). Memorandum to Sargent Shriver. Improving the opportunities and achievements of the children of the poor. Unpublished.

Costello, J., & Binstock, E. (1970). Review and summary of a national survey of the Parent-Child Center Program. Yale Child Study Center, New Haven, CT.

Cronbach, L. (1969). Heredity, environment, and educational policy. *Harvard Educational Review, 39*, 338–347.

Datta, L. (1976). The impact of the Westinghouse/Ohio evaluation on the development of Project Head Start. In C. C. Abt (Ed.), *The evaluation of social programs* (pp. 129–181). Beverly Hills, CA: Sage.

Datta, L. (1983). A tale of two studies: The Westinghouse-Ohio evaluation of

Project Head Start and the Consortium for Longitudinal Studies Report. *Studies in Educational Evaluation* 8 (3), 271–280.

Finkelstein, N. W., Dent, C., Gallagher, K., & Ramey, C. T. (1978). Social interaction of infants and toddlers in a day care setting. *Developmental Psychology, 14,* 257–262.

Garber, H. (1975). Intervention in infancy: A developmental approach. In M. Begab & S. Richardson (Eds.), *The mentally retarded and society: A social science perspective.* Baltimore: University Park Press.

Garber, H., & Heber, R. (1977). The Milwaukee Project. In P. Mittler (Ed.), *Research to practice in mental retardation.* Baltimore: University Park Press.

Gray, S. W., & Wanderson, L. P. (1980). The methodology of home-based intervention studies: Problems and promising strategies. *Child Development, 51,* 933–1009.

Grotberg, E. (1980). The federal role in parenting. ERIC Clearinghouse on Elementary and Early Childhood Education.

Hamilton, M. (1972). Evaluation of a parent and child center program. *Child Welfare, 51,* 248–258.

Heber, R., & Garber, H. (1975). The Milwaukee Project: A study of the use of family intervention to prevent cultural-familial mental retardation. In B. Z. Friedlander, G. Sternih, & G. Kirk (Eds.), *Exceptional infants. Assessment and intervention* (Vol. 3). New York: Brunner/Mazel.

Hertz, T. W. (1977). The impact of federal early childhood programs on children. Office of the Assistant Secretary for Planning and Evaluation.

HEW Region III (1977). Head Start Assessment. Washington, DC.

Kirschner Associates, Inc. (1970). A national survey of the impact of Head Start centers on community institutions. Albuquerque, NM.

Krech, D., Crutchfield, R. S., & Ballachey, E. L. (1962). Individual in society. New York: McGraw-Hill.

Lamb-Parker, F. (1983). Project Head Start, a supportive institutional social network: The effects of parental utilization on psychological well-being. Unpublished Ph.D. dissertation. New York: New School of Social Research.

Lazar, I. (1981). Early intervention is effective. *Educational Leadership, 303–305.*

Magidson, J., & Dorbom, D. (1980). Adjusting for confounding factors in quasi-experiments: Another reanalysis of the Westinghouse Head Start evaluation. Paper presented at the annual meeting of the American Statistical Association, Houston, Texas, August 9–12.

Malof, M., & Lott, A. (1962). Ethnocentrism and the acceptance of Negro support in a group pressure situation. *Journal of Abnormal and Social Psychology, 65,* 254–258.

Midco Educational Associates, Inc. (1972). Investigation of the effects of parent participation in Head Start. Final Technical Report. 251. Denver, CO.

Monroe, E., & McDonald, M. A follow-up study of the 1966 Head Start program. Unpublished manuscript. Rome, GA: Rome City Schools.

Morris, W. N., & Miller, R. S. (1975). The effects of consensus-breaking and consensus-preempting partners on reduction in conformity. *Journal of Experimental Social Psychology, 11,* 215–223.

O'Keefe, F. (1978). What Head Start means to families. Washington, DC: Administration for Children, Youth, and Families (DHEW).

Page, E., & Grandon, G. (1981). Massive intervention and child intelligence: The Milwaukee Project in critical perspective. *Journal of Special Education, 15*, 239–256.

Project Developmental Continuity: Guidelines for a planning year. (1974). Mimeo. Washington, DC: DHEW, Office of Child Development.

Ramey, C. T., Collier, A. M., Sparling, J. J., Loda, B. A., Campbell, F. A., Ingram, D. L., & Finklstein, N. W. (1976). The Carolina Abecedarian Project: A longitudinal and multidisciplinary approach to the prevention of developmental retardation. In T. Tjossem (Ed.), *Intervention strategies for high-risk infants and young children*. Baltimore: University Park Press.

Rapoport, R. (1985). Research and action. In R. Rapoport (Ed.), *Children, youth, and families: The action-research relationship* (pp. 1–25). Cambridge, MA: Cambridge University Press.

Smith, M. S., & Bissell, J. S. (1970). Report analysis: The impact of Head Start. *Harvard Educational Review, 40*, 51–104.

Stubbs, J. L. (1980). National Head Start Parent Involvement Study. Part I: Opportunities for Parent Involvement Study. United Research and Development Corporation.

Travers, J., Beck, R., & Bissell, J. (1982). Measuring the outcomes of daycare. In J. Travers and R. Light (Eds.), *Learning from experience: Evaluating early childhood demonstration programs* (pp. 169–173). Washington, DC: National Academy Press.

Travers, J., & R. J. Light (Eds.) (1982). *Learning from experience: Evaluating early childhood demonstration programs.* Washington, DC. National Academy Press.

Valentine, J., & Stark, E. (1979). The social context of parent involvement in Head Start. In F. Zigler & J. Valentine (Eds.), *Project Head Start: A legacy of the war on poverty* (pp. 291–315). New York: The Free Press.

Weiss, H. (1983). *Strengthening families and rebuilding the social infrastructure. A review of family support and education programs.* Washington, DC: Urban Institute

Weiss, H. (1985). The contribution of qualitative methodology to the understanding of the ecology of human development. Unpublished manuscript.

Weld, L. A. (1973). Family characteristics and profit from Head Start. Dissertation Abstracts International 34(3-B):1172.

Westinghouse Learning Corporation (1969). The impact of Head Start: An evaluation of the effects of Head Start on children's cognitive and affective development. Vol. I-II. Athens, OH: Ohio University.

Zigler, E. (1979a). *Head Start: Not a program but an evolving concept.* In E. Zigler & J. Valentine (Eds.), *Project Head Start: A legacy of the war on poverty* (pp. 367–379). New York: The Free Press.

Zigler, E. (1979b). Project Head Start.. Success or failure? In E. Zigler & J. Valentine, (Eds.), *Project Head Start: A legacy of the war on poverty* (pp. 495–509). New York: The Free Press.

Zigler, E., & Berman, W. (1983). Discerning the future of early childhood intervention. *American Psychologist, 38*, 894–906.

Zigler, E., & Trickett, P. K. (1978). IQ, social competence, and evaluation of early childhood education programs. *American Psychologist, 33*, 789–798.

Zigler, E., & Weiss, H. (1985). Family support systems: An ecological approach to child development. In R. Rapoport (Ed.), *Children, youth, and families: The action-research relationship* (pp. 166–205). New York: Cambridge University Press.

PART III/TYPES OF FAMILY
SUPPORT PROGRAMS

5 FAMILY BEGINNINGS: INFANCY AND SUPPORT

Jack P. Shonkoff

No society can survive unless its members reproduce themselves. No child can survive unless he or she is nurtured both before and after the moment of birth. The way in which that nurturance is provided reflects the broad diversity of goals and values that shape different social systems. In this regard, the growing influence of the family support movement on childbirth and infancy in the United States represents a cultural revolution.

The dramatic transformation over the past two decades in our approach to the beginning of life reflects the impact of a number of sociopolitical, economic, and professional/academic influences that are described throughout this volume. Like most successful revolutionaries, the architects of perinatal family support programs have succeeded because of their ability to identify critical vulnerabilities in the existing order as well as to articulate inspired alternatives. For women, childbearing is being recaptured as a natural process to be experienced fully and not a pathological condition to be treated medically. For men, the course of pregnancy, labor, and delivery is being redefined as a family experience to be shared intimately and not simply a woman's exclusive function to be tolerated sympathetically. For infants, the early months of life have become recognized as a period of important development to be mastered actively and not a time of mere growth to be experienced passively. The forces that have combined to bring about such fundamental changes in our approach to the beginning of family life, the manifestations of these changes, and an agenda of unfinished business for the future are the subjects of this chapter.

A HISTORICAL PERSPECTIVE ON CHILDBIRTH

During the colonial period and through the end of the eighteenth century, childbirth in America was a social event managed exclusively by women. Its success depended upon the technical assistance of a midwife (whose competence varied from superb to poor), in conjunction with the social support provided by female family members and friends. The typical "lying in" period extended over three to four weeks, during which time the mother remained in bed to rest and nurse her baby while others took over her household responsibilities and offered emotional support. At the end of her "confinement," the new mother hosted a "groaning party" for the women who cared for her, to express her appreciation and to mark her return to regular routines. Men were excluded from all phases of the perinatal process, and such "social childbirth" represented an important vehicle for female solidarity (Wertz & Wertz, 1977).

During the nineteenth century, women's control over the childbirth process began to wane. While female midwives continued to be accepted in Europe, the practice of midwifery in the United States was severely curtailed by competition from a variety of empirical healing sects (such as the botanical movement, hydrotherapy, and homeopathy) and the emerging, male-dominated medical profession. The empirics, who believed in the healing powers of natural plant products and water, made up the so-called Popular Health Movement. They advocated a disease-preventing lifestyle (including exercise, moderate diet, and fresh air), supported the concept of individual responsibility for health, and accepted female practitioners (Wertz & Wertz, 1977). The "regular" medical profession, on the other hand, was virtually closed to women, focused more on therapeutics than preventive strategies, and promoted dependency on the medical management of labor and delivery, even though most physicians could not match the practical experience of a seasoned midwife.

The childbirth options for the American woman of the nineteenth century were multiple, and choice generally varied with social class. Immigrant groups and many lower socioeconomic-class women continued to use midwives. The empiric sects remained influential throughout the century, with the botanists achieving most of their following in the rural Midwest and South and homeopathy retaining some success among the urban upper classes in the East because of its popularity among European nobility. The greatest growth in influence among the middle and upper classes, however, was achieved by the medical profession. Although rigorous medical educational standards were not established until after the publication of the Flexner Report in 1910, and many nineteenth-century American physicians obtained diplomas after only a few months of attendance at a proprietary school that provided no clinical or laboratory experiences, the American medical profession successfully marketed an elitest attitude against the unorthodox empirics and gained a growing dominion over the obstetrical management of middle- and upper-class women. The abandonment of the female midwife and acceptance of the role of the male doctor, despite the pervasive influence of Victorian modesty, reflected a growing belief that childbirth was not as simple and natural as was previously believed and that a greater margin of safety could be secured only through the technical expertise and "cool, detached competence" of a male physician. However, while the number of medically attended deliveries continued to rise, childbirth in the nineteenth century remained a home-based event.

In the early decades of the twentieth century, the risks of medical complications affecting labor and delivery outcomes were increasingly apparent, and physicians moved to solidify their responsibilities for the management of the entire perinatal period. Immediately after the Children's Bureau was established in 1912, its first investigation focused on the problem of infant mortality. The importance of prenatal care began to be appreciated during this period. As the demand for improved pregnancy outcomes intensified and the process of pregnancy and childbirth came increasingly under the control of physicians, medical interventions in the course of labor and delivery became commonplace, and the shift of childbirth from home to hospital proceeded rapidly. What was formerly viewed as a normal process to be shared exclusively by women was transformed into a potentially pathological condition with risks of complications that required close medical supervision.

This attitude was graphically reflected in an article published in the *American Journal of Obstetrics and Gynecology,* in which a prominent obstetrician wrote:

> It always strikes physicians as well as laymen as bizarre to call labor an abnormal function, a disease, and yet it is a decidedly pathological process. Everything, of course, depends on what we define as normal. . . . If a baby were to have its head caught in a door very lightly, but enough to cause cerebral hemorrhage, we would say it is decidedly pathologic, but when a baby's head is crushed against a tight pelvic floor, and a hemorrhage in the brain kills it we call this normal, at least we say that the function is natural, not pathogenic. . . . So frequent are these bad effects, that I have often wondered whether Nature did not deliberately intend women to be used up in the process of reproduction, in a manner analogous to that of the salmon, which dies after spawning. (DeLee, 1920, pp. 39–41)

Throughout the first half of the twentieth century, American women continued to surrender their autonomy and control over childbirth.

While initially they were motivated by issues of safety, these were soon accompanied by a growing interest in the pharmacologic relief of pain. Interestingly, early advocates of the use of morphine and scopolamine (so-called twilight sleep) in the 1920s and 1930s included leading feminists, suffragists, and socialites. By the outbreak of World War II, childbirth in the United States was treated like an illness, requiring medication, instrumentation, prolonged hospitalization, and separation from family and friends. The average ward patient remained hospitalized for two postpartum weeks, and private patients stayed for three (Wertz & Wertz, 1977). Women welcomed the disrupted consciousness and amnesia of twilight sleep, and men continued to accept their exclusion from the process without protest.

CHANGING CONCEPTS OF INFANCY

Changing attitudes toward infants and the role of the family during the early months of life present another interesting window through which one can view shifting cultural values. Colonial America considered babies to be "born in sin" and emphasized the spiritual salvation of the young as the primary task of early child rearing. Strict discipline was the hallmark of model parenting, and submission the sign of "a good baby." During the nineteenth century, as the Puritan influence was supplanted by a more secularized culture, the physical survival of infants became a greater priority than their moral redemption. Thus, while the medicalization of childbirth was gaining popular acceptance to assure the survival of both mother and neonate, the medicalization of infancy was seen as a way to increase the baby's chances of survival into the later childhood years.

The final decades of the nineteenth century witnessed the birth of a host of professional groups concerned with the well-being of young children. These included social-welfare activists, proponents of early childhood education, those in the field of child study itself, and pediatricians as subspecialists within the medical profession. As the early pediatricians focused their attention on the physical needs of young children, their growing professional status had a significant influence on child-rearing attitudes. In a classic textbook on *The Diseases of Infancy and Childhood*, one of the most prominent pediatricians of the early twentieth century wrote: "The physical development of the child is essentially the product of the three factors—inheritance, surroundings, and food. The first of these it is beyond the physician's power to alter; the second is largely and the third almost entirely within his control, at least in the more intelligent classes of society. These two subjects, infant hygiene and infant feeding, are the most important departments of pediatrics" (Holt, 1897,

p. 1). Physical survival was precarious, and the priorities of infant care were cleanliness, fresh air, and minimal stimulation. In fact, attempts to stimulate early development, as practiced today, were discouraged actively by early pediatricians:

> Great injury is done to the nervous system of children by the influences with which they are surrounded during infancy, especially during the first year. . . . Playing with young children, stimulating [them] to laughter and exciting them by sights, sounds, or movements until they shriek with apparent delight, may be a source of amusement to fond parents and admiring spectators, but it is almost invariably an injury to the child. . . . It is the plain duty of the physician to enlighten parents upon this point, and insist that the infant shall be kept quiet, and that all such playing and romping as has been referred to shall, during the first year at least, be absolutely prohibited. (Holt, 1897, p. 5)

During the early decades of the twentieth century, the combined influences of improved prenatal health care and obstetrical practices and advances in infant feeding practices contributed to a steady decline in the infant mortality rate in the United States. As the fear of death diminished, interest in the early development of infants grew. Whereas pediatricians had delivered rigid prescriptions to assure the physical survival of the child, behavioral psychologists began to bombard parents with rigid child-rearing guidelines suggesting that they had complete responsibility (but little ability) for facilitating the emerging competence and ultimate success of their children. In a popular book, one of the foremost child psychologists wrote: "Since the behaviorists find little that corresponds to instincts in children, since children are made not born, failure to bring up a happy child, a well adjusted child—assuming bodily health—falls upon the parents' shoulders. The acceptance of this view makes child rearing the most important of all social obligations" (Watson, 1928, p. 8).

By the 1940s, the professionalization of bearing and raising children was in high gear, and parent empowerment was thoroughly devalued. The process of childbirth had been passively turned over to the complete control of physicians. Popular treatises on child rearing reinforced the harsh message that the care and nurturance of infants was too important to be left to the natural instincts of parents and required the guidance of highly prescriptive experts. In a society that worshiped science and professional knowledge, family support around the birth and early care of children consisted of the provision of externally imposed technical competence with little demonstrated interest in the promotion of individual control, autonomy, or independent decision-making. In this context, one can appreciate the magnitude of change reflected in the first edition of Spock's famous child-care manual, which sought to reaffirm family instincts by saying to parents: "Trust yourself" (Spock, 1945).

RESTORING THE POWER OF THE FAMILY

In the years following World War II, as the popular culture embraced the traditional virtues of home and family and the baby boom erupted, a combination of forces began to transform American attitudes toward childbirth and the care of infants. At first this was a modest attempt by some parents to participate actively and reassert individual judgment. For a few, it escalated to a crusade against all forms of professionalism and authority.

The first significant challenge to the medical domination of birth in the United States was launched by a British obstetrician whose widely read book, *Childbirth Without Fear* (originally published in the 1930s and reissued in 1959), suggested that a properly prepared woman could participate in the delivery of her baby with minimal anaesthesia, manageable discomfort, a higher level of personal satisfaction, and greater safety for the baby (Dick-Read, 1959). As the popularity of "natural childbirth" grew in the 1940s and 1950s, the media extolled this approach to childbearing as the reemergence of the essence of womanhood.

While Dick-Read promised childbirth without fear, the next wave of alternative birthing practices offered "natural" liberation from pain. Two French physicians, Lamaze and Vellay, advocated a drug-free method of pain control ("psychoprophyllaxis") achieved through preparatory training in mental-concentration techniques. This "improvement" upon nature, based on the behavioral psychology of Pavlov, gained rapid popularity in the United States, aided by a widely read book by Marjorie Karmel, *Thank You, Dr. Lamaze: A Mother's Experience in Painless Childbirth* (1959).

The initial response of the medical profession to the growing demand for natural-childbirth options was less than enthusiastic. Some critics pointed out the irony that the emerging focus on the personal experience of labor and delivery was made possible largely by advances in the medical management of childbirth which had lessened the physical risks for both mother and baby. Others were more extreme in their condemnation of what they described as the "mass application of Pavlovian principles by [the Soviet] government to reshape the behavior of its citizens" (quoted in Wertz & Wertz, 1977, p. 194). Most agreed, however, that the growing demand by women for greater control of the birth process confronted the medical profession with a potent challenge.

The liberal use of obstetrical anaesthesia was the first medical intervention to fall. Forceps-assisted deliveries and the routine performance of episiotomies were reevaluated, and indications for Caesarian sections were challenged. As the turbulent 1960s came to a close, medical domination over childbirth remained strong, but women were gaining a recognition of their right to be conscious participants in the birthing process and to share in some of the decisions that had to be made.

While the women of the 1960s asked for personal involvement in childbirth, those of the 1970s demanded power and control. Whereas the former wanted to modify the behavior of physicians, the latter considered rejecting their intervention entirely. Whereas the 1960s father paced in the waiting room, his 1970s counterpart was becoming an expected participant in all phases of labor and delivery. If the 1960s began with a romantic vision of the limitless possibilities of American technology, the 1970s witnessed a growing cynicism about its limitations and dehumanizing consequences. The promises of the "Great Society" yielded to themes of "self-help," "personal development," "back to basics," and "all natural." The 1960s political rhetoric of brotherhood and the "family of man" yielded to the "sisterhood" of the 1970s and the subsequent reconceptualization of family roles that has continued into the 1980s. Throughout this period of cultural upheaval and social reorganization, popular demands for greater attention to family needs received critical support from concurrent research on attachment behaviors, parent-child interaction, and the development of young children.

CONTRIBUTIONS OF ACADEMIC RESEARCH

An examination of the interplay among research findings, sociopolitical forces, and the transformation of perinatal services in the United States starts with an analysis of the work of Klaus and Kennell. Beginning with their first report published in the prestigious *New England Journal of Medicine*, these two pediatricians and their colleagues spearheaded a series of investigations into the process and consequences of maternal–infant bonding within the first hours of life (Klaus et al., 1972). On the basis of data obtained from studies of avian, ungulate, and primate behavior, they postulated a sensitive period for the optimal development of parent–infant attachment in human neonates. In their popular book entitled *Maternal-Infant Bonding*, Klaus and Kennell (1976) asserted: "This original mother-infant bond is the wellspring for all the infant's subsequent attachments and is the formative relationship in the course of which the child develops a sense of himself. Throughout his lifetime the strength and character of this attachment will influence the quality of all future bonds to other individuals" (pp. 1–2).

Skin-to-skin contact between an awake mother and an alert newborn immediately after birth was believed to promote optimal bonding. The availability of such bonding opportunities reportedly led to more sensitive and appropriate maternal behavior toward the infant and optimal developmental progress by the young child. Voluminous data have been collected over the past decade in an attempt to document these relationships. Investigators have studied full-term as well as premature populations with varying degrees of vulnerability. They have examined a wide range of short-term and long-term dependent variables, including such behavioral measures as duration of breast-feeding, maternal responsiveness to baby's crying, mother–child social interactions, and infant developmental test scores (Ali & Lowry, 1981; O'Connor et al., 1980; Siegal et al., 1980; Sosa, Klaus, Kennell, & Urrutia, 1976).

Unlike researchers who leave the practical application of their data to others, many of the investigators engaged in bonding studies became vigorous and effective advocates for change in perinatal medical practices during the 1970s. Greater facilitation of early bonding was proposed as an effective preventive measure to combat such enduring social problems as child abuse, developmental attrition, and delinquency. Lozoff and her colleagues (1977) charged:

> The widespread disturbance in parenting and the fragmentation of families in the United States suggest the need for reexamination of those medical practices that affect the involvement of parents with their children. Throughout most of known history, anatomic, physiologic, and behavioral adaptations within the mother-infant relationship have been capable of providing the nutrition, protection, and social stimulation necessary for the infant's survival and development. Perinatal medical care was introduced in this century with the purpose of further decreasing mortality and morbidity by preventing infection and managing physical problems. There is now a growing body of evidence that these advances inadvertently alter the initiation of the mother-infant relationship, and that some mother-infant pairs may be strained beyond limits of their adaptability. (p. 1)

They went on to recommend:

> Any aspect of peripartum care not based on sound scientific evidence should be left to parental choice. . . . There is no medical reason why healthy mothers and babies should not be together from the time of birth to the time of discharge from the hospital. (pp. 8–9)

Critics of the bonding literature have noted methodological problems in many published studies (Klaus & Kennell, 1983; Lamb & Hwang, 1982). Some point out research-design limitations that preclude the rejection of alternative explanations for demonstrated positive impacts. Others highlight the failure of some studies to replicate previous findings. The absence of documented long-term effects of extended mother–neonate contact has also been problematic. Some observers have expressed particular regret over the increased anxiety and guilt generated among mothers whose birthing experiences prohibited extended neonatal contact (Chess & Thomas, 1982). Others have attempted to soften the emphasis on the first hours of life by rejecting what McCall (1982) called the "epoxy" theory of bonding in which "mother and infant must be brought together before the glue dries." However, whether true believers or skeptics, almost all acknowledge the remarkable contributions of Klaus, Kennell, and their colleagues to the dramatic transformation of American hospital-based childbirth practices. Less than a decade after the publication of their early studies, active maternal involvement in the process of delivery and the promotion of intimacy between a mother and her newborn had become accepted features of standard obstetrical procedures.

Closely related to the study of parent–neonate attachment has been an interest in the reciprocal interaction between an infant and his or her primary caregiver and the effect of that ongoing relationship on the development of competence in young children. From the painstaking documentation of the capacity of the newborn to process auditory, visual, and tactile stimuli through the analyses of an infant's growing ability to understand the properties and rules of the inanimate and social world in which he or she lives, developmental researchers in the past twenty years have dramatically extended our knowledge of the origins of human abilities (Mussen, 1983). In the laboratory setting, video-taped interactions have provided vivid illustrations of the influence of infants and their caregivers on each other's behavior. In the clinical research setting, assessment techniques such as the Neonatal Behavioral Assessment Scale (Brazelton, 1973) are a vehicle for quantifying the individual differences in physiological and neurological organization that newborns bring to their developmental tasks.

Like the effect of bonding research on the organization and delivery of obstetrical services, new insights into the development of social competence and learning abilities in young infants, combined with an awareness of the needs of their families, have been translated into "early interventions" designed to promote optimal outcomes for a variety of target populations. Programs have been designed for premature or disabled babies, infants of vulnerable caregivers, such as adolescent mothers, and the "normal" offspring of ambitious, middle-class families wishing to maximize their child's developmental competence. Examples of such efforts are described below.

CURRENT MODELS OF FAMILY SUPPORT

Programs and policies that provide support for families during the prenatal period, the childbirth process itself, and/or early infancy embody a wide range of formats and utilize a variety of personnel. A comprehensive overview of such programs would itself fill an entire volume. This chapter briefly describes selected examples of three representative models: family-centered maternity services, institutionally based support programs, and home visitation.

Family-Centered Maternity Services

In 1978, the Interprofessional Task Force on Health Care of Women and Children (representing the views of the American Academy of Pediatrics, the American College of Nurse-Midwives, the American College of Obstetricians and Gynecologists, the American Nurses Association, and the Nurses Association of the American College of Obstetricians and Gynecologists) issued a joint policy statement, which was also supported by the American Hospital Association, endorsing the concept of family-centered maternity care as an acceptable approach to maternity/neonatal health services. The task force defined such care as "the delivery of safe, quality health care while recognizing, focusing on, and adapting to both the physical and psychosocial needs of the client-patient, the family, and the newly born . . . with emphasis on the provision of maternity/newborn health care which fosters family unity while maintaining physical safety" (p. 55). General guidelines called for hospital policies that allowed the husband or "supporting other" to remain part of the childbirth process "as much as possible," encouraged family-newborn interaction immediately after birth, and provided for flexible rooming-in arrangements. Specific implementation plans were left to individual communities and providers. The importance of educational programs for hospital staff as well as families was underlined, and the major change needed to convert existing maternity services to a family-centered model was identified as "attitudinal." Although the task force concluded that "the hospital setting provides the maximum opportunity for physical safety and for psychological wellbeing," it endorsed the need for "a team effort of the woman and her family, health care providers, and the community" (Interprofessional Task Force, 1978, p. 56).

During the past several years, family-centered maternity programs have proliferated across the United States. Declining birth rates, highly selective consumer demands, and aggressively marketed alternative childbirth services have forced hospitals to invest both capital and imagination in the development of competitive programs. Free-standing childbearing centers, hospital-affiliated alternative birth centers, and birthing rooms within traditional obstetrical services are some of the many options available.

The Childbearing Childrearing Center (CCC) affiliated with the University of Minnesota presents one interesting alternative model linked to a traditional medical facility (Rising & Lindell, 1982). An outreach clinic of University Hospital in Minneapolis, the CCC offers complete child-bearing, child-rearing, and well-woman care through individual visits, formal educatonal programs, and discussion/support groups. Most of the services are provided by expanded-role nurses (certified nurse-mid-wives, pediatric nurse-practitioners, adult nurse-practitioners, and ma-ternity nurse-practitioners) in a house located off campus. The center provides "wellness care" that emphasizes health promotion and mainte-nance with backup from the university medical system for the care of pathologic conditions. A survey of CCC consumers found a high level of satisfaction with its services, particularly with its respect for women's de-sire to have control over their own experiences, its family-centered ori-entation, and its provision of peer support.

It is clear that the roles of health care institutions, and hospitals in particular, are being reassessed critically. Greater attention to the impor-tance of psychosocial support, attempts to provide a less medicalized en-vironment for childbirth without compromising accessibility to technical sophistication, and a general shift toward a nonpathological approach to labor and delivery are some of the central features of the trend toward family-oriented models in traditional medical settings. Home deliveries and sibling participation in the birthing process are less common but significant alternatives that raise yet greater challenges to our ability to balance responsiveness to the needs of families with a retention of the positive contributions of modern health-care technology.

Institutionally Based Support Programs

Whereas family-centered maternity programs address specific needs around the childbirth process itself, a wide variety of comprehensive support services has been developed for many other aspects of early family functioning. Some programs serve a diverse range of families. Others are targeted to meet the needs of vulnerable subgroups for whom childbirth and its aftermath involve specific additional stressors (for example, single, adolescent mothers or families of premature infants).

Programs for low-risk families offer a range of services. *COPE* (Cop-ing with the Overall Pregnancy/Parenting Experience), a well-estab-lished prototype, is a licensed counseling, education, training, and re-source center in Boston that specializes in perinatal mental health. Originally organized as a system of peer-led support groups for preg-nant women and new parents, COPE has expanded to a highly profes-sionalized, multidimensional mental health clinic that has recently aug-mented its program offerings to address the needs of working parents through such activities as employer-sponsored seminars and information/referral services (*Programs to Strengthen Families*, 1983).

The Parenting Program at Booth Maternity Center in Philadelphia is another example of a high-quality professional service that has developed in response to requests from average families for more support and information during the early infancy period. Its many creative components include a trained parent volunteer ("Booth Buddy") who contacts first-time parents three weeks after their hospital discharge; thirty to forty activities a month, including parent-child playgroups, that involve several hundred families; and a monthly newsletter ("Listening Booth") that describes available activities. Whereas individualized services are limited to families who use the prenatal/maternity services at Booth Maternity Center, group activities are open to anyone in the local community (*Programs to Strengthen Families*, 1983).

Unlike programs that depend upon individual family-initiated referrals, the *Infant Care Program* at Evanston Hospital in Evanston, Illinois, routinely establishes contact with "all families of newborn infants, full-term and premature, healthy and critically ill, from affluent families and from impoverished homes, born to women in their thirties and to children barely in their teens" (Ceithaml, 1984). Staff members offer demonstrations of the Brazelton Neonatal Behavioral Assessment Scales to parents as an integral component of the maternity service, and work in a complementary manner with other specific hospital- or community-based programs when indicated.

Support programs designed specifically for mothers of premature babies represent another prototype with widespread replication. *Project Welcome*, a collaborative effort administered through Wheelock College and The Children's Hospital in Boston, is an example of a large demonstration project that succeeded in coordinating sophisticated medical, educational, and social-support services for infants admitted to neonatal intensive care units and for their families. Three phases of program activity were designed and implemented: *family support*, including both professional and peer channels; a *transition* program that linked the infant and family to an integrated system of continuous service including intensive care units, community hospitals, primary-care physicians, and community-based early-intervention programs; and a program of *outreach/liaison* that provided extensive educational experiences and disseminated materials for over 1,000 health and early intervention professionals on the special needs of families with premature babies who require intensive care. *Project Welcome Outreach*, a follow-up service, has provided training, consultation, and enrichment activities for program replication in more than 30 demonstration sites in 13 states and the District of Columbia (Gilkerson, 1985).

A number of investigators have conducted studies on the impacts of support services for families of premature or sick newborns. At the Hospital for Sick Children in Toronto, a ten-week discussion group led by a nurse coordinator and a "veteran mother," who had given birth to a premature infant within the previous year, was found to have a range of beneficial effects. When compared to matched controls, mothers who attended the discussion group visited their infants significantly more often in the hospital; touched, talked, and looked at them more during those visits; and rated themselves as more competent on a number of infant care measures. Three months after the babies were discharged from the hospital, the experimental mothers showed greater involvement with their children during feedings and expressed more concern about their development (Minde et al., 1980).

Zeskind and Iacino (1984) evaluated a program designed to increase mothers' visits to their premature babies by scheduling weekly appointments for them in the neonatal intensive care unit. A controlled study showed that this simple intervention increased the frequency of independent maternal visitation beyond the scheduled appointments, brightened the mothers' perceptions of their infants' prognosis, and decreased the length of the child's hospitalization. Although the mothers in the experimental group had more negative perceptions of their infants' behaviors, the authors speculated that this reflected their more realistic observations based upon greater contact and familiarity with their babies. Furthermore, such additional contact was hypothesized to have facilitated the infants' recovery, attested to by their earlier discharge.

Support programs for families with special vulnerabilities have also proliferated significantly over the past several years. *The Caring Connection* in Racine, Wisconsin, for example, is a hospital-based program that has demonstrated the successful use of volunteer perinatal coaches to provide education and support for teenage parents from the prenatal period through labor and delivery and into early infancy (*Programs to Strengthen Families*, 1983).

Similar efforts for adolescent mothers or isolated mothers with young children have been established in a variety of community-based settings, and some of these programs have been evaluated systematically. In one such study of preterm infants born to teenage, lower socioeconomic status, black mothers in Miami, Widmayer and Field (1981) found that the simple and relatively inexpensive demonstration of a Brazelton Neonatal Behavioral Assessment Scale at birth and weekly for four weeks after the baby's discharge was effective in facilitating more responsive parent-infant interactions. Although a great deal more work is needed in this area, the potential benefits of supportive interventions for high-risk parents and their infants appear promising.

Home Visitation

The practice of routine home visitation by public health nurses during the prenatal and early infancy period is widespread in many Western societies. In some countries, such as Great Britain, regular home visitors collect important epidemiologic data while they provide a range of basic health-maintenance services, including immunizations and surveillance of the child's growth and development. Although the implementation of this simple family-support service has traditionally been relatively limited in the United States (in part because of concerns about the preservation of privacy), such programs are being established with increasing frequency in a variety of settings throughout the country in an effort to reach high-risk mothers who are unlikely to utilize institutionally based services.

Family Support Services, Inc. in Denver offers a Lay Home Visitor Program in both an urban and a rural model. Participants are recruited during their pregnancy and include families at risk for parenting problems because of social isolation and a history of child abuse or neglect, marital discord, or substance abuse. Home visitors are selected for their personal qualities of warmth, empathy, and a history of having been well-nurtured children and successful parents themselves. Emotional support, role modeling, and concrete assistance are provided within the context of an ongoing relationship in which the home visitor may serve as a surrogate friend (*Programs to Strengthen Families*, 1983).

Neighborhood Support Systems for Infants in Somerville, Massachusetts, uses a team model in which weekly home visits are made by a nonprofessional "core mother" who meets regularly with a professionally trained case manager to review the implementation of an individual program plan designed for each family. This program model illustrates the effective use of lay workers who are given initial training and ongoing supervision by an experienced professional staff. Preference for enrollment is given to low-income and high-risk families. Monthly "drop-ins" at the center focus on activity-oriented interactions, which have been found to be more acceptable and efficacious than discussion groups for this high-risk population (*Programs to Strengthen Families*, 1983).

The Prenatal Intervention Project in Montreal provides home visits through a hospital-based service project with a sophisticated research component. In a study of the impact of this home-visitor program designed to influence mother-child interaction, home environment, and well-child care for working-class families, Larson (1980) documented minimal gains when visits were begun in the infant's sixth week of life, as compared to a control group receiving no services. For families that received home visits beginning in the prenatal period, however, the experimental group showed significant benefits as reflected in reduced accident rates for children, higher scores on assessments of the home environment and maternal behavior, and a lower prevalence of mother-infant interaction or feeding problems and of nonparticipant fathers. In analyzing his findings, Larson suggested that the impact of such programs might be affected by the timing of the initial encounter, which influences the development of the parent-home visitor relationship.

Perhaps the best studied home-visitor demonstration project is the *Prenatal/Early Infancy Project* in Elmira, New York. In an evaluation of comprehensive prenatal services provided by nurse home visitation, Olds and his collaborators (1986b) documented a broad range of positive outcomes that supported the efficacy of such services in improving the social and health context for childbearing among socioeconomically disadvantaged families. In a series of papers reporting several aspects of their multidimensional study, they reported that, compared to women randomly assigned to contrast groups, nurse-visited women became more aware of community services, attended childbirth classes more frequently, improved their dietary habits, were more likely to be accompanied by a support person during labor, and reported more frequent communication with family and friends about their pregnancy and personal problems. Younger adolescents gave birth to babies who averaged 395 grams heavier; smokers had a 75 percent reduction in the incidence of preterm delivery; women who had not finished high school at the time of their registration in the program returned to school more often in the first two postpartum years; poor, unmarried adolescents had fewer subsequent pregnancies; and unmarried nonadolescent women were employed for a greater number of months after childbirth (Olds et al., in press). Moreover, among the women identified as having the greatest risk for parenting difficulties, those who were nurse-visited had fewer verified cases of child abuse and neglect during the first two years. They also were observed during home visits to provide more appropriate play materials and to restrict and punish their children less frequently, and their babies were seen in the hospital emergency room less frequently in the first year of life (Olds et al., 1986a). These findings provide an impressive argument in favor of expanded home-visitor services, with ongoing evaluation of their impacts, for high-risk families during the prenatal and early infancy period.

THE UNFINISHED AGENDA

Despite the growing popular demand for more family-oriented childbirth practices and the greater availability of supportive services for infants and their parents, much unfinished business remains if family support programs are to endure and thrive. Research needs in this area remain substantial. Although associations between social support and positive outcomes for both pregnancy and parenting have been demonstrated, the mechanisms that mediate such relationships have not been elucidated (Crnic et al., 1983; Crockenberg, 1981; Nuckolls, Cassel, & Kaplan, 1972). Further investigation of individual differences among children and families is a necessary prerequisite to matching specific program models and appropriate service recipients.

Available data on the short- and long-term impacts of alternative birthing practices on family functioning are limited (Committee on Assessing Alternative Birth Settings, 1982). Despite a great deal of anecdotal information, we know very little about the relative safety of different methods of delivery for mother and baby. While some studies have shown beneficial results of psychoprophyllaxis during labor (that is, fewer medical complications), others (for example, investigations of the Leboyer method) have merely failed to demonstrate any increased risks (Nelson et al., 1980; Scott & Rose, 1976). Considerations regarding the physical well-being of the mother and the fetus/neonate, as well as the psychosocial needs of the family unit, require sensitive and systematic study. If a variety of delivery options are to be made available and if families are expected to make informed choices, then much work remains to develop criteria for evaluating levels of risk that might warrant recommendations for different degrees of medical supervision or other professional intervention.

As described earlier in this chapter, the research on mother-neonate bonding has been extensive but remains inconclusive. Few disagree with the intrinsic value of close contact among mother, father, and newborn immediately after birth. The degree to which such an opportunity makes the birth experience more meaningful for the family unit needs no further justification. Assertions regarding the long-term developmental-behavioral impacts of early extended contact, however, remain speculative. Whether ongoing parent-child interactions are influenced in a significant way by the experiences of a sensitive period in the early minutes or hours of life is not clearly established. How such early contact affects the later developmental competence of infants requires a great deal more investigation.

The extent to which supportive services affect the developing mother-child relationship in high-risk circumstances is another important area for further study. In a recent investigation of neonatal intervention in a middle-class population, Belsky (1985) found no significant differences among groups with passive exposure to the Brazelton Neonatal Behavioral Assessment Scale and those who actively participated in its administration, involving either both parents or mothers alone. In examining past reports of positive effects, Belsky emphasized the need to be cautious in interpreting the impact of minor interventions and the importance of considering the possibility of differential effects on groups of varying vulnerability.

Finally, much research obviously remains to be done on the early role of the father and its impact on child and family development. In a critical review of available data on the effects of a father's birth attendance and early or extended contact with his newborn, Palkovitz (1985) observed that no conclusive statements can be made at this time regarding the influence of paternal involvement in the newborn period on either subsequent father-child relationships or developmental outcomes for the children.

Aside from continuing research, bridge-building remains another critical prerequisite to the effective provision of family support during pregnancy, delivery, and the early infancy period. Persistent long-standing tensions between physicians and nonmedical birthing personnel have deep cultural, political, and economic roots. Conflict between pregnant women and the medical profession spans a range of intensity from individuals who simply desire a more personalized involvement in the delivery of their babies to organized groups that see themselves as engaged in a holy war against the menace of modern obstetrics. The recent transformation of the childbirth process into a marketing battle among entrepreneurs presents a critical challenge to assure that the competition for customers and the quest for profit do not generate unsafe maternity services. Communication and collaboration are needed between professionals and consumers, among diverse professional groups, and across community-based services that have an interest in the development of a supportive milieu for family life.

Finally, the specific goals of family support in the prenatal, newborn, and early-infancy periods need to be clarified. Social support during pregnancy may affect the baby's birthweight and/or the mother's hopes or expectations for her own development. Parental fulfillment during childbirth and positive developmental outcomes for the family are both desirable but are not inevitably linked in a cause-effect relationship. Some advocate infant intervention programs for their presumed influence on the child's cognitive competence; others seek impact on affective well-being. Some search for methods to facilitate all aspects of family and child function; others oppose any intrusion into the early parent-child relationship.

Individuals' values and needs vary considerably. Long-standing conflicts between professional technology and natural, humanistic values are not necessarily irreconcilable. Some prefer one over the other. Many seek a mixture of both. The simple fact is that, despite significant differences in personal style and individual aspirations, increasing numbers of American families are defining their own goals and recapturing control of pregnancy, childbirth, and early infancy through the family support movement.

REFERENCES

Ali, Z., & Lowry, M. (1981). Early maternal-child contact: Effects on later behavior. *Developmental Medicine and Child Neurology, 23*, 337.

Belsky, J. (1985). Experimenting with the family in the newborn period. *Child Development, 56*, 407–414.

Brazelton, T. B. (1973). *Neonatal Behavioral Assessment Scale.* London: Spastic International Medical Publications.

Ceithaml, C. (1984). The infant care program at Evanston Hospital: Putting research to work. *Zero to Three, 5*(2), 1–5.

Chess, S., and Thomas, A. (1982). Infant bonding: Mystique and reality. *American Journal of Orthopsychiatry, 52*, 213–222.

Committee on Assessing Alternative Birth Settings. Institute of Medicine and National Research Council. (1982). *Research Issues in the Assessment of Birth Settings.* Washington, DC: National Academy Press.

Crnic, K., Greenberg, M., Ragozin, A., Robinson, N., & Basham, R. (1983). Effects of stress and social support on mothers and premature and full-term infants. *Child Development, 54*, 209–217.

Crockenberg, S. (1981). Infant irritability, mother responsiveness, and social support influences on the security of infant-mother attachment. *Child Development, 52*, 857–865.

DeLee, J. (1920). The prophylactic forceps operation. *American Journal of Obstetrics and Gynecology, 1*, 34–44.

Dick-Read, G. (1959). *Childbirth without fear.* 2d rev. ed. New York: Harper & Row.

Flexner, A. (1910). *Medical education in the United States and Canada: A report to the Carnegie Foundation for the Advancement of Teaching.* Bulletin No. 4. Boston: Updyke.

Gilkerson, L. (1985). Personal communication.

Holt, L. E. (1897). *The diseases of infancy and childhood.* New York: D. Appleton.

Interprofessional Task Force on Health Care of Women and Children. (1978). Joint position statement: The development of family-centered maternity/newborn care in hospitals. *Journal of Obstetric, Gynecologic, and Neonatal Nursing, 7* (5), 55–59.

Karmel, M. (1959). *Thank you, Dr. Lamaze: A mother's experience in painless childbirth.* Philadelphia: Lippincott.

Klaus, M., Jerauld, R., Kreger, N., McAlpine, W., Steffa, M., & Kennell, J. (1972). Maternal attachment: Importance of the first post-partum days. *New England Journal of Medicine, 286*, 460–463.

Klaus, M., & Kennell, J. (1976). *Maternal-Infant Bonding.* St. Louis: C. V. Mosby.

Klaus, M., & Kennell, J. (1983). Parent to infant bonding: Setting the record straight. *Journal of Pediatrics, 102*, 575–576.

Lamb, M., & Hwang, C. (1982). Maternal attachment and mother-neonate bonding: A critical review. In M. Lamb and A. Brown (Eds.), *Advances in Developmental Psychology*, Vol. 2. Hillsdale, NJ: Erlbaum.

Larson, C. (1980). Efficacy of prenatal and postpartum home visits on child health and development. *Pediatrics, 66*, 191–197.

Lozoff, B., Brittenham, G., Trause, M., Kennell, J., & Klaus, M. (1977). The mother-newborn relationship: Limits of adaptability. *Journal of Pediatrics, 91*, 1–12.

McCall, R. (1982). A hard look at stimulating and predicting development: The cases of bonding and screening. *Pediatrics in Review, 3*, 205–212.

Minde, K., Shosenberg, N., Marton, P., Thompson, J., Ripley, J., & Burns, S. (1980). Self-help groups in a premature nursery—a controlled evaluation. *Journal of Pediatrics, 96*, 933–940.

Mussen, P. (Ed.). (1983). *Handbook of child psychology.* New York: Wiley.

Nelson, N., Enkin, M., Saigal, S., Bennett, K., Milner, R., & Sackett, D. (1980). A randomized clinical trial of the Leboyer approach to childbirth. *New England Journal of Medicine. 702*, 655–60.

Nuckolls, K., Cassel, J., & Kaplan, B. (1972). Psychological assets, life crisis and the prognosis of pregnancy. *American Journal of Epidemiology, 95*, 431–441.

O'Connor, S., Vietze, P., Sherrod, K., Sandler, H., & Altemeier, W. (1980). Reduced incidence of parenting inadequacy following rooming-in. *Pediatrics, 66*, 176–182.

Olds, D., Henderson, C., Chamberlin, R., & Tatelbaum, R. (1986a). Preventing child abuse and neglect: A randomized trial of nurse home visitation. *Pediatrics, 78*, 65–78.

Olds, D., Henderson, C., Tatelbaum, R., & Chamberlin, R. (1986b). Improving the delivery of prenatal care and outcomes of pregnancy: A randomized trial of nurse home visitation. *Pediatrics, 77*, 16–28.

Olds, D., Henderson, C., Tatelbaum, R,, & Chamberlin, R. (in press). *Improving the life-course development of socially disadvantaged parents. A randomized trial of nurse home visitation.*

Palkovitz, R. (1985). Father's birth attendance, early contact, and extended contact with their newborns: A critical review. *Child Development, 56*, 392–406.

Programs to strengthen families: A resource guide. (1983). New Haven, CT: Yale University Bush Center in Child Development and Social Policy (available from the Family Resource Coalition, 230 North Michigan Avenue, Suite 1625, Chicago, IL 60601).

Rising, S., & Lindell, S. (1982). The childbearing childrearing center: A nursing model. *Nursing Clinics of North America, 17* (1), 11–21.

Scott, J., & Rose, N. (1976). Effect of psychoprophylaxis (Lamaze preparation) on labor and delivery in primiparas. *New England Journal of Medicine, 294*, 1205–1207.

Siegal, E., Bauman, K., Schaefer, E., Saunders, M., & Ingram, D. (1980). Hospital and home support during infancy: Impact on maternal attachment, child abuse and neglect, and health care utilization. *Pediatrics, 66*, 183–190.

Sosa, R., Klaus, M., Kennell, J., & Urrutia, J. (1976). The effect of early mother-infant contact on breast-feeding, infection and growth. In K. Elliott (Ed.), *Breast-feeding and the mother.* Amsterdam: Elsevier.

Spock, B. (1945). *The common sense book of baby and child care.* New York: Duell, Sloan and Pearce.

Watson, J. B. (1928). *Psychological care of infant and child.* New York: Norton.

Wertz, R., and Wertz, D. (1977). *Lying-in: A history of childbirth in America.* New York: The Free Press.

Widmayer, S., & Field, T. (1981). Effects of Brazelton demonstrations for mothers on the development of preterm infants. *Pediatrics, 67,* 711–714.

Zeskind, P., & Iacino, R. (1984). Effects of maternal visitation to preterm infants in the neonatal intensive care unit. *Child Development, 55,* 1887–1893.

6 FAMILY SUPPORT AND THE PREVENTION OF CHILD MALTREATMENT

James Garbarino

Child maltreatment has replaced "educational disadvantage" at the cutting edge for those who favor an activist policy of public intervention into the private lives of children and their families. Much as the many Head Start-related programs aimed at improving children's cognitive and academic development were central to early intervention in the 1960s, so the prevention and remediation of child abuse and neglect are the focal point of early intervention in the 1980s. The issues display several significant similarities: The demographic and socioeconomic profiles of the children at greatest risk bear a family resemblance; the poor, young, single parent and her children are the most salient target for intervention. Academic discussions of the proper labels and conceptualization for the problem have proceeded along similar paths.[1] In both academic failure and child maltreatment, a commitment to either "bad parents" or "bad environments" has been singled out as the primary problem (with the former position being accused of "blaming the victim" and the latter of "simplistic environmental determinism"). And both issues have been granted the respect implied by the use of multivariate analyses and interactive models of the transactions between individual and environment.

While recognizing these similarities, we still need to acknowledge some important differences between educational disadvantage and child maltreatment as focal points for early intervention. The former has much less moral stigma attached to it. The latter is caught up in the ongoing debate over criminal-justice versus mental-health models for dealing with deviant behavior. In the case of educational disadvantage the public is more willing to recognize positive motives on the parents' part, in contrast to its perception of parents who maltreat their children. For the purposes of the present discussion, however, the major characteristic of intervention in child maltreatment that distinguishes it from intervention in educational disadvantage is the intense dynamic linking nurturance and control as necessary conditions for success.

For intervention to succeed on a widespread basis it must link the nurturance of individuals who have been subjected to circumstantial stress and to their own psychological inadequacy, on the one hand, with explicit sanctions and stringent vigilance against further dysfunction (that is, social control), on the other (Belsky, 1980; Garbarino, 1977a). The mixture of social control and social nurturance required for comprehensive intervention to prevent and remediate child maltreatment raises what for the United States may be insurmountable cultural challenges, including political decisions about the social costs of freedom (are we willing to give up personal autonomy for greater community authority?), the constitutionality of socially desirable information systems (is it legal to require people to register their movements, to require that children receive routine medical care and that health visitors have access to children?), and the citizenship and rights of children versus parents (if someone's rights must be compromised, should it be the parent's autonomy or the child's right to adequate care?) (Garbarino & Gilliam, 1980). Thus we begin by addressing this strategic issue directly before proceeding to a series of tactical questions for which the support/control question serves as a backdrop.

WHAT KIND OF SOCIETY PERMITS CHILD MALTREATMENT?

A prominent child psychiatrist has offered the following assessment of where preventing child maltreatment stands in our hierarchy of values and commitments:

> Tragically, the violent physical abuse and murder of children by adults, often parents, is as old as recorded human history; and sad as it may seem, most of us would not want to live in a society that was able to prevent every single instance of child abuse because that could only be carried out in a prison-like state. At the same time, all of us would like to prevent as much child abuse as is possible to prevent in a relatively free society in which the democratic values of family privacy and the pluralism of differing life styles are protected and supported. (Solnit, 1980, p. 135)

Solnit is on the mark in recognizing that *total* prevention is rather unlikely and that the prevention of child maltreatment is bound up in mechanisms for social control. But this bleak picture is not the whole story. There is a basic misconception about our efforts to understand and enhance family support programs as a way of preventing child maltreatment. This misconception is driven by our society's ambivalence concerning the need to balance collective and individual rights. Using the prison as a metaphor for a society that could prevent all child maltreatment has an ironic element. As research on institutional maltreatment makes clear, prisons are probably *less* capable of preventing abuse and neglect than any other social context. Even in rehabilitation (as opposed to penal) settings, institutional abuse (abuse by staff) and abuse in institutions (abuse by fellow inmates) are intractable problems (Rabb & Rindfleisch, 1985). Indeed, victims of maltreatment in the family are likely to describe their homes as prisons in that they feel locked into a pattern of exploitation and brutality. To draw out this image still further, the neighborhoods in our society with the highest rates of child maltreatment often are themselves the most prison-like of social environments, dominated by a police presence contesting with a criminal element for control while the bulk of the "inmates" do their time for the economic "crime" of poverty (cf. Garbarino & Sherman, 1980). It seems that the answer to preventing child maltreatment does not lie in a prison-like society—at least not one modeled after our prisons. Our kind of society permits child maltreatment *and* has one of the highest rates of incarceration among the world's industrialized societies.

THE ROLE OF SUPPORT SYSTEMS IN PREVENTING CHILD MALTREATMENT

The prevention of child maltreatment involves more than mechanisms of social control. In that it requires the joining together of social nurturance and social control, it contrasts with the inapplicable prison model. The linking of social nurturance and social control, the essential element of effective family-support programs to prevent child maltreatment, flows directly from the concept of support systems as articulated by Caplan and his colleagues over the years (Caplan & Killilea, 1976). In this view support systems are

> continuing social aggregates that provide individuals with opportunities for feedback about themselves and for validations for their expectations about others, which may offset deficiencies in these communications within the larger community context. . . . People have a variety of specific needs that demand satisfaction through enduring interpersonal relationships, such as for love and affection, for intimacy that provides the freedom to express feelings easily and unself-consciously, for validation of personal identity and worth, for satisfaction of nurturance and dependency, for help with tasks, and for *support in handling emotion and controlling impulses.* . . . They tell him [the individual] what is expected of him and guide him in what to do. They watch what he does and they judge his performance. (italics added; Caplan, 1974, pp. 4–6)

The key is nurturance *and* control; social resources *and* feedback. This becomes particularly important in preventing child maltreatment, for families at risk are likely to face a deficit of both nurturance and feedback (Garbarino & Gilliam, 1980). Families involved in maltreatment are likely to be cut off from prosocial support systems—in part because of their own "distancing" behaviors and lack of social skills (Polansky et al., 1981). And yet, we have anecdotal observation and systematic empirical evidence to substantiate the contention that families at high risk for maltreatment can participate in and profit from family support programs (Cohn, 1979).

Successful support programs in this area have the ability to accomplish five goals. The first is improving the social skills of the individual parent, perhaps by modeling and reinforcing such skills. The second is enlarging the resource base of the parent's social network, usually by an infusion of new skills, financing, participants, or all three. The third involves enhancing the prosocial orientation of the network by linking the parent to mainstream community values and institutions. This means stimulating participation in the institutional life of the community—for example, PTA, church, and civic groups—and seeking to change the beliefs and values of the network where necessary through parent education programs. The fourth is reducing the degree to which the parent is a resource drain on the network. Networks are reciprocal, and individuals who only take and have nothing to give in exchange (or feel they have nothing) may be expelled or withdraw. High-risk parents need individualized support to build up their capacity to contribute in peer networks, perhaps through skills training and income enhancement. The fifth goal is providing greater positive surveillance for the family. This means frequent, regularized occasions for community representatives to observe family functioning and child welfare and development to detect incipient maltreatment. With this in mind, an examination of model programs aimed at preventing child maltreatment follows.

COSTS AND BENEFITS OF FAMILY SUPPORT SYSTEM INTERVENTIONS

On the one hand, the results of several model programs tell us that prevention is possible. On the other hand, these programs tell us that success does not come cheaply. There are financial and social costs to be borne and difficult choices to be made. For example, several programs aimed at improving the prenatal, childbirth, and early childhood experiences of high-risk families have reported preventive effects (Gray et al., 1977; O'Connor et al., 1977; Olds, 1980; Olds et al., 1985). However, some programs with similar goals have not reported such success (Siegel et al., 1980).

Olds and his colleagues (1985) have conducted a family support program with high-risk mothers that is unusual in combining significant intervention with a sophisticated research design (including random assignment to conditions). Its rigor justifies a detailed description of its findings. The critical test contrasted the assignment of a home health visitor (a registered nurse) to the family during the pregnancy and continuing for the first two years of life (beginning with weekly visits that tapered off to monthly visits) with three "smaller" forms of intervention incorporating a prenatal health visitor, free transportation to health clinics, and screening/diagnostic testing. Results indicate a significant preventive effect among poor unmarried mothers 19 years of age or younger. Among this group the rate of maltreatment (as determined from official reports) in the first two years was 4 percent for the longer health-visitor treatment versus 19 percent in the other intervention conditions. Olds (personal communication) speculates that the long-term health visitors developed a relationship characterized by both nurturance and feedback with their young clients.

Backing up the lower reported rates of child maltreatment in the nurse-visitor treatment is the finding that these same young mothers also described their babies in more positive terms, their children had fewer hospital emergency-room visits for ingestions and accidents (.91 times versus 1.70 times), and the mothers reported that they spanked their six-month-old infants an average of .02 times in two weeks versus 1.89 times in the other intervention conditions.

One indicator of the social-control function is that home health visitors initiated discussions that led to voluntary termination of parental rights at birth by two women who prenatally exhibited very high risk for child maltreatment. The home health visitors sought to change values, clarify the consequences of alternative paths for family development, and empower socially responsible behavior. Evidence of the success of this effort is the finding that only 13 percent of the poor unmarried teenage women in the long-term nurse visitor group gave birth a second time within two years as opposed to 54 percent in the comparison groups.

Interestingly (and possibly very significantly for programming and policy), Olds reports that the most negative side effects (for example, conflict with relatives) and the least positive results (the smallest preventive effects) observed were functions of being married and being older. Young unmarried mothers manifested more positive effects than older, married women, presumably because they were more responsive to social supports, more willing to change, and less enmeshed in a negative social system. This finding underlines that the key issue is isolation from *prosocial* support systems (Garbarino, 1977a). As Straus (1980) reports in his study of two-parent families, when the only involvement a parent has is with kin (who presumably reinforce problematic behaviors and attitudes), the result as measured by rates of child abuse is worse than that of simple social isolation. It appears that support systems are more likely to be prosocial if they are diverse and extend beyond kin.

This hypothesis is in keeping with the general principle that pluralistic social environments facilitate prosocial individual development (Garbarino & Bronfenbrenner, 1976) and highlights the important point that powerful preventive interventions are not psychologically and socially "free." They exact real psychological and financial costs in the form of conflict over rights and values and heightened need for community development (for example, creating family centers, improved day care, and health programs) and social network change (for example, value change, linking professionals with networks, and infusing resources) as components of positive interventions aimed at the parent-child relationship. The care, the attention to detail, and the persistence of Olds' study make clear that preventive intervention cannot be casual or half-hearted if it is to succeed. But Olds' work does demonstrate better than any other single project that prevention is possible. To quote from his report: "The pattern of results from this investigation provides coherent evidence that nurse home visitors are capable of preventing a number of caregiving dysfunctions, including child abuse and neglect. The positive effects of the program were concentrated on those women at greatest risk for caregiving dysfunction" (p. 17).

Olds' findings are consistent with the experience of the Denver-based Lay Health Visitor Program (Gray & Kaplan, 1980), suggesting that health-system-related family support does effectively capitalize upon the authority and legitimacy of medicine and nursing in American society. Reviewing the records of 550 high-risk families receiving the service over an 18-month period, Gray and Kaplan report that no children were seriously damaged because of parental maltreatment. These results correspond to those of an earlier experimental study of the program (Gray et al., 1977). In the 18-month follow-up, it appeared that the majority of the high-risk families could be phased out of routine visitation by the end of the third month after childbirth while in one-third of the families (the most "chaotic and prone to violence") visitation continued past the sixth month. However, Siegel and colleagues (1980) did not report significant preventive effects in their study of early contact and home visiting. Unlike Olds' study this study did not examine the possibility that preventive effects were confined to (or at least intensified among) families that were at highest risk and perhaps specially susceptible to the intervention.

Family-centered childbirth constitutes a second, related class of family support to prevent child maltreatment. Kennell, Voos, and Klaus (1976) reported that lack of parental visits to infants receiving intensive care predicted substantially greater risk of child maltreatment—23 percent for infrequently visited infants versus 2 percent for the frequently visited. We do not know if this constitutes a direct effect of early visiting or simply means that high-risk parents are more likely to withdraw from the relationship early on. Gray and her colleagues (1977) concluded that this finding reflects a more generalized link between disruptions in early maternal-infant interaction and later maltreatment. In their study they found no reported cases in the group classified as low risk on the basis of assessments of the mother-infant relationship conducted by the nurses versus 8 percent in the high-risk group. The family-centered childbirth intervention (rooming in, early contact, father involvement, breast-feeding) implemented by O'Connor and her colleagues (1977) in a sample of high-risk mothers resulted in a child-maltreatment incidence of .7 percent in the treatment group and 6 percent in the no-treatment control.

Directed self-help groups constitute a third class of family support relevant to preventing child maltreatment. Most of the examples cited here involve prevention at the secondary (preventing high-risk parents from abusing their children) or tertiary (preventing abusive parents from repeating the abuse) level. The best-known example is the national network of Parents Anonymous, groups of abusive parents who meet to help one another eliminate abuse in their families. Each group has a professional facilitator and uses the mutual-disclosure and solidarity techniques pioneered by Alcoholics Anonymous and used by other self-help and mutual-help groups (cf. Whittaker, Garbarino, & Associates, 1983). Evaluation of the programs has been encouraging (Lieber & Baker, 1977; Behavior Associates, 1977)— including assessments of their cost effectiveness (Cohn, 1979). A recent study (Roth, 1985) reports that children of parents who have a good attendance record at Parents Anonymous meetings behave better in a group setting led by adults. The study did not establish that participation in the Parents Anonymous group was the cause, but this congruity between parents' involvement and children's improved behavior is one of the important goals for such programs. This lends credence to recent Parents Anonymous efforts to create and maintain "Kids' Groups."

A fourth class of family support aimed at preventing child maltreatment involves efforts at the neighborhood or community level to empower social networks to provide more nurturance and feedback to families. The rationale and mechanisms for such an approach have been laid out by Alice Collins, Diane Pancoast, and others (see Garbarino, Stocking, & Associates, 1980; Whittaker, Garbarino, & Associates, 1983).

Briefly, the approach involves an effort to understand the social structure in the target community. Who are the sources of information? Whom do you go to for help? Who keeps an eye on children and young parents? The answers to questions like these provide a basis for opening channels of communication between professionals and the "lay helpers," "central figures," and "natural neighbors." These channels eventually become a two-way street of mutual information and consultation.

The Michigan Maximization Project (located in Inkster, Michigan) is an illustrative effort to implement this concept. The project involves creating a community council to build up informal social-support networks throughout the community and enhance collaboration between formal and informal helping resources as a way of improving social nurturance and control and, ultimately, preventing child maltreatment. Other projects exist with similar goals. Wayne State University's Neighborhood Family Resource Center Project reports (Smock, 1982) that its efforts resulted in a 52 percent increase in neighborhood involvement by participating families. This reduction in social isolation is critical. What is more, the skills-building and personal-enhancement aspects of the programs were similarly successful (as judged by participants' self-reports). "Using Informal Resources in Child Protective Services," a handbook developed by Bertsche and his colleagues at the University of Montana School of Social Work (Sudia, 1982), is an effort to codify this approach.

It is worth noting here that parent-education programs frequently play a role in all four categories of social-support intervention. Parent education (discussed in detail by Wandersman (chap. 11) provides the content goals for many of the interactions that take place—both formally as programs and informally as agendas in the day-to-day contact between professionals or lay helpers and clients or network members. Helping parents understand their child's capabilities so that their expectations are realistic is one important way in which parent education can help prevent child maltreatment.

The apparent success of some model programs encourages speculation about the effect of nationwide implementation, although the very prospect invokes troublesome issues of resource availability and allocation (how effectively does child welfare compete with national security for financial resources?), political ideology (how can constitutional guarantees of privacy be reconciled with the level of surveillance, supervision, and social control necessary for comprehensive participation in powerful programs?), and technique (can programs be replicated on the scale necessary for the diverse populations involved?).

The programmatic and policy issues involved in implementing an effective national effort to prevent child abuse are the topic of several recent analyses (Cohen, Gray, & Wald, 1984; Cohn, 1983; Gelles, 1984;

Rosenberg & Reppucci, 1985). Cohen, Gray, and Wald (1984) reviewed a variety of programs emphasizing early contact, perinatal support, parent education, and/or counseling/behavior modification. They conclude:

> Ideally, we would be able to list those prevention strategies that really do effectively counteract each underlying cause [of child abuse]. But we still know far too little to be able to hand out that kind of prescription. We can, however, make some educated guesses. That is the role that the evaluation studies . . . can play. While they are still too few to allow bold claims, they do suggest that much of what we have been trying may benefit at least a subgroup of that risk population. (p. 20)

What does all this imply for our efforts? It has important implications for the way we evaluate family support programs aimed at child maltreatment as well as which programs we support. It steers us toward a series of propositions concerning programs aimed at preventing child maltreatment (Garbarino, 1986).

PRINCIPLES FOR PREVENTING CHILD MALTREATMENT

1. Prevention goals and their limitations should be stated as precisely as possible. For example, some forms of abuse may be more preventable by family support programs than others, and this should be acknowledged. We should also acknowledge the distinction between reducing incidence and reducing severity. It may well be possible to reduce severity in cases where complete prevention is not possible. Indeed, one of the commonly cited prevention programs (the home-health-visitor program in Denver: Gray et al., 1977) is perhaps better understood as reducing severity than preventing abuse. It resulted in fewer *serious injuries* but not in fewer cases of maltreatment overall.

2. We should recognize that prevention efforts may be effective only under specified conditions. For example, some family support programs may work only for unmarried young mothers. Olds' results are consistent with this hypothesis. Others may work only for families with adequate economic resources. This suggests that a realistic strategy may involve matching programs to targeted groups. Thus, for example, while family-centered childbirth may be a key family-support program for dealing with abuse among primiparous mothers it may be less useful in dealing with neglect in a family that already has several children.

3. In any overall claims about reducing child abuse in a given community, or across the whole society, we must clearly specify the appropriate base rates and must take into account changes in underlying social and economic conditions and variations in definition and case identification. We must avoid obscuring prevention effects by these factors. For exam-

ple, we must be aware that changes in definition and reporting procedures could affect the officially recorded rate of abuse. Prevention and treatment programs may uncover new cases and thus may appear to increase the incidence of child abuse (see Conte, Rosen, & Saperstein, in press). Prevention programs are often undertaken in a climate of heightened public concern, which itself can lead to an increase in *reported* incidence. It is worth noting, however, that in some areas, reporting of certain kinds of maltreatment may have evolved to the point where there is no reservoir of unreported abuse cases.

4. A complete strategy will involve both generalized primary prevention and programming targeted at high-risk groups. Evaluation of these interventions may be profitably based on comparisons of similar groups randomly assigned to different treatment conditions. Indeed, the need for prospective evaluation studies is critical. After reviewing the knowledge base on preventing child abuse, Rosenberg and Reppucci (1985) conclude: "Although we have come a long way in terms of child abuse research and operationalization of prevention approaches, we will go no further in our goal of eradicating child abuse until evaluation of prevention programs is taken as seriously as the ideas that formulate the programs. It is this task that confronts the serious prevention researcher and practitioner over the next decade."

5. Comparable communities can be the targets for intervention so that studies using before/after designs can note and control for broad economic and social effects in analyzing results. This will also permit estimates of the incidence of abuse where the program does not exist. Making use of "natural experiments"—such as using as controls people who are on the waiting list to join a family support program, and any naturally occurring *random* differences in who gets what services when—is vital because the logistical and technical challenges of using "comparable" communities as the units of analysis are often daunting and sometimes overwhelming. Such controlled experimentation is crucial. It requires that we have sufficient numbers of programs and/or communities (or community subunits such as neighborhoods) to permit the use of statistical procedures that control for several dimensions of community variability in assessing the impact of programs aimed at preventing child abuse.

6. Evaluation efforts must utilize multiple measures. We should not limit ourselves to measures of reported child abuse. A complete approach will include efforts to assess changes in the incidence of child death and serious injury, the costs and outcomes of treatment (on the assumption that prevention programs may affect the "treatability" of cases that do occur), hospital emergency-room treatment, standards for disciplinary practices (for example, spanking in the first year of a child's

life), and knowledge and attitudes concerning the range of behaviors that constitute or increase the risk for abuse. Measures of parent and child behavior are the bottom line, and it will not suffice to substitute measures of attitude alone (which are usually easier to obtain).

7. Prevention efforts can include both measures designed to control or restrain destructive patterns *and* measures designed to replace these destructive patterns with positive patterns that are incompatible with abuse. Quality out-of-home child care appears to serve a useful function in modeling effective relationships.

8. Two basic approaches to prevention exist. One argues that we can tackle discrete pieces of the problem of child abuse in isolation from the broader socioeconomic, cultural, and political context. The other derives from the view that total social reform is a prerequisite (and a vehicle) for significant progress in preventing child abuse. We can refer to the former view as "patchwork prevention" and the latter as "total reform prevention." Although existing research does seem to demonstrate the possibility of altering families and their social relations without fundamental community change, we should not too readily discard the hypothesis that sustained widespread prevention will come only as a feature of efforts more in keeping with "total reform prevention" (such as reducing poverty)

IS THE COMMUNITY PARENT TO THE FAMILY?

A family support approach to child maltreatment is necessarily a community-focused endeavor. It asks that the community assume comprehensive responsibility for families. To put this in another way, it demands that the community be parent to the family. This approach confronts some basic issues of authority and responsibility. Does the community stand in the same relation to parents as parents do to their children? If it does, the vast body of research, theory, and practice of parenting becomes relevant. This literature tells us that offering unconditional regard and acceptance is vital but leads to competence and appropriate independence most reliably when coupled with a disciplinary style that emphasizes reciprocity. Reciprocity here refers to parent and child sharing power as a function of the child's growing competence in self-management and decision-making. It begins in infancy as parental responsiveness to the child's needs and eventually becomes a partnership of approximate equals in adulthood.

Diana Baumrind's studies (1979) of child-rearing styles and their consequences for development provide an insightful look at how important reciprocity is to the family microsystem. She found that when reciprocity was upheld in day-to-day interaction (what she called an "authoritative" orientation), the child is provided with the greatest number of opportunities to develop social competence. When it was systematically violated in an "authoritarian" style, the child's development suffered. This style violated the principle of symmetry by lodging excessive power in the hands of the parent and thus placing the child in a passive role. On the other hand, a "permissive" pattern inappropriately gave free rein to the child and his unformed drives and thus placed the parent in a passive role. Neither the authoritarian nor the permissive style does justice to the family. Healthy parent-child relations require large doses of *both* demands and responsiveness. As Baumrind (1979) puts it:

> The most effective parents regard their parental rights and obligations as complementary to the duties and rights of the child. . . . Authoritative parents see the balance between the rights of parents and those of children as a changing function of the child's stage of development as well as an expression of the norm of reciprocity by which they operate and which they wish their children to adopt. (p. 641)

What happens if we substitute "community" for "parents" and "parents" for "children" in Baumrind's analysis?

> The most effective communities regard their community rights and obligations as complementary to the duties and rights of the parents. . . . Authoritative communities see the balance between the rights of communities and those of parents as a changing function of the parents' stage of development as well as an expression of the norm of reciprocity by which they operate and which they wish parents to adopt.

If the community is parent to the family, this is an appropriate model. It offers just what most high-risk families need—at least initially, when the issue is whether the family *can* be stabilized in a pattern of relating that does not involve maltreatment. It recognizes that mature and effective parents can and should assume leadership roles in improving the community's systems that care for children. This is exactly what happens in social support networks in general and in family support programs that incorporate mutual-help groups in which successful clients become lay helpers (Whittaker, Garbarino, & Associates, 1983).

However, many voices are raised to dispute the concept of community "parenthood" of the family. The preferred orientation is community as parent-of-last-resort. This requires a "clear and present" danger to the child before the privacy of the family and the "rights" of the parents are "violated." If we are limited to being invited into families that are motivated to seek help or bullying our way in after a tragic event or a pattern of maltreatment is well established, then we usually end up trying to lock the barn door after we have removed the horse. Is this our cultural destiny?

North American social history is pervaded with a cultural and structural ambivalence concerning individualism and collectivism, freedom and authority, privacy and social integration. This dynamic has been variously identified. Thirty-five years ago James Webb called it "the Parabola of Individualism" and David Riesman labeled it "the Lonely Crowd." Fifteen years ago Philip Slater termed it "the Pursuit of Loneliness." Privacy has both ideological and structural value, as is evident in the high value we Americans place on owning our own homes. Opportunities for privacy have increased markedly in recent decades, often under the protective rationale of civil liberties. However, privacy provides a potentially dangerous context for parent-child relations when it generates isolation in a context characterized by personal and social stress and professional and political attitudes favoring independence over interdependence (Garbarino, 1977b).

Elder (1974) noted that middle-class observers were often dismayed by the ways that working-class families shared with kin during the Great Depression. Stack's (1974) account of black kinship sharing notes that the typical professional evaluation of such behavior is that it is irrational and self-defeating. In a study of Jewish social workers and clients, Leichter and Mitchell (1967) report differences in attitudes and values. The more traditional clients (and their parents) expressed belief in the rights, wisdom, and obligation of kinship, and the more modern caseworkers downgraded kinship networks in favor of personal freedom, autonomy, and privacy. Campbell (1975) remarks the ideological commitment of most modern psychologists to liberation of the individual from collective bonds. He questions the wisdom of this approach on the grounds that it tends to release antisocial impulses and, in the long run, cannot indefinitely increase satisfaction. In Campbell's view, psychologists who council liberation are embarking on a socially dangerous course in conflict with the need for structure, obligations, and the "ties that bind" in human life. Yet, the "liberation" perspective is strong among many professionals and much of the general public.

The allure of privacy is great. It permits individuals to flourish and insulates the family against external meddling by persons who may have their own interests to advance. This "protective" function seems a major attraction to professional helpers. Privacy provides the potential for a "quiet" atmosphere, whereas social support system intrusion is psychologically "noisy." The latter exacts real social-psychological costs, including the dangers that powerful elites will impose *their* values inappropriately and that meddlesome individuals will misuse community authority to sanction unwarranted intrusions. Are we willing to pay those costs to prevent child maltreatment? If not, are we willing to let children pay the price for privacy? Each community must answer these tough questions if we are to confront the problem of child maltreatment.

Some ask: Who owns the children? We reject that question because we reject the idea of children as property in favor of the idea of children as citizens, as junior partners in the life of the community. So we might better say, "Who has custody of the children?" One model replies, "Parents do." Another asserts, "Parents have custody but the community has visiting rights." Perhaps the answer most likely to preserve and protect children while supporting and encouraging parents is to say that parents and the community have joint custody. Such an answer provides the foundation for an approach to family support systems that we can live with. What is more, it offers a level of community commitment to child welfare that children in high-risk families cannot live without.

NOTE

1. For example, see Steven Tulkin, An analysis of the concept of cultural deprivation, in *Developmental Psychology*, 1972; and Eli Newberger's efforts to redefine the "battered child syndrome" as "social pediatric illness," in Newberger, ed., *Child Abuse*, 1982.

REFERENCES

Baumrind, D. (1979). A dialectical materialist's perspective on knowing social reality. *New Directions in Child Development, 2*, 61–82.

Behavior Associates. (1977). *Parents Anonymous self-help for child-abusing parents project: Evaluation report.* Tucson, AZ: Behavior Associates.

Belsky, J. (1980). Child maltreatment: An ecological interaction. *American Psychologist, 35*, 320–335.

Berkeley Planning Associates. (1977). *Evaluation of child abuse and neglect demonstration projects, 1974–1977. Volume III. Adult client impact.* Final Report to the National Center for Health Services Research, Hyattsville, MD.

Bronfenbrenner, U. (1972). *Two worlds of childhood: U.S. and U.S.S.R.* New York: Simon and Schuster (Touchstone Edition).

Campbell, D. (1975). On the conflict between biological and social evaluation and between psychology and moral tradition. *American Psychologist, 30*, 598–627.

Caplan, G. (1974). *Support systems and community mental health.* New York: Behavioral Publications.

Caplan, G., & Killilea, M. (1976). *Support systems and mutual help: Multidisciplinary explorations.* New York: Grune and Stratton.

Cohen, S., Gray, E., & Wald, M. (1984). *Preventing child maltreatment: A review of what we know.* NCPCA, Working Paper No. 24.

Cohn, A. H. (1979). Essential elements of successful child abuse and neglect treatment. *Child Abuse and Neglect: The International Journal, 3*, 491–496.

Cohn, A. H. (1983). *An approach to preventing child abuse.* Chicago: NCPCA.

Conte, J., Rosen, C., & Saperstein, L. (In press). An analysis of programs to prevent the sexual victimization of children. *Journal of Primary Prevention.*

Elder, G. H. (1974). *Children of the Great Depression.* Chicago: University of Chicago Press.

Garbarino, J. (1977a). The human ecology of child maltreatment: A conceptual model for research. *Journal of Marriage and the Family, 39,* 721–736.

Garbarino, J. (1977b). The price of privacy: An analysis of the social dynamics of child abuse. *Child Welfare, 56,* 565–575.

Garbarino, J. (1986). Can we measure success in preventing child abuse? Issues in policy, programming, and research. *Child Abuse and Neglect: The International Journal, 10,* 143–156.

Garbarino, J., & Bronfenbrenner, U. (1976). The socialization of moral judgment and behavior in cross-cultural perspectives. In T. Lickona (Ed.), *Moral development and behavior.* New York: Holt, Rinehart, & Winston.

Garbarino, J., & Gilliam, G. (1980). *Understanding abusive families.* Lexington, MA: Lexington Books.

Garbarino, J., & Sherman, D. (1980). High-risk neighborhoods and high-risk families: The human ecology of child maltreatment. *Child Development, 51,* 188–198.

Garbarino, J., Stocking, S. H., & Associates. (1980). *Protecting children from abuse and neglect: Developing and maintaining effective support systems for families.* San Francisco, CA: Jossey-Bass.

Gelles, R. (1984, August 7–10). Applying our knowledge of family violence to prevention and treatment: What difference might it make? Paper presented to the Second National Conference for Family Violence Researchers, Durham, NH.

Gerbner, G., Ross, C., & Zigler, E. (1980). *Child abuse: An agenda for action.* New York: Oxford University Press.

Gray, J., Cutler, C., Dean, J., & Kempe, C. H. (1977). Prediction and prevention of child abuse and neglect. *Child Abuse and Neglect, 1,* 45–58.

Gray, J., & Kaplan, B. (1980). The lay health visitor program: An eighteen-month experience. In C. H. Kempe & R. Helfer (Eds.), *The battered child* (pp. 373–378). Chicago: University of Chicago Press.

Kennell, J., Voos, D., & Klaus, M. (1976). Parent-Infant bonding. In R. Helfer & C. H. Kempe (Eds.), *Child abuse and neglect: The family and the community* (pp. 25–53). Cambridge, MA: Ballinger.

Leichter, H., & Mitchell, W. (1967). *Kinship and casework.* New York: Russell Sage.

Lieber, L., & Baker, J. (1977). Parents Anonymous and self-help treatment for child abusing parents: A review and an evaluation. *Child Abuse and Neglect, 1,* 133–148.

Newberger, E. (Ed.). (1982). *Child abuse.* Boston: Little, Brown.

O'Connor, S., Vietze, P., Hopkins, J., & Altemeir, W. (1977). Postpartum extended maternal-infant contact: Subsequent mothering and child health. *Sociological Pediatric Research* (Abstract).

Olds, D. (1980). Improving formal services for mothers and children. In J. Garbarino, S. H. Stocking, & Associates (Eds.), *Protecting children from abuse and neglect.* San Francisco: Jossey-Bass.

Olds, D., Chamberlin, R., Henderson, C., & Tatelbaum, R. (1985). *The prevention of child abuse and neglect: A randomized trial of nurse home visitation.* Rochester, NY: Department of Pediatrics, University of Rochester.

Polansky, N., Chalmers, M., Buttenwieser, E., & Williams, D. (1981). *Damaged parents*. Chicago: University of Chicago Press.

Rabb, J., & Rindfleisch, N. (1985). A study to define and assess severity of institutional abuse/neglect. *Child Abuse and Neglect, 9*, 285–294.

Riesman, D. (1950). *The lonely crowd*. New Haven, CT: Yale University Press.

Rosenberg, M., & Reppucci, N. D. (1985). Primary prevention of child abuse. Unpublished paper, University of Virginia.

Roth, H. (1985). Relationship between attendance at a Parents Anonymous Adult program and children's behavior at the Parents Anonymous child care program. *Children and Youth Services Review, 7*, 39–44.

Siegel, E., Bauman, K., Schaefer, E., Saunders, M., & Ingram, D. (1980). Hospital and home support during infancy: Impact on maternal attachment, child abuse and neglect, and health care utilization. *Pediatrics, 66*, 183–190.

Slater, P. (1970). *The pursuit of loneliness*. Boston: Beacon Press.

Smock, S. (1982). *Neighborhood Family Resource Centers Project*. Wayne State University, Detroit, MI.

Solnit, A. (1980). Too much reporting, too little service: Roots and prevention of child abuse. In G. Gerbner, C. Ross, & E. Zigler (Eds.), *Child abuse: An agenda for action* (pp. 124–146). New York: Oxford University Press.

Stack, C. (1974). *All our kin: Strategies for survival in a black community*. New York: Harper & Row.

Straus, M. (1980). Stress and child abuse. In R. Helfer & H. Kempe (Eds.), *The battered child*. Chicago, IL.: University of Chicago Press.

Straus, M., Gelles, R., & Steinmetz, S. (1980). *Behind closed doors*. New York: Doubleday.

Sudia, C. (1982). Using informal resources to prevent abuse and strengthen families. *Caring, 7* (4), 2ff.

Tulkin, S. R. (1972). An analysis of the concept of cultural deprivation. *Developmental Psychology, 6*, 326–339.

Webb, W. (1952). *The great frontier*. Austin: University of Texas Press.

Whittaker, J., Garbarino, J., & Associates. (1983). *Social support networks in the human services*. New York: Aldine.

7 DAY CARE AS A FAMILY SUPPORT SYSTEM

Douglas R. Powell

A high-quality child-care arrangement is one of the most important family-support systems for working parents of young children. Performance in the work setting, parent-child relations, and other key aspects of individual and family functioning are influenced directly by the quality of child care. The recent dramatic growth in the number of women in the work force and the concomitant increase in the use of day care suggest that out-of-home child care is no longer a marginal feature of American life. For parents in all economic strata, day care increasingly is an essential component of the family's external support system.

In the past two decades, public policies and programs have demonstrated three contrasting perspectives on the relationship between the family and out-of-home child care. In one view, day care is a positive influence on family functioning that provides a child development program while freeing parents for work and other meaningful activities. According to this view, day care is a service for children with positive benefits for families. The spirit of this view was reflected in federal legislative efforts of the 1970s making day care universally available (for example, the Mondale–Brademas Comprehensive Child Development Act of 1971).

A second perspective construes day care as a compensatory program for children from inadequate families. This orientation has its roots in the history of day care. Early forms of child care were intended for children whose families were deemed unable to fulfill their child-rearing responsibilities owing to poverty, family structure, or some other indicator of atypical status (Fein & Clarke-Stewart, 1973). Under these circumstances, day care is seen as providing cognitive and socialization experiences that parents are unable or unwilling to supply.

A third perspective suggests that day care is disruptive to family life. In this view, day care is a deviant form of child rearing, significantly inferior to maternal care in the home. Day care is thought to supplant the family. President Nixon's veto of the Mondale–Brademas bill was indicative of this orientation. He noted the undesirability of "communal approaches to child rearing," which work "against the family-centered approach" (Nixon, 1971, pp. S21129–30).

It is difficult to determine which perspective dominates the field today. Clearly the growing use of day care by "mainstream" families with no apparent negative effects on children or families (Belsky, 1984) seems to have weakened the idea that day care poses a threat to home and family. The first perspective—day care as a supplement to the family—is popular in rhetoric, but the extent of its actual implementation is not known. At the same time, remnants of the view of day care as a substitute for the family—as a "savior" of the child—still exist although generally not at a surface level. Studies of judgmental attitudes of caregivers toward parents (Kontos & Wells, 1986) and strained parent-teacher relations in public school (Lightfoot, 1978) and preschool (Joffe, 1977) settings suggest that the relationship between families and child-rearing institutions may be characterized by an undercurrent of tension and occasional overt conflict.

Day care has not evolved in this country as a family support program. Conceptually and operationally, the primary client has been the child. Day care typically does not operate as a family support program akin to many other family-based services represented in this book. It is, however, a rapidly growing institution that could be strengthened through closer ties with families.

Under what conditions are day-care services supportive of family values and functioning? Which program strategies improve the chances of a good match and close communication between two major socialization agencies—day care and the family? Responses to questions of this type must be more speculative than empirical. Most day-care research has examined effects on children (for reviews, see Belsky, 1984; Belsky & Steinberg, 1978; Belsky, Steinberg, & Walker, 1981); day-care effects on the family have not been studied in great detail. Yet life for all members of a nuclear family—not just the child—may change markedly with the use of day care. Consider, for example, the positive correlation between marital satisfaction and satisfaction with a day-care arrangement (Meyers, 1973).

This chapter moves toward a fourth perspective on the relationship between day care and the family, suggesting that there should be a good match and a close relationship between the family and the child care resource. This is crucial because in day care the intimate and value-laden family function of child rearing is being shared with an extrafamilial system. This view transcends the first perspective (day care as a supplement) by suggesting that day care should be more than a high-quality child-development program that frees parents to pursue work. It should be a support, not a supplement, to the family.

This chapter investigates two dimensions of the role of day care as a family support system: the process of matching day-care services to families and subsequent interactions between families and day-care settings. Within each of these areas attention is given to issues and research pertinent to the design of strategies to improve relations between families and day care.

MATCHING DAY-CARE RESOURCES TO FAMILY NEEDS

At the most general level, an examination of day care as a family support system must consider the quality of care provided. The negative influences of large group size, high staff-child ratios, inadequately trained caregivers, and inappropriate curriculum approaches are not limited to the child but also may have deleterious effects on the family. Although we know very little about the impact of poor-quality child care on parents and the parent-child dyad, a large-scale study of infant-toddler day care found that infants in low-quality settings (characterized, for instance, by infrequent play and frequent negative interactions) were less sensitive (that is, no distress) to mother-infant separations than were infants from high-quality centers (Kermonian, 1980). The investigators suggested that low-quality care might increase the development of dysfunctional infant-mother attachment.

A child's reluctance to go to a child care center or provider in the morning, troubling behavior at the end of the child care day, and signs of stress or burnout from a dysfunctional child care environment may prompt strained relations within the family. Parental guilt about the use of day care may be heightened by a child's difficult experiences in a low-quality child care setting.

Efforts to enhance the role of day care as a family resource must be geared partly toward ensuring conditions under which quality is likely to flourish: precise and monitored standards; adequate financial resources for staff and facilities; staff training; and a healthy level of professional self-assessment among child care providers. Societal support for day care in the United States is inexcusably weak, although there are some recent important initiatives to improve caregiver qualifications and center quality.[1] Much of the high-quality child care found in this country is due largely to the willingness of exceptionally talented and dedicated caregivers to work for minimal pay, often with limited materials and physical facilities.

Systematic data on how much quality care exists in this country today are not available. Until recently the push for quantity has overshadowed the struggle for quality (Greenman, 1984). Serious efforts to enhance day care's role as a family resource, however, must begin with a careful assessment of the quality of care provided and existing structures (for example, financial resources and staff training) to support the enterprise.

Quality care, characterized by such indicators as are noted above, is crucial if day care is to serve as a family support program. Quality care also must be available in a variety of forms and settings. Diverse types of care are needed to meet varying child and family needs. A freely operating child care market is potentially more responsive to family needs than a massive system dominated by a uniform type of care. For some children, the optimal child care environment may be a small, mixed-age family day-care home (an arrangement where a provider cares for a small group of children in her own home). Other children may function best in a same-age classroom of as many as eighteen children.

Responsive day care also is compatible with the logistics of family life. Hours of service, location, and flexibility in entry and exit times are among the key determinants of the extent to which day care coincides with parental work schedules and transportation logistics. The provision of afterschool child care is a good example of problems in matching day-care services to family lifestyles. Many center-based afterschool programs operate from the end of the school day until 5:30 or 6:00 P.M. To be financially viable, most programs must impose a fee schedule that assumes the child is present five days a week for at least an hour a day. This arrangement is probably a useful resource for a parent who consistently works until 4:30 or 5:00 P.M. But for parents whose work day ends within 30 to 40 minutes of the child's departure from school, or whose work schedule is inconsistent from week to week, the financial and logistical costs of accommodating an afterschool program may outweigh the benefits.

Diverse forms of child care are also needed to satisfy the range of child-rearing values found among American families. Parents differ markedly in their ideas of what constitutes a good environment for children. A critical characteristic of a quality day-care arrangement is congruence of child-rearing values between family and child care setting. A greater diversity of child care forms maximizes the opportunity for parents to find an arrangement that reflects their values and beliefs.

Information and Referral as Matchmaker

In view of family lifestyle differences and child-rearing diversity, it would seem that the potential for day care to function as a family support system depends in part on the degree of match between a particular day-care resource and a particular family's needs and values. The critical task is for a family to find a satisfactory child care resource. The steps involved include an assessment of child and family needs for child care; an identification of options; and knowledge of, and the ability to assess, indicators of quality. Typically all of this must be done without a child care counterpart to a Michelin guide. Several studies indicate that parents would welcome assistance with the process (Powell & Eisenstadt, 1980; Rhodes & Moore, 1975).

One of the most promising strategies to help parents find child care is the establishment of local child care information and referral services (Zigler & Hunsinger, 1977). The need for information and referral (I&R) services has been emphasized in several major public-policy analyses (for example, Keniston & Carnegie Council on Children, 1977) and has received support in arguments against an increased federal role in the provision of day-care services (for example, Woolsey, 1977). It has been argued that child care I&R services are among the most politically feasible mechanisms for the development of future day-care policy (Levine, 1982). I&R services are thought to function as a "broker," linking parents with existing day-care services. Thus, the idea emphasizes family choice in child-rearing decisions and does not involve large sums of money to develop new day-care resources. The concept holds promise of improving the child care market by increasing parents' access to child care services, matching supply and demand, and maximizing consumer choice.

The vast majority of out-of-home child care in this country occurs in day-care homes, not in centers. One of the expected tangible benefits of I&R is to make family day care more visible and therefore more accessible. Another important expectation is that I&R services would help parents become informed consumers of child care by providing public education about characteristics of quality care (for example, through disseminating brochures and checklists of quality criteria). The notion here is that parents, in their roles as consumers, would influence the standards operating in the local child care marketplace by avoiding low-quality services.

Despite the popularity of the concept, in 1985 it was estimated that there were only slightly more than 200 agencies in the United States devoted exclusively to child care I&R (P. Seigel, personal communication, Sept. 6, 1985). This is an increase from the 50–60 such services found in a 1979 study by the American Institutes for Research. This study found that an average of 115 requests a week were handled by child care I&R services. The typical agency response was to give the names of two or three day-care centers and/or family day-care homes. Information also was supplied about sources of financial assistance for child care (for example, tax credits) and criteria for selecting a child care provider (American Institutes for Research, 1979). The vast majority of child care I&R services are located in California, a state that has provided child care I&R funding.

Although in theory the I&R concept appears promising, crucial questions must be asked about its design and implementation. What are the most effective ways to provide I&R in different types of communities? In urban settings, for instance, are centralized or decentralized (neighborhood based) services more useful to parents? What types of information should be disseminated? What role does I&R play in monitoring the quality of child care services? To what extent should informal sources of information be incorporated into the structure of an I&R service? Regarding this last question, Collins and Watson (1976) have proposed that in almost all neighborhoods where there are young families with children there are "day care neighbors"—individuals who provide child care and also serve as matchmakers between parents and family day-care providers. One image of an I&R operation, then, is a grassroots approach: provide technical assistance to the existing informal day-care matchmakers rather than create a new bureaucratic layer of information disseminators.

Findings of a study of urban parents' strategies for locating child care have implications for the design of a child care I&R service in an urban setting (Powell & Eisenstadt, 1982). The research involved structured interviews with a sample representative of Detroit households with one or more children under 6 years of age. The general pattern was for parents to begin the search for child care with nuclear family members and/or close friends and gradually move out to more peripheral ties such as nonnuclear relatives, acquaintances from work or other organizations (for example, church), and even strangers. Formal sources such as newspapers, agencies, and telephone directories tended to be used toward the end of the search, and sometimes not at all.

These findings suggest a tendency for parents to view child care as a private family matter. Peripheral ties were used when the inner circle of sources proved ineffective. Although many parents knew of at least one community agency that might have child care information, they did not use these sources initially in their searches for child care. Parents who used their relatives extensively in the child care search showed the least amount of interest in using an I&R service (Powell & Eisenstadt, 1983). Perhaps parents trusted their personal social networks to lead to quality child care services that were compatible with their child-rearing values and practices. Rearing children in a personalized network of kin and kith is a venerable American tradition.

Given these findings, what type of I&R service might be useful? A strategy that provides effective assistance to some parents might not be effective with other parents. A key variable seems to be neighborhood age, defined as the length of time most residents had lived in the parents' neighborhood. For instance, the need for an I&R service seemed greatest in neighborhoods where most people had resided for less than five years, since the "youth" of the neighborhood may have worked against the development of effective informal communication structures. Parents in these neighborhoods used help from formal sources, particularly newspapers. Print sources seem to be a likely way for an I&R to become visible among these parents, whereas informal neighborhood matchmakers probably would not be effective.

These data raise questions that future research needs to address. Under what conditions do parents view a formal agency as an appropriate source of information about child care? What properties of a formal institution prompt parents to perceive it as a keeper of useful information? The findings of the Powell and Eisenstadt study give the impression that a locally based information service may be viewed as a more appropriate source of child care information than a distant, centrally organized service. This impression needs careful examination.

The type of information disseminated by an I&R service is another major issue. Should it recommend or rate providers (for example, a "five-star" center), or should it disseminate objective data about day care resources that parents should judge? From the perspective of the service, generally there are limited resources for conducting assessments of child care providers on which to base recommendations to parents. There also is the legal issue of liability involved in recommending a child care facility that subsequently is judged to be of poor quality. Some parent-consumers have a strong desire for a recommendation; objective information is not enough. In the study of day-care search strategies, single parents with limited income were most likely to utilize the advice of others regarding the selection of care. Other parents (typically from two-parent households) assumed a more active stance in making their own decisions about day care. Presumably they would want facts, not judgments, from an I&R (Powell & Eisenstadt, 1983). An I&R that provides professionally determined recommendations about child care is modifying the principle of family decision-making about child care inherent in the concept of child care I&R. Yet for resource-pressured parents, advice may be more useful than such information as a list of providers that a parent has no time to assess and act upon.

The experiences of well-established I&R services in this country challenge the assumption that a supply of quality care exists in a given community, and the task for an I&R is to match day-care resources to parents' needs. The *I* in I&R is being transformed from *information* to *resource* in some operations. The change reflects the perceived need to take an active role in upgrading quality through training and developing new day-care options. A recent evaluation report by Bank Street College on the I&R program of the Child Care Council of Westport–Weston, Connecticut, sets forth a rationale representative of this shift. The report indicates that the change "reflects the fact that as demand for quality child care of all kinds increases, the agency finds it difficult to offer parents information on child care programs that are filled and have waiting lists or that plainly do not exist. The challenge becomes to develop new child care resources to meet new needs—from new centers to in-home care" (Mitchell, 1984, p. 8).

Information and referral holds much promise of matching families with appropriate day-care resources. Future research and program development need to address matters regarding the design, scope, and implementation of I&R services. It is important not to expect too much of child care I&R (Levine, 1982). It cannot satisfy the nation's growing need for day care, and its ability to have significant impact on the improvement of day-care quality in a local community is not clear. However, in a marketplace of diverse and largely invisible forms of child care, an I&R service appears to be a practical and necessary first step in helping families negotiate a child-rearing resource that is responsive to their needs and values.

DAY-CARE–FAMILY INTERACTIONS

A popular notion in the child development field is that parents should maintain close ties with day-care providers. Previous work has noted the theoretical argument that children's socialization experiences are improved when there is close coordination and communication between two or more socialization agents (Bronfenbrenner, 1979; Lippitt, 1968). While conventional wisdom suggests that the child benefits from a close relationship between parent and child care setting, an important question is whether the parent or family is influenced by the quality of the interaction between home and child care setting.

Studies of relationships between parents and caregivers in group child-care programs paint a gloomy picture. Zigler and Turner (1982) found that parents spent an average of only 7.4 minutes a day in a university-based child care program which was heavily committed to the principle of parent involvement. This included drop-off and pick-up times, conferences with center staff, time observing children, and participation in group meetings. A study of parent-caregiver relationships in 12 Detroit metropolitan area day-care centers revealed that most parents and caregivers communicated almost daily at the "transition point" when parents picked up and dropped off their child. However, interaction surrounding substantive issues was considerably less frequent—and one-third of the parents did not communicate with a particular staff member consistently; here communication was spread among two or more caregivers, seemingly at random (Powell, 1978a).

Strategies to Improve Day-Care—Family Interactions

There is a long tradition of interest in improving interactions between families and early childhood environments in the field of early childhood education and day care. The extent to which this interest has been acted upon programmatically in full-day child care programs is not known. Proposed and actual day-care practices to improve relations with families fall into three broad categories: increased communication, parent education, and parent involvement in policymaking.

Conventional efforts to improve communication include group meetings and individual conferences with parents, and caregiver visits to the home. Many early childhood education textbooks (for example, Hess & Croft, 1981) discuss these avenues of communication, but the Detroit study of parent-caregiver relationships in group child-care settings found that formal conferences were infrequent and caregiver visits to the child's home seldom occurred. In view of the finding that most parent-staff communication took place at the transition points of the day, it might be advantageous to attempt to enhance this informal context of communication at pick-up and drop-off points. Attention should be paid to the physical ecology of the setting (for example, is there a space conducive to communication?) as well as staffing patterns (for example, in centers, an aide might be added so the main provider has fewer child responsibilities and more time for parents) (Powell, 1980). Some day-care programs, especially centers, also attempt to incorporate the family into the curriculum by having parents share special talents with the children; by featuring a child's family for a week with pictures and descriptions of family activities; or by experiencing and discussing a cultural tradition of a particular family using the program.

A descriptive study of exemplary child care programs, conducted by Galinsky and Hooks (1977), uncovered many intentional efforts to improve parent-staff communication. For instance, at the Preschool Development Program at the National Institutes of Health, parents completed an extensive form about the goals for their child. The completed form was given to the program director and all the teachers and served as a basis for teacher reports to parents during informal periods (drop off, pick up) and twice-yearly parent conferences. The conferences typically lasted about an hour and were organized around a four-page form completed by the teacher to describe the child's behavior and development in relation to the center's and parents' goals. The program staff also suggested parent-child activities for the home.

At Mesa: Children's World Play School Learning Center in Colorado Springs, Colorado, the underlying assumption of staff in relating to parents was that parents are busy working people. Parent meetings were designed to be pleasant family occasions. There were breakfasts, teas, and potluck suppers. Informal social gatherings were thought to be a good time to get to know parents. The staff believed that true feelings were more likely to be expressed in an informal setting than at a more rigid formal meeting.

In Pasadena, California, Debbie Sakach, a family day-care provider, initiated her relationship with parents with an interview in which she made clear her own values and goals regarding child care (for example, she did not believe in a rigidly structured program). She used the pick-up time to communicate highlights of the child's day. Ms. Sakach attempted to develop a "sisterly" relationship with the child's parents; she believed the lack of extended family ties among many of the highly mobile residents of California might be mitigated through a family approach to child care (Galinsky & Hooks, 1977).

There is evidence to suggest that when there is increased interaction between parents and a child care center, the center seems to function as an informal resource for typical family and parent needs. In the Detroit study of parent-caregiver relationships, as communication became more frequent, so did the proportion of parent- and family-related topics discussed increase—topics such as the parent's job, social life, and family problems. Joffe (1977) discovered a child care program "under-life" where staff provided a range of informal services negotiated privately between individual parents and staff members. The network of activity included afterschool chauffeuring, legal and medical advice, and career counseling. It appears, then, that in some situations the child care program may contribute to an alteration or expansion of parents' social network ties. Future research should explore the conditions under which child care resources fulfill traditional extended family functions for participants.

The formal and informal exchanges between parents and caregivers may have long-term effects on parent behavior. A ten-year follow-up study of the effects of a family support program which included day care for children of low-income families found that program mothers were more self-initiating in contacts with their child's teacher than control-group mothers (Seitz, Rosenbaum, & Apfel, 1985). The investigators speculate that this active style of dealing with the schools arose from earlier interactions with day-care staff which led parents to expect an exchange of information between parents and child care institutions. Apparently, mothers felt competent to deal with whatever information emerged from such exchanges.

Similar findings of parental empowerment through day-care use were uncovered in a study of a high-quality day-care program for children of low-income parents (Ramey, Dorvall, & Baker-Ward, 1983). After approximately five years of day-care involvement, mothers of day-care children, when compared to control mothers, were less likely to say they were powerless to influence the schools and that teaching is not the parent's job (Schaefer, cited in Ramey et al., 1983). Whether interactions with the child care program or some other variable (for example, participation in the work force) contributed to these differences is not clear.

A second strategy espoused by some child care programs to improve relations with parents is providing parent education. Discussions, lectures, and workshops on child development topics are typical forms of this effort. Again, research is needed on the extent to which day-care programs provide parent education and on the level of parent participation. A frequent topic at professional conferences of day-care providers is concern over the lack of attendance at parent meetings.

Parents' interactions with day-care staff and other parents may serve as an informal and subtle form of parent education (Powell & Stremmel, in press). Discussions with caregivers and other parents may alter parents' perceptions of their child and may prompt self-examination of child-rearing practices. Hughes (1985) found that both center and family day-care providers reportedly used an active helping response in dealing with parents' questions and concerns about their child. Frequent caregiver responses were to ask questions, offer sympathy, present alternatives, and share personal experiences. Although little is known about the effects of caregiver responses on parents, anecdotal evidence suggests that day-care settings may be powerful sources of informal parent education (Belsky, Steinberg, & Walker, 1982). For instance, consider the potential effect on the parent of hearing a caregiver casually tell how the parent's child acted in a mature and helpful manner toward another child. The impact of this type of information may be especially significant if it conflicts with existing parental constructs of the child. Observing how caregivers and other parents interact with children (for example, respond to a child's temper tantrum at pick-up time) may expose parents to new ways of relating to children. The day-care setting is a rich public arena for observing a variety of parenting practices.

A third potential strategy for improving parent-child care program communication is to involve parents in decisions about program policy and operation. This approach is a component of Head Start and parent cooperative nursery schools (Fein, 1980) but appears to be rarely practiced in day-care programs. In some centers there are parent advisory (not decision-making) committees that typically have program development and advocacy as a primary concern. For instance, advisory committees may be involved in fund-raising, equipment procurement and maintenance (for example, building a playground), lobbying activities with funding agencies, and appearance at local, state, or national demonstrations regarding child care policies. Research is needed on how these entities function and how they affect parents and center operations.

Throughout the country there is a handful of parent-controlled child care centers. For instance, Galinsky and Hooks (1977) found that parents were deeply involved in decision-making at the Children's Pumphouse in New York City's Harlem. Every parent was a member of the Pumphouse board. Meetings were held each month, and attendance was mandatory; there was a fine if parents missed two consecutive meetings. Galinsky and Hooks note that the realization that "parents would have to do things for themselves rather than depend on others has served as the sustaining strength for the center" (p. 82). For parents, being a part of the Pumphouse program has been a two-way venture. In addition to being a learning center for the children, the program has exposed parents to new information about child rearing and parenthood (for example, there have been parent training sessions on child development, black history, and community organizing skills). At the Preschool Development Program, National Institutes of Health, parents managed the program through Parents of Preschoolers, Incorporated, a nonprofit, tax-exempt corporation. At the time of enrollment, each parent joined the corporation and signed a contract for a minimum of 20 hours annually of volunteer service to the center (for example, service as room parent, help with field trips, participation in fund-raising). The child care field needs further experimentation with parent-controlled day care. Its effects on staff, families, and children need to be investigated.

The effects of efforts to strengthen interaction between families and day care probably vary according to family characteristics. How do such factors as family structure, parental perceptions of the day-care provider, and parental feelings about the use of day care mitigate the effects of day care? For instance, single parents were found to communicate significantly less with group child-care staff than mothers from two-parent families in the Detroit day care study (Powell, 1978b), although Zigler and Turner (1982) failed to find a similar pattern in a university-based day-care center. Parental perceptions of the day-care provider as a person "who watches my kid" versus a person with expertise in child care may also mediate effects of the day-care experience on parents. Steinberg and Green (1979) report that parents with children in day-care centers claimed to learn more about parenting than parents with children in family day-care homes. Also, mothers who are in the work force but would prefer to be at home with their child may approach the provider differently from mothers who are not in conflict over their role and child's care. It is not clear how parental guilt over or ambivalence toward the use of day care influences parent–day-care interactions; resentment of the provider's relationship with the child might be a response.

Future Directions and Critical Issues in Improving Day-Care–Family Interactions

At leadership levels in the early childhood field there is growing support for closer ties between families and day-care programs. Consider the following developments. Prominent spokespersons have argued that quality child care functions as an extended family (for example, Caldwell, 1985). The National Association for the Education of Young Children (NAEYC) annual meeting now includes a substantial number of presentations and workshops on current conditions of family life and strategies for involving families in early childhood programs. The NAEYC has established a national accreditation project for early childhood programs that considers parent involvement as a component of quality programming. The Child Development Associate, a competency-based credential for early childhood practitioners, emphasizes caregiver sensitivity to family child-rearing values and professional skills in relating to parents. These latter efforts are especially important because they incorporate a view of day care as a family support system into standards of professional practice.

A significant increase in the level of professional education and training regarding work with families is needed to complement these preeminent trends in the field. Child care professionals need concrete, practical assistance to enhance their relations with families, especially information on how to talk with parents and conduct parent programs, and on community resources available to parents (Hughes, 1985).

Professional training programs may need to focus on caregiver attitudes toward parents as much as on specific skills in relating to parents. Findings of a recent investigation (Kontos & Wells, 1986) suggest that child care staff ideas about "good" parenting may need to be broadened to include a wider range of behavior in the acceptable category. The study found that parents held in low esteem by caregivers engaged in parenting practices that caregivers deemed less than desirable and violated expectations of parent adherence to center policies and procedures (for example, late payments). Compared to a group of parents held in high esteem by caregivers, the low group included a significant number of divorced mothers as well as women with less education. Low group mothers could rarely rely on a spouse or neighbor for assistance and were more likely to express guilt over the use of day care. Communication with staff generally was limited to the child's behavior in the center whereas the high group parents tended to establish more personal relationships with the day-care staff. Low group mothers were less likely than high group mothers to see the center as a resource for child-rearing advice. Kontos and Wells suggest that these low-esteem judgments of parents by caregivers may be in response to parent attitudes and behaviors typically associated with less education and role overload. Perhaps the mothers most in need of support or assistance from the child care staff are those least likely to get it.

In addition to professional education and training surrounding caregiver relations with parents, the child care field would benefit from more program demonstrations of innovative approaches to parent education and support. Careful scrutiny of the lifestyles and interests of working parents may lead to offering formal programs at times of the day (for example, noon) and on topics (for example, accommodating work and family life) that depart from the traditional evening lecture on ages and stages of child development. The growing interest in parent support programs suggests that many families would respond positively to opportunities to extend their social network ties within the day-care setting. Staff-dominated parent education meetings may be of less value than peer-dominated discussions of parenthood and child-rearing issues.

At least three critical issues must be addressed in designing efforts to improve interactions between families and child care programs: the service boundaries of the child care resource, the professional status of child care providers, and conflicts over who is the primary client of child care services.

If communication between families and day-care services is increased in frequency and broadened in substance, questions must be asked about the scope of information exchanged and the services provided. For instance, how does a caregiver respond to a parent's announcement: "I found out this weekend my husband wants a trial separation. I'm devastated. What should I do?" What does it mean for a day-care program to be a family support system under these circumstances? Does the caregiver function as an active listener? Suggest ways to save the marriage? Refer the parent to a community service? Try to focus the parent's attention on the child's responses? The service boundaries of the day-care program are being challenged here. Most day-care providers lack the appropriate training, experience, and time to serve as family counselors. Yet when day care sees itself as a family resource, clarification of the substantive parameters of the service is needed.

A high level of day-care responsiveness to family life also raises questions about the autonomy and professional status of caregivers. A characteristic of a profession is freedom from client control of services. In the eyes of public school teachers, for instance, the ideal parent does not attempt to influence the curriculum or classroom activities (Lortie, 1975). Although early childhood education is not a high-status profession, it has strong strivings toward increased professionalism (Powell, 1982). It is doubtful that many caregivers would be eager to implement parents' ideas about desirable day-care experiences for their children, especially when the ideas conflict with the caregivers' judgments. Nonetheless, a certain level of negotiation is necessary if family values are to be incorporated into a day-care environment. (Readers are referred to Joffe [1977] for an insightful analysis of how early childhood teachers accommodated the interests of black and white parents.)

Day-care providers who wish to be responsive to families may need to revamp the traditional image of professionalism. In particular, the idea that the work of professionals should be relatively free of lay (parent) interference may need modification in the early childhood field. Collaborative relationships with parents appear to be more appropriate than roles where the professional assumes all-knowing expert status. In the Galinsky and Hooks (1977) examination of exemplary child care programs, no staff members believed they were a substitute for the family or had more influence on the child than the parents.

Related to these two concerns is a third issue: Who is the client of day-care services: the parent or the child? This is a difficult ethical issue in early childhood education (Katz, 1984). While most caregivers would probably say the child is their client, in fact parents determine whether the service is used and in most cases provide the financial base of the day-care operation. For day care to be supportive of families, do parents' needs outweigh the child's needs? This is not an easy issue to resolve. For instance, Katz (1984) offers an example of conflict between the needs of a parent and a child in which the day-care professional believes it is in the child's best interests to take a nap in the afternoon at the day-care program but the parent protests because the nap makes the child unwilling to go to bed early in the evening at home. If a child's staying up later contributes to negative interactions with a tired parent, one could argue that a day-care program would be supportive of family life by not having the child take a nap. But would the child's interests be best served by this approach? When day-care programs seek to be sensitive to family values and needs, questions must be addressed regarding what services are provided to whom.

Parents must increasingly serve as coordinators of their child's life in this country (Keniston & Carnegie Council on Children, 1977). They must identify, select, and coordinate the caregivers who help rear their children. More and more of this coordination is outside the trusted network of kin. Whether day-care resources become a part of this trusted network of family helpers depends on many factors. This chapter has suggested that two major elements are the appropriateness of the match between quality day-care resources and family needs, and the level of communication between parents and child care providers.

A critical day-care issue today is the congruence of day care and family systems. A critical family life issue today is how to find and maintain a high-quality day-care arrangement. Future research and program development should improve our understanding of ways to strengthen the match between family needs and day care services and ways to incorporate families into the life of day care settings. The first major step in this direction is to conceptualize day care as a family resource, for children cannot be disconnected from their family environments.

NOTE

1. A significant effort to improve the quality of child care centers in the United States has been launched by the National Association for the Education of Young Children through the establishment of the National Academy of Early Childhood Programs. The academy is a national, voluntary accreditation system for early childhood centers and schools. Another major attempt to improve the quality of early childhood programs is the Child Development Associate credential, which is awarded to early childhood professionals who meet specified field-based competencies.

REFERENCES

American Institutes for Research. (1979). *Project Connections: A study of child care information and referral*. Phase I results. Cambridge, MA: American Institutes for Research.

Belsky, J. (1984). Two waves of day care research: Developmental effects and conditions of quality. In R. Ainslie (Ed.), *The child and the day care setting*. New York: Praeger.

Belsky, J., & Steinberg, L. (1978). The effects of day care: A critical review. *Child Development, 49*, 929–949.

Belsky, J., Steinberg, L., & Walker, A. (1982). The ecology of day care. In M. E. Lamb (Ed.), *Nontraditional families: Parenting and child development* (pp. 71–116). Hillsdale, NJ: Erlbaum.

Bronfenbrenner, U. (1979). *The ecology of human development: Experiments by nature and design.* Cambridge, MA: Harvard University Press.

Caldwell, B. (1985). What is quality child care? In B. Caldwell & A. Hilliard (Eds.), *What is quality child care?* (pp. 1–16). Washington, DC: National Association for the Education of Young Children.

Collins, A., & Watson, E. (1976). *Family day care: A practical guide for parents, caregivers and professionals.* Boston: Beacon Press.

Fein, G. (1980). The informed parent. In S. Kilmer (Ed.), *Advances in early education and day care, Vol. 3* (pp. 155–185). Greenwich, CT: JAI Press.

Fein, G., & Clarke-Stewart, A. (1973). *Day care in context.* New York: Wiley.

Galinsky, E., & Hooks, W. (1977). *The new extended family: Day care that works.* New York: Houghton Mifflin.

Greenman, J. (1984). Perspectives on quality day care. In J. Greenman & R. Fuqua (Eds.), *Making day care better* (pp. 3–20). New York: Teachers College Press.

Hess, R., & Croft, J. (1981). *Teachers of young children.* Boston: Houghton Mifflin.

Hughes, R. (1985). The informal help-giving of home and center childcare providers. *Family Relations, 34,* 359–366.

Joffe, C. (1977). *Friendly intruders: Childcare professionals and family life.* Berkeley: University of California Press.

Katz, L. (1984). *More talks with teachers.* Urbana, IL: ERIC Clearinghouse on Elementary and Early Childhood Education.

Keniston, K., & Carnegie Council on Children. (1977). *All our children: The American family under pressure.* New York: Harcourt Brace Jovanovich.

Kermonian, R. (1980). Type and quality of care: Mediating factors in the effects of day care on infant responses to brief separation. Paper presented at the International Conference on Infant Studies, New Haven, CT.

Kontos, S., & Wells, L. (1986). Attitudes of caregivers and the day care experiences of families, *Early Childhood Research Quarterly, 1,* 47–67.

Levine, J. (1982). The prospects and dilemmas of child care information and referral. In E. Zigler & E. Gordon (Eds.), *Day care. Scientific and social policy issues* (pp. 378–401). Boston: Auburn House.

Lightfoot, S. (1978). *Worlds apart: Relationships between families and schools.* New York: Basic Books.

Lippitt, R. (1968). Improving the socialization process. In J. Clausen (Ed.), *Socialization and society* (pp. 321–374). Boston: Little, Brown.

Lortie, D. (1975). *Schoolteacher.* Chicago: University of Chicago Press.

Meyers, L. (1973). The relationship between substitute child care, maternal employment and female marital satisfaction. In D. Peters (Ed.), A summary of the Pennsylvania Day Care Study, Pennsylvania State University (mimeo).

Mitchell, A. (1984). *Evaluation report: Child Care Council of Westport-Weston, Inc.* New York: Bank Street College of Education, Child Care Consultation Service.

Nixon, R. (1971). Text of veto message of Comprehensive Child Development Act of 1971. *Congressional Record,* Dec. 10, 1971, pp. S21129–30.

Powell, D. (1978a). The interpersonal relationship between parents and caregivers in day care settings. *American Journal of Orthopsychiatry, 48,* 680–689.

Powell, D. (1978b). Correlates of parent-teacher communication frequency and diversity. *Journal of Educational Research, 71*, 333–341.

Powell, D. (1980). Toward a socioecological perspective on relations between parents and child care programs. In S. Kilmer (Ed.), *Advances in early education and day care* (pp. 203–226). Greenwich, CT: JAI Press.

Powell, D. (1982). The role of research in the development of the child care profession. *Child Care Quarterly, 11*, 4–11.

Powell, D., & Eisenstadt, J. (1980). *Finding child care: A study of parents' search processes.* Detroit, MI: Merrill-Palmer Institute.

Powell, D., & Eisenstadt, J. (1982). Parents' searches for child care and the design of information services. *Children and Youth Services Review, 4*, 239–253.

Powell, D., & Eisenstadt, J. (1983). Predictors of help-seeking in an urban setting: The search for child care. *American Journal of Community Psychology, 11*, 401–422.

Powell, D., & Stremmel, A. (in press). Managing relations with parents: A study of teachers' intentions. In D. Peters & S. Kontos (Eds.), *Advances in applied development psychology, Vol. II: Continuity and discontinuity of experience in child care.* Norwood, NJ: Ablex.

Ramey, D., Dorval, B., & Baker-Ward, L. (1983). Group day care and socially disadvantaged families: Effects on the child and the family. In S. Kilmer (Ed.), *Advances in early education and day care* (pp. 69–132). Greenwich, CT: JAI Press.

Rhodes, T., & Moore, J. (1975). *National child care consumer study: 1975, Vol. I.* Arlington, VA: Unco.

Seitz, V., Rosenbaum, L., & Apfel, N. (1985). Effects of family support intervention: A ten-year followup. *Child Development, 56*, 376–391.

Steinberg, L., & Green, C. (1979). How parents may mediate the effect of day care. Paper presented at the biennial meeting of the Society for Research in Child Development, San Francisco.

Woolsey, S. (1977). Pied piper politics and the child-care debate. *Daedalus, 106*, 127–145.

Zigler, E., & Hunsinger, S. (1977). Bringing up day care. *APA Monitor, 8* (43).

Zigler, E., & Turner, P. (1982). Parents and day care workers: A failed partnership? In E. Zigler & E. Gordon (Eds.), *Day care: Scientific and social policy issues.* Boston: Auburn House.

8 FAMILY SUPPORT AND EDUCATION IN EARLY CHILDHOOD PROGRAMS

Heather Weiss

Over the past twenty years, a significant subset of programs designed to help young children develop the cognitive, social, and other skills necessary for school and presumably life success has moved from an almost exclusive focus on children in center-based programs to a more ecological systems approach, emphasizing and supporting the roles of parents, other family members, and community in child development. Underlying this broader focus is the ecological principle that, since the family is the primary institution that shapes a child's development, family-support and education programs can effectively promote child development by helping parents to provide the best possible environment for the child (Bronfenbrenner, 1979; Travers & Light, 1982). This subset of family-support and education programs typically provides services in each of the domains that social support researchers included in the core concept of social support (House & Kahn, 1984; Cleary, in press); they supply information (for example, about child health and development), emotional support (for example, attention, feedback, and reinforcement to adults in parenting roles), and instrumental assistance (for example, transportation, referrals to other services). The designation of "Family Support and Education" for these programs has been chosen to underline both their social-support aspects and the prevalence of parent and family education components among them. This diverse subset includes federally funded community-based programs such as Head Start and related experimental programs (Home Start, Child and Family Resource Centers, and Parent Child Development Centers), research and demonstration programs such as those that banded together to form the Consortium for Longitudinal Studies (Lazar & Darlington, 1982), and various foundation- and community-funded efforts (Bryant & Ramey, 1984; Pierson, Walker, & Tivnan, 1984; Slaughter, 1983).

Accumulating experience with these programs has had a pronounced effect on practice and research designed to promote child development and strengthen families. Program providers, for example, have developed new ways for parents and professionals to work together and to harness community resources for the benefit of families. In the process, they have helped to define, to refine, and develop new ways to provide both formal and informal social support for young families (Zigler & Weiss, 1985). Efforts to evaluate these programs have invigorated applied child-development research and provoked significant rethinking of evaluation methodology. As two recent reviewers of the early childhood literature have argued, evaluation research on these programs, along with research on day care, has helped lay the groundwork for a new and potentially fruitful field-based research paradigm for the study of child development (Clarke-Stewart & Fein, 1983). In addition, the promise, popularity, and early indications of the effectiveness of these more ecologically oriented interventions have attracted the interest of policymakers at the state level, a number of whom have begun major program initiatives (Winter, 1985; Committee on Four Year Olds, 1985; Minnesota Council on Quality Education, 1981). These initiatives reflect concern about the effects of stress on families and the ways in which it affects their capacity to rear the next generation for independent and productive lives in an advanced technological society.

This interest in family support and family-focused interventions is accompanied by a renewed optimism about early childhood intervention, fueled by positive results from longitudinal research on an earlier generation of programs. Typifying the media response is a recent editorial in the *New York Times* declaring: "After all the years of experiment and disappointment, American society does know one sure way to lead poor children out of poverty. It has different names—Project Head Start, developmental daycare, nursery school—but the idea is the same: high quality preschool education and it works" (September 13, 1984, p. 123). Endorsement of preschool programs, especially for the disadvantaged, has recently come from corporate America in the form of recommendations for changes in the educational system issued by the Committee for Economic Development (*New York Times*, September 26, 1985, p. A-34).

This very heartening attention to and recognition of the importance of early childhood programs have spurred a round of state-sponsored early childhood legislation and programs, including the family-oriented ones described above. In more than a third of the states such legislation is pending or has been passed as of the fall of 1985, and more states are likely to follow suit (Schweinhart, 1985). However, it is crucial not to forget an important lesson learned from the War on Poverty's round of social experimentation: "Although optimism is a great promoter of action, danger lies in the inevitable counterreaction of pessimism" when expectations are set unrealistically high (Zigler & Berman, 1983, p. 898). Those involved in this new and expanded round of interest in early childhood—policymakers, parents, researchers, and programmers—need to walk a narrow and uncharted path between two dangers. One is the Scylla of overstating the case for what early childhood programs can realistically accomplish. The other is the Charybdis of understating it and thereby undermining the current momentum that could lead to quality programs for young children and their families. With this in mind, this chapter examines both what is and what is not known about the implementation and effectiveness of family-oriented as opposed to child-centered early childhood programs.

THE EVIDENCE· IS THE CUP HALF EMPTY OR HALF FULL?

The proliferation of ecologically oriented early childhood programs makes the job of a reviewer particularly difficult. The relevant literature is vast and is to be found not only in books and journals but also in unpublished reports, conference presentations, and other sources beyond the reach of many literature search techniques. A recent study by White (1984) suggested that reviewers of this literature need to be especially conscious of their procedures and of potential biases. He examined 64 reviews of research on early intervention with disadvantaged and handicapped children published between 1966 and 1982. Among them 630 primary research studies were cited. What was striking was how little overlap there was in the studies that reviewers examined: only one study was cited in common by as many as 24 of the 64 reviews. This led White to question not only the generalizability of the conclusions but also the objectivity of the reviews.[1] After examining individual program studies, literature reviews, and reviews of literature reviews, I would describe the state of our knowledge of these programs and their effectiveness at this juncture as a cup that is both half full and half empty (Weiss & Jacobs, 1984).

The cup is half full because there are now several well-designed and mutually reinforcing longitudinal evaluations of early childhood programs that involve parents and that have demonstrated lasting positive effects for children (Berrueta-Clement et al. 1984; Deutsch, Jordan, & Deutsch, 1985; Lazar & Darlington, 1982; Ramey, 1985; Research and Training Associates, 1985). As Clarke-Stewart and Fein (1983) have warned, it is important not to overgeneralize from the results of a few studies. Nonetheless, given the difficulties attendant in the conduct and funding of high-quality longitudinal research, the existence of these studies represents a real watershed for advocates of preschool programs designed to work with parents to promote child development. Several other evaluations have indicated that these programs may also have positive effects for parents and families (Seitz, Rosenbaum, & Apfel, 1985; Slaughter, 1983; Travers, Nauta, & Irwin, 1982). Further, indirect supporting evidence is mounting about the importance of formal and informal social support for positive child and family functioning in both the program-evaluation and child-development literatures (Bristol & Gallagher, 1982; Colleta, 1981; Crnic et al., 1983; Olds et al., 1983). In their longitudinal study of the development of a group of Hawaiian children considered vulnerable because of a set of socioeconomic, biological, and family factors, for example, Werner and Smith (1982) found that the presence of an informal multigenerational network of kin providing support with child rearing distinguished the children who grew into competent adults from those who did not.

Finally, the cup is also half full because past critiques have informed a number of recent and ongoing evaluations that are yielding useful information about both program implementation and effectiveness and are suggesting creative solutions to some of the methodological problems that have plagued program evaluation in the past (Bryant & Ramey, 1984; Halpern & Bond, in press; Seitz, Rosenbaum, & Apfel, 1985; Travers, Nauta, & Irwin, 1981; Weiss & Jacobs, in press).

The cup is half empty because relatively few programs have been systematically evaluated and, with a few notable exceptions, program evaluations have focused very narrowly on changes in the child's I.Q. Equally important, until recently, the concept of evaluation itself has been narrowly defined. As a result, most evaluations have looked almost exclusively at global outcomes; they have therefore provided little information about *what* programs work for *whom, when, how,* and *why.* The relative lack of program process and implementation data has also inhibited the contributions these programs can make both to the elaboration of ecological theories of child development and to program development. It also forces reviewers to depend primarily on program descriptions and a few in-depth process or ethnographic studies to address key issues about how these programs actually work—for example, do they create dependence on professionals? Do they empower parents, and, if so, how? At this stage in the development of family support and education programs, these few in-depth studies serve primarily to raise questions about program implementation, reinforcing the distinction between a program on paper and one in actual operation and throwing down warning flags about problem areas for other programs.

Finally, the cup is half empty because until recently there has been little convergence between researchers who examine naturally occurring social support as it affects health, development, and well-being and those who evaluate socially supportive interventions for children and families (Rook & Dooley, 1985; Zigler & Weiss, 1985). The former often end their articles by saying their research has unspecified implications for practice, while the latter, until recently, have failed to take account specifically of the social support aspects of their family support and education interventions. If more cross-fertilization between social support researchers and these support programs occurs, it may be possible to determine whether some of the positive effects of naturally occurring social support on coping, well-being, and various child and parent outcomes also accrue from these programs' more formal support efforts.

Carrying the cup metaphor one step further, because these programs have been a part of a larger long-term cycle of social-program experimentation, feedback, and revision (Zigler, 1979), both how to fill the cup and what to fill it with have become clearer (Zigler & Weiss, 1985). It is fashionable now to say that social programs do not work. This ignores a substantial legacy of hard-won knowledge about how to design, implement, and evaluate interventions for children and families—knowledge that comes from both successes and failures of programs and evaluations. After examining the evolution and basic characteristics of more ecologically oriented early childhood programs, this chapter examines the accumulated knowledge in two areas: parent roles and relationships with professionals, and program effectiveness and evaluation. The first area deserves close scrutiny both because parents are such an essential part of these programs' service delivery systems and because of the dilemmas inherent in parent-professional relations. The second area, program effectiveness and evaluation, is covered here in some detail; first, because evaluation data are playing a significant role in generating the current widespread interest in early childhood programs, and second, because, given heightened interest in measuring the results of human-service investments (U.S. Department of Human Development Services, 1985), program evaluation is likely to have an important place in new program initiatives. Therefore this is a crucial juncture at which to examine the implications of past evaluation efforts for future evaluation design and practice.

EVOLUTION AND CHARACTERISTICS OF ECOLOGICALLY ORIENTED EARLY CHILDHOOD PROGRAMS

The War on Poverty in the 1960s, which attempted to promote equal educational opportunity for poor children through better preschool preparation, provided the initial thrust for the recent cycle of more eco-logically oriented programs. At that point, program developers and policymakers were forced to make an important choice with respect to the design of interventions aimed at maximizing the chances of school success for poor children: should they serve only the child or involve the parents and family as well? A number of programs chose the latter course and designed parent and family education and support pro-grams with services such as home visits, parent groups, and referral to other community services. These programs are premised on three as-sumptions about promoting child development, assumptions that in-cidentally have guided various intervention efforts since at least the nineteenth century (Weiss, 1979).[2] These assumptions are: (1) early childhood is a critically important time in an individual's development; (2) the home is the crucial place for early development to take place, with the corollary that the mother is the child's most significant teacher; and (3) the parents of young children need and will use advice and support with child rearing.

Reinforcing the Family's Role in Human Development

This programmatic emphasis on parent involvement and family support was stimulated fairly early on by two influential analyses of the results of a number of 1960s early childhood research and demonstration pro-grams for disadvantaged children. Bronfenbrenner (1974) and Good-son and Hess (1975) examined data on 23 and 29 programs, respec-tively, and addressed the question of whether parent involvement made a difference in program impact. Each came to the conclusion, necessarily tentative given the limitations of the data, that a parent component did appear to result in a more successful intervention, where success was de-fined as the maintenance of the child's I.Q. test gains after program ter-mination. In an effort to explain this, Bronfenbrenner suggested a set of hypotheses about the role of reciprocal interaction in a child's develop-ment. Specifically, he posited that programs that stress parent-child in-teraction around a joint task or activity early in the child's life are of immediate and perhaps longer term benefit to the child because they reinforce the parent-child system. By affirming and informing the parental role in development, these programs may "maximize the possi-bility that gains made by the child will be maintained" because the system develops its own momentum (Bronfenbrenner, 1974, pp. 291–92). Bronfenbrenner's analysis and his subsequent book on the ecology of human development (1979) have had a powerful impact on early child-hood program development. They have been cited frequently in sup-port of family-oriented programs perhaps because they help to ground sometimes atheoretical programs in an illuminating developmental theory, thereby offering justification for a shift in direction that some programs have made on the basis of instinct and experience.

Substantial parent involvement in programs also received considerable thrust from another source that should not be minimized: the War on Poverty's emphasis on "maximum feasible participation." During the 1960s and early 1970s considerable attention was paid to the role of parents, in part because parents themselves demanded a greater part in the design and implementation of programs intended for their children. As a result, programs such as Head Start and Follow-Through and legislation such as the Education for All Handicapped Children Act (P.L. 94-142) mandate various forms of parent involvement (Haskins & Adams, 1983; Pizzo, 1983; Valentine & Stark, 1979).

Reinforcing the Community Role in Family Development

In addition to working with the family, programs now increasingly emphasize the importance of creating and reinforcing links between families and external sources of support, both formal (for example, local social and health services) and informal (for example, opportunities to meet neighbors, utilization of natural helpers in programs). This emphasis is the result of research in child development and human service delivery as well as of evolving program experience. First, efforts by ecologically oriented child development researchers to understand the ways in which child and family development is influenced by forces outside the immediate family have served as a catalyst for program change (Bronfenbrenner, 1979; Cochran & Brassard, 1979; Crockenberg, 1981; Hobbs, 1979). For example, they have documented the sense of loneliness and isolation felt by many families with young children (Weiss, 1979) and have indicated the sometimes negative consequences of isolation for parenting behavior (Garbarino & Sherman, 1980; Wahler, 1970). Research on what resources parents actually use and find helpful has indicated the importance of social networks and social support (Collins & Watson, 1976; Stack, 1974). Research on less formal nonprofessional efforts has suggested both their power and utility; for example, peer-support groups have been shown to be not only popular but also effective in enhancing parenting behaviors and aspects of parent-child interaction (Boukydis, 1982; Minde et al., 1980; Slaughter, 1983). Disillusionment with some professional services, diminished program budgets, the desire for greater service efficiency and coordination through better case management, and recognition of the power and utility of mediating structures (such as churches and neighborhood organizations) have stimulated efforts to link families with informal as well as formal external support. Finally, the movement toward better understanding of how to build and reinforce formal as well as informal support for families parallels similar developments within child welfare (Whittaker, 1986), public health (Chamberlin, 1984), and human services (Whittaker & Garbarino, 1983).

Importance of Diffuse and Individualized Family Support

As interest in parent involvement and family support has increased, so has recognition of the value of diffuse and individualized support. This recognition stemmed from the influences noted above, but also from the fact that even the fairly didactic early childhood interventions with parent components designed in the 1960s and early 1970s took place *at least* partially on the parent's turf, literally so in the case of home visits. As a result, these programs had to be more responsive to parent and family needs. If for no other reason than to maintain rapport and participation, task-oriented home visitors intent on demonstrating ways a mother could play with her child with an age-appropriate toy, for example, probably provided a variety of forms of information and support as they sat and chatted with mothers at their kitchen tables. This support probably ran the gamut from opportunities to talk about child or family problems and to "brag" about the child to information and referrals to other community agencies. Many programs have peer-support groups as one of their parent components. There is some evidence to suggest that parent participation is also facilitated by giving them the opportunity to express their personal and parental concerns in discussions (Joffe, 1977; Slaughter, 1983; Weiss, 1979).

Examination of the program development and evaluation literature suggests that there have been three stages in the recognition and documentation of the significance of these more diffuse and individualized forms of family support: the initial stage, when this support was provided but not recognized as such; an intermediate stage, when the possible value of more diffuse support for families was recognized but not evaluated (Bromwich, 1981; Dawson, Robinson, & Johnson, 1982), and the current stage, in which many programs are both consciously providing such social support and directly evaluating its impact on the child and the family (Bryant & Ramey, 1984; Olds et al., 1983).

Program Characteristics: Similarity in Diversity

The evolution to a more ecological approach is evident in the development of the Head Start program (Zigler and Freedman, chap. 4 above) as well as in the design of numerous other early childhood programs begun during the past twenty years. Examples of non-Head Start programs include:

1. the school-sponsored Brookline Early Education Project (Pierson et al., 1984), a comprehensive family-oriented early childhood program

providing home visits, parent groups, developmental assessments, play groups, and prekindergarten programs to a broad socioeconomic mix of families;

2. the Yale Child Welfare Research Project (Provence & Naylor, 1983; Seitz et al., 1985), a comprehensive family-oriented program providing medical, educational, social, and psychological services to a group of low-income families through home visits, pediatric care, day care, and developmental exams;

3. the Boston Children's Museum Early Childhood Program (*Programs to strengthen families*, 1983), a family-oriented drop-in center designed to create environments, materials, and programs to promote positive parenting in a natural setting for anyone in a large urban area; and

4. the Center for the Development of Non-Formal Education (*Programs to strengthen families*, 1983), a community-based bilingual learning center for early childhood, adult, and family education providing home visits, parent groups, and various kinds of emergency survival assistance for Hispanic families.

These programs illustrate the diversity of early childhood family support and education programs. As will become evident, diversity is one of the chief characteristics of these programs.

Within the general framework of providing support and education to families with young children, the programs vary on a number of key dimensions. It should by no means be assumed, for example, that they are found primarily in schools, that they are staffed only by early childhood educators, or that the participants are exclusively low-income children and their parents. Some of the major differences among programs occur on the following dimensions, listed here to underscore the wide range of variation on critical program variables: *auspices* (public-private, educational, mental health, day care, Head Start, local-state-federal); *setting* (home-center, educational-therapeutic, and others); *funding amount and source(s)*; *client characteristics* (family and child type defined by income, ethnicity, risk, and other factors); *staff characteristics* (amount and type of training, staff diversity, paid-volunteer status, and so forth); *number and types of service delivery mechanisms* (for example, parent groups, home visit, parent classes, and information and referral services); *curriculum and philosophy of child and family development; degree of coordination with other community services; program size* (small single site to large multisite programs); *program duration and intensity* (number of program components, frequency and length of participation, etc.); and *parental roles* (such as parent as teacher, parent as program staff, and parent as board member). At this point there is no comprehensive source of information that indicates the distribution of programs along these dimensions. The few existing program surveys confirm the presence of considerable variation (Hite, 1985; Ramey et al., 1983). Current heightened interest in early childhood and in the coordination of preventive community services for young children and families could usefully stimulate more studies to obtain even basic descriptive information about the distribution of these program characteristics.

Roots of Diversity

The diversity noted above is partly attributable to the fact that many communities have deliberately developed new programs or tailored existing ones to accord with local needs, resources, and inclinations. Head Start, for example, was structured to provide for community input in program design (Zigler & Anderson, 1979). That this has in fact been the case was recently corroborated by a political scientist examining the positive aspects of the program for conservatives intent on curbing federal programs and promoting local initiatives for children and families (Skerry, 1983). Skerry argued that with its emphasis on self-help, individual sacrifice, substantial parent participation, responsiveness to the local community, and flexible and nonbureaucratic service provision, Head Start shows that "conservative goals can sometimes coexist with— even be fostered by—government programs" (p. 20). Even when major adjustments to local circumstances were not necessarily intended, as in the case of Head Start's experimental eleven-site Child and Family Resource Program, the program's evaluators found substantial variation in program goals, services, and implementation across sites. They concluded that indeed, the program "was invented eleven times" (Nauta & Travers, 1982, p. 3).

Experience with these Head Start programs as well as other programs initially designed to be uniform across sites suggests that some cross-site variation is inescapable and that programs need to and will respond to local circumstances. Further, in order for program personnel and perhaps the host community to become invested in an imported program, it may be necessary for them to put their own mark on it. Although program variability causes difficulties for evaluators of multisite interventions, it is increasingly clear that a program's ability to adapt to its setting may be a prerequisite for program implementation, effectiveness, and survival (McLaughlin, 1980; Travers & Light, 1982). This is not meant to imply that each program must start from scratch; only that there are many viable points on the program-development continuum including exact replication and flexible adaptation of existing models as well as starting from scratch. Rather than investing energy at either end of this continuum, particularly if the goal is widespread development of quality programs grounded in local communities, it would be more appropriate to develop a middle course. To pursue this, we should develop mechanisms to encourage sharing and networking among programs, disseminate diverse promising models, and test the proposition that successful programs cannot be uniformly produced on an assembly line. This middle course makes sense for many reasons, not the least of which is the fact that at this point there is mounting evidence that a number of kinds of family support and education programs appear to benefit children and families.

The evidence from Head Start and the experience of the State of Minnesota's Early Childhood and Family Education Program (Minnesota Council on Quality Education, 1981)—the latter with state sponsorship of diverse local programs—indicate that federal and state governments can fund and encourage programs that are at heart responsive to local communities. As states develop early childhood programs and policies, it will be important to compare the experiences of those that implement fairly uniform programs from the top down and those that set up systems to enable program variation in accord with a bottom-up community approach. The points of comparison should include measures of program effectiveness, community and family investment in the program, and ease of implementation and monitoring.

These programs also share some important characteristics beyond their commitment to a more ecological approach, their diversity on key program variables, and their responsiveness to local circumstances. Many of them have moved from preestablished services for everyone toward more individualized services based on formal or informal assessment of each family's strengths and needs. The fact that different families may receive somewhat different treatment has created further problems for program evaluators (Hewett & DeLoria, 1982), but it may also have increased the program's appeal for parents and the public at large, as well as its effectiveness.

By definition, another common characteristic of these programs is their substantial and varied involvement with parents. As the next section suggests, parent involvement is an area in which family support and education programs are charting new ground and confronting some difficult dilemmas.

PARENT AND PROFESSIONAL: ROLES AND RELATIONSHIPS IN THE AGE OF ECOLOGY

Insightful analyses of an emerging field often come from outsiders, and in the case of the relationships of parents and professionals, some of the most thought-provoking work has been done by historians. In his examination of professional involvement with families during the twentieth century, Christopher Lasch (1977) argues: "Having first declared parents incompetent to raise their offspring without professional help, social pathologists 'gave back' the knowledge they had appropriated— gave it back in a mystifying fashion that rendered parents more helpless than ever, more abject in their dependence on professional option" (p. 18). There is no doubt that such criticism should be taken very seriously and that parent-oriented programs should be carefully scrutinized to see if this criticism proves to be well-founded. It should also be pointed out, however, that implicit in Lasch's charge is the assumption that parents are incapable of rejecting or selectively accepting so-called expert information and advice. This assumption at best is unproved; at worst it suggests the same negative views of parental competence that Lasch criticizes in professionals. As historian Laurence Stone has suggested, recent analyses of the relationships between families and the helping professions have involved either "savage polemic or Panglossian optimism" (Stone, 1977, p. 12).

The few studies that have examined the relationship between parents and those who provide them with information and support find that some programs do appear to enhance parental autonomy (Weiss, 1979) but that this is not uniformly the case (Travers et al., 1982). Research on the unanticipated negative consequences of these programs is imperative; they can sometimes undermine parental well-being, as is illustrated by the following remark made by one young, single, depressed, and very poor mother who participated in the Brookline Early Education Project (BEEP): "They have shown me what I should do, and I feel bad because I can't." In future examinations of these programs we would do well to heed the admonition of David Rothman (1978), historian of reform in the progressive era, and begin to ask a different set of questions: "Rather than wondering how professional expertise and discretionary authority can be exercised in the best interest of the client or patient," he suggests, "we should ponder how the objects of authority can protect themselves against abuse without depriving themselves of the benefits that experts can deliver" (p. 95).

Analyzing Parent-Program Relations: A Continuum

A useful way to analyze parent-program relationships is in terms of a continuum varying both by source of support and by relationship between supporter and supported (Zigler & Weiss, 1985). At one end of the continuum is the unilateral relationship in which the parent is seen as an empty vessel, passively waiting to be filled with professional expertise. In the middle are more bilateral relationships in which the parent is viewed as the partner of the professional. Programs at this point on the continuum typically indicate that both parents and professionals are "experts" with respect to the child, albeit in different but presumably complementary ways. Toward the other end are more multilateral arrangements in which information and support are both formal and informal and come from professionals, peers, and nonprogram sources. In this last case the parent is both recipient and provider of support through such means as peer support and informal helping arrangements. Inherent in the movement toward multilateral programs is a nondeficit service philosophy, which values efforts to work with and reinforce family strengths rather than simply remediate weaknesses. Professionals and program staff do not do things *to* but *with* parents (Cochran & Woolever, 1982; Weiss, 1983b). In fact, efforts to change relationships between parents and programs are one of the hallmarks of these programs and what one program analyst has labeled the Age of Ecology (Schaefer, 1983).

The need for a nondeficit approach to practice, as well as a nondeficit program ideology underscoring family strengths and empowering parents, has been widely argued (Bronfenbrenner & Weiss, 1983; Cochran & Woolever, 1982). Part of the widespread popularity of this approach —as evidenced in program brochures, staff training, and analytical literature—is perhaps explained by its ability to counter earlier criticisms of the judgments of "culture of poverty" proponents about the inadequacy of low-income homes and parenting. Because nondeficit approaches are based on the assumptions that parenting is not completely instinctive, that it is a demanding job, and that all parents can benefit from support and reinforcement, the approach can also counteract the still strong public perception that participation in parenting programs implies some serious parent or family inadequacy. The idea of empowering parents also speaks to the concern that these programs have a debilitating effect on families because they foster dependence on professionals (Donzelot, 1979; Lasch, 1977; Weiss, 1979; Zigler & Berman, 1983).

Ultimately, the argument for nondeficit approaches in family programs hinges as much on the value placed on respecting family diversity and promoting self-sufficiency as on data about the effectiveness of such programs. Nonetheless, it is unfortunate that there is so little pertinent research about program and parent interactions, about staff and parent attitudes toward each other, and the like, that would help in identifying the crucial features and practices of nondeficit programs and in answering the question of whether these programs are in fact empowering. Overall, the field is now long on prescription and short on description and analysis of nondeficit partnership and of multilateral program models. It is *because* the values implicit in nondeficit models are so important that it is necessary to determine how best to incorporate them in family programs. At this juncture, clarity with respect to what nondeficit programs are and do as well as careful implementation are crucial if the pendulum is not to swing back to unilateral programs ruled by experts. The relative lack of knowledge about nondeficit models may be remedied as program evaluators broaden their concept of evaluation to include studies of implementation and program processes.

Family programs include a number of roles for parents. Chief among them are the parent as his or her own child's teacher; as recipient of parent education and other services to meet adult and family needs; as program resource through such means as program aides and participation in peer support; and as decision-maker through such means as board participation and program advocacy.[3] The remainder of this section examines some of the lessons learned and questions raised as programs have worked with parents in these expanded program roles.

Working with Families: Tensions and Dilemmas

There is considerable evidence, described in the last section, that through careful work with parents it is possible to promote adult as well as child development. Nonetheless, the experience of the Child and Family Resource Program (CFRP) points to the fact that working with parents on their personal and social needs as well as their child's development can strain program resources, particularly in the case of very distressed families. CFRP's evaluators found that parental needs and child-development goals can conflict. Specifically, ethnograhic observations of home visits revealed that often more time was spent helping low-income mothers deal with pressing personal, economic, and housing problems than on child-development-related activities. The evaluators suggest that this in part explains why the program failed to have measurable effects on children's social and cognitive development (Travers, Nauta, & Irwin, 1982). CFRP did have significant positive effects on mothers' feelings of efficacy and sense of control over their lives and expanded their awareness of their role as the child's teacher; these changes may later engender child development gains. Nonetheless, the CFRP experience documents some of the difficulties in providing services to meet both child development and family needs, especially in families experiencing multiple personal and socioeconomic stresses. It also underscores the need for adequate funding and careful staff training and supervision in such efforts (Travers et al., 1982).

Programs that work with parents—usually mothers, despite many efforts to involve fathers (Hite, 1985; Weiss, 1979)—must be especially sensitive about respecting the parents' own child-rearing philosophies and practices, especially in view of the fact that there is no research or professional consensus on what constitutes the range of good parenting.

Interviews with a sample of mothers who participated in BEEP indicated their feeling that the following aspects of the project's style contributed to their positive interaction with staff: openness and accessibility, many positive statements about parent behaviors, a nonjudgmental attitude, the exploration of alternatives rather than the provision of advice or child-rearing directives, two-way communication and feedback, and the noncoercive quality of the interactions (Weiss, 1979). As the creators of another early childhood family support and education program have noted, a central challenge for those working with parents is to "distinguish in one's work . . . between outreach and intrusiveness, between guiding parents and lecturing them, between providing them with the tangible supports they appear to need and enabling them to get these for themselves, between imposing, even in a benevolent fashion, one's own goals for them and helping them to define and consider their goals for themselves (Provence & Naylor, 1983, p. 161).

In a thought-provoking essay on parent education and cultural pluralism, Laosa (1983) has posed difficult questions concerning the extent to which programs respect different cultural standards with regard to appropriate child and parent behaviors and development. His questions are particularly pertinent for publicly funded family support and education programs because many such programs are targeted at cultural and racial minorities and many have parent-education components (Hite, 1985). In his analysis of ecologically oriented early childhood programs, Powell (1982) raises a parallel question with respect to class: Are programs imposing middle-class child and family values on other groups? Consideration of cultural and class diversity also raises questions about just how generic parent education about child and family development can be. In this regard it is noteworthy that one widely used parent education curriculum, Systematic Training for Effective Parenting (STEP), has offered a religious version of its material (STEP Biblically) and one for a teen audience (STEP/Teen) but nothing tailored to the needs or experiences of different racial or cultural groups (American Guidance Service, 1985). As is further discussed by Williams (chap. 16) and Jenkins (chap. 15) in this volume, finding ways to acknowledge and respect a variety of child-rearing philosophies and child development goals is central to the creation of nondeficit programs.

Importance of Other Parents: Peer Support, Community-Building, and Social Action

The programs under examination here are attempting to affect the family's external environment and the availability and uses of support through a variety of formal and informal means, including involving parents themselves in the role of program resource. Parents are increasingly serving as a resource through their participation in programs' formal peer-support groups and through informal contacts with other parents as well as in the obvious role of program aide. Peer-support groups appear to be part of the core of more ecologically oriented programs (Hite, 1985), and there is some evidence that peers in similar circumstances can be a powerful source of support, first by sharing common concerns and problems and then by sharing solutions (Boukydis, 1982; Weiss, 1979). Analysis of the experience of these groups suggests that flexibility—opportunities for parents to shape the agenda and to deal with problems in individual and unstructured ways ("my kid . . ." kinds of discussions)—contribute to the popularity and perhaps effectiveness of these groups (Joffe, 1977; Slaughter, 1983; Weiss, 1979). Through drop-in centers, parent resource rooms, parent "talk-back" boards, and other devices, many programs also encourage informal sharing and networking among parents.

Despite problems of attrition, which indicate that parent groups are not appropriate for everyone, there is initial evidence that they can promote parental self-esteem and personal growth with ultimately positive effects for the parent-child system (Slaughter, 1983). Opportunities for peer support are also important because they allow parents to give as well as receive support, which may in turn enhance self-esteem. As one self-described shy mother participating in BEEP said about her group experience: "I just found that I gained a lot from what they said—and they seemed to be listening to what I said, which surprised me even more" (Weiss, 1979, p. 195). Provisions for formal and informal peer contact and multilateral support interventions may further militate against any parents' tendency to depend excessively on professionals and may create bonds and sources of support that outlive the period of program participation (Weiss, 1983a). Another hypothesis worthy of empirical research is that which relates reciprocity (opportunities for parents to give as well as receive support) with aspects of personal growth and program effectiveness. Such research would also contribute significantly to our understanding of nondeficit program models.

It would be reasonable to expect, although it remains to be empirically tested, that positive experiences in programs alter the ways in which parents form social networks and seek help outside of or after the period of program involvement (Gottlieb, 1981). I have argued elsewhere that family support and education programs are promising not only because they benefit children and families but also because of the potential they have to strengthen the local social infrastructure (Weiss, 1983). Some of these programs may strengthen the bonds among people in the community, thereby increasing the availability of informal supports and enriching the community environment for families. The community-building aspects of these programs therefore deserve serious attention from evaluators and program analysts.

Examination of a variety of parent-oriented early childhood programs suggests, as Valentine and Stark (1979) have found with regard to the history of parent involvement in Head Start, that the emphasis on parents as program decision-makers or governors has receded in favor of parents in less political and more educational roles, particularly in demonstration research projects. It is unclear what the implications of this are for the resolution of staff-parent conflicts or for collective community action on behalf of children and families. An individual-consumer model now seems to underlie many programs. It stresses empowerment through the provision of information and support so that parents can make informed choices about parenting and child development. Although many programs thus emphasize individual rather than institutional change, this does not necessarily preclude parents from banding together to identify common concerns and to lobby for needed services or changes in local institutions, as has been the case, for example, with some of the CFRP programs (*Programs to strengthen families*, 1983). However, given the trend toward emphasizing individual change, it is important to ask if parents in these programs become involved in social action to improve community policies and conditions for children and families. Serious consideration should also be given to the question of whether it is a prerequisite for programs aimed at empowering parents to have a formal, systematic means of obtaining parent feedback and of giving parents a meaningful, ongoing role in program design and governance.

High-Risk versus Community Programs

Before concluding this discussion, the connection between family-respecting program ideology and practice and social policy for targeting these programs to particular groups needs to be made. As has been noted, many family-support and education programs are now available only to so-called high-risk families. Is it possible to implement nondeficit programs for such families when they are labeled "high risk"? This question requires a lengthy discussion; it is sufficient here to say that the argument for concentrating resources exclusively on the neediest versus that for some provision of family support for everyone is one that deserves considerably more discussion. It is unrealistic to expect that the intensive and costly services provided by some of the most comprehensive programs will or should be universally available for all young families. However, it may be realistic to have a more graduated set of services available in every community so that some less intense ones such as parent support groups and a few afterbirth home visits are available to everyone. This sort of community-wide approach to prevention (with services available to everyone) might remove some of the stigma from family support services as well as reducing child and family problems in the community (Chamberlin, 1984).

FROM EQUAL OPPORTUNITY TO THE PREVENTION OF DEPENDENCE: PROGRAM EFFECTIVENESS AND FUTURE EVALUATION CONSIDERATIONS

At the outset, I suggested that the cup of knowledge about the effectiveness of family support and education programs is both half-empty and half-full. The studies reviewed below are described in order to examine the case in favor of more ecological and family-oriented early childhood interventions and to suggest some useful future directions for evaluators intent on generating knowledge both for program improvement and for policy formation.

Several recent reviews indicate that early childhood programs, including family-oriented ones, can have significant short-term effects on children's IQs (Ramey et al., 1983; White, 1984). The longer term maintenance of gains after program completion and the issue of whether IQ gains affect later life success have been more difficult to assess (Bronfenbrenner, 1974). Few projects collected postprogram follow-up data from participants until a small group of programs banded together to locate and examine their program and control groups with a set of common measures. This Consortium for Longitudinal Studies collected data on 2,000 low-income children who had participated in various interventions during the 1960s and 1970s. These data were used to address two central questions: Would differences favoring participants over controls persist long after the interventions ended? And do these programs really make a difference in various measures of real world performance? The consortium found that program children outscored controls on the Stanford-Binet Intelligence Test for up to three years after the intervention and that they fared better with respect to two school-performance measures. Specifically, program children were significantly less likely to be assigned to special classes or to be retained in grade (Lazar & Darlington, 1982).

Two consortium members, the Perry Preschool Project (Berreuta-Clement et al., 1984) and the Institute for Developmental Studies Program (Deutsch et al., 1985), have continued to follow their participant and control groups into their late teens. Each has found dramatic differences between the treatment and control groups on various measures of independence and life performance. These outcomes include retention in grade, assignment to special education classes, unemployment, school dropout, teenage pregnancy, and juvenile delinquency. Because the results of these two studies are mutually corroborating, they have provided support for those interested in more widespread early childhood programs. As a result of these evaluations and the consortium's work, IQ is used less readily as a proxy for diverse program effects in order to demonstrate both short- and longer-term personal and societal benefits from early childhood intervention programs with low-income children.

Over ten years ago, Bronfenbrenner (1974) raised the question of whether early intervention programs for disadvantaged children that work with parents as well as children are more effective than those for children alone. As White (1984) has concluded after his recent meta-analysis of data on the effects of these programs on poor and handicapped children, we have made remarkably little progress in answering this question, particularly given its importance.

The evidence we have on the question is suggestive, not definitive. Both programs with longitudinal results (described above) provided intensive center-based programs for children, but they varied in terms of the roles that parents played in them. Although their evaluation designs do not permit the contribution of the parent components to be assessed directly, their administrators suggest that parent involvement was important to program success (Weikert, Bond, & McNeil, 1978; Cynthia Deutsch, personal communication, September 1985).[4] The recent results of two other family-oriented early childhood programs provide additional evidence about the value of family support and education approaches for enhanced child development.

Post-program follow-up of the children who participated in the Brookline Early Education Project and the Yale Child Welfare Research Project, two programs that had intensive family support and education components, showed significant differences favoring the program groups on selected measures of school adjustment and performance (Pierson et al., 1984; Seitz et al., 1985). That neither program showed differences on intelligence measures suggests the limits of those measures and the importance of performance-based indicators in evaluating such programs. In addition, these two programs are notable not only for their parent-education and family-support components, which their evaluators argue were central to their success (Pierson et al., 1985; Seitz et al., 1985), but also for their incorporation of a strong health component in the form of access to medical information and diagnostic services (Levine & Palfrey, 1982; Provence & Naylor, 1983).

While these various studies help make the case for the expansion of more family-oriented early-childhood programs, that case will be considerably strengthened when more direct confirmatory data are available from programs with random assignment to contrasting treatment groups, particularly child-centered versus more ecologically oriented programs. One such experiment, Project Care, is now under way. It was designed so that low-income families with infants were randomly assigned to one of two treatments or a control group. The first treatment group received educational day care, family education through weekly home visits, pediatric care, and social work services. The second group received all these services except day care. At thirty-six months, the children who received both day care and family education were rated higher on several child development measures than those who did not (Bryant & Ramey, 1984). These results raise the question of whether it is necessary to work with both the parents and the child.

At this point, program development is far ahead of program evaluation; however, evaluators and practitioners are beginning to reframe and broaden the questions they ask about these programs to produce a deeper understanding of how they work (see Weiss & Jacobs, in press, for a discussion of broader measures for family support and education programs). Specifically, some evaluations now employ broader outcome measures related to changes in parents, parent-child interaction, and aspects of social support. Some are also expanding their conceptions of appropriate evaluation methodology to include mulitimethod qualitative and quantitative examination of program processes and implementation. These changes will help both program designers and policymakers in that they address the crucial question of *what* programs work *when*, for *whom, how*, and *why*.

Use of broader outcome and process measures will also lead to a better sense of the complex causal sequence underlying more ecologically oriented programs. This complexity and the possibility of far-reaching outcomes is evident from the evaluation of the Yale Child Welfare Research Project, one of the few that has examined the effects of a family support program on adult and family variables. This longitudinal study found that the program's major contribution was its long-term impact on family patterns such as limitations on family size, improvements in residence, educational advancement, and economic self-sufficiency (Seitz et al., 1985). The evaluators hypothesize that the main mediating factors of such interventions may be interpersonal and motivational. Social support contributes to the development of self-esteem and enlarges parents' personal aspirations. This, in turn, has positive consequences for adult development, family functioning, and the quality of the parent-child relationship. In their skeptical assessment of the effectiveness of more parent-focused as opposed to child-focused early-childhood interventions, Clarke-Stewart and Fein (1983) point out that even if changes in maternal behavior accompany changes in child performance, they may not cause the changes in children; in fact, sometimes the reverse may occur. Longitudinal examination of the relationship between changes in parents and children is necessary if we are to understand the complex and nonlinear causal processes underlying changes in children, parents, and family processes, as these two reviewers suggest.

Evaluation designs that include systematic attention to program process and implementation through careful qualitative research will further our understanding of how and why these programs do and do not work and will facilitate successful replication of effective programs. Qualitative assessments, including intensive interviews and ethnographic observations about program processes, are useful in at least four ways: they can reveal unanticipated positive and negative consequences of the intervention; they help capture practical knowledge; they address the question of whether the program was implemented as designed; and they can help explain the pattern of quantitative program outcomes (Zigler & Weiss, 1985). The utility of an ethnographic component as part of a comprehensive evaluation design is illustrated by the previously described results from the CFRP evaluation. In that case the ethnographic data revealed tension between the program's social service and child development activities, which appear to have resulted in an insufficiently intense child development intervention (Travers et al., 1982).

Just as we need to identify the crucial features and practices of nondeficit programs, we need to develop ways of assessing whether these programs are in fact empowering. Can empowerment be measured by improvement in individual self-concept, by a family's increased use of appropriate services, or by its involvement in collective action to bring about improved community services or conditions for young children and their families? Whether empowerment is a means to enhanced human development or an end in itself, it is important to establish the comparative effectiveness of programs that practice a nondeficit, empowerment approach.

Interest in early childhood programs has been rekindled not least because of the recent attention of some prescient evaluators and funding agencies to policy-relevant long-term outcomes and issues such as cost effectiveness. Cognizant of the larger policy implications of their work, some of these evaluators have included cost-effectiveness studies and have begun to grapple with the difficulties of conducting them in the human service context (Seitz et al., 1985; Weber, Foster, & Weikart, 1978). Others have raised questions about how these programs fit into the system of services within local communities (Travers et al., 1982) and about which community institutions are appropriate hosts for the programs (Hobbs et al., 1984; Jacobs, 1986). It may well be that some institutions are better implementors of child-focused programs and others are better equipped to provide more ecologically oriented early childhood interventions. In any case, data about program and host interactions will be increasingly relevant as local and state policymakers oversee the broader implementation of early childhood programs.

In the twenty years since Head Start and a small group of early childhood demonstration programs began the effort to improve the life chances of poor children, the goals of federal social policy for the poor have shifted from the provision of equal opportunity to the prevention of dependence. This shift is evidenced in the introduction to the Office of Human Development Service's fiscal year 1986 Discretionary Grant announcement thus: Given shifts in the age structure and the composition of the population and "the reconfiguration of the American family, HDS seeks approaches that begin to invest in strategies to prevent future dependency and to assure maximum opportunities for self-sufficiency for HDS populations between now and the year 2000" (U.S. Department of Health and Human Services, 1985, p. 35907). As a result of the evidence reviewed above, these programs have taken on the character of a Man for All Seasons; they are once again at the heart of contemporary discussions of public policy for children and families. It remains to be seen if the change in rhetoric reflects a more realistic sense of what these programs can achieve or diminished commitment and expectations. It is important to consider that public rhetoric may affect not only program design but individual achievement motivation and expectations.

In sum, it is fair to say that early childhood programs that provide support and education to families as well as children are eminently worthy of careful consideration by contemporary policymakers for several reasons. First, longitudinal data suggest that these programs can be a cost-effective way to help ensure the preparation of a future generation of independent and productive adults. Second, these programs appear to hold substantial promise for promoting adult development and strengthening families; these are not trivial considerations as communities grapple with ways to help increasingly stressed families. Third, the existence of diverse high-quality program models and substantial practice knowledge means that there is much expertise to draw on as state and local groups design programs adapted to their particular needs. Finally, it is the responsibility of those who advocate more ecologically oriented approaches to early childhood programming to help steer the narrow channel between over- and understating what these programs can deliver with respect to two enduring public goals: the prevention of dependence and the promotion of equal opportunity.

NOTES

1. Mindful of the problems involved both in choosing what data to examine and in interpreting them, since data do not speak for themselves, even for meta-analysts, I com-

mend several other reviews to the other reader's attention. These reviews cover a range of sometimes overlapping studies, and perhaps more important, of thoughts about the utility and future development of parent and family support and education within the context of early childhood programs (see Bronfenbrenner, 1974; Goodson & Hess, 1975; Gray & Wandersman, 1980; Powell, 1982; Travers & Light, 1982; Clarke-Stewart & Fein, 1983; Ramey, Bryant, & Suarez, 1983; Haskins & Adams, 1983; Zigler & Berman, 1983; White, 1984; Weiss & Jacobs, 1984; Halpern, 1984; Zigler & Weiss, 1985).

2. Weiss (1979) contains a discussion of nineteenth-century child-rearing literature and evidence for the view that the assumptions behind many contemporary interventions date from this period or earlier.

3. See Goodson & Hess, 1979, and Gotts, Spriggs, & Saltes, 1979, for other classifications of parent involvement.

4. The Institute for Developmental Studies Program had parent classroom aides who also helped families obtain community services, a parent drop-in center in a church, a home visit prior to program entry, occasional parent meetings and classes on topics such as nutrition (personal communication with Cynthia Deutsch, September 1985). The Perry Preschool Project provided weekly home visits aimed at acquainting teachers with children in their family and neighborhood contexts and at familiarizing parents with the child's teacher and educational program (Weikart, Bond, & McNeil 1978).

REFERENCES

American Guidance Service catalog. (1985). Circle Pines, MN: American Guidance Service.

Berrueta-Clement, J., Schweinhart, L., Barnett, W., Epstein, A., & Weikert, D. (1984). Changed lives: The effects of the Perry Preschool Program on youths through age 19. Monographs of the High/Scope Educational Research Foundation, 8.

Boukydis, C. F. Z. (1982). Support groups for parents with premature infants in NICU's. In Marshall, Karman, & Cope (Eds.), Coping with and caring for sick newborns (pp. 215–222). Philadelphia, PA: Saunders.

Bristol, M., & Gallagher, J. (1982). A family focus for intervention. In C. T. Ramey & P. O. Trohanis (Eds.), Finding and educating the high risk and handicapped infant (pp. 137–161). Baltimore, MD: University Press.

Bromwich, R. (1981). Working with parents and infants. Baltimore, MD: University Park Press.

Bronfenbrenner, U. (1974). Is early education effective? Columbia Teachers College Record, 76, 279–303.

Bronfenbrenner, U. (1979). The ecology of human development: Experiments by nature and design. Cambridge, MA: Harvard University Press.

Bronfenbrenner, U., & Weiss, H. (1983). Beyond policies without people: An ecological perspective on child and family policy. In E. Zigler, S. Kagan, & E. Klugman (Eds.), Children, families and government: Perspectives on American social policy (pp. 393–414). Cambridge: Cambridge University Press.

Bryant, D., & Ramey, C. (1984, March). Results from Project Care: An early intervention comparison study. Paper presented at the Gatlinburg Conference, Gatlinburg, TN.

Can it be? A path out of poverty? (1984, September 13). *The New York Times*, p. 22.

Chamberlin, R. (1984). Strategies for disease prevention and health promotion for maternal child health: The "ecologic" versus the "high risk" approach. *Journal of Public Health Policy, 5*, 185–197.

Clarke-Stewart, K. A., & Fein, C. G. (1983). Early childhood programs. In P. H. Mussen (Ed.), *Handbook of child psychology: Vol. 2. Infancy and developmental psychobiology* (pp. 917–999). New York: Wiley.

Cleary, P. (in press). Measuring social support. In H. Weiss & F. Jacobs (Eds.), *Evaluating family programs*. Hawthorne, NY: Aldine.

Cochran, M., & Brassard, J. (1979). Child development and personal and social networks. *Child Development, 50*, 601–616.

Cochran, M., & Woolever, F. (1982). Beyond the deficit model: The empowerment of parents with information and informal supports. Unpublished manuscript, Cornell University.

Colletta, N. (1981). Social support and the rise of maternal rejection by adolescent mothers. *Journal of Psychology, 109*, 191–197.

Collins, A., & Watson, E. (1976). *Family day care*. Boston: Beacon Press.

Committee on Four Year Olds, Their Families, and the Public Schools. (1985, April). *Four year olds: Who is responsible?* A report presented to the Connecticut Board of Education, Hartford, CT.

Crnic, K., Greenburg, M., Ragozin, A., Robinson, N., & Basham, R. (1983). Effects of stress and social support on mothers and premature and full-term infants. *Child Development, 54*, 209–217.

Crockenberg, S. (1981). Infant irritability, mother responsiveness, and social support influences on the security of infant-mother attachment. *Child Development, 52*, 857–865.

Dawson, P., Robinson, T., & Johnson, C. (1982). Informal social support as an intervention. *Zero to Three, 3* (2), 1–5.

Deutsch, M., Jordon, T., & Deutsch, C. (1985). *Long-term effects of early intervention: Summary of selected findings*. New York: New York University Institute for Developmental Studies.

Donzelot, J. (1979). *The policing of families*. New York: Random House.

Garbarino, J., & Sherman, D. (1980). High-risk neighborhoods and high-risk families: The human ecology of child maltreatment. *Child Development, 51*, 188–198.

Goodson, B., & Hess, R. (1975). Parents as teachers of young children: An evaluative review of some contemporary concepts and programs. Unpublished manuscript, Stanford University.

Gottlieb, B. (1981). Preventive interventions involving social networks and social support. In B. Gottlieb (Ed.), *Social networks and social support*. Beverly Hills, CA: Sage.

Halpern, R. (1984). Lack of effects for home-based early interventions? Some possible explanations. *American Journal of Orthopsychiatry, 54*, 33–42.

Halpern, R., & Bond, T. (in press). The role of cross-project evaluation in the Child Survival/Fair Start Initiative. In H. Weiss & F. Jacobs (Eds.), *Evaluating family programs*. Hawthorne, NY: Aldine.

Haskins, R., & Adams, D. (1983). Parent education and public policy: Synthesis and recommendations. In R. Haskins & D. Adams, *Parent education and public policy*. Norwood, NJ: Ablex.

Hewett, K., with the assistance of De Loria, D. (1982). Comprehensive family service programs: Special features and associated measurement problems. In J. Travers & R. Light (Eds.), *Learning from experience: Evaluating early childhood demonstration programs* (pp. 203–253). Washington, DC: National Academy Press.

Hite, S. J. (1985). Family support and education programs: Analysis of a national sample. Unpublished E.D. dissertation, Harvard University Graduate School of Education, Cambridge, MA.

Hobbs, N. (1979). Families, schools, and communities: An ecosystem for children. *Teachers College Record, 79*, 756–766.

Hobbs, N., Dokecki, P., Hoover-Dempsey, K., Moroney, R., Shayne, M., & Weeks, K. (1984). *Strengthening families*. San Francisco: Jossey-Bass.

House, J. S., & Kahn, R. L. (1984). Measures and concepts of social support. In S. Cohen & L. Syme (Eds.), *Social support and health* (pp. 83–108). New York: Academic Press.

Jacobs, F. (1986). *Public education and family-involved programming: A match made in heaven?* Harvard Family Research Project Policy Paper Series, No. 2.

Joffe, C. (1977). *Friendly intruders*. Berkeley: University of California Press.

Laosa, L. (1983). Parent education, cultural pluralism, and public policy: The uncertain connection. Unpublished manuscript, Educational Testing Service, Princeton, NJ.

Lasch, C. (1977). *Haven in a Heartless World*. New York: Basic Books.

Lazar, I., & Darlington, R. B. (1982). Lasting effects of early education: A report from the Consortium for Longitudinal Studies. *Monographs of the Society for Research in Child Development, 47* (2–3, Serial No. 195).

Levine, M., & Palfrey, J. (1982). The health impact of early childhood programs: Perspectives from the Brookline Early Education Project. In J. Travers & R. Light (Eds.), *Learning from experience: Evaluating early childhood demonstration programs* (pp. 57–108). Washington, DC: National Academy Press.

McLaughlin, M. (1980). Evaluation and alchemy. In J. Pincus (Ed.), *Educational evaluation in the public policy setting* (pp. 41–47). Santa Monica, CA: The Rand Corporation.

Minde, K., Shosenberg, N., Marton, P., Thompson, J., Ripley, J., & Burns, S. (1980). Self-help groups in a premature nursery: A controlled evaluation. *Journal of Pediatrics, 96*, 933–940.

Minnesota Council on Quality Education. (1981, February). *A study of policy issues related to early childhood and family education in Minnesota: A report to the Minnesota legislature*. St. Paul, MN: Minnesota Council on Quality Education.

Moynihan, D. (1985). *Family and nation*. Cambridge, MA: Godkin Lectures, Harvard University.

Nauta, M., & Travers, J. (1982, September). *The effects of a social program: Executive summary of CFRP's Infant-Toddler Component*. Cambridge, MA: ABT Associates.

Office of Human Development Services, U.S. Department of Health and

Human Services. (1984, November 26–28). *Social services in the year 2000: Proceedings of a symposium.* Washington, DC: Office of Human Development Services.

Olds, D., Henderson, C., Birmingham, M., & Chamberlain, R. (1983). *Final report: Prenatal/early infancy project.* Prepared for the Maternal and Child Health and Crippled Children's Services Research Grants Program, Elmira, NY.

Pierson, D., Walker, D., & Tivnan, T. (1984). A school-based program from infancy to kindergarten for children and their parents. *Personnel and Guidance Journal, 62,* 448–455.

Pizzo, P. (1983). *Parent to parent.* Boston: Beacon Press.

Powell, D. (1982). From child to parent: Changing conceptions of early childhood intervention. In W. M. Bridgeland & E. A. Duane (Eds.), *The annals of the American Academy of Political and Social Science, 461,* 135–144.

Programs to strengthen families: A resource guide. (1983). New Haven, CT: Yale University Bush Center in Child Development and Social Policy (available from the Family Resource Coalition, 230 North Michigan Ave., Suite 1628, Chicago, IL, 60601).

Provence, S., & Naylor, A. (1983). *Working with disadvantaged parents and their children.* New Haven, CT: Yale University Press.

Ramey, C. (1985, October). Does early intervention make a difference? Paper presented at the National Early Childhood Conference sponsored by the Council for Exceptional Children. Denver, CO.

Ramey, C., Bryant, D., & Suarez, T. (1983). Preschool compensatory education and the modifiability of intelligence: A critical review. In D. Detterman (Ed.), *Current topics in human intelligence* (pp. 1–49). Norwood, NJ: Ablex.

Research and Policy Committee of the Committee for Economic Development. (1985). *Investing in our children: Business and the public schools.* New York: Committee for Economic Development.

Research and Training Associates. (1985). *New parents as teachers project: Evaluation.* Overland Park, KS: Research and Training Associates.

Rook, K., & Dooley, D. (1985). Applying social support research: Theoretical problems and future directions. *Journal of Social Issues, 41,* 5–28.

Rothman, D. J. (1978). The state as parent: Social policy in the progressive era. In W. Gaylin, I. Glasser, S. Marcus, & D. Rothman (Eds.), *Doing good: The limits of benevolence* (pp. 67–96). New York: Pantheon.

Schaefer, E. S. (1983). Parent-professional interaction: Research, parental, professional, and policy perspectives. In R. Haskins & D. Adams, *Parent education and public policy* (pp. 283–303). Norwood, NJ: Ablex.

Schweinhart, L. (1985, October 24). Changing lives through high quality early childhood development programs. Presentation at the Principals' Center, Harvard Graduate School of Education, Cambridge, MA.

Seitz, V., Rosenbaum, L., & Apfel, N. (1985). Effects of family support intervention: A ten-year follow-up. *Child Development, 54,* 376–391.

Skerry, P. (1983, Fall). The charmed life of Head Start. *The Public Interest, 73,* 18–39.

Slaughter, D. (1983). Early intervention and its effects on maternal and child development. *Monographs of the Society for Research in Child Development, 48* (4), serial No. 202.

Stack, C. B. (1974). *All our kin: Strategies for survival in the Black community.* New York: Harper & Row.

Standing up for schools. (1985, September 26). *The New York Times,* p. A-34.

Stone, L. (1977). *The family, sex and marriage in England, 1500–1800.* New York: Harper & Row.

Travers, J., & Light, R. (1982). *Learning from experience: Evaluating early childhood demonstration programs.* Washington, DC: National Academy Press.

Travers, J., Nauta, M., & Irwin, N. (1981, December 15). *The culture of a social program: An ethnographic study of CFRP* (summary volume). Cambridge, MA: ABT Associates.

Travers, J., Nauta, M., and Irwin, N. (1982). *The effects of a social program: Final report of CFRP's infant-toddler component.* Cambridge, MA: ABT Associates.

U.S. Department of Health and Human Services. (1985, September 4). Fiscal year 1986 Coordinated Discretionary Funds Program; availability of funds and request for applications; announcement. *Federal Register, 50.*

Valentine, J., & Stark E. (1979). The social context of parent involvment in Head Start. In E. Zigler, & J. Valentine (Eds.), *Project Head Start: A legacy of the War on Poverty* (pp. 291–314). New York: Free Press.

Wahler, R. G. (1970). The insular mother: Her problems in parent-child treatment. *Journal of Applied Behavior Analysis, 13.*

Weber, C., Foster, P., & Weikart, D. (1978). An economic analysis of the Ypsilanti–Perry Preschool Project. *Monographs of the High/Scope Educational Research Foundation* (5).

Weikart, D., Bond, J., & McNeil, J. (1978). *The Ypsilanti–Perry Preschool Project: Preschool years and longitudinal results through fourth grade.* Ypsilanti, MI: High/Scope Educational Research Foundation.

Weiss, H. (1979). Parent support and education: An analysis of the Brookline Early Education Project. Unpublished E.D. dissertation, Harvard University Graduate School of Education.

Weiss, H. (1983a). Strengthening families and rebuilding the social structure: A review of family support and education programs. A State-of-the-Art paper prepared for the Charles Stewart Mott Foundation.

Weiss, H. (1983b, May). The state-of-the-art of family-oriented support programs: Early childhood intervention. Paper presented at the Conference on Family Support Programs, Yale Bush Center in Child Development and Social Policy, New Haven, CT.

Weiss, H., & Jacobs, F. (1984). The effectiveness and evaluation of family support and education programs. A final report to the Charles Stewart Mott Foundation by the Harvard Family Research Project.

Weiss, H., & Jacobs, F. (Eds.). (in press). *Evaluating family programs.* Hawthorne, NY: Aldine.

Werner, E., & Smith, R. (1982). *Vulnerable but invincible: A longitudinal study of resilient children and youth.* New York: McGraw-Hill.

White, K. (1984, February). The different and legitimate roles of advocacy and science. Paper presented to the CEC/DEC Conference, Greeley, CO.

Whittaker, J. (1986). Formal and informal helping in child welfare services: Implications for management and practice. *Child Welfare, 65*, 17–25.

Whittaker, J., & Garbarino, J. (1983). *Social support networks: Informal helping in the human services.* Hawthorne, NY: Aldine.

Winter, M. M. (1985, May). Parents as first teachers. *Principal, 64*, 22–24.

Zigler, E. (1979). Project Head Start: Success or failure? In E. Zigler & J. Valentine (Eds.), *Project Head Start: A legacy of the War on Poverty* (pp. 495–507). New York: Free Press.

Zigler, E., & Anderson, K. (1979). An idea whose time had come: The intellectual and political climate. In E. Zigler & J. Valentine (Eds.), *Project Head Start: A legacy of the War on Poverty* (pp. 3–19). New York: Free Press.

Zigler, E., & Berman, W. (1983, August). Discerning the future of early childhood intervention. *American Psychologist, 38* (8), 894–906.

Zigler, E., & Weiss, H. (1985). Family support systems: An ecological approach to child development. In R. Rapoport (Ed.), *Children, youth and families: The action-research relationship* (pp. 166–205). New York: Cambridge University Press.

9 HOME-SCHOOL LINKAGES: HISTORY'S LEGACIES AND THE FAMILY SUPPORT MOVEMENT

Sharon L. Kagan

Bombarded by charges of ineffectiveness and mediocrity, public schools are undergoing diligent scrutiny (Fiske, 1983). Demands, criticisms, and paradoxes beleaguer American education, leaving school personnel dismayed and perplexed by their plight. Cries of fewer resources, more challenging children, layers of regulation, and intransigent bureaucracies reverberate through the nation's schools. Simultaneously, the American family is undergoing its own transformation. With more women in the work force, more single parents, fewer children per family, and more variegated family patterns, the very structure and function of American families are being tested and modified.

Can it be mere coincidence that the two institutions that most directly influence children are in such flux simultaneously? If not coincidence, then what are the phenomena shaping schools and families in the 1980s? And what are the consequences for children when their two primary institutions are caught at the vortex of a social and technological revolution? There is no dearth of evidence supporting the contention that families and schools have absorbed and accommodated previous social changes. Similarly, the literature is replete with information on family adaptations to changing demographics. What is less well understood is the relationship between families and schools as they interact and synergistically deal—in planned and unplanned ways—with social phenomena. What is the nature of reciprocity between them? How do and can they support each other, given the demands and constraints borne by each? What can be expected from the press for, and the promise of, family-school partnerships?

HISTORICAL OVERVIEW

Formal education in the United States had its beginnings in Colonial times, when the school was charged with instructing children in areas now referred to as the basics: reading, writing, and arithmetic (Kerensky & Logsdon, 1979). The family and the church were considered the primary educators, responsible in the long run for developing ethical character. Lawrence Cremin (1977), a respected educational historian, has noted the dichotomy between schooling and education that was prevalent in Colonial times. He points out that American schools at this time had only marginal influence as compared to that of the family. Then, families provided children with ideas about the world and how they should behave in it, and, later, provided youth with apprentice opportunities, where learning by trial and error and self-education predominated.

As society expanded, the family continued to supplement the basic instruction afforded in the school. While schools were accorded importance, crops and other life necessities were given priority. Advancements in schooling appeared, yet schools continued to be regarded as places where specific information was provided during specified periods of the day and year.

Home and family were the seat of education in early America, but by the time of Horace Mann (1796–1859), the early nineteenth century, the face of schooling had changed so dramatically that, along with other concerns, educators were becoming distressed by the pervasive alienation that characterized home-school relations. These tensions were exacerbated as society became more industrialized and education grew to be a more bureaucratic and professional endeavor. By the late nineteenth century, organizational responses emerged. In the 1890s, numerous parent organizations, usually dominated by women, were preoccupied with the issue of fostering positive home-school relationships. Without quarreling with the traditional idea that women's place was in the home, women activists rejected the notion that there was any conflict between domestic identity and a broader social commitment (Reese, 1978). Armed with a new self-image, "the hand that rocks the cradle is the hand that rules the world" (Capitol Park Parent Teachers Association Minute Book, October 16, 1903), women became "municipal housekeepers"—social reformers who agitated for pure food, clean streets, and any educational improvement that would guarantee the welfare of urban schoolchildren (Reese, 1978).

Inspired by visions of a better America and faced with the economic depression of 1893 (the most severe depression Americans had experienced until that time), women mobilized to aid the poor, and children in particular. The idea that poverty resulted from sinfulness or laziness was now challenged by a more encompassing social and economic catastrophe. Poverty became a social problem, and education was seen as a panacea. Consequently, schools were charged with broader mandates of feeding the poor and socializing immigrants by teaching them English and acculturating them to American values.

Concern about schools stemmed not just from the emphasis on the poor and the new Americans but from the demands of middle-class families who were interested in the possibilities schools could afford their children. Hence, the decades from the 1890s to World War I witnessed a widespread tendency for parents from many socioeconomic groups to participate in school organizations. Reese indicates that in 1908 a University of Chicago professor wrote: "The Parents' Association seems to be a veritable exception to the general statement that there is nothing new under the sun" (Reese, 1978, p. 9).

A plethora of organizations whose main aim was to foster cooperation between home and school came into existence. In subsequent years, they played an important role in introducing and improving instruction in music, art, foreign languages, manual skills, and domestic science as well as in establishing school gardens, kindergartens, and playgrounds. Some districts had impressive records of accomplishments which helped to extend the social functions of public education to include health and nutrition services. A case in point is the Womans' School Alliance of Milwaukee, which became involved in a controversy over who was to provide school lunches for needy children. These women, undaunted, served lunches in their own homes (1,000 each year) and remained the leading agitators for a publicly funded school lunch program.

It is important to note that organized parents and clubwomen did have success in expanding the functions of urban education. Schools took on the responsibility for educating, not merely schooling, children and youth. This is not to imply that the reformers were solely responsible for all changes or that they reached all their goals. Rather, within limits, they legitimized citizen participation in education and, in so doing, altered the services provided by schools and changed the nature of relationships between parents and schools.

Although accolades heralding the accomplishments of home/school councils reverberated through many local districts, this publicity, in some cases, piqued the anxieties of school personnel concerned that parents were impinging on their authority. Antagonisms flared and clashes between home and school ensued in some districts, minimizing the euphoria that existed. Nationally, a variegated pattern of parental involvement emerged, with some municipalities enjoying the benefits of involved parents while others were quite content to forestall supportive family-school partnerships.

During the period between the Progressive movement and the mid-

1960s, parent-school relations were for the most part overshadowed by preoccupations with war and postwar and cold-war adjustments. No one can doubt the educational impact of the launching of Sputnik, which heralded an emphasis on mathematics, science, and foreign languages. Yet mechanisms for home-school cooperation had been set in place, and efforts to cement cooperation continued, if not center-stage, certainly in full view.

One very important effort, the modern community school movement, took root in the 1930s, rose to prominence in the 1950s, and remains today a significant force in fostering family support. Devoting its 1952–53 annual yearbook to community education, the National Society for the Study of Education reported that a community school has two distinct emphases: to serve the entire community, not merely school-age children; and to discover, develop, and use resources of the community as part of the educational facilities of the school (Henry, 1953). The community school was therefore designed to serve the needs of children, youth, and adults and became a unifying force in the community. Under its aegis, a number of support programs were initiated, including adult classes, recreation programs, senior citizen services, job preparation, and parent-child hobby clubs.

With the same commitment to serve parents and other citizens and to include them in decision-making, the community school effort has since been expanded to a community education concept, thereby broadening education beyond the school-based focus. While not a consuming movement, today about 17 percent of the nation's school districts have community education programs, and about 10 percent of the nation's schools are community schools. The 1974 Community Schools Act and the 1978 Community Schools and Comprehensive Community Education Act helped accelerate interest in and support for the community education effort.

Concurrent with the development of community education, another force propelled parent-school relations to the fore, primarily in urban areas. This force arose largely in reaction to the failure of schools to respond to the 1954 Supreme Court desegregation decision and is characterized by parents confronting school bureaucracies and demanding control of personnel (hiring, firing, and evaluating) and budgetary practices. Emerging in the 1960s as the community control movement, its accomplishments were often mitigated by bureaucratic resistance. Seeley (1981) offered an accurate assessment: "We cannot tell whether community control could be an educational success because thus far it has been a political failure" (p. 117). Yet the movement was a visible and vocal attempt to significantly alter relationships between schools and families.

A second form of parent participation in schools, primarily an out-growth of, but very different from, the first, took the form of working *within* school bureaucracies to achieve reform. As opposed to the community control movement, which worked outside and more often than not in opposition to the bureaucracy, this latter movement legitimated efforts to work cooperatively within the structure. It was accelerated by federal mandates that required parental involvement as a condition of funding. As a result, parents (usually urban and poor) joined school committees and councils in concert with school professionals. Yet the long-term impact of this form of participation remains questionable. Davies (1978), in the most comprehensive study done to date, indicates that, owing in part to structural and bureaucratic inefficiencies, mandated participation has generally produced little reform.

A third response to the push for improved home-school relations took a different route—that of establishing *new* agencies, programs, and subsystems outside of mainstream bureaucracies. In these efforts, the focus was not placed on bridging the gap between parents and schools, but on creating alternatives to conventional schooling. Efforts to create new programs came from the federal government, foundations, universities, and local community groups. The federal government created and funded Head Start while small local groups instituted independent, sometimes storefront, schools. The not-infrequent, though often short-lived, successes of these efforts came from the fact that parents were motivated by a vision that did not threaten existing bureaucratic structures.

In spite of very rocky existences, many home-school linkage efforts of the 1960s did have positive impacts on individuals and institutions. Impressive changes in parents' involvement in school, sense of self-worth, and actual competence and employability have been documented (Henderson, 1981; Kagan, 1984). Widespread social gains existed in and for communities where parents were actively involved in schools and Head Start programs (*National survey*, 1970). There is also strong evidence of academic gains for children resulting from parents' involvement in their education (Della-Piana, Stahmann, & Allen, 1968; Iverson, Brownlee, & Walberg, 1981; Mann, 1975; Rankin, 1967). Thomas (1980) and Duncan and Fitzgerald (1969) have demonstrated correlations between parent involvement and improved student attendance, a reduction in suspension rates for disciplinary reasons, and an improved attitude toward homework. Moreover, a great deal was learned about the process of facilitating quality relationships between school staff and parents and about strategies to engage parents in school life in a meaningful way (Becker & Epstein, 1982; Sowers, Lang, & Gowett, 1980; Wimpelberg, 1982).

Equally important, the concept of parent-school *reciprocity*, while not new, took hold. Historically, parents had been primarily involved in improving schools for the benefit of their own and others' children. They "gave" their children to the schools; they gave money (via taxes) and support. Now, spurred by federal mandates for parent involvement and the needs and demands of urban and low-income parents, some schools not only "received" from parents but "gave" in return. Specific efforts undertaken by schools included courses for parents in child development, prevocational training, teacher aide preparation, and school decision-making. More generally, the prevailing ethos begged schools to envision their charge more holistically (Davies, 1976; Goodlad, 1981). Parents were no longer the isolated responsibility of the school social worker or the adult education department: many school personnel had a stake in the quality of the relationships between parents and schools. The vision and practice of the 1960s led to schools acknowledging a more comprehensive commitment to children and their families, and in particular to families with low incomes.

HISTORY'S LEGACY

Although accomplishments of parent-school relations have been documented, the legacy of many decades of school reform is quite mixed. Left in the wake of history are many ironies, ambiguities, and assumptions, all of which are essential to explore because they help shape patterns of family-school relationships as they emerge in the 1980s.

Ironies rooted in the earliest days of American educational experience have salience today. Is it not ironic that education had its origins in the family but that, as the academic system evolved, schooling grew so separate from the family that it took the force of federal mandate to open schools to all the people? Is it not ironic that families and schools have been and are engaged, as Lightfoot (1978) notes, in complementary sociocultural tasks, yet have been in such conflict with one another? Is it not ironic that the goals of schooling, pristinely clear when schooling in America was established, became more controversial and contested in each subsequent generation?

Beyond these ideological ironies, history has also left us with a very practical ambiguity. As efforts to involve parents waxed and waned, definitional questions arose. People spoke about "parent involvement," "citizen participation," "community control," "parenting education," and "parenting support" as synonymous terms without delineating their unique contributions or orientations. In trying to wade through definitional problems, academics have developed typologies to clarify different approaches. For example, Ira Gordon (1979) developed a three-part impact model that looked at parent-school relationships in terms of their effects on parents, schools, or communities. Another model type, exemplified by Arnstein (1971) and Adams (1976), described levels of parent participation. A third classification schema, proposed by Stearns and Peterson (1973) and Mann (1975), described the hierarchy of effects of different degrees of parent involvement. Gotts, Spriggs, and Sattes (1979) classified programs according to their theoretical orientations, such as (1) a prevention focus versus a correction focus or (2) the orientation of programs toward parents as autonomous and resourceful adults rather than as helpless, victimized, and dependent beings. Although interest in classifying programs continues, to date there is no single generally accepted schema. Hence definitional ambiguities persist.

But perhaps more influential than these ironies and ambiguities are the inherent assumptions that have evolved over time and persist today. Never mandated or consciously constructed, these shadowy assumptions lurk behind and quietly taint current home-school relations and family support efforts.

ASSUMPTION 1: THE FAÇADE OF CONGRUENT VALUES

Steeped in idealism, theorists and lay people alike often assumed that the values and wills of families were and should be congruent with those of schools. However, common sense, fortified by scholarly analysis, indicates that compatibility, not congruency, should be the goal. Comer's work in the New Haven schools, beautifully described in *School Power* (1980), led him to underscore the need for consonance of values as a prerequisite for stabilizing schools and establishing school climates where effective learning can take place.

The reason for the emphasis on harmonious but not identical values is that there are inherent differences in the roles of parents and teachers and in the function of schools and families. Litwak and Meyer (1973) clarify these differences by distinguishing between primary groups (families) and bureaucratic organizations (schools), although they suggest that most major tasks, including education and socialization, are carried out by both. Each has its own strengths and properties: bureaucratic organizations stress merit, expert knowledge, and transitory membership while primary groups stress permanent membership and personal ties. Organizations operate by standard rules and procedures while primary groups are more flexible and adaptive. Because of these differences, Litwak and Meyer (1974) suggested that if each institution is to function smoothly, distance between them must be maintained. Without implying that communication or cooperation between schools and families is undesirable, they caution against equating the roles of the two. Lightfoot (1978) has further pointed out inherent conflicts in the relationship between families and schools. She suggested that different priorities (concern for the individual vs. responsibility for the group) place families and schools in conflict over the means and strategies of accomplishing essentially common goals. She went on to suggest that collaboration is generally a one-way accommodation—that of families accommodating to schools.

These inherent structural differences, reinforced by experiences from the past, indicate that distance between families and schools exists, is unavoidable, and must be understood as a natural dynamic. As relationships between families and schools are forged, it is well to remember that a façade of commonality may mask functional realities. Often hidden by social graces, tensions remain beneath the surface and are ultimately counterproductive. By acknowledging inherent differences, parents and schools may be able to build more lasting, productive relationships.

ASSUMPTION 2: THE MYTH OF PHYSICAL PRESENCE

During the 1960s and 1970s, when parent involvement was given credibility in legislation and regulation, program effectiveness was often measured by how many hours parents were in direct contact with the school or school personnel. The tendency, however misguided, was to equate parents' physical presence in schools with program success. It is interesting that now, over a decade later, the major school-effectiveness models, advanced by Lezotte, Edmonds, and others, do not consistently cite parental involvement as a criterion for an effective school. Why this change?

Several reasons help explain this change in attitude, and indicate why the mere physical presence of parents in schools may not induce or be indicative of school effectiveness. During the 1960s, parents entered schools, whether by mandate or choice, as consumers—as lay people. Schools and school personnel were the producers, "the experts." This role dichotomy extended the psychological power of the bureaucracy and alienated, rather than endeared, parents. Something other than physical presence, a more fundamental parent involvement in and support for the educative process, needed to be present.

Lezotte and Edmonds, along with other analysts, indicate that it is not the physical presence of parents that counts so much but, rather, the existence of a consonance of educational will and values between home and school. Litwak and Meyer (1973) carry this notion a step further with their construct of social distance. They, too, suggest that when goals and values of parents and school personnel are harmonious, physical distance is acceptable. Conversely, when no value congruence between families and schools exist, social distance is large, and physical presence may be necessary to maximize educational effectiveness. Linney and Vernberg (1983) point out that although these hypotheses lack empirical suport, they have heuristic and intuitive appeal with regard to the responsiveness of schools to families. They suggest that in districts where social distance is high, schools have to be most sensitive and responsive to family needs, instituting special services and taking care to develop mechanisms that link schools and families.

ASSUMPTION 3: THE MYTHS OF EQUITY AND SAMENESS

Questions of social and educational equity have been dominant themes in American education for the past quarter century. Mired in debates about equal educational opportunity, our school systems have perpetuated inequity while seeking equity. This is nowhere more apparent than in the history of parent-school relations. First, historically, low-income and minority parents had little impact on public schools, whereas mainstream parents were able to institute at least modest reforms. Second, little equity exists with respect to the types of reforms that were incorporated into the ongoing life of the school. Programs that survive— kindergarten, home economics, and physical education—are those that served the total population, not the targeted few. Many parent-initiated reforms, established in a quest for equity, actually did little to redress basic differences between the haves and have-nots. Certainly, some programs targeted for the poor have continued, but many worthwhile efforts have been summarily eliminated. Interestingly, those targeted efforts that have remained operative without major budget cuts have been fortihed by strong, vocal constituencies.

The legacy of parent-school interactions belies not only the myth of equity but also another particularly strange myth, that of the sameness of American schools. When America speaks about its schools, it assumes that "schools" are alike, overlooking the rich diversity that prevails in American education. While it is well-known that the Constitution leaves responsibility for education to the states and that many states further delegate large segments of this function to municipalities, the concept of an American education and an American school system persists. Scholars have attempted to debunk the "sameness" myth. John Goodlad (1983), in his epic study of schooling, points out the particularist and unique nature of schools and schooling. Sarason (1971) indicated that each school's institutional regularities and history help create its unique culture. With this diversity, it is inaccurate, although convenient, to postulate one model of home-school collaboration that will have universal appeal.

These myths strikingly call attention to the fact that the needs of individuals are different, as are the needs of institutions. Establishing simple models and applying them equally in all locales perpetuate history's legacy of equity and sameness. Rather, programs and services that link parents and schools need to be tailored by individual parents and their schools.

The review of the relationship between families and schools reveals that advances in family support efforts are tied to broader social events. A negative consequence of tagging school reform to societal trends is that education is accused of following fads or responding to pendulum swings. Nonetheless, this history clearly indicates that during crisis periods effective school reform has emerged. It is well to remember this when we consider the present context for family-school interactions.

THE CURRENT CONTEXT

If relationships between families and schools intensify at times of rapid social reform, the 1980s should indeed prove an era worthy of attention. Rapid demographic changes including declining birth rates, the burgeoning of women in the work force, the postponement of marriage and child bearing, the increase in divorce and single parenting, and the participation of children in serial or simultaneous families characterize this decade.

While the literature is replete with the effects of changing demographics on family life (Kamerman & Hayes, 1982), the demographic revolution is not the only one that confronts us. The 1980s witness a revolution in the technological and communication fields. The age is characterized by conversion from product to service industries, the transition from smokestack to high-tech markets, and the explosion of the information-transfer industry, to name but a few. The development and use of robots, shorter work weeks (32 hours by 1990 and 25 hours by 2000), and longer life spans (83 years for children born in 1982) have all been predicted by knowledgeable trend forecasters (Cetron & O'Toole, 1982). Perched on the horizon, technological advances will have significant impact on families and schools, but unfortunately, because they have not yet been systematically assessed, their future impact remains a mystery.

Joining demographic and technological transformations on the list of reforms that have characterized the 1980s is the changing role of the federal government and other organizational structures. During the 1960s and 1970s a government role in child and family policy was acknowledged, and programs that supported that function were launched, such as Head Start and the Elementary and Secondary Education Act.

In the 1980s, the Reagan administration's philosophy of a markedly reduced federal role has led to the federal divestiture of responsibilities
for children and families. These responsibilities are being foisted on and
picked up by others. For example, communities no longer routinely look
to the federal government for regulations and funding. Practitioners,
reconditioned to create innovative funding packages, seek support from
local, state, or regional agencies and foundations. Under the familiar rubric of "partnerships," agencies and corporations across America are
sharing responsibility for children, schools, and social service agencies in
new and demonstrable ways. Perhaps the biggest change is in corporations, who are easing the federal burden by adopting programs such as
employer-supported child care, flexible work options, employee assistance programs, and flexible benefit plans.

Not only are institutions reaching out to fill gaps left by the federal
government, but individuals themselves are seeking solutions to unmet
needs via family support programs. These support efforts, to which
school-related efforts are closely aligned, refute traditional approaches
to human services in four major ways. First, for the most part the programs tend to be antibureaucratic, informally mediating between large
formal organizations and small units, like the family. Second, professionals play a reduced role: more often than not, programs are built on a
partnership model, in which parents and volunteers render support to
each other while professionals take a backseat. Third, program intimacy
or small scale allows for flexibility and adaptability to individual or community needs. For example, programs routinely respond to community
crises such as plant closings and natural disasters. Finally, many of these
programs are preventive in that they are set up to offer support before a
problem occurs. Thus they are providing new approaches to human
service delivery—approaches that might reduce not only costs but the
stigma traditionally associated with human services.

Another important trend that is shaping the current context is the
strong movement away from categorical or targeted services to a more
holistic approach. New services are less likely to be targeted to a child's
specific deficit. Further, the family rather than the child is becoming the
unit of intervention. As a consequence of this more holistic orientation,
as well as reduced funding, single-purpose agencies are being forced to
look outward and work collaboratively. For example, between sectors,
schools and corporations are working together via loaned executive and
adopt-a-school programs. In these cases, corporations lend executives
who may be skilled in areas (for example, finance) needed by school districts, or corporations may "adopt" a single school, thereby providing financial support. Or corporations may sponsor special school activities
or projects. Even within a sector, cooperation is increasing. Within the

mental health field, for example, planning councils are fostering net-working, interagency agreements, and employee swaps, with each com-munity sculpting its own structure—a decided contrast to the single fed-eral "model" that predominated in the 1960s and 1970s. This holistic orientation alters the *kinds* of services that are offered and the ways orga-nizations come together to deliver services. Essentially, then, the sub-stance and structure of many human services are being reshaped.

Another change characterizing today's society and relevant to family support is the ready availability of information on children, and parents' willingness to use that information. Researchers have become more in-terested in making their findings available to the public, and now that over 50 percent of women with children are in the paid labor force, magazines and media are realizing that coverage of women's issues is quite lucrative. Magazines such as *Savvy*, *Working Mother*, and *Working Woman* have emerged. Even more traditional magazines are modifying their editorial policy to carry articles of appeal to women and to families with children. Routinely, the *New York Times* and *Wall Street Journal* now afford issues related to children and families front-page coverage, catapulting them to national prominence. Day care and schooling at age four, for instance, are no longer buried in "Women's" or "Living" sections or assigned to the society editor. Armed with new information and an ever-increasing number of resources, adults are seeking to make informed consumer and life choices. Handbooks on how to do, have, or make just about anything exist. More so than at any earlier time in our history, parents, learning from research, are aware of their critical roles in influencing their children's development.

One consequence of the media explosion is that parents are seeking information and supports that will help them parent more effectively. Snow (1982) found this interest in obtaining help in child rearing across income levels. Of the 231 parents in the study, 73 percent of low-income and 79 percent of higher-income parents surveyed agreed that "in to-day's world, everyone needs some kind of help in rearing children." In-terestingly, Snow found that parents sought support primarily from other parents, friends, neighbors, and churches. Noticeably absent from this list are schools.

Perhaps because family support efforts are burgeoning in so many sectors, schools, the most bureaucratic of institutions, are not routinely considered sources of support—despite the fact that they have long served parents and communities. The potential consequence of this per-ception may be perilous indeed. With only one-quarter of our popula-tion having children in the schools, with reduced overall school popu-lations, and with the graying of America, the schools' constituency is di-minishing. Educators must understand that their success is contingent upon the support they generate for and from parents and the community at large. For schools and school personnel, family support can no longer be a gracious gesture. Rather, because family support is key to children's success and to the very success of public education, productive parent-school interaction is imperative (Kagan & Schraft, 1983).

FAMILY SUPPORT PROGRAMS FOR WHOM?

As noted earlier, differences in schools' responses to poor and middle-class families began early in our history and have persisted. Gordon (1977) pointed out that parent involvement followed two main directions: the first involved middle-class and well-educated people, who for the most part generated activities that elaborated and supported the institution's values. Examples of this direction can be found in the PTA and Child Study movement. This tradition was voluntary, self-selective, and self-managed with content based upon parents' perceptions of need. The second direction worked to teach the poor about middle-class values. This tradition was usually programmatic, funded or connected to a government agency, run by professionals, and based upon "expert" perception of needs.

Despite its strong history, current demographics are forcing the collapse of this two-tiered system. Poor and more affluent families alike are subject to stresses such as separation, divorce, and drug and alcohol abuse. Although still weighted toward minority and low-income families, need for support has expanded across races and classes. Precisely because needs are more pervasive, family support programs within the context of schools may be more likely to be implemented and sustained. This hypothesis is substantiated by the previously reviewed history, throughout which the most global programs have proved the most durable.

More specifically, who are the families in need of services? Snow (1982) has identified six family types with special needs, "meaning they have certain unique characteristics which we hypothesize call for special understanding and adjustments on the part of the schools if the home and school are to work together cooperatively" (p. iv). The types are families with low socioeconomic status, single-parent families, two-job families, families with chronically ill or handicapped children, isolated rural families, and minority families. Upon closer scrutiny, differences among family types and within each type emerge. For example, Snow differentiates the two-job family into the two-worker family, where the wife's commitment to work is less than her husband's, and the two-career family, where a high commitment to career exists for both people. To further complicate matters, families do not neatly fit only one of the categories suggested, but instead fall into multiple categories. A family may be poor, rural, single-parent, minority, and have a handicapped child simultaneously.

These variegated patterns of family structure and family need suggest that the scope and structure of family support services in schools must vary accordingly, and in fact, vast differences in home–school family support efforts do exist. For example, legislatively more sophisticated than other family categories, parents with handicapped children have been successful in altering many school practices. Supported by federal mandate and money, services to families with handicapped children are broad in scope and exist in school districts throughout the country. In contrast, services to single-parent and two-job families tend to be initiated locally, with no federal financial support, and exist sporadically from district to district. What is important to understand is that these differences may be developmental (a function of time) or they may be structural. Will two-worker families, as they grow in number and organizational sophistication, become more legislatively oriented, or will they want to maintain an essentially grassroots structure, meeting needs on an ad hoc basis? While answers to these and other questions regarding family types cannot be predicted, it is certain that lessons can and must be learned from current practice.

PROGRAM MODELS

Because current efforts to support families via the schools are so diverse in orientation, activities, and outcomes, two distinct perspectives will be presented. First, one family type will be discussed and current and possible strategies to meet their needs will be reviewed. Second, an "aerial view" of several innovative programs that are meeting needs of an array of family types will be presented. Although each viewpoint employs a case study approach and neither presumes to be comprehensive, the first is essentially a family perspective whereas the second presents a school's perspective. In reality, in any setting, these perspectives exist simultaneously.

The First Perspective: Two-Job Families

Demographics indicate that in nearly 60 percent of married couples with children, both adults were in the paid work force in 1980. In view of increasing economic pressures and changing attitudes toward the roles of men and women, it is predicted that this trend will continue at least through 1990, when 56 million women and 66 million men will be wage earners (Masnick & Bane, 1980). As indicated earlier, two-job families differ considerably, yet they share concerns about care of their children and a minimum of time. While *two-career* families may have the advantage of being able to afford services—child care, housekeepers, lessons for their children—*two-job* families typically do not. Role sharing, shift scheduling, and informal networking are strategies used to meet the press of parental employment for many couples.

As is the case for single parents, logistics are not the only problem for two-job families. For both groups, negative social stigmas as well as institutional regulations have posed difficulties that are only now beginning to abate. There are still criticisms of teachers who maintain stereotypes about neglectful or unconcerned working parents and about schools unwilling to reschedule routine but important visits so that working parents may attend. Yet research (Kamerman & Hayes, 1982) has shown that many two-worker and two-career families retain high degrees of commitment to the schools and great concern over obtaining quality services for their children. Many of their career decisions about where to work, for how long, and at what times are influenced by concern for their youngsters.

Some schools have been responsive to the pressures faced by two-job families and have ameliorated tensions by altering schedules and establishing special practices. For example, the provision of child care, particularly after school hours, has been instituted in some areas to relieve pressures on two-job families. In other cases, Saturday or evening sessions have been added to the traditional times for parent-teacher conferences.

Still, the interaction between schools and working parents needs considerable attention. Relevant evidence comes from Snow's (1982) findings that "the schools do not expect a high level of involvement from two-job parents and the parents do not expect the schools can do anything to make their involvement more possible" (p. 45). Since there is no doubt that positive home-school relationships influence children, this business as usual attitude minimizes possible gains that students could be achieving if positive and productive home-school relations existed. Instead of accepting the status quo, the goal of an effective partnership is optimizing positive support and involvement.

The Second Perspective: Program Models

Many school districts in America have made major advances in developing programs of family support. Some programs, aided by departments of education, serve entire states or school districts; in other cases, only one school is involved. More typically, programs are funded fully by local sources, including businesses and industries. The programs are staffed differently, some relying heavily on volunteers while others use paid professional and paraprofessional staff.

Although the programs highlighted here vary in every way—services, funding, longevity, staffing, and scope—all have at their core a commitment to partnership and to a broad definition of education. They recognize that families and schools diverge in missions and wills, but are not thwarted by this reality. They also acknowledge limitations, realizing that no single program can meet the needs of all people. They continually strive to learn from the past in making improvements in school practices and policies. The following are selected examples of family support efforts functioning in conjunction with schools:

New Parents as Teachers. Operating in Missouri school districts, this program provides information and services to any family with a child under three. Families are helped to provide a home environment that aids child development. The schools reach out to parents before the child is born and continue providing support until the child reaches age three. Multiple services include drop-in child care, home visitor programs, lending library, newsletters, joint parent-child activities, information and referral systems, parent support and education groups, and a "warm-line."

Peralta Year Round School. Serving a multiethnic community in California, the Peralta School operates on a year-round schedule. This and other policy changes were developed by parents to meet their needs. Afterschool services are provided for children of working parents, and night parent education and support groups are maintained as well as a networking line and information and referral services.

Parent Education Resource Center (PERC). Operating in the Davis County School District in Utah, PERC is a resource center that lends some 28,000 books, tapes, educational toys, and filmstrips on child development and parenting to families each year. Utilizing local resources, including representatives from community health, mental health, social and family service agencies, and the PTA, PERC sponsors many workshops, serving 5,000 parents each year. Public agencies refer parents to PERC and, conversely, PERC refers families to community services. Preventive in nature, PERC receives full financial support from the school district.

Parents in Touch. In Indianapolis, Indiana, Parents in Touch promotes the direct participation of parents in the education of their children while strengthening communication and cooperation between home and school. Through a well-coordinated system including parent-teacher conferences, workshops, homework hotlines, Dial-A-Teacher, home visits, and a parent line that offers recorded messages ranging from school holiday dates to tips on preparing a child for examinations, Parents in Touch permeates every facet of the Indianapolis School District. Offering support for teachers and parents, this comprehensive model helps parents guide their children's development.

It is important to note that these and other programs chronicled in several well-researched resource guides (for example, Family Resource Coalition, 1982) are scattered samples of what can be done. These are by no means the only kinds of family support efforts under way in American schools. On the contrary, many other programs exist. For example, quality teen parenting, drug and alcohol abuse, and adopt-a-grandparent programs operate across the country (Furniss, 1982). Further strides are being made in state capitols. Legislation has been passed in Missouri and Minnesota, for instance, that supports parenting education through departments of education. Finally, many organizations exist to foster home-school interactions and family support. In addition to the Parent Teachers Association, important contributions have been made by the Institute for Responsive Education (Boston, Mass.), the Home-School Institute (Washington, D.C.), and the National Committee for Citizens in Education (Columbia, Md.).

In spite of the existence of these programs, legislation, and organizations, family support efforts in schools remain few. The Missouri and Minnesota legislation are vanguard steps—and are not being quickly adopted in other states. Similarly, the specific programs listed above are not representative of what is happening in schools but are exceptions. Unearthing them was a difficult task, yet worthwhile because their very existence indicates that the family support movement can and does function under a formalized aegis—namely, the schools.

IMPLICATIONS

A review of family support efforts in schools clearly indicates that a new movement, different in character, orientation, and mission from efforts of the past, is taking hold. While deeply rooted in past traditions of family-school relationships, the current family support movement emerges directly from the needs of modern families themselves. Often created by parents' initiatives, family support efforts are not established primarily "by" and "for" others. Do-good helping professionals and bureaucratic government support are ancillary to the 1980s' version of family support. Emphasis is on individuals who have needs helping themselves and others, as can be seen in the heterogeneous nature of this movement, which includes a mix of families that are not the traditional participants in social service programs. These programs are designed to meet the diverse needs of families be they minority or white, low income or middle class, two worker or unemployed. As discussed elsewhere in this volume, this broad base of participants demands acceptance of the strengths of cultural pluralism and ethnic diversity.

Family support today is becoming essentially a partnership movement where the façade of equality of the 1960s has given way to cooperative and collaborative planning and decision-making. Instead of seeking control of schools or of planning, parents are making a unique and enriching contribution. As the role of the government has diminished, autonomy at the local level has grown. National program models may be adapted for local use, but most frequently programs are locally created. Local design permits flexibility and allows programs to respond to demographic, social, and economic changes in a community.

Although control exists at the local level, some of the exemplary programs did receive their initial financial support from federal or state funds. Thus, although not a precondition, outside support accelerates the inception of these efforts. To ensure that new efforts continue to emerge, incentives for school systems to initiate effective parent-school links should be established by federal or state governments. This is particularly appropriate since, after outside seed funds are exhausted, localities (either through municipal governments, local nonprofit organizations, or businesses and industry) frequently sustain the efforts. While governmental *financial* support has been helpful, federal mandates that restrict the options and creativity of local program planners and implementers have not. Regulation accompanying federal support must enable localities to tailor programs. With this freedom comes responsibility for local planners.

Learning from the past, advocates of family support programs in the schools must recognize the need not only to develop program components but to ensure longevity. As we have seen, educational practice is replete with programmatic add-ons that have had little long-term effect on schools and schooling. Adding on programs and support groups to meet the immediate needs of single parents, for instance, is not enough to guarantee their success. Rather, structural changes are needed so that the relationship between parents and schools can become a true partnership.

The very process of establishing support programs in the schools, a collaboration between schools and families, begins the realignment of their relationship that Seeley (1981) says is necessary, not simply for family support, but for the entire educational enterprise in America. Seeley has indicated that continued emphases on the inputs and outputs of education clouds the issue. He contends that schools will not be able to do their jobs until a fundamental reordering of relationships between parents and schools is accomplished. Family support efforts can be an effective tool in achieving this aim.

Given that family support efforts have value in and of themselves, and given that they can be effective in improving education generally, what must be done to ensure their existence? Because these efforts are so new, several important steps to sustain them must be undertaken immediately. First, information regarding family support programs, their strategies and effects, should be disseminated to potential adapters so that they may benefit from the knowledge and experience of others. An education campaign should also be launched so that the American public will be better informed about family strengths and needs and about constructive proactive efforts of schools. Second, longitudinal evaluations of family support programs must be initiated and sustained, with results made available for national dissemination and utilization. Studies should focus on program effects on families, children, and home-school relationships. Finally, an analysis of how public policies can be developed to be sensitive to family functions without overtaking them is warranted.

What little data we have to date reveal that where family support programs in schools exist, the immediate and pressing needs of today's families are being addressed, communication between home and school is improving, and parents are more satisfied with, and supportive of, their schools. While not a panacea that can ameliorate the effects of rapid demographic and technological changes on children, families, and schools, school-related family support efforts seem to be effective on many counts. As such, they are an important vehicle for helping individuals and institutions meet today's challenges head-on.

REFERENCES

Adams, D. (1976). *Parent involvement: Parent development.* Berkeley, CA: Center for the Study of Parent Involvement.

Arnstein, S. R. (1971). A ladder of citizen participation. In E. S. Cahn & B. A. Passett (Eds.), *Citizen participation effecting community change* (pp. 69–91) Praeger Special Studies in U.S. Economic and Social Development. New York: Praeger.

Becker, H. J., & Epstein, J. L. (1982). *Influences on teachers' use of parent involvement at home.* Baltimore, MD: Johns Hopkins University, Center for the Study of Social Organization of Schools.

Capital Park Parent Teachers Association Minute Book. (1903, October 16). Des Moines, IO: Wallace School.

Cetron, M., & O'Toole, T. (1982). *Encounters with the future: A forecast of life into the 21st Century.* New York: McGraw-Hill.

Comer, J. (1980). *School power.* New York: Free Press.

Cremin, L. (1977). *Traditions of American education.* New York: Basic Books.

Davies, D. (1976). *Schools where parents make a difference.* Boston: Institute for Responsive Education.

Davies, D. (1978). *An overview of the status of citizen participation in educational decision making.* Washington, DC: Institute for Responsive Education and the Education and Human Resources Development Division of Optimum Computer System.

Della-Piana, G., Stahmann, R. F., & Allen, J. E. (1968). Parents and reading achievement: A review of research. *Elementary English, 45* (2), 190–200.

Duncan, L. W., & Fitzgerald, P. W. (1969). Increasing the parent-child communication through counselor-parent conferences. *Personnel and Guidance Journal, 47,* 514–517.

Family Resource Coalition Program Directory, (1982, August). Chicago: Family Resource Coalition.

Fiske, E. B. (1983, April 27). Commission on education warns "Tide of mediocrity" imperils U.S. *The New York Times,* pp. A1, B6.

Furniss, T. (1982, June 2). Schools: What works. *Education Week,* p. 19.

Goodlad, J. J. (1981). Education, schools, and a sense of community. In D. Davies, (Ed.), *Communities and their schools* (p. 31). New York: McGraw-Hill.

Goodlad, J. J. (1983, March). A study of schooling: Some findings and hypotheses. *Phi Delta Kappan, 64* (7), 465–470.

Gordon, I. J. (1977, February). *Parent education and parent involvement: Retrospect and prospect.* Paper presented at Towards the Competent Parent Conference, Georgia State University, Atlanta.

Gordon, I. J. (1979). The effects of parent involvement on schooling. In R. S. Brandt (Ed.). *Partners: Parents and schools.* Alexandria, VA: Association for Supervision and Curriculum Development.

Gotts, E. E., Spriggs, A. M., & Sattes, B. D. (1979). *Review of major programs and activities in parenting.* Charleston, WV: Appalachia Educational Laboratory.

Henderson, A. (Ed.). (1981). *Parent participation—student achievement: The evidence grows.* Columbia, MD: National Committee for Citizens in Education.

Henry, N. B. (1953). *The fifty-second yearbook of the National Society for the Study of Education, Part II: The community school.* Chicago: University of Chicago Press.

Iverson, B. K., Brownlee, G. D., & Walberg, H. J. (1981). Parent-teacher contacts and student learning. *Journal of Educational Research, 74* (6), 394–396.

Kagan, S. L. (1984). *Parent involvement research: A field in search of itself.* Boston: Institute for Responsive Education.

Kagan, S. L., & Schraft, C. M. (1983). Developing parent commitment to public education: New directions for the 1980s. In R. L. Sinclair (Ed.), *For every school a community: Expanding environments for learning* (pp. 24–38). Boston: Institute for Responsive Education.

Kamerman, S. B., & Hayes, C. D. (Eds.). (1982). *Families that work: Children in a changing world.* National Research Council, Panel on Work, Family and Community, Washington, DC: National Academy Press.

Kerensky, V. M., & Logsdon, J. D. (1979). *A new foundation: Perspectives on community education:* Washington, DC: Community Education Program, United States Office of Education.

Lightfoot, S. L. (1978). *Worlds apart-Relationships between families and schools.* New York: Basic Books.

Linney, J. A., & Vernberg, E. (1983). Changing patterns of parental employment and the family-school relationship. In C. D. Hayes & S. B. Kamerman (Eds.), *Children of working parents: Experiences and outcomes* (pp. 73–99). Washington, DC: National Academy Press.

Litwak, E., & Meyer, H. J. (1973). The school and the family: Linking organizations and external primary groups. In S. P. Sieber & D. E. Wilder (Eds.), *The school in society: Studies in the sociology of education* (pp. 425–435). New York: Free Press.

Litwak, E., & Meyer, H. J., with Mickelson, C. E. (1974). *School, family and neighborhood: The theory and practice of school-community relations.* New York: Columbia University Press.

Mann, D. (1975). *Ten years of decentralization: A review of the involvement of urban communities in school decision making.* New York: Institute for Urban and Minority Education, Columbia University.

Masnick, G., & Bane, M. J. (1980). *The nation's families, 1960–1990.* Boston: Auburn House.

National survey on impacts of Head Start centers on community institutions. (1970). Washington, DC: Office of Child Development, U.S. Department of Health, Education and Welfare.

Rankin, P. T. (1967, February). The relationship between behavior and achievement of inner-city elementary children. Paper presented at the meeting of the American Educational Research Association, Washington, DC.

Reese, W. J. (1978, November). Between home and school: Organized parents, clubwomen, and urban education in the Progressive era. *School Review*, pp. 3–28.

Sarason, S. (1971). *The culture of the school and the problem of change.* Boston: Allyn and Bacon.

Seeley, D. (1981). *Education through partnership: Mediating structures and education.* Cambridge, MA: Ballinger.

Snow, M. (1982). *Characteristics of families with special needs in relation to schools.* (Technical Report, School-Family Relations Program Deliverable #2-A). Charleston, WV: Appalachia Educational Laboratory.

Sowers, J. C., Lang, C., & Gowett, J. M. (1980). *Parent involvement in the schools: A state of the art report.* Newton, MA: Education Development Center.

Stearns, M. S., & Peterson, S. (1973). *Parent involvement in compensatory education programs.* Washington, DC: Office of Planning, Budgeting, and Evaluation, U.S. Office of Education.

Thomas, W. B. (1980). Parental and community involvement. RX for better school discipline. *Phi Delta Kappan, 62,* 203–204.

Wimpelberg, R. K. (1982, March). Redefining lay participation in educational politics: Parental activity at the levels of school and classroom. Paper presented at the meeting of the American Educational Research Association, New York.

10 PARENT INVOLVEMENT: SUPPORT FOR FAMILIES OF CHILDREN WITH SPECIAL NEEDS

Ronald Wiegerink and
Marilee Comfort

Federal policies require that parent-involvement strategies be part of publicly funded services for children with special needs. These strategies are intended to offer support to families of children who are handicapped by physical, mental, and/or emotional disabilities. One indicator of the implementation of these policies is that in 1982 parents of more than 3 million handicapped children participated in the development of their children's special educational programs. The reasons for this mandated participation are many and diverse, as are those behind all political policies of importance. The current practices can be traced back to at least 1866, when Seguin, a physician and advocate of education for mentally retarded individuals, wrote:

> Who could watch over the tardy coming of these [delayed] functions better than a mother, if she were timely advised by a competent physician? . . .
> As soon as any function is set down as deficient at its due time of development, the cause must be sought and combated. . . . The arm of the mother . . . becomes a swing or a supporter; her hand a monitor or a compressor; her eye a stimulant or a director of the distracted look; the cradle is converted into a classroom, gymnasium, etc. . . .
> . . . it [maternal involvement] will in the end save the State and families the expense of several years of after-teaching, besides accomplishing more fully the object of the treatment. (pp. 88–89)

A century later, in the early 1960s, pioneering preschool intervention services with low socioeconomic families by Weikart (Weikart et al., 1970; Schweinhart et al., 1985) and Gray (Gray, Ramsey, & Klaus, 1982) included a focus on parental participation. Their work established a firm foundation for Head Start policy and later guided services for handicapped children and their families. In 1966 Head Start gave impetus to the development of current policies for early childhood special education programs by establishing parent involvement as a cornerstone of its project (Zigler, 1973).

In 1969 Congress enacted PL 90–538, authorizing the Handicapped Children's Early Education Program (HCEEP). This is a series of projects designed to demonstrate different methods and models that assist handicapped infants and preschool children in overcoming their handicapping conditions to the maximum extent possible. Since 1970, 280 HCEEP programs have been funded nationwide and form the foundation of services for young handicapped children in our country.

The authorizing legislation mandated that parents be encouraged to participate in the development and operation of these programs. The HCEEP regulations call for parent involvement through (1) assistance in program planning, development, operation, and evaluation; (2) training in parenting skills; (3) parent participation in educational and therapeutic components; and (4) opportunities for parents to advise and assist in information dissemination.

An expanded role for parents is also a major feature of PL 94–142, the Education for All Handicapped Children Act (1975). The act includes (1) an opportunity for the parent to participate in the writing and approval of his/her child's individualized education plan; (2) extensive due-process procedures (for example, the right to notification upon initiation or change of child's placement); (3) procedures for parental consultation and review of evaluations, reports, applications of local education agencies, state plans for educational services, and overall policies and procedures involved in educating handicapped children; and (4) the appointment of parents to an advisory council by the governor of each state to advise the governor on needs, policies, and programs involving the education of handicapped children (Pelosi & Hocutt, 1977).

The history and development of programs for children with special needs deal with two related populations—children in disadvantaged home environments and those with handicapping conditions—both of which are groups at risk for developmental delays. Therefore, both populations can benefit from special educational and/or therapeutic services. Although the literature for each population provides insight into the needs and services for the other, for the purposes of this chapter the focus will be on handicapped children and their families.

THEORETICAL RATIONALE FOR PARENT INVOLVEMENT

The ultimate rationale for parent involvement in early childhood special education programs for children at risk due to handicapping conditions is to promote improved outcomes for children (Karnes & Lee, 1980). After reviewing educational programs for young children at risk for developmental delay, Bronfenbrenner (1975) concluded that active involvement of parents in early childhood programs is vital to the development of the child and to the success of programs. Since Bronfenbrenner's proclamation over a decade ago, parent involvement has been considered an efficacious means not only to bring about initial child progress (Casto & Lewis, 1984) but also to extend program effects into later childhood and adolescence (Lazar & Darlington, 1982).

Programmatic reasons also have been cited in support of parent involvement in early childhood special education programs. Training parents as teachers of their children can be a cost-effective administrative strategy as a partial solution to staffing shortages (Clements & Alexander, 1951; Ora, 1973; Reisinger, Ora, & Frangia, 1970). When parents are considered members of a treatment team, they can instruct staff members in how to motivate their children and increase their responsivity (Hanson, 1985). Moreover, parent participation in program planning and implementation may increase the accountability of the program to the public (Ora, 1973).

Parent-involvement activities may also accrue benefits for parents. In an interview study of parents participating in early-intervention services for developmentally disabled infants, mothers receiving home-based services showed gains in positive attitudes toward their children and in child-care information and decreases in stress in relation to intervention (Moran, 1985). Parents of handicapped infants and toddlers enrolled in home- and center-based programs demonstrated improvements in parent-child interaction (Hanson, 1985; Kelly, 1982; McCollum & Stayton, 1985) and in teaching skills (Rosenberg & Robinson, 1985).

Parent involvement in early childhood special education programs has the following aims:

1. to increase the competence of children as a result of educational and therapeutic intervention by parents,
2. to improve information sharing between staff and parents,
3. to increase public confidence in program accountability,
4. to provide instruction in parent-child interaction and teaching, and
5. to provide emotional and informational support for parents.

CRITICISMS OF THE PARENT INVOLVEMENT CONCEPT

Although most researchers and practitioners assume that parent involvement in all early childhood education programs is beneficial, some challenging criticisms have appeared in the literature. Four points capture the minority opinion. First the deficit model (already discussed in this volume), which creates a hierarchy of professional and parental roles, was generalized to work with families of handicapped children. Although responsibility for the education and treatment of children was shared, professionals generally focused on the weaknesses of parents in dealing with child behaviors. Parents were, therefore, taught how to teach, feed, or how to manage child behavior, while little attention was given to other parent or family needs that may have been more pressing (Johnson & Chamberlin, 1983).

From a more recent perspective, many human service providers see parents and other family members as competent caregivers of their children who do what is feasible given the personal characteristics, environmental circumstances, and resources at hand (Moroney & Dokecki, 1984). This viewpoint, however, does not necessarily preclude the need for or benefits of parent involvement in early childhood programs. Rather, it underlines the utility of flexible, individualized roles for parents in providing care and education for young children with special needs (Schaefer, 1983).

Second, Farber and Lewis (1975) cautioned against the involvement of parents as teachers, not because of a theoretical model, but because the educational system as currently constituted must demonstrate both profitability and fiscal responsibility. They proposed that the system had embraced parent involvement as a "fad" adopted to reduce costs, with the added advantage of helping to transfer to parents the responsibility for educational failure. In addition, they feared that parents would be co-opted by the school and that efforts to make parents educators would impair their roles as parents. This reasoning assumes incorrectly that responsibility for child development must rest with either the school or the home, rather than with both, and that parents can enact only one role vis-à-vis their children.

Third, Stevens (1978) expressed concern about unanticipated detrimental effects on parents' and children's behavior as a result of careless planning of parent educational activities in programs. For example, it would be futile to organize a behavior management workshop for families of Down's syndrome infants, whose current priorities are to facilitate independent sitting and crawling. Stevens believes that such "haphazard programs may operate to shake the confidence a parent has acquired" (p. 64) and cautions that programs need to plan, evaluate, and adjust their services to meet the specific needs of families.

Fourth, Rutherford and Edgar (1979) stated that whereas parents should be involved in policy-oriented areas of their children's programs, they should not be involved in the classroom, simply because they need a respite from parenting the handicapped child. They asserted that relief from the stress associated with difficult parenting would allow the parents to attend to their own needs and pleasures. Winton and Turnbull (1981) agree that the relief and rest that parents receive while their children attend preschool special education programs might ultimately be more beneficial for both parent and child than would parental involvement in classroom activities. Rather than discard the concept of parent involvement altogether, however, programs could provide an array of choices that includes nonparticipation as one option.

The criticisms leveled at the parent-involvement concept have been answered largely by changes within the field of early intervention during the past fifteen years. Professionals' views of parents have changed, from regarding them as inadequate to competent caregivers, as lay teachers to team members, and as consumers to advocates for their children and themselves. Parents are considered to be capable of enacting several roles and engaging in various activities simultaneously (if they so desire) within early childhood special education programs. In short, in exemplary programs parents are becoming active participants in intervention as opposed to passive recipients of child-oriented services.

PARENT-INVOLVEMENT ROLES AND ACTIVITIES

A sizable amount of descriptive information is available regarding the various parent roles and activities offered by early childhood programs to meet the needs of families with handicapped children (see, for example, Karnes & Lee, 1980; Karnes, Linnemeyer, & Myles, 1983; and Lillie & Trohanis, 1976). Although the early intervention literature often refers to parent involvement as if it were a singular concept, it is multifaceted and is operationalized in numerous ways across programs. Gordon (1977) identified six roles that parents can play in educational settings for young disadvantaged children that apply equally well to programs for handicapped children: (1) parent as audience, bystander, or observer; (2) parent as learner; (3) parent as teacher of his/her own child; (4) parent as volunteer; (5) parent as professional; and (6) parent as decision-maker.

A survey of HCEEP projects conducted at the Frank Porter Graham Child Development Center at the University of North Carolina at Chapel Hill in 1980 (Hocutt & Wiegerink, 1983) found 34 different activities utilized to involve parents. Among the most common activities listed were systematic observation of children and attendance at individual parent-teacher conferences. Other frequent examples cited included regularly scheduled home visits, counseling or therapy, and individualized instruction regarding teaching tasks and techniques. Less commonly identified activities were those involving parent assistance with

TABLE 10.1
Parent Involvement Activities in a Prototypic Project

Rank	Activity
1	Participate in development of child's Individual Education Plan
2	Receive information regarding support services of programs offered by other agencies
3	Receive systematic reports of child's progress
4	Receive information concerning the legal rights of child and parents
5	Receive instruction in educational techniques to use with child
6	Receive information concerning the behavioral and/or other effects of medicine
7	Work with child at home to carry out the child's educational or therapeutic program
8	Meet with child's teacher for informal exchange of information about the child
9	Observe child in activities at home at the request of project staff
10	Receive a formal orientation to the project (philosophy, methodologies, services, and so forth)
11	Assist in the screening/assessment of their own child
12	Assist in setting project goals and objectives
13	Be members of a project advisory board
14	Participate in project evaluation activities
15	Receive instruction in normal/exceptional child development
16	Participate in parent discussion groups to discuss problems associated with having a handicapped child
17	Receive regularly scheduled home visits
18	Receive their own (the parents') individualized program
19	Observe their child at the preschool on a regularly scheduled basis

Source: Hocutt & Wiegerink, 1983.

administrative tasks (for example, fund-raising and program evaluation). A panel of experts selected 19 of these 34 activities as important strategies to be included in a prototypic program for handicapped preschoolers and their parents (see table 10.1).

In spite of legislative trends mandating parental involvement in policy-oriented activities, descriptive data indicate that the majority of parents are active in more traditional roles. In the 1980 HCEEP survey, Hocutt and Wiegerink (1983) found that high percentages of parents were involved in passive parent-training activities, receiving information from professionals rather than participating actively in program planning, development, or operations. For example, parents were more likely to take part in observational activities or parent-teacher conferences than to train other parents or serve as program evaluators.

Ideally, parents of children with special needs should be offered an array of parent-involvement activities so as to fit the diverse demographic and cultural profiles that exist in American society as well as changes in the needs of child and family over time (Bernheimer, Young, & Winton, 1983; Silva, 1981). This is not a new appeal. For more than a decade researchers have called for responsive family programming (Karnes & Zehrbach, 1975). This goal can be accomplished by negotiating parent and professional roles with individual families (Schaefer, 1983) and by offering flexible options for parent-involvement activities that meet individual family needs (Turnbull & Winton, 1984).

SPECIAL NEEDS OF PARENTS

There is a considerable body of literature that describes the special needs of parents of handicapped children and supports the importance of services for them (Gallagher & Vietze, 1986). This information comes from two kinds of sources: (1) research describing the impact of the handicapped child on the family (see, for example, Beckman, 1983; Darling, 1983; Paul, 1981; Waisbren, 1980); and (2) reports of parents of handicapped children (Gallagher, Beckman, & Cross, 1983; Turnbull & Turnbull, 1978).

The most frequent need reported by parents is for accurate information regarding their child's diagnosis and prognosis (Beckman-Bell, 1981). In retrospect, parents often criticize physicians for disregarding early concerns about child development in apparent attempts to alleviate parental fears (Cunningham & Sloper, 1977). Practitioners also are faulted for withholding diagnostic information when they suspect a handicapping condition until anxious parents question developmental lags or inappropriate child behaviors (Gayton & Walker, 1974). Physicians' perceptions of their conversations with parents sometimes differ from those of parents (Shapiro et al., 1983). Nevertheless, many parents would prefer that practitioners communicate with them openly about their children's handicapping conditions (Cunningham & Sloper, 1977; Turnbull & Turnbull, 1978). Information then becomes a shared commodity that facilitates interaction between parents and professionals in meeting family and child needs (Schaefer, 1983).

In addition to information about their child's impairment, parents require consultation regarding the availability of appropriate educational and therapeutic services. Human service professionals must be aware of a variety of community resources in order to help parents in selecting services to meet their family's needs. Even so, frustrations such as clinic eligibility requirements or elusive explanations of services may encourage "shopping behavior" from parents—that is, displaying their dissatisfaction with one agency or practitioner by going to another one (Bernheimer et al., 1983; Darling, 1979). For many families with handicapped children, consultation regarding services becomes a lifelong necessity for assistance with case management and coordination of multiple services.

Once the family locates an appropriate program, parents require a clear explanation of the rationale, goals, and options for parental and child participation in it. Optimally, exchange of information between staff and family is an integral part of every level of early intervention services, from assessment of the child to evaluation of the program. Whether or not parents are able or willing to participate in parent involvement activities, they deserve to be well informed about their child's program and progress, as well as the option of not engaging in structured program activities (Winton & Turnbull, 1981).

For some families, financial responsibilities associated with child health care, specialized equipment, and therapeutic or educational services become a major burden. Private insurance coverage and government funding vary greatly among families, programs, and locales (Ireys, 1980). Parents need up-to-the-minute counsel regarding sources of financial support and the most cost-efficient sources of equipment and services.

Information and counsel, however comprehensive and continuous, are not the only types of support that families require. A pervasive need that seems to touch all families and circumstances is the need for emotional support. Raising a handicapped child entails not only personal and familial adjustment but also anticipation of the reactions of kin, neighbors, and the community (Darling, 1979). The extent of need and preferred source of support may vary depending on a family's past experience and the resources at hand. Although people usually turn to family and friends before seeking aid from professionals (Gourash, 1978), the birth of an impaired child may tax natural support sources beyond their abilities to provide the specific assistance required by parents.

The need for assistance with routine activities of caring for a child with a developmental disability is frequency underestimated (Beckman-Bell, 1981). Parents report the impact of a handicapped child on virtually every aspect of family life including health, finances, and family relations. Empirical evidence documenting the stress of parenting a child with impairments is mounting (Crnic, Friedrich, & Greenberg, 1983; Gallagher et al., 1983; Murphy, 1982).

Although practitioners are well aware of the variability in family needs and resources, the long-standing focus on the child in early intervention has made them less than skilled in family-oriented intervention techniques. Few practitioners in early intervention programs are trained to assess families, and few programs are prepared to offer the broad range of services necessary to address the diverse individual profiles of families with young children with special needs (Bailey & Simeonsson, 1984). Although many programs continue to emphasize the child-related needs of parents, this approach contrasts with family support programs that focus on the whole family as a target for intervention.

FAMILY SUPPORT PROGRAMS

Some educational and health service programs attempt to meet families' child-related needs by focusing directly on parents. In these programs parents are more than *involved* in intervention; they are the targets of strategies designed to meet their needs for information, emotional support, and skills training. Several examples of parent-oriented programs are delineated in table 10.2. These are not intended to be exhaustive. Instead, they illustrate the breadth of possible strategies that can be implemented to involve parents with their children while simultaneously meeting parental needs. (For a review of parenting education programs, see Joy et al., 1980.)

Before we discuss the selected programs, three overriding points require explanation. First, programs that include parents as targets of intervention may take either a preventive or a reactive approach to services. Preventive services intervene with high-risk populations to guard against infant or family problems. For example, comprehensive counseling and education programs for parents of babies in neonatal intensive care units are designed to decrease the incidence or severity of developmental disabilities and to increase parental competencies in caring for a fragile baby. In contrast, reactive services aim to ameliorate extant problems such as asynchronous interactions between parents and their severely handicapped children. Both categories of services are necessary because problem conditions cannot always be predicted in advance or prevented from occurring. Although they are less likely to draw public support and funding, preventive services are more cost-beneficial in the long run (Bartel, 1981; Clement et al., 1984; Seitz, Rosenbaum, & Apfel, 1985).

Second, the majority of early childhood special education programs identify the child, the mother, or the mother-child dyad as the target of intervention. The current literature on child development, however, increasingly emphasizes the salient roles played by fathers (Lamb, 1981), siblings (Skrtic et al., 1984), grandparents (Tinsley & Parke, 1984), and the extrafamilial social support network (Bronfenbrenner, Moen, &

TABLE 10.2
Family Support Programs

Type of intervention/ program name	Target population	Timing of intervention	Goal of intervention	Focus of intervention	Format of intervention	Effects of intervention
Parent-professional communication and support Infant Referral Center (Taylor & Hall, 1980)	Parents of infants admitted to regionalized neonatal intensive care unit (NICU)	Prenatal to neonatal Frequent contacts as needed	Facilitate psychological adaptation of parents to premature or high-risk infant	Parent-professional communication Interstaff communication Parent-infant relationship	Anticipatory tour of hospital facilities and NICU for medically high-risk mothers Continual procedural orientation and status consultations with both parents during hospitalization of baby Liaison nurse facilitates communication between nursery and obstetrics Transfer of mothers with baby to regionalized center whenever possible Phone contacts between referring physicians and regionalized center staff	Brief case study examples indicate improved communication between parent and professionals and among practitioners Enhanced parent-infant relationships

TABLE 10.2 (Continued)

Type of intervention/ program name	Target population	Timing of intervention	Goal of intervention	Focus of intervention	Format of intervention	Effects of intervention
Parent-to-parent support Parent Helpers Program (Davidson & Dosser, 1982)	Parents of developmentally disabled newborns	Neonatal contacts as needed	Facilitate a positive climate in which parents of newborn developmentally disabled infants can maximize their adjustment to family crisis	Psychological adaptation to birth of infant with handicap	Visits in hospital by trained parent helper	Anecdotal reports from parents and parent helpers indicate increased acceptance of handicapped infant and increased use of community support agencies
Professional support Family Care Program (Siegel, 1982)	Families of infants transferred from Neonatal Intensive Care Unit	Transfer from NICU to hospital discharge Periodic professional consultations, peer support, and parent group meetings	Facilitate attachment and reorganization of family	Physical caregiving Family-child interactions Family functioning Support for families	Individualized teaching and counseling for parents during infant's hospitalization in transitional nursery Written information regarding NICU staff, common problems, and local accommodations Parent-to-parent contacts Parent support group Follow-up assessments	Results forthcoming

TABLE 10.2 (Continued)

Type of intervention/ program name	Target population	Timing of intervention	Goal of intervention	Focus of intervention	Format of intervention	Effects of intervention
Parent education and support Supporting Extended Family Members Program (Meyer et al., 1982; Klinman & Kohl, 1984; Vadasy et al., 1984)	Fathers of handicapped infants or preschoolers	Infancy to early childhood	Promote father's understanding and enjoyment of handicapped child to enable him to play active and informed role in child's development	Father-child interaction Paternal caregiving role Child development Intra- and extra-familial support	Saturday sessions: • group play • discussion • community professional speakers	Pilot vs. newly enrolled fathers: • lower paternal depression scores • more positive perceptions of interactions with their children • greater access to social support
Parent education to enhance parenting skills and personal competence Regional Intervention Program: Parent-to-parent training and support (Wiegerink & Parish, 1976)	Parents of behaviorally disruptive children under 5	Preschool age (up to 5) 6 months of parent/child interaction training	Increase parental skills of behavioral observation and functional analysis of behavior. Emphasis on positive reinforcement and behavioral generalization training	Parent-child interaction during tutorial sessions, in a classroom, in an apartment-like room, and at home	Parent and child are observed and data recorded during 30-minute sessions. Parents are tutored by reviewing data, video tapes, and are also encouraged to be positive toward emerging behaviors	Pre-post comparisons: • increased verbal and cooperative behavior in children • improved self-image of parents 3-yr and 10-yr follow-up: • reduced institutionalization • increased normal behavior in regular classrooms over projected rates

Garbarino, 1984) with respect to child and family outcomes. In the selection of exemplary programs for this chapter, favor was given to programs that included total families and that promoted linkages with the social context in which the family is embedded.

Finally, only one of the programs described here reported systematic pre-post comparisons to evaluate the effectiveness of its interventions with parents. Although a gap in evaluation is not unusual in many health and educational programs, this lack of validating data seriously limits program planning, accountability, and policy decisions regarding family support.

The first three programs listed in table 10.2 offer information and emotional support to parents already experiencing a family crisis related to the birth of their baby. The target encompasses both parents. The onset, duration, and setting of intervention (that is, intervention during hospitalization from birth until discharge) are narrow. All three programs seek to facilitate family adaptation to difficult birth situations and to enhance optimal family relationships during a short but critical time span. The foci of intervention vary from specific to broad—from parental psychological adaptation to all aspects of adaptive family functioning. Likewise, formats range from simple parent-to-parent conversation to a full array of individualized and group strategies for transforming the baby's hospitalization into a family experience. Unfortunately, little information was reported to evaluate the efficacy of the interventions outlined in table 10.2.

The last two programs in table 10.2 concern parents of children with identified problems. The goals, however, concentrate more on parents' personal resources than do those of the aforementioned programs. The positive short- and long-term effects of parental training in behavior management skills lend credence to this approach with families of young children who exhibit behavioral problems.

Overall, the intervention programs described in table 10.2 illustrate the diversity of goals and service formats utilized to meet parent needs. Unfortunately, programs such as these are not offered universally. When they do exist, it may be difficult for parents to gain access to them without direct referrals. Typically, assorted child- and parent-oriented services are sponsored by different private or public agencies in the community. If collaborative linkages could be established among family support programs in neonatal intensive care units, home-based health and educational services, and later, early childhood special education programs, this would foster continuity of care over time to meet each family's needs at critical junctures during the early years of the child's life (McPherson, 1983).

RESEARCH ON IMPACT AND EFFECTIVENESS

Despite the widespread involvement of parents in programs for their young handicapped children the impact and effectiveness of this strategy of early intervention continue to be debated (Casto & Lewis, 1984; Casto & Mastropieri, 1986a, 1986b; Strain & Smith, 1986). Much of the parent-involvement literature to date has been descriptive (for example, Karnes & Lee, 1980), and the efficacy research often has been of limited conclusive value (Bricker & Casuso, 1979; Dunst & Rheingrover, 1981; Simeonsson, Cooper, & Scheiner, 1982). However, program administrators cannot be assigned full blame for the inconclusive evaluations of these services. They are dealing with varied populations that thrive on individualized treatments and call for complex evaluation and research strategies.

Most of the literature regarding parent participation has focused on parent satisfaction with the child's treatment or educational program. Traditionally, parents of handicapped children have not been very satisfied with the services they have received (Barclay et al., 1962; Koch et al., 1959; Waskowitz, 1959). In a 1959 survey of parent members, the National Association for Retarded Citizens found that only 25 percent of the parents were satisfied with their contacts with professionals. This is an especially low rate of satisfaction when one considers that the respondents were active members in a parent group.

Anderson and Garner (1973) found that parent satisfaction with professional contacts was poor. They concluded from their interviews with 23 mothers who did not participate in their retarded children's preschool programs "that professional people may play a role in producing parent dissatisfaction" (p. 39). In a 1974 analysis of the same study, Anderson contended that dissatisfaction with parental services contributes to the shopping behavior mentioned above where parents visit professionals with no resolution of their problems. Parents in these studies showed dissatisfaction with multiple and conflicting diagnoses, excessive time lag between diagnosis and treatment, lack of practical assistance with parenting skills, and lack of child progress during treatment.

One hundred parents of exceptional children in the public schools were contacted in a survey of services for the handicapped (Becker, Bender, & Kawabe, 1976). The programs involving these parents indicated that they were effectively serving parents. However, the parents themselves expressed mixed feelings. The major finding from this study is that parents were unaware of the services available in the school district, owing to lack of involvement in the planning or supervision of the programs.

On the other hand, a 1976 report on the HCEEP program (Bureau of Education for the Handicapped, 1976) found that 97 percent of the parents were pleased with services and 80 percent reported personal benefits from their involvement. In studies conducted from 1977 to 1982, Hocutt and Wiegerink (1983) found similarly high levels of satisfaction among parents. One difference between the HCEEP programs and those investigated in earlier surveys was the active form that parent involvement took in the former. Many of HCEEP's parent activities were included in the prototypic program list (table 10.1).

An examination of the empirical literature reveals that researchers have endeavored to go beyond self-reported satisfaction to substantiate the positive effects of early intervention, including parent involvement (Dunst & Rheingrover, 1981). Although the clinical evidence is strong, well-designed studies are lacking (Simeonsson et al., 1982). In an effort to produce specific answers to practical questions, the original research problem concerning education for young children—"Is Early Intervention Effective?" (Bronfenbrenner, 1975)—has been divided into more meaningful queries. For example, do biweekly home visits increase child progress more rapidly than bimonthly visits? Not necessarily; frequent home visits may lead to dependence on the home interventionist, which may hinder parental competence (Sandow & Clarke, 1978). Can the home training system be used effectively with families of children with varying degrees and types of handicapping conditions? It appears so (Revill & Blunden, 1979). Because the answers to these and other questions are equivocal, however, multiple outcome measures are called for in the literature (Denhoff, 1981; Johnson & Chamberlin, 1983; Wiegerink et al., 1980; Zigler & Balla, 1982).

Two reviews of intervention-program evaluations for biologically handicapped children criticized the methodology of recent studies. Dunst and Rheingrover (1981) asserted that 71 percent of the 49 studies they examined were inconclusive because of inattention to internal validity factors (for example, maturation, testing, attrition, history, selection). In another analysis, Simeonsson et al. (1982) found that 48 percent of the 27 articles selected demonstrated statistical proof of a program's success while 93 percent claimed efficacy. In addition to the methodological problems that contributed to this discrepancy, the evaluations often suffered from tunnel vision; that is, they looked at child progress alone. Simeonsson and his colleagues found that 26 of the 27 studies measured program effectiveness primarily in terms of child progress. Clearly, intervention and parent involvement are much more complex than these single-factor analyses suggest.

Casto and Mastropieri (1986c) reported that "parents can be effective intervenors but that they are probably not essential to intervention success, and those intervention programs which utilize parents are not more effective than those which do not" (p. 421). This statement was based on the findings of a meta-analysis of 74 early intervention studies of programs for handicapped preschoolers. The conclusions drawn from the meta-analysis contradict the beliefs of early intervention researchers and practitioners and have been debated vigorously (Casto & Mastropieri, 1986a, 1986b; Dunst & Synder, 1986; Strain & Smith, 1986). However, the significance of this study lies in the substantial gap the authors identified in the early intervention literature. Few studies specifically examined the efficacy of parent involvement in early childhood programs for handicapped children. In many studies the extent and type of parent involvement activities were not well-documented. Furthermore, the conclusions of the meta-analysis were based largely on changes in child IQ as a measure of parent effectiveness because other variables (for example, language development, play skills, social competence, and parent-child interaction) were usually not measured by individual program evaluations.

When evaluating studies of programs for families of young handicapped children, numerous researchers have suggested the need to utilize other measures than IQ to capture program effects on a variety of child behaviors and on family members that may be more amenable to change (Dunst & Rheingrover, 1981; Simeonsson et al., 1982; Stoneman & Brody, 1984). Although the criticism by Casto and Lewis is startling initially, it simply emphasizes the need for more rigorous research to determine what amount and types of parent involvement are effective in early childhood programs for children with special needs.

Overall, future research regarding early intervention programs for families of young children with special needs requires systematic planning and evaluation strategies. Program evaluations need to incorporate a broad range of outcome measures, including process-oriented assessments (for example, parent-child interaction and parent-professional role sharing) in order to document the functional effects of intervention. In addition, program effects on multiple levels of the family ecology—on the child, the family, the social network, the community—need to be evaluated. Finally, several types of evaluations, such as experimental comparisons and cost-benefit analyses of alternative intervention techniques, need to be conducted. Such research strategies will help determine which aspects of early intervention services are effective for particular families with special needs (Ramey et al., 1982).

THE CHANGING FOCUS OF EARLY INTERVENTION SERVICES

Parent participation in child-related activities is currently the typical strategy for serving parents in the majority of programs for young handicapped children. Staff members provide educational information and skills training to enable parents to effectively change child behavior. For some families, however, information and skills training are not the primary needs. Before some parents are able to learn skills, they may require assistance with basic family needs such as food, housing, and employment. Other families may be quite competent in child care and in promoting their child's developmental skills but may need aid with family communication. To accommodate these families, one intervention program implemented a two-pronged parent component consisting of (1) social services/counseling, and (2) education/child advocacy. The program goals for parents were (1) to teach them to independently solve family problems related to survival and family well-being, and (2) to teach them to be effective change agents for their children's behavior (Bricker & Casuso, 1979).

A number of early intervention programs are now adopting a more comprehensive approach that takes family needs as well as child needs into account (Foster, Berger, & McLean, 1981; Hanson, 1981; Gabel & Kotsch, 1981). In fact, home-based early intervention services with handicapped children are entering a new phase of development (Bailey & Simeonsson, 1984). Over the past fifteen years the focus of services has moved from child to mother to family. The first phase, direct child training, emphasized acceleration of child progress in all areas of development (for example, motor, language, cognitive, and socioemotional). This phase was a natural outgrowth of the comprehensive preschool programs for disadvantaged children that proliferated in the 1960s.

The second phase focused on training mothers and, indirectly, children. This transition can be attributed partially to the initial evaluation of Head Start, which questioned the lasting positive effects of center-based early intervention programs for three- and four-year-olds (Westinghouse Learning Corporation, 1969). Educators surmised that perhaps intervention should begin earlier in the child's life and include direct services to parents. At the same time, they recognized mothers as the primary caregivers and teachers of their young impaired children and the most powerful reinforcement agents for teaching them new skills. Interventionists therefore began teaching parents to be effective caregivers and systematic teachers by demonstrating appropriate physical care, behavior modification techniques, and developmental activities (Finnie, 1975; Karnes & Lee, 1980; Lillie & Trohanis, 1976).

Now entering a third phase in the development of early intervention, practitioners are broadening their perspectives to include total families (Bailey et al., 1986; Bricker & Casuso, 1979; Foster et al., 1981). Recent changes in the prevalence of single-parent families and maternal employment and the sharing of child care responsibilities among several caregivers require revisions in services (Garbarino, 1982; Parke, 1981; Pederson, 1980). The entire family is becoming an appropriate target for intervention because the total caregiving environment plays a major role in overcoming the disabilities of the child (Werner & Smith, 1982). The current transactional view of child development suggests that the characteristics of child, parents, and environment interact in a mutual, ongoing fashion to determine child outcome (Sameroff & Chandler, 1975).

The systems perspective regarding family functioning complements this view. According to family systems theory, each member and dyad within the family interacts reciprocally with every other, continually adapting to changes in personal characteristics and the environment (Belsky, 1984; Minuchin, 1985). These perspectives regarding child and family functioning require practitioners to consider the entire family system when planning for intervention.

For families of some handicapped children, progress as a result of early intervention may be more apparent in other family members than in the child, so that program effectiveness can be documented better by means of family rather than child assessment. In order to maximize intervention effects, then, practitioners are looking beyond the child and the mother-child dyad to consider effects on various members of the family system (Sheehan & Keogh, 1982; Simeonsson et al., 1982).

Although child development continues to be the ultimate goal in this third phase of early intervention, the needs of parents are now being acknowledged alongside those of the child. A firm base of family-focused services during the early years of the child's life is likely to facilitate optimal ties between parents and professionals that may generalize to the preschool program, where the parent-involvement concept was launched. The recent passage of PL 99–457 (1986) requires the use of Individualized Family Service Plans in federally funded programs for families with developmentally delayed children from birth through two years of age to ensure the inclusion of families in the intervention process. As the family-focused perspective is adopted by an increasing number of early intervention programs, parent-involvement activities will become more clearly defined as only one of many strategies to support families with special needs.

Effective family-focused intervention will require systematic evaluation comparing strategies for meeting family needs. The multifaceted needs of the family, the mandate for services to younger children, and the financial retrenchment of the 1980s will press public and private agencies to coordinate existing health, education, and social services from the local to the federal levels. Given these requisites, practitioners will need training in family assessment, planning, and evaluation aimed at interdisciplinary intervention. Without question, parent involvement is already a fixed feature and family-focused services are the latest development in early intervention for handicapped children. Careful research, training, and interagency collaboration will enable parents and professionals to match intervention services to the special needs of families with young handicapped children.

REFERENCES

Anderson, K., & Garner, A. (1973). Mothers of retarded children: Satisfaction with visits to professional people. *Mental Retardation, 22,* 36–39.

Bailey, D. B., & Simeonsson, R. J. (1984). Critical issues underlying research and intervention with families of young handicapped children. *Journal of the Division for Early Childhood, 9,* 38–48.

Bailey, D. B., Simeonsson, R. J., Winton, P. J., Huntington, G. S., Comfort, M., Isbell, P., O'Donnell, K. J., & Helm, J. M. (1986). Family-focused intervention: A functional model for planning, implementing, and evaluating individualized family services in early intervention. *Journal of the Division for Early Childhood, 10,* 156–171.

Baker, B. L. (1984). Intervention with families with young, severely handicapped children. In J. Blacher (Ed.), *Severely handicapped young children and their families: Research in review* (pp. 319–375). New York: Academic Press.

Barclay, A., Goulet, L. R., Holtgrewe, M. M., & Sharp, A. R. (1962). Parental evaluations of clinical services for retarded children. *American Journal on Mental Deficiency, 67,* 231–237.

Bartel, J. M. (1981). Economics of early intervention. In R. Wiegerink (Ed.), *A review of early childhood services.* Series paper No. 24. Chapel Hill: University of North Carolina.

Becker, L. D., Bender, N. N., & Kawabe, K. K. (1976). *Exceptional parents: A survey of programs, services, and needs.* Riverside: University of California School of Education.

Beckman, P. (1983). Influence of selected child characteristics on stress in families of handicapped infants. *American Journal of Mental Deficiency, 88,* 150–156.

Beckman-Bell, P. (1981). Needs of parents with developmentally disabled children. In R. Wiegerink (Ed.), *A review of early childhood services.* Series paper No. 18. Chapel Hill: University of North Carolina.

Belsky, J. (1984). The determinants of parenting: A process model. *Child Development, 55,* 83–96.

Bernheimer, L. P., Young, M. S., & Winton, P. J. (1983). Stress over time: Parents with young handicapped children. *Developmental and Behavioral Pediatrics, 4,* 177–181.

Bricker, D. (1978). Early intervention: The criteria of success. *Allied Health and Behavioral Sciences, 1,* 567–582.

Bricker, D., & Casuso, V. (1979). Family involvement: A critical component of early intervention. *Exceptional Children, 46,* 108–116.

Bromwich, R. (1976). Focus of maternal behavior in infant intervention. *American Journal of Orthopsychiatry, 46,* 439–446.

Bronfenbrenner, U. (1975). Is early intervention effective? In B. Z. Friedlander, G. M. Sterritt, & G. E. Kirk (Eds.), *Exceptional infant: Assessment and intervention* (Vol. 3) (pp. 449–475). New York City: Brunner/Mazel.

Bronfenbrenner, U., Moen, P., & Garbarino, J. (1984). Child, family, and community. In R. D. Parke (Ed.), *Review of child development research* (Vol. 7) (pp. 283–328). Chicago: University of Chicago Press.

Bureau of Education for the Handicapped. (1976). *Battelle Report: A summary of the evaluation of the Handicapped Children's Early Education Program (HCEEP)*. Washington, DC: Department of Health, Education and Welfare.

Casto, G., & Lewis, A. C. (1984). Parent involvement in infant and preschool programs. *Journal of the Division for Early Childhood, 9*, 49–56.

Casto, G., & Mastropieri, M. A. (1986a). Much ado about nothing: A reply to Dunst and Snyder. *Exceptional Children, 53*, 277–279.

Casto, G., & Mastropieri, M. A. (1986b). Strain and Smith do protest too much: A response. *Exceptional Children, 53*, 266–268.

Casto, G., & Mastropieri, M. A. (1986c). The efficacy of early intervention programs for handicapped children: A meta-analysis. *Exceptional Children, 52*, 417–424.

Clement, J. R. B., Schweinhart, L. J., Barnett, W. S., Epstein, A. S., & Weikart, D. P. (1984). *Changed lives: The effects of the Perry Preschool Program on youths through age 19*. Ypsilanti, MI: High Scope Press.

Clements, J. E., & Alexander, R. N. (1975). Parent training: Bringing it all back home. *Focus on Exceptional Children, 7*, 1–12.

Crnic, K. A., Friedrich, W. N., & Greenberg, M. T. (1983). Adaptation of families with mentally retarded children: A model of stress, coping, and family ecology. *American Journal of Mental Deficiency, 88*, 125–138.

Cunningham, C. C., & Sloper, T. (1977). Parents of Down's syndrome babies: Their early needs. *Child: Care, Health and Development, 3*, 325–347.

Darling, R. B. (1979) *Families against society: A study of reactions to children with birth defects*. Beverly Hills, CA: Sage.

Darling, R. B. (1983). The birth defective child and the crisis of parenthood: Redefining the situation. In E. J. Callahan & K. A. McCluskey (Eds.), *Life-span developmental psychology: Nonnormative life events* (pp. 115–143). New York: Academic Press.

Davidson, B., & Dosser, D. A. (1982). A support system for families with developmentally disabled infants. *Family Relations, 31*, 295–299.

Denhoff, E. (1981). Current status of infant stimulation of enrichment programs for children with developmental disabilities. *Pediatrics, 67*, 32–37.

Dunst, C. J., & Rheingrover, R. M. (1981). An analysis of the efficacy of infant intervention programs with organically handicapped children. *Evaluation and Program Planning, 4*, 287–323.

Dunst, C. J., & Snyder, S. W. (1986). A critique of the Utah State University early intervention meta-analysis research. *Exceptional Children, 53*, 269–276.

Farber, B., & Lewis, M. (1975). The symbolic use of parents: A sociological critique of educational practice. *Journal of Research and Development in Education, 8*, 34–43.

Finnie, N. R. (1975). *Handling the young cerebral palsied child at home* (2d. ed.). New York: Dutton.

Foster, M., Berger, M., & McLean, M. (1981). Rethinking a good idea: A reassessment of parent involvement. *Topics in Early Childhood Special Education, 1*, 55–65.

Gabel, H., & Kotsch, L. S. (1981). Extended families and young handicapped children. *Topics in Early Childhood Special Education, 1* (3), 29–36.

Gallagher, J. J., Beckman, P., & Cross, A. H. (1983). Families of handicapped children: Sources of stress and its amelioration. *Exceptional Children, 50*, 10–19.

Gallagher, J. J., & Vietze, P. M. (Eds.). (1986). *Families of handicapped persons: Research, programs, and policy issues.* Baltimore: Paul H. Brookes.

Garbarino, G. (1982). Social policy, children and their families. In G. Garbarino, *Children and families in the social environment* (pp. 208–230). New York: Aldine.

Gayton, W. F., & Walker, L. (1974). Down syndrome: Informing the parents: A study of parental preferences. *American Journal of Diseases in Childhood, 127*, 510–512.

Gordon, I. (1977). Parent education and parent involvement: Retrospect and prospect. *Childhood Education, 54*, 71–79.

Gourash, N. (1978). Help-seeking: A review of the literature. *American Journal of Community Psychology, 6*, 413–423.

Gray, S. W., Ramsey, B. K., & Klaus, R. A. (1982). *From 3 to 20: The Early Training Project.* Baltimore, MD: University Park Press.

Hanson, M. J. (1981). A model for early intervention with culturally diverse single and multiparent families. *Topics in Early Childhood Special Education, 1* (3), 37–44.

Hanson, M. J. (1985). An analysis of the effects of early intervention services for infants and toddlers with moderate and severe handicaps. *Topics in Early Childhood Special Education, 5* (2), 36–51.

Hocutt, A., & Wiegerink, R. (1983). Perspectives on parent involvement in preschool programs for handicapped children. In R. Haskins & D. Adams (Eds.), *Parent education and public policy* (pp. 211–229). Norwood, NJ: Ablex.

Ireys, H. T. (1980). Health care for chronically disabled children and their families. In *Better health for our children: A national strategy. The report of the select panel for the promotion of child health* (pp. 321–353). (Vol. 4). Background Papers. Washington, DC: Government Printing Office.

Johnson, N. M., & Chamberlin, H. R. (1983). Early intervention: The state of the art. In *Developmental handicaps: Prevention and treatment* (pp. 1–23). Washington, DC: American Association of University Affiliated Programs for Persons with Developmental Disabilities.

Joy, L. A., Davidson, S., Williams, T. M., & Painter, S. L. (1980). Parent education in the perinatal period: A critical review of the literature. In P. M. Taylor (Ed.), *Parent-infant relationships* (pp. 211–237). New York: Grune and Stratton.

Karnes, M. B., & Lee, R. C. (1980). Involving parents in the education of their handicapped children: An essential component of an exemplary program. In M. J. Fine (Ed.), *Handbook on parent education* (pp. 201–225). New York: Academic Press.

Karnes, M. B., Linnemeyer, S. A., & Myles, G. (1983). Programs for parents of handicapped children. In R. Haskins & D. Adams (Eds.), *Parent education and public policy* (pp. 181–210). Norwood, NJ: Ablex.

Karnes, M. B., & Zehrbach, R. (1975). Matching families and services. *Exceptional Children, 41,* 1–4.

Kelly, J. F. (1982). Effects of intervention on caregiver-infant interaction when the infant is handicapped. *Journal of the Division for Early Childhood, 5,* 53–63.

Klinman, D. G., & Kohl, R. (1984). *Fatherhood U.S.A.: The first national guide to programs, services, and resources for and about fathers.* New York: Garland.

Koch, R., Graliker, B. R., Sands, R., & Parmelee, A. H. (1959). Attitude study of parents with mentally retarded children. *Pediatrics, 23,* 582.

Lamb, M. E. (Ed.). (1981). *The role of the father in child development* (rev. ed.). New York: Wiley.

Lazar, I., & Darlington, R. (Eds.). (1982). Lasting effects of early education: A report from the Consortium for Longitudinal Studies. *Monographs of the Society for Research in Child Development, 47,* (2–3, Serial No. 195).

Lillie, D. L., & Trohanis, P. L. (Eds.). (1976). *Teaching parents to teach.* New York: Walker.

McCollum, J. A., & Stayton, V. D. (1985). Infant/parent interaction: Studies and intervention guidelines based on the SIAI Model. *Journal of the Division for Early Childhood, 9,* 125–135.

McPherson, M. G. (1983). Improving services to infants and young children with handicapping conditions and their families: The Division of Maternal and Child Health as collaborator. *Zero To Three, 4,* 1–6.

Meyer, D. J., Vadasy, P. F., Fewell, R. R., & Schell, G. (1982). Involving fathers of handicapped infants: Translating research into program goals. *Journal of the Division of Early Childhood, 5,* 64–72.

Minuchin, P. (1985). Families and individual development: Provocations from the field of family therapy. *Child Development, 56,* 289–302.

Moran, M. (1985). Families in early intervention: Effects of program variables. *Zero To Three, 5,* 11–14.

Moroney, R. M., & Dokecki, P. R. (1984). The family and the professions: Implications for public policy. *Journal of Family Issues, 5,* 224–238.

Murphy, M. (1982). The family with a handicapped child: A review of the literature. *Developmental and Behavioral Pediatrics, 3,* 73–82.

Ora, J. (1973). Involvement and training of parent and citizen workers in early education for the handicapped. In M. B. Karnes (Ed.), *Not all little wagons are red.* Reston, VA: Council for Exceptional Children.

Parke, R. (1981). *Fathers.* Cambridge, MA: Harvard University Press.

Paul, J. L. (Ed.). (1981). *Understanding and working with parents of children with special needs.* New York: Holt, Rinehart & Winston.

Pedersen, F. (1980). Research issues related to fathers and infants. In F. Pederson (Ed.), *The father-infant relationship* (pp. 1–20). New York: Praeger.

Pelosi, J., & Hocutt, A. (1977). *The Education for All Handicapped Children Act: Issues and implications.* Chapel Hill, NC: Developmental Disabilities Technical Assistance System.

Ramey, C. T., Sparling, J. J., Bryant, D. M., & Wasik, B. H. (1982). Primary prevention of developmental retardation during infancy. *Preventive Human Services, 1,* 61–83.

Reisinger, J. J., Ora, J. P., & Frangia, G. W. (1970). Parents as change agents for their children: A review. *Journal of Consulting Psychology, 4,* 108–123.

Revill, S., & Blunden, R. (1979). A home training service for preschool developmentally handicapped children. *Behavior Research and Therapy, 17,* 207–214.

Rosenberg, S. A., & Robinson, C. C. (1985). Enhancement of mothers' interactional skills in an infant education program. *Education and Training of the Mentally Retarded, 20,* 163–169.

Rutherford, R. B., Jr., & Edgar, E. (1979). *Teachers and parents: A guide to interaction and cooperation.* Boston: Allyn and Bacon.

Sameroff, A., & Chandler, M. (1975). Reproductive risk and the continuum of caretaking casualty. In F. Horowitz (Ed.), *Review of child development research,* (pp. 187–244). (Vol. 4). Chicago: University of Chicago Press.

Sandow, S., & Clarke, A. D. B. (1978). Home intervention with parents of severely sub-normal, preschool children: An interim report. *Child: Care, Health and Development, 4,* 29–39.

Schaefer, E. S. (1983). Parent-professional interaction: Research, parental, professional, and policy perspective. In R. Haskins & D. Adams (Eds.), *Parent education and public policy* (pp. 283–303). Norwood, NJ: Ablex.

Schweinhart, L. J., Berrueta-Clement, J. R., Barnett, W. S., Epstein, A. S., & Weikart, D. P. (1985). Effects of the Perry Preschool Program on youths through age 19: A summary. *Topics in Early Childhood Special Education, 5,* (2), 26–35.

Seguin, E. (1866). *Idiocy and its treatment by the physiological method.* New York: William Wood.

Seitz, V., Rosenbaum, L. K., & Apfel, N. H. (1985). Effects of family support intervention: A ten-year follow-up. *Child Development, 56,* 376–391.

Shapiro, M. C., Najman, J. M., Chang, A., Keeping, J. D. Morrison, J., & Western, J. S. (1983). Information control and the exercise of power in the obstetrical encounter. *Social Science and Medicine, 17,* 139–146.

Sheehan, R., & Keogh, B. K. (1982). Design and analysis in the evaluation of early childhood special education programs. *Topics in Early Childhood Special Education, 1* (4), 81–88.

Siegel, R. (1982). A family-centered program of neonatal intensive care. *Health and Social Work, 1,* 50–58.

Silva, M. (1981). Ethnic and cultural differential factors among Spanish surnames and Spanish-speaking populations: Implications for delivery of services to the developmentally disabled. In D. Brantley & S. Wright (Eds.), *Coordinating comprehensive child health services: Service, training, and applied research perspectives* (pp. 76–90). Birmingham, AL: Center for Developmental and Learning Disorders.

Simeonsson, R. J., Cooper, D. H., & Scheiner, A. P. (1982). A review and analysis of the effectiveness of early intervention programs. *Pediatrics, 69,* 635–641.

Skrtic, T. M., Summers, J. A., Brotherson, M. J., & Turnbull, A. P. (1984). Severely handicapped children and their brothers and sisters. In J. Blacher (Ed.), *Severely handicapped young children and their families: Research in review* (pp. 215–246). New York: Academic Press.

Stevens, J. H. (1978). Parent education programs: What determines effectiveness? *Young Children, 33*, 59–65.

Stoneman, Z., & Brody, G. (1984). Research with families of severely handicapped children: Theoretical and methodological considerations. In J. Blacher (Ed.), *Severely handicapped young children and their families: Research in review* (pp. 179–214). New York: Academic Press.

Strain, P. S., & Smith, B. J. (1986). A counter-interpretation of early intervention effects: A response to Casto and Mastropieri. *Exceptional Children, 53*, 260–265.

Taylor, P. M., & Hall, B. L. (1980). Parent-infant bonding: Problems and opportunities in a perinatal center. In P. M. Taylor (Ed.), *Parent-infant relationships* (pp. 315–334). New York: Grune & Stratton.

Tinsley, B. R., & Parke, R. D. (1984). Grandparents as support and socialization agents. In M. Lewis (Ed.), *Beyond the dyad* (pp. 161–194). New York: Plenum Press.

Turnbull, A., & Turnbull, J. R. (Eds.). (1978). *Parents speak out: Growing with a handicapped child.* Columbus, OH: Charles E. Merrill.

Turnbull, A. P., & Winton, P. J. (1984). Parent involvement policy and practice: Current research and implications for families of young, severely handicapped children. In J. Blacher (Ed.), *Severely handicapped young children and their families: Research in review* (pp. 377–400). New York: Academic Press.

Vadasy, P. F., Fewell, R. R., Meyer, D. J., Schell, G., & Greenberg, M. T. (1984). Involved parents: Characteristics and resources of fathers and mothers of young handicapped children. *Journal of the Division for Early Childhood, 8*, 13–25.

Waisbren, S. E. (1980). Parent's reactions after the birth of a developmentally disabled child. *American Journal of Mental Deficiency, 84*, 345–351.

Waskowitz, C. H. (1959). The parents of retarded children speak for themselves. *Journal of Pediatrics, 54*, 319–332.

Weikart, D. P., Deloria, D. J., Lawsen, S. A., & Wiegerink, R. (1970). *Longitudinal results of the Ypsilanti Perry Preschool Project.* Ypsilanti, MI: High Scope Educational Research Foundation.

Werner, E. E., & Smith, R. S. (1982). *Vulnerable but invincible: A longitudinal study of resilient children and youth.* New York: McGraw-Hill.

Westinghouse Learning Corporation. (1969). *The impact of Head Start on children's cognitive and affective development.* Athens: Ohio University Press.

Wiegerink, R., Hocutt, A., Posante-Loro, R., & Bristol, M. (1980). Parent involvement in early education programs for handicapped children: A review. In J. J. Gallagher (Ed.), *New directions in exceptional children: Ecology of exceptional children* (pp. 67–85). San Francisco: Jossey-Bass.

Wiegerink, R., & Parrish, V. (1976). A parent-implemented preschool program. In D. L. Lillie & P. L. Trohanis (Eds.), *Teaching parents to teach* (pp. 149–162). New York: Walker and Company.

Winton, P., & Turnbull, A. (1981). Parent involvement as viewed by parents of preschool handicapped children. *Topics in Early Childhood Education: Families of Handicapped Children, 1*, 11–19.

Zigler, E. (1973). Project Head Start: Success or failure? *Learning, 1*, 43–48.

Zigler, E., & Balla, D. (1982). Selecting outcome variables in evaluations of early childhood special education programs. *Topics in Early Childhood Special Education, 1*, 11–22.

11 NEW DIRECTIONS FOR PARENT EDUCATION

Lois Pall Wandersman

> *Employment Opportunities:*
> One couple to procreate and raise a child. No experience neces-
> sary. Applicants must be available 24 hours per day, 7 days per
> week, and must provide food, shelter, clothing, and supervision.
> No training provided. No salary; applicants pay $140,000 over
> the next 18 years. Accidental applications accepted. Single peo-
> ple may apply but should be prepared for twice the work.
> (Dangel & Polster, 1984, p. 1)

No job is more important to the future of our society than parenting.
Yet, in the United States we spend more time, money, and energy inves-
tigating the raising of pigs, cows, and chickens than the rearing of hu-
mans (Lane, 1976). For almost all parents, learning to be a parent is a
trial-and-error process with countless frustrations. Parent education is
one strategy for making the job of parenting less frustrating and more
rewarding to parents and children.

Parent education is based on the principle that parenthood is an extremely complex and demanding job, and that education can help parents perform their job more effectively. This principle sounds incontro-
vertible. Yet, in American society there is a deeply held belief that being
a parent is an instinctual process and that families should solve their own
problems. Parents are often reluctant to admit that they might benefit
from education.

While its proponents have viewed parent education as a panacea for
poverty, mental illness, crime, and divorce, opponents have regarded it
as an intrusion into family life and a threat to individual freedom and
cultural diversity (Dokecki & Moroney, 1983; Mundel, 1983).

The only unanimous conclusion about the effectiveness of parent education is that the available data are insufficient as a basis for conclusions (Clarke-Stewart, 1983; Harman & Brim, 1980; Haskins & Adams, 1983). Analysis of the efficacy of parent education is greatly hampered by the paucity of published documentation and evaluations of parent education programs. Only a tiny fraction of the programs, primarily those that have been university-based or federally funded, have disseminated program descriptions or collected evaluation data. In many programs, parent education is combined with other services, such as day care or job training, so that the effect of the parent-education component per se cannot be determined.

DEFINING PARENT EDUCATION

Parent education has been defined as an organized effort with clear content, target population, and goals aimed at changing parental role performance (Harman & Brim, 1980). It incorporates a variety of educational experiences that give parents added knowledge and understanding, thus causing them to question their habitual ways of thinking, feeling, and acting. These experiences can help parents develop new methods of dealing with their children, with themselves, and with the social environment when necessary (Hammer & Turner, 1985, p. 21).

There is no single model of parent education. It involves a wide range of strategies including handbooks and manuals; child development and parenting courses; self-help and support groups; home-visiting programs; and television, radio, and magazine series. It takes place in varied settings, including schools, universities, hospitals, health centers, mental health clinics, day-care centers, churches, libraries, community centers, shopping malls, and wherever else parents are likely to gather. Target groups include future parents, single parents, adolescent parents, grandparents, divorced parents, parents of children with special needs, and parents of infants, preschool, school-age and teen-age children. Goals of programs range from the relatively specific, such as improving verbal communication, discipline, or health care, to the more global, such as expanding parents' knowledge of child development or parenting skills in order to prevent mental illness, educational failure, or poverty.

Parent education is distinguished from clinical or counseling approaches to helping parents by its focus on building strengths in normal families in order to prevent subsequent problems. Parent education and clinical approaches may use similar techniques and types of programs, for example, behavior-management skills training (Dangel & Polster, 1984) or communication training (Gordon, 1975). Substantively, however, parent education differs from therapy in its emphasis on (1) normative developmental and family problems rather than individual personality and family dysfunctions, (2) techniques that provide support rather than conflict and confrontation, and (3) goals that increase self-confidence and satisfaction rather than restructure personality or family dynamics.

The purpose of this chapter is to set forth more realistic expectations of the potential of parent education and to suggest some promising future directions. The chapter relies heavily on published accounts but also draws on informal communication with parent educators and on my own experiences in developing, leading, and evaluating several parent education programs. It focuses on parent education programs that center on active interactions with parents of young children rather than communications through the mass media. The programs considered fall into three primary types: in *home-based* programs, a home visitor individualizes the educational program for each parent; in *group discussion* programs, a parent educator leads discussions tailored to parents' concerns, and in *parent training* programs, parent educators use a structured didactic model to teach parenting skills.

BRIEF HISTORY

Some form of parent education and support has probably existed since the first parents, or at least the first grandparents. Child-rearing suggestions in print go back over 2,000 years (Dangel & Polster, 1984), and handbooks for parents appeared as early as 1633 (Fein, 1980). Older manuscripts suggest such techniques as submerging babies in freezing water to increase their strength or using opium to quiet a cranky baby (Dangel & Polster, 1984).

In this century, the variety, quantity, and quality of parent education have increased dramatically. At the turn of the century, many mothers joined others to share common parental concerns, and these groups banded together to form what became the Parent-Teachers Association (PTA). Since the 1920s a movement rooted in the Child Study Association has attempted to use scientific knowledge of child development to raise the standards of parental performance and ultimately cure all of society's problems (Schlossman, 1983). Harman and Brim (1980) have related the rise in parent education to the breakdown in cultural traditions and intergenerational interaction and the development of an empirical knowledge base about child development.

In the 1960s and 1970s the focus of the parent education movement shifted from middle-class self-improvement to the disadvantaged. As part of the War on Poverty the federal government funded a variety of comprehensive programs that stressed parent education. These programs were aimed at reducing educational inequality and eventually poverty (Schlossman, 1978). Comprehensive programs like the Parent and Child Development Centers (PCDCs) (Dokecki, Hargrove, & Sandler, 1983) and Home Start (Love et al., 1976) were optimistically developed to communicate scientific views of child development to low-income mothers in order to help them promote competence in their young children and thus prevent the children's failure in school and subsequent poverty. While these programs for high-risk families generally demonstrated positive effects on mother-child interactions and the children's cognitive functioning, the results were more modest than the initial hopes; they did not erase educational or social inequality (Bronfenbrenner, 1974; Gray & Wandersman, 1980). Some critics argue that these programs place the blame for social and educational inequality on poor families (Laosa, 1983; Schlossman, 1978). Other policy analysts and policymakers conclude that parent education has not proved to be cost effective in reducing social problems in a period of fiscal conservatism (Haskins & Adams, 1983; Mundel, 1983).

In spite of the questions as to the effectiveness of parent education, parents continue to express interest in it (Schaefer, 1983; Sparling & Lowman, 1983). This can be attributed to several developments (Hammer & Turner, 1985): (1) the publicity given to the long-term effectiveness of some comprehensive early-intervention programs (see, for example, Lazar & Darlington, 1982); (2) social changes that have intensified the stress on parents—such as increases in the proportion of working, single, and adolescent mothers; and (3) increased attention to the problems of child abuse and neglect and delinquency. This changing social climate has given rise to a new generation of parent education programs.

Parent education, like other components of family support, has been affected by cuts in federal funding for major national experiments. Innovative, locally funded, low-cost programs have been initiated by parents or service agencies to meet community needs (Family Resource Coalition, 1982). Second, as understanding of the ecology of family development has increased, programs have shifted their attention from the child to the family. They view the family, in turn, as a system within its social network, neighborhood, and larger community (Weiss, 1983). Consequently, parent education today is often incorporated into a broader approach to strengthening families within their ecological context. Finally, as awareness of individual and cultural diversity has sharpened, programs have emphasized building on the strengths of each family.

PARENT EDUCATION AND FAMILY SUPPORT

In this chapter parent education is considered to be a central component of an integrated approach to family support. The Family Resource Coalition, a national organization of family support programs, defines it as one of the basic elements of family support (Family Resource Coalition, 1982, p. 2).

To be supportive, parent education must be geared to the strengths, styles, and needs of individual families. While the term *family support* is recent, a longstanding tradition of home-based parent education (Gray & Wandersman, 1980) and parent discussion groups (Auerbach, 1968) has emphasized an individualized approach to building on family strengths. Parent education can positively affect the satisfaction and functioning of families by communicating knowledge about human development and relationships that increases their understanding, providing alternative models of parenting that widen their choices, teaching new skills, and facilitating access to community resources.

Parent education, however, has sometimes been accused of not being supportive of families. Parenting "cookbooks" and courses with "the answer" to every parenting dilemma may be detrimental to families if they find the approach difficult to tailor to their unique situations. Some programs have been accused of being insensitive to the strengths and values of minority families while attempting to impose middle-class values. Implemented in this way the expert-professional model can erode the confidence of parents, ignore their needs and strengths, and promote dependency (Fein, 1979). This chapter examines the implicit values of and the empirical data on parent education and suggests ways in which parent education can become more effective in strengthening and supporting families.

PREVELANCE OF PARENT EDUCATION

Parent education appears to be increasingly prevalent and accepted. Professionals argue that most parents need education about child development and parenting (Huntington, 1979; Lane, 1976), and parents tend to agree. For example, a Gallup poll of public school parents indicated that 78 percent thought it was a good idea to have school courses for parents "to help them help their children in school," and 52 percent were willing to pay additional taxes to support such a program (Schaefer, 1983). In a survey of adolescent mothers, three-quarters thought parent education would be very useful to them (Crockenberg, 1985). To meet this rising interest, childbirth and prenatal classes, parenting centers, and parent groups are springing up around the country (Mason, Jensen & Ryzewicz, 1979; *Programs to Strengthen Families*, 1983).

There is little information about the number or type of parents who are involved in parent education programs. One parent training program, Parent Effectiveness Training, reports that a quarter of a million parents have taken its course (Gordon, 1975). In contrast, federal education programs aimed at high-risk parents—such as Home Start, the Parent-Child Centers, and the Parent and Child Development Centers (PCDCs)—have involved fewer than 40,000 parents since their inception almost two decades ago (Fein, 1980).

Although there are few statistics, Harman and Brim used descriptive and other informal evidence to compile a profile of the type of parents involved in parent education.

> The prototypical parent education client emerges as a white, middle- or upper-middle-class mother with a relatively high level of formal education whose participation parallels the first years of her child's growth, lowers during her child's primary school years, and increases with the onset of the child's adolescence. The form of parent education most likely to appeal to this clientele is that manifest in various printed forms followed by attendance at lectures and consultation with professionals (particularly physicians) and last by organized programs of systematic instruction. Surrounding the main group are others, smaller in both size and proportion, consisting of high school pupils, pregnant teenagers and adolescent mothers, and mothers from disadvantaged backgrounds. (Harman & Brim, 1980, p. 107)

An inconsistent picture emerges in which parent surveys generally indicate a high level of interest in parent education but many programs have difficulty attracting parents and keeping them in the program (Gray & Wandersman, 1980). This raises major questions concerning what type of parents participate in what type of programs, why more parents do not participate, and how to make programs more responsive to parents' needs. The following section addresses these questions.

KEY ELEMENTS OF SUPPORTIVE PARENT EDUCATION

Across a broad range of types of programs and types of participants, programs that include parent education have shown small but important effects on parents and their children (Harman & Brim, 1980). Examples of short-term beneficial effects include greater maternal warmth and skill (Dokecki, Hargrove, & Sandler, 1983); more appropriate responsiveness of parents (Dickie & Gerber, 1980); fewer accidents and feeding problems for children and less paternal nonparticipation in child care (Larson, 1980); higher developmental status of the child who is the focus of the intervention (Beller, 1979) as well as of younger siblings (Gray,

Ramsey, & Klaus, 1982); and lower incidence of child abuse and neglect (Olds, 1985). Recently, evidence for long-term impact is emerging in follow-ups of high-risk samples. Examples of long-term effects of programs that include parent education are (1) reduced incidence of special education or grade retention for children (Lazar & Darlington, 1982); (2) reduced rate of later behavior problems (Johnson & Breckenridge, 1982); (3) higher educational achievement of parents and less welfare support (Naylor, 1982); and (4) lower subsequent birth rate of mother (Badger, 1981; Seitz, Rosenbaum, & Apfel, 1985).

In many of these programs, parent education is part of a comprehensive approach including such services as child care or health care, so that the effect of parent education cannot be isolated. Nevertheless, the positive effects across different types of programs and of parents suggest that parent education may play an important role in improving family functioning. The finding that very different programs can positively affect parent-child interaction and children's development suggests that the key to success lies less in specific curricula or structure than in the quality of the programs and the relationships they foster.

It would seem that a crucial effect of interventions is that

> the recipients come to believe that the service providers value them as people and consider their development and achievement as an important goal worth striving for. Perhaps of equal importance, the intervention helps parents to see that their own behaviors are important in influencing the course of their children's educational, social, and emotional development. (Rescorla & Zigler, 1981, p. 12)

By helping parents to believe that they are valued and able to affect their children's lives, parent education programs can potentially influence the lives of families long after the program ends.

The following strategies are proposed to increase the effectiveness of parent education by making it more supportive of families and more responsive to their needs. The list is meant to be not exhaustive but suggestive of promising directions for future programs. It also indicates areas in which our knowledge is incomplete, making further research a prerequisite to developing the most effective programs.

Designing Programs to Be Responsive to Family Needs

One reason that parent education may not have reached more parents is that educators have tried to develop a model program that would demonstrate long-term effectiveness and then could be widely implemented (for example, PCDCs: Dokecki et al., 1983). But families vary tremendously in their structures, values, needs, and resources. As Powell indicates in chapter 17 of this volume, individual differences can affect who participates in a parent education program, the ways they participate, and their perception of the program.

Prior to beginning programs, extensive measures of the strengths, needs, and attitudes of parents and their social networks are essential. More attention is needed to the influence on participation of elements of the family's ecology, including other family members, networks, neighborhoods, and cultural values. Knowing the characteristics of people who choose to attend particular types of programs versus those who do not can help in tailoring a program to those it attracts and developing other kinds of programs to reach those who want support but do not participate.

Research on social support suggests that parents may differ in their ability to seek and use different types of education and support and in the kinds of education and support they want from experts, peers, and family. Whether an individual seeks and uses support in a stressful period depends not just upon support availability but on the person's competence in eliciting help and on the coping strategies he or she has used in the past (Heller & Swindle, 1983). For example, middle-income fathers who attended parent groups initially reported better marital adjustment and fussier babies than fathers who did not attend, suggesting that they had both marital support for attending and a high need for information (Wandersman, 1982). In a higher risk sample, adolescent mothers who thought that parent education would not be useful to them had lower levels of perceived family support than those who thought it would be useful (Crockenberg, 1985). These examples suggest that the needs and social-support resources of parents influence their interest in parent education.

A certain level of personal resources (for example, confidence, social competence, social support) is likely to be necessary for people to participate in and benefit from parent education. Fein (1979), for example, found that parents and children with a large supporting family benefited most from parent education and that lonely, isolated people benefited least. A collaborative study of behavioral parent skills training programs in mental health clinics found that parents who are most likely to receive and persist with some forms of behavioral family intervention are those whose family composition (for example, two parent) and relatively high occupational prestige indicate competence in pursuits other than child rearing (Blechman, 1984). Blechman suggests that less competent parents who have inadequate problem-solving skills and high levels of stress may not respond well to parent education on child rearing. These families may require alternative approaches prior to parent education, such as school programs for the children and self-control, self-sufficiency, or marital problem-solving training for the parents.

Parent education programs interact with the existing informal network and may sometimes augment contacts and emotional support by working with the individual on effective ways to elicit and use support, by working with the network to provide support that is better suited to the individual's needs, or by adding similar others (for example, program participants) to the network (Gottlieb, 1981). However, parent education programs may also conflict with the existing network by increasing the participant's stress. For example, Olds (1985) suggests that home visits by nurses may have interfered with the fragile marital dynamics of teenage mothers and led to their showing more negative parenting behaviors than control mothers. In a more middle-income sample, McGuire and Gottlieb (1979) found that participants in postpartum support groups discussed child-rearing matters more frequently with members of their own networks, but that this was not accompanied by lower levels of reported stress or more positive ratings of their well-being. Gottlieb (1981) suggests caution in increasing contact when the informal social network is not equipped to offer support or recommends unproductive coping strategies.

One strategy for increasing the congruence between parent education programs and the social network is to involve family members, boyfriends, and other important friends directly. This approach may be especially important for groups such as adolescent mothers who are very dependent on their networks and express interest in having their families involved (Crockenberg, 1985). But in precisely the situation that *most* calls for the commitment of parents' friends and relatives—that is, when parents have low social support—it is likely to be most difficult to involve network members. And these are also the parents who tend to show lower levels of participation in parent education (Wandersman, in press). Innovative approaches to parent education that capitalize on needs expressed by parents *and* network members may be effective in reaching some of these parents. For example, parent education might be integrated with quality health care or day care (Provence & Naylor, 1983) or job training (Field, 1981). To encourage the participation of network members, a program for teenage mothers might provide child care in order to spell the grandmother—often the primary caregiver—so that she can attend group meetings.

By involving parents in specifying their needs, programs can become more congruent with the goals of participants. While the community development movement has advocated matching programs to participants' needs since the 1950s, the efficacy of the matching approach has never been evaluated (Harman & Brim, 1980).

Rather than assume that families need a particular type of parent education or support, programs should assess what kinds of education and support parents need, from which sources, when, and with what effect on their satisfaction and adjustment. For instance, Powell (1983) found that patterns of participation in neighborhood parent discussion groups varied with parents' needs and resources. Parents with high levels of stress and economic hardship tended to use professional staff services more, whereas parents with more supportive social networks tended to interact more with other parents in the program.

The finding that effectiveness is not related to many parent education variables (for example, age of the child, curriculum content, curriculum type, degree of detail in instruction, and professional/paraprofessional education) (Florin & Dokecki, 1983) may indicate that different types of programs have different effects for different parents at different stages of the life cycle. Some parents might benefit more from a structured behavioral curriculum, others from a less structured discussion curriculum. When all parents are lumped together for evaluation purposes, these variables may not show effects. While the quality of the relationship between educator and parent may be the critical element across programs and parents, the role of specific program variables needs to be evaluated in relation to individual differences among parents.

Many recent parent education and support programs offer a tempting array of services including workshops, support groups, children's programs, counseling, libraries, equipment exchanges, babysitting pools, telephone warm-lines, and drop-in centers (*Programs to Strengthen Families*, 1983). The programs allow parents to choose the aspects of parent education best suited to their needs at a particular period. However, some parents under stress may feel overwhelmed by the range of choice offered by multifaceted programs. Evaluations of some parent education programs emphasize the significance of the participant's relationship with a few caring people who focus on the individual and provide continuous, individualized education and support as well as coordinating other services (Bromwich, 1981; Provence & Naylor, 1983). A single liaison person who reaches out to parents and serves as a bridge to other services may increase the effectiveness of this menu approach for parents who are not reached by these programs.

It is important to devise strategies to match parent education programs to family strengths and needs. Typologies of parent education might be developed to aid liaison parent educators trained to coordinate parents and programs. Matching might involve the following considerations, among others: parents with fewer personal resources (for example, lacking transportation, social skills) might prefer and benefit more from a more individualized, home-based approach, whereas more socially oriented parents (for example, adolescents) might prefer peer discussion groups. For parents of infants, a home-based approach may be more effective, while later a combination of toddler play group and group discussion might be useful. Groups of parents with special needs are more feasible in large cities than in rural areas, where pairing with an experienced parent might be more practical.

Such matching would have to be an ongoing process. Education and support needs can change even during the span of participation in a program (Powell & Eisenstadt, 1985). For example, Haffey and Levant (1984) suggest that low-income parents may be more responsive initially to parent education that focuses on their interest in learning skills to increase their children's obedience. Once this concern is met, they may become more interested in learning ways to improve communication.

Essentially, I am suggesting that parent education programs move from standardized, unidirectional structures to more flexible, collaborative processes. Programs might experiment with developing collaborative models in which parents consult with parent educators to evaluate the parents' needs and resources, to match them with the needed services, and to evaluate their progress toward their goals.

An integrated, flexible approach makes it impossible to determine which aspects of a program are critical for success. But the effort to do so may be as fruitless and as pointless as attempting to determine whether parents need to provide food, love, and limits for their children to develop competency (Seitz et al., 1985). Each aspect influences the others, and children and programs need a balance of all. To help parents with the critical job of parenting, programs need to have a multidisciplinary approach.

Collaborating with Parents

The goals of parent education programs are often vague, ambitious, and general; for example, "to strengthen families and prevent child abuse and juvenile delinquency" (*Programs to Strengthen Families*, 1983, p. 78) or "to promote the optimal development of children during the first three years of life by enhancing parental confidence" (ibid., p. 82). Stating explicit goals for parent education is difficult since there is little information about what constitutes good parenting, and definitions are based primarily on values and assumptions.

Some parent educators try to avoid the value issues by claiming to base their programs on research knowledge. Although communicating research evidence is clearly an advance over relying solely on instinct or personal preference, there are several reasons to be cautious. Clarke-Stewart summarizes the major lines of research that have been used as a basis for parent education programs and concludes that the evidence for making recommendations is shaky:

> All [lines of research on which parent education is based] point in the same direction: the environment, particularly parental behavior, does seem to have an effect on development throughout childhood (not just early childhood), and the kind of parental behavior that is most predictive of good child development outcomes is stimulating, consistent, moderate, and responsive. But this evidence is not incontrovertible. Each line of research has serious limitations. (Clarke-Stewart, 1981, pp. 52–53)

Extreme care is needed before leaping from research based on small samples and flawed designs to general principles for all families. The dangers of overgeneralizing from research are greatest when recommendations for one group are based on research with members of another race, ethnic group, income group, age, sex, or family structure (Laosa, 1983). For example, Field (1981) cautions against using infant-stimulation programs designed for high-risk babies of teenage mothers to accelerate the development of babies who are developing adequately.

Instead of avoiding values in stating goals, it may be advantageous to make them explicit. Harman and Brim advocate using parent education to help parents examine, select, and reach their own child-rearing goals.

> An acceptable statement of aims of many programs is to increase parent competence and rationality in role performance through making parents better able both to select their own values for the child and to achieve these through child-rearing practices. In part, this position suggests that parent education should support and encourage as much variability in the aims of parents as parent educators urge parents to give their children. Of course, this position is not value-free. Its ramifications are that resulting programs select approaches on the democratic end of the presentation continuum and allow participants the maximum possibility for raising, airing, and examining their own values. (Harman & Brim, 1980, p. 78)

Even when diversity is encouraged, value conflicts are likely. For example, in the author's program with adolescent mothers, an early issue in training was how home visitors could work with parents who had an opposing view on spanking infants. Brim's suggestions for handling value conflicts remain useful:

> The objective is to achieve an educational program which speaks with moral conviction on some matters and assists the parent toward his own ends in others. The educator must know and state his own values, work with parents to do the same with theirs, assist in the achievement of those which are agreed upon, seek democratically to win the parent to his point of view, where they disagree, by rational persuasion, and finally, withdraw and refuse to help where the parent insists on the pursuit of goals which the educator believes to be evil. (Brim, 1959, p. 90)

Thus the goals of the program are likely to vary with the needs, strengths, and values of the participants. One way to avoid giving advice based on inadequate research or conflicting values is to teach parents skills to facilitate their own goals. It may be possible to help parents articulate and pursue short- and long-term goals based on an integrated view of human development and on their own needs and resources.

Helping parents achieve their goals might follow a pattern similar to Mahoney's SCIENCE (Mahoney, 1977) approach to teaching coping skills. Adapting this approach, the parent educator would be a coach who encourages the parent to try different behaviors and evaluate their effectiveness. SCIENCE involves several steps: s:specify general area (for example, decrease baby's crying); c:collect data (note the circumstances when baby cries the most and least); i:identify patterns or sources (see if baby cries less when held); e:examine options (figure out ways for baby to be close or for others to hold him or her); n:narrow and experiment (try out acceptable options); c:compare data (see which ways get best results for parent and child); e:extend, revise, or replace.

Although this approach appears to be quite abstract and complicated, elements of this type of cognitive-behavioral parent training have been used successfully with a variety of clinical and volunteer populations (Dangel & Polster, 1984). The advantage is that the parents are actively involved in learning new skills that are consistent with their own goals, needs, styles, and resources and that can be generalized to new situations. A possible risk in this approach is focusing on short-term problem behaviors and losing sight of long-term developmental issues. To avoid a short-sighted approach, it is important to integrate parenting skills into the larger view of goals and values concerning human development.

Emphasizing the Parent-Staff Relationship

Reviews of parent education research generally indicate that the duration of a program influences its effectiveness (Florin & Dokecki, 1983; Harman & Brim, 1980). One reason for this may be that it takes time to build a relationship of trust between parents and staff and to tailor program content to the pace and the needs of the parents. Time is also essential for helping parents generalize what they have learned to new situations.

Parent educators sometimes forget that learning is an active process of assimilation and accommodation and that they do not simply pour information into a void. Parents sort, fit, and modify new information according to their assumptions, values, and level of reasoning about the parent-child relationship (Newberger & Cook, 1983). For example, parents who see their role as organized around their own needs may be uninterested in information about the child's needs. Levels of parental awareness may be deeply ingrained, not controlled by conscious choice, and sustained by longstanding patterns of interaction (Harman & Brim,

1980). They may be difficult to change—even by direct intervention (Sandy, 1983). From this perspective, parent education is not a unidirectional transfer of facts from expert to parent but a mutual interaction process in which, ideally, education starts at the parents' level and educators and parents come to understand and enrich each other's perceptions over a period of time.

This kind of mutual interaction requires considerable skill, warmth, patience, and perceptiveness from parent educators. Parent educators generally agree about the importance of the personal qualities of the staff, and some attention has been paid to their training (Harman & Brim, 1980; Provence & Naylor, 1983). In most programs, staff, recruited for their warmth and personal skills, create the magic that leads to effective relationships and quality parent education. Nevertheless, little is known about how staff qualities influence program effectiveness. How are parents' perceptions of the program and its impact affected by variations in the styles of discussion group leaders or home visitors? in the participants' enthusiasm, needs, or strengths? in the content of questions, answers, and topics? For example, McGuire and Gottlieb (1979) reported increases in perceived social support for participants in a parent discussion group led by one doctor, but not in a group led by a different doctor. We do not know, however, how the groups differed in leader characteristics, participants' characteristics, or the content of instruction. An observational study by Powell and Eisenstadt (1985) of interaction in discussion groups found that the actual level of leader domination diverged from the planned democratic role of the leader.

Empirical studies have not shown differential effectiveness for paraprofessional and professional parent educators (Florin & Dokecki, 1983). Personal characteristics of warmth, flexibility, organization, and commitment may be more important than background or professional training. The ability of the educator to act as an appropriate model is also likely to be important. More research is needed to understand how the characteristics of educators and participants interact and how this relationship can help the parent to grow.

Coordinating Services and Advocating

Many families have very real needs—for money, food, job training, housing, child care—which cannot be met by parent education. In fact, their needs may be more acute if parent education programs encourage families under stress to take control when few resources are available to them (Schlossman, 1978). For example, in my own program in a rural area with few day-care facilities and few jobs, encouraging teenage mothers to return to school could put additional stress on the already overburdened grandmother and increase the teenager's sense of hopelessness. Fein (1979) cautions against using parent education and support to increase the family's burdens.

> We react with panic as divorce rates increase and as mothers in growing numbers join the work force. In panic we cry, "support the family" and then create social programs such as home-based education to provide this support. The problem is this: if the abandonment of public institutions places an excessive burden on the family, our good intentions to support the family may, in fact, increase the burdens placed upon it. Perhaps we need to encourage the involvement of parent and child with public institutions rather than their involvement with one another. (Fein, 1979, p. 2)

Some programs (for example, PCDCs) have dealt with these critical needs by building coordinated services into their programs such as health care, day care, and job training. As funding for comprehensive programs has decreased, some communities have formed coalitions to coordinate services. For example, in Ohio, 170 programs banded together to form United Services for Effective Parenting (USEP) to generate public support and local funding, to involve existing resources, to expand promising new programs, and to refer parents to appropriate programs (Badger & Burns, 1980).

Another approach often taken by parent educators is to become community advocates for basic resources and to empower parents to advocate for their own needs. For example, the finding that children who had been in early intervention programs were less likely to be retained in grade or to require special education has been attributed in part to their parents' greater confidence and activity in working with the educational system (Lazar & Darlingon, 1982; Seitz et al., 1985).

Another potentially effective strategy for coordinating services and empowering parents is to build parent education into existing services and environments. Child development information, peer interaction, and referral can be incorporated into many community settings, churches, hospitals, and health departments. Parent education need not be isolated in a few intensive programs but could be part of the training, philosophy, and approach of all who work with families (Schaefer, 1983).

Grotberg provides a synthesis of ideas on how programs may educate and empower families in suggesting the following policy guides:

> Each program affecting parents and children, whether child care, education, health, nutrition, or social services, must empower parents to participate in decision-making and in developing and carrying out the program.

> Each program which is intended to affect the lives of children must have a parent education component so that parents might develop skills, acquire information, and become knowledgeable about parenting. The parent educa-

tion component should be linked to informal networks (such as mutual support or self-help groups) and to the formal program structure.

Each program which is intended to serve the needs of family members must demonstrate the ways in which the program will provide support to the entire family, preserve its integrity, and respect its uniqueness. Programs emphasizing prevention of family break-up must clarify the elements of the program that are preventive. (Grotberg, 1983, p. 329)

The different approaches to coordinating services and empowering parents emphasize the need for parent education to be integrated within the community. Rather than attempt to develop a single effective model of parent education, it may be more productive to find ways for parent education programs to become more responsive to the social context.

DEVELOPING REALISTIC EXPECTATIONS FOR PARENT EDUCATION

Although a variety of parent education programs have shown positive effects on parents and their children, the results have been smaller than originally expected, and parent education has not had as great an impact on societal problems as was hoped. After reviewing the parent education research from public-policy criteria of effectiveness, Haskins and Adams reach a conservative verdict: "Defining the societal problem as one of inadequate child development and conceptualizing parent programs as a method of attacking this problem, we have not found empirical evidence to strongly support the efficacy of the approach. The strongest conclusion that seems permitted by the evidence is that parent programs are moderately effective in solving the problem" (Haskins & Adams, 1983, p. 368). Perhaps moderate effectiveness is enough to expect of parent education. Initial hopes that it could be a panacea for all society's problems were too high and bound to lead to disappointment. Parent education and support programs should not become a substitute for other resources that parents need (Weiss, 1983).

Parenting *is* a stressful and complex job, and parents generally report feeling more confident as a result of being in parent education programs (Wandersman, 1982). But parenting behavior and attitudes are deeply ingrained and difficult to change (Harman & Brim, 1980). Often the immediate impact of parent education is intangible and difficult to quantify—feeling that being a parent is important, feeling more confident and less anxious, enjoying parenting more. While these gains in satisfaction with parenting may not lead to a sharp rise in children's IQ or even in parents' skills, they can have a substantial and lasting impact on the family environment and children's development. Unfortunately, parent education programs do not usually measure these subjective variables. When subjective measures are assessed, they are often discounted by hard-nosed critics as not behavioral, objective, or significant.

We know little about the long-term effects that these changes in satisfaction and confidence might have. Yet there is some beginning evidence that comprehensive programs that *include* parent education can be cost effective in reducing the need for remedial services for high-risk families (Lazar & Darlington, 1982; Naylor, 1982). These results are exciting but may not be replicated by less intensive programs with less high-risk samples.

Ultimately, the final evaluation of the efficacy of parent education programs involves subjective values about the importance of parenting. Endorsement of the need for parent education would require a national shift in thinking from the current state of "valuing the atomistic individual and family to valuing the individual and family within community, and from valuing a society based on economics to valuing a society based on human development" (Dokecki & Moroney, 1983, p. 48). And while some parent education programs, as we have indicated, may demonstrate cost-effective benefits, other programs may not. Can we justify parent education on the ground that most participants feel it improves their quality of life? We do not base the decision to teach algebra on its effects on the students' lives (or their children's lives) ten years hence but on its inherent value. We need to develop realistic expectations of what parent education can accomplish based on empirical research on objective and subjective effects.

Parent education is not without risks and costs. It costs participants and taxpayers money and uses professional resources and participants' time. A poorly designed program can offer inappropriate advice or undermine parents' values, confidence, and relationships with their network. The risks are substantial and essential to consider.

Nevertheless, when parent education is carefully designed to be supportive to families, it has much potential. This chapter has suggested some strategies for increasing the effectiveness of parent education programs. These suggested future directions would further move parent education from a unidirectional expert model in which professionals teach to a collaborative model in which "families define their own needs and play an active role in a process of self-development" (Florin & Dokecki, 1983, p. 58). Perhaps the time has come to realize that families are our nation's most valuable natural resource and that we need to develop strategies to conserve and nurture the family environment of our future generation.

REFERENCES

Auerbach, A. B. (1968). *Parents learn through discussion: Principles and practices of parent group education.* New York: Wiley.

Badger, E. (1981). Effects of parent education program on teenage mothers and their offspring. In K. G. Scott, T. Field, & E. Robertson, (Eds.), *Teenage parents and their offspring* (pp. 283–310). New York: Grune & Stratton.

Badger, E., & Burns, D. (1980, September). Promoting infant development: A coalition model for community service delivery. Paper presented at the Annual Meeting of the American Psychological Association, Montreal.

Beller, E. K. (1979). Early intervention programs. In J. D. Osofsky (Ed.), *Handbook of infant development* (pp. 852–894). New York: Wiley.

Blechman, E. A. (1984). Competent parents, competent children: Behavioral objectives of parent training. In R. E. Dangel & R. A. Polster (Eds.), *Parent training* (pp. 34–63). New York: Guilford Press.

Brim, O. G. (1959). *Education for child rearing.* New York: Free Press.

Bromwich, R. (1981). *Working with parents and infants.* Baltimore, MD: University Park Press.

Bronfenbrenner, U. (1974). *Is early intervention effective?* (Publication No. OHD 74–25). Washington, DC: Department of Health, Education and Welfare.

Clarke-Stewart, K. A. (1981). Parent education in the 1970s. *Educational Evaluation and Policy Analysis, 3* (6), 47–58.

Clarke-Stewart, K. A. (1983). Exploring the assumptions of parent education. In R. Haskins & D. Adams (Eds.), *Parent education and public policy* (pp. 257–276). Norwood, NJ: Ablex.

Crockenberg, S. (1985). Professional support for adolescent mothers: Who gives it, how mothers evaluate it, what they would prefer. Paper presented at the Society for Research in Child Development, Toronto.

Dangel, R. E., & Polster, R. A. (Eds.). (1984). *Parent training.* New York: Guilford Press.

Dickie, J. R., & Gerber, S. C. (1980). Training in social competence: The effect on mothers, fathers, and infants. *Child Development, 51,* 1248–1251.

Dokecki, P. R., Hargrove, E. C., & Sandler, H. M. (1983). An overview of the Parent Child Development Center social experiment. In R. Haskins & D. Adams (Eds.), *Parent education and public policy* (pp. 80–109). Norwood, NJ: Ablex.

Dokecki, P. R., & Moroney, R. M. (1983). To strengthen all families: A human development and community value framework. In R. Haskins & D. Adams (Eds.), *Parent education and public policy* (pp. 40–64). Norwood, NJ: Ablex.

Family Resource Coalition (1982, Fall). *Statement of Philosophy, Goals and Structure.* Chicago: Family Resource Coalition.

Fein, G. (1979, April). Socio-cultural issues: Privacy, needs, and benevolence. Paper presented at the Biennial Meeting of the Society for Research in Child Development, San Francisco.

Fein, G. (1980). The game of social criticism. *Merrill-Palmer Quarterly, 26* (4), 429–439.

Field, T. M. (1981). Intervention for high-risk infants and their parents. *Educational Evaluation and Policy Analysis, 3* (6), 69–78.

Florin, P. R., & Dokecki, P. R. (1983). Changing families through parent and family education: Review and analysis. In I. Sigel & L. Laosa (Eds.), *Changing families* (pp. 23–65). New York: Plenum Press.

Gordon, T. (1975). *Parent effectiveness training.* New York: New American Library.

Gottlieb, B. (1981). Preventive interventions involving social networks and social support. In B. Gottlieb (Ed.), *Social networks and social support* (pp. 201–232). Beverly Hills. CA: Sage.

Gray, S., Ramsey, B., & Klaus, R. (1982). *From 3 to 20—The early training project.* Baltimore, MD: University Park Press.

Gray, S., & Wandersman, L. P. (1980). The methodology of home-based intervention studies: Problems and promising strategies. *Child Development, 51,* 993–1009.

Grotberg, E. (1983). Integration of parent education into human service programs. In R. Haskins & D. Adams (Eds.), *Parent education and public policy* (pp. 324–330). Norwood, NJ: Ablex.

Haffey, N. A., & Levant, R. F. (1984). The differential effectiveness of two models of skills training for working class parents. *Family Relations, 33* (2), 209–216.

Hammer, T. J., & Turner, P. H. (1985). *Parenting in contemporary society.* Englewood, NJ: Prentice-Hall.

Harman, D., & Brim, O. G., Jr. (1980). *Learning to be parents: Principles, programs and methods.* Beverly Hills, CA: Sage.

Haskins, R., & Adams, D. (1983). Parent education and public policy: Synthesis and recommendations. In R. Haskins & D. Adams (Eds.), *Parent education and public policy* (pp. 346–373). Norwood, NJ: Ablex.

Heller, K., & Swindle, R. W. (1983). Social networks, perceived social support and coping with stress. In R. D. Fellner, L. A. Jason, J. Moritsugu, & S. S. Farber (Eds.), *Preventive psychology: Theory, research and practice in community intervention* (pp. 87–103). Elmsford, NY: Pergamon Press.

Huntington, D. S. (1979). Supportive programs for infants and parents. In J. D. Osofsky (Ed.), *Handbook of infant development* (pp. 837–851). New York: Wiley.

Johnson, D. L., & Breckenridge, J. H. (1982). The Houston Parent-Child Development Center and the primary prevention of behavior problems in young children. *American Journal of Community Psychology, 10,* 305–316.

Lane, M. B. (1976). *Education for parenting.* Washington, DC: National Education Association of Young Children.

Laosa, L. M. (1983). Parent education, cultural pluralism, and public policy: The uncertain connection. In R. Haskins & D. Adams (Eds.), *Parent education and public policy* (pp. 331–341). Norwood, NJ: Ablex.

Larson, C. P. (1980). Efficacy of prenatal and postpartum home visits on child health and development. *Pediatrics, 66,* 191–197.

Lazar, I., & Darlington, R. (1982). Lasting effects of early education: A report from the Consortium for Longitudinal Studies. *Monographs of the Society for Research in Child Development, 47* (2–3), No. 195.

Love, J. M., Nauta, M. J., Coelen, C. G., Hewett, K., & Ruopp, R. R. (1976). *National Home Start evaluation: Final report, findings and implications*. Ypsilanti, MI: High Scope Educational Research Foundation.

Mahoney, M. J. (1977). Personal science: A cognitive learning therapy. In A. Ellis & R. Grieger (Eds.), *Handbook of rational-emotive therapy* (pp. 352–366). New York: Springer-Verlag.

Mason, D., Jensen, G., & Ryzewicz, C. (1979). *How to grow a parents' group*. Milwaukee, WI: International Childbirth Education Association (P.O. Box 20852).

McGuire, J. C., & Gottlieb, B. H. (1979). Social support groups among new parents: An experimental study in primary prevention. *Journal of Clinical Child Psychology, 8*, 111–115.

Mundel, D. S. (1983). The apparent lack of connection between congressional concerns and those of parent program proponents. In R. Haskins & D. Adams (Eds.), *Parent education and public policy* (pp. 65–69). Norwood, NJ: Ablex.

Naylor, A. (1982). Child day care: Threat to family life or primary prevention? *Journal of Preventive Psychiatry, 1* (4), 431–441.

Newberger, C. M., & Cook, S. J. (1983, April). *The study of cognition in parenthood: The parental awareness measure*. Paper presented at the Society for Research in Child Development, Detroit.

Olds, D. (1985). Professional support for adolescent mothers: Effectiveness varies with risk. Paper presented at the Society for Research in Child Development, Toronto.

Powell, D. R. (1983). Individual differences in participation in a parent-child support program. In I. Sigel & L. Laosa (Eds.), *Changing families* (pp. 203–224). New York: Plenum Press.

Powell, D. R., & Eisenstadt, J. (1985). Life in parent discussion groups: An observational study. Paper presented at the Society for Research in Child Development, Toronto.

Programs to Strengthen Families: A resource guide. (1983). New Haven, CT: Yale University Bush Center in Child Development and Social Policy (available from The Family Resource Coalition, 230 North Michigan Ave., Suite 1625, Chicago, IL 60601).

Provence, S., & Naylor, A. (1983). *Working with disadvantaged parents and their children*. New Haven: Yale University Press.

Rescorla, L. A., & Zigler, E. (1981). The Yale Child Welfare Research Program: Implications for social policy. *Educational Evaluation and Policy Analysis, 3*, 5–14.

Sandy, L. R. (1983, April). Parent intervention and the development of parental awareness. Paper presented at the Society for Research in Child Development, Detroit.

Schaefer, E. S. (1983). Parent-professional interaction: Research, parental, professional, and policy perspectives. In R. Haskins & D. Adams (Eds.), *Parent education and public policy* (pp. 283–303). Norwood, NJ: Ablex.

Schlossman, S. L. (1978). The parent education game: The politics of child psychology in the 1970s. *Teacher's College Record, 79* (4), 788–808.

Schlossman, S. L. (1983). The formative era in American parent education: Overview and interpretation. In R. Haskins & D. Adams (Eds.), *Parent education and public policy* (pp. 7–39). Norwood, NJ: Ablex.

Seitz, V., Rosenbaum, L. K., & Apfel, N. H. (1985). Effects of family support intervention: A ten-year follow-up. *Child Development, 56* (2), 376–394.

Sparling, J., & Lowman, B. (1983). Parent information needs as revealed through interests, problems, attitudes, and preferences. In R. Haskins & D. Adams (Eds.), *Parent education and public policy* (pp. 304–323). Norwood, NJ: Ablex.

Wandersman, L. P. (1982). An analysis of the effectiveness of parent-infant support groups. *Journal of Primary Prevention, 3,* 99–115.

Wandersman, L. P. (in press). Parent-infant support groups: Matching programs to needs and strengths of families. In Z. F. Boukydis (Ed.), *Research on support for parents in the postnatal period.* Norwood, NJ: Ablex.

Weiss, H. (1983). Yale Bush Conference highlights—Family support programs: The state of the art. *The Networker* (Newsletter of the Bush Programs in Child Development and Social Policy), *4* (4), 4–6.

12 PARENT-TO-PARENT SUPPORT GROUPS: ADVOCATES FOR SOCIAL CHANGE

Peggy Pizzo

An ever-widening grassroots movement of parent-initiated organizations is afoot in America. Whatever their particular pursuits, these organizations share a common belief that in mutual support and action, parents can effectively confront and reduce feelings of helplessness and isolation to better protect and nurture their children.

Parents turn their powerful protective energies outward for two reasons. First, when it takes more than private efforts to stave off harm from children or to acquire the resources basic to a child's fair chance at life, the passionate commitment of the parent-child bond propels parents outward into connection with others. Second, the help available to deal with sometimes excruciating parent stress is often *un*helpful or just not helpful enough.

Three underlying objectives characterize the parent self-help movement: mutual support among parents; work for professional and institutional change; and enactment/enforcement of new or improved laws.[1] This chapter examines these objectives within the context of the cultural and historical origins of this movement and the accomplishments of parent-to-parent groups. Finally, it offers some recommendations for parent, professional, and policymaker adaptations requisite to a fuller realization of the promise of successful parent advocacy for social change.

In the past two decades, parents have founded support groups centering on concerns ranging from childbirth to child abuse, from single parenting to drunk driving. Schools, hospitals, adoption agencies—all our most cherished institutions for helping children—have felt the

heat (and sometimes the sting) of parent advocacy for social change.
The growth of these groups has been remarkable. To cite just a few
examples:

- The Mother's Center originated in suburban Long Island in 1975,
  when a group of new mothers came together to share their experiences around childbirth. By 1982, other Mothers' Centers, modeled
  on the original Long Island group, were being established in places as
  far away as Missouri, Georgia, and Florida.
- In New York City, in the early 1980s the Sisterhood of Black Single
  Mothers spread itself out over the city's five boroughs from its storefront in Bedford-Stuyvesant, creating a network of empathetic telephone accessibility and mutual support.
- In Washington, D.C., the National Coalition of Title I Parents, whose
  children are eligible for federal funds for educationally disadvantaged
  children, reaches out with information and support to thousands of
  low-income parents in central cities, backwoods and barrios across the
  country.
- Another self-help and advocacy group, the National Society for Autistic Children, is now headquartered in Washington, D.C., after organizing and winning many legislative battles from the kitchens and living
  rooms of its members. For years parents of autistic children were
  blamed for their children's strange, sometimes self-destructive behavior; prolonged parental and child therapy was offered as the only cure.
  In the late 1960s, a handful of parents put together a national organization and helped to blaze new paths of understanding about autism.
- Also in the nation's capital, the North American Council on Adoptable
  Children (NACAC) encourages its several hundred member organizations to develop parent-to-parent support and counseling for adoptive
  parents and to work for laws to assure permanent homes for the hundreds of thousands of children needlessly growing up in institutions or
  foster homes. NACAC is widely respected for its participation in the
  successful passage of the Opportunities for Adoption Act and the
  Adoption Assistance and Child Welfare Reform Act, recent national
  laws that help homeless children.
- Just across the District of Columbia border, in Silver Spring, Maryland, is the headquarters of the National Federation of Parents for
  Drug Free Youth (NFP), a nationwide federation of local groups established in 1980 to use parent peer pressure to *prevent* drug use by children. In 1982, representatives of over 2,000 groups met at the White
  House to discuss the parent movement for prevention of drug use.
  By 1985, the membership had grown to almost 9,000 groups. NFP
  strongly encourages parent-to-parent support both to prevent and
  free teenagers from drug addiction.

- Another parent-initiated organization, Parents without Partners (PWP), is based in nearby Bethesda, Maryland. From 25 people in 1957, PWP grew in two decades to 150,000 members with chapters in every state of the union and in Canada. Parents without Partners offers support groups for single parents as well as planned social events that help leaven the serious (and isolating) child-rearing responsibilities of divorced or widowed parents. PWP also supports policy changes to secure better day care and child support and improved protection against child abduction by noncustodial parents.
- Finally, a city with the peaceful name of Fair Oaks, California, is the place of origin for a mothers' movement whose initials spell MADD. These are mothers with good cause for anger: their children have been killed or crippled by drunk drivers. So Mothers Against Drunk Drivers—founded in 1980 by a mother whose thirteen-year-old daughter was hit and killed while walking to church—counsels other stricken parents, refers them to bereavement groups, and crusades for stiffer federal and state legislation against intoxicated drivers. Between 1980 and 1982, MADD inspired the passage of major federal legislation by Congress and legislative and enforcement changes by nearly half the nation's states.

There are hundreds of other groups, not mentioned above, criss-crossing the country. Local parent action groups have sprung up around many school systems; in several states divorced fathers are coming together to help one another and to argue for changes in child custody laws; and all over the country, parents whose children's mental, emotional, or physical health has been impaired in some way keep a watchful eye on special education, on both private and public residential institutions, and on the health care system (Pizzo, 1983).

To understand the subject of informal support among parents, it is important to understand the powerful feelings that propel parents toward participation in a mutual support group. One member of a support group for parents worried about abusing their children describes how she felt:

> I had created in my mind a very detailed picture of the ideal mother *I* would be and the ideal child my *baby* would be. The day the baby came into our home I wanted out! I didn't know what to do when he cried. Nothing I did pleased him. I started to panic. (He was not at all the bubbling, bouncing, Gerber baby I'd planned on.)
>
> I felt enclosed and alone in this panic. . . . I recall how desperately I needed someone to show me that I was not alone. That there were several solutions to my problems. . . . If it's possible for me to reach one person who feels as alone as I did, who wants help as much as I did, I want them to know we are here. (Anonymous, 1975)

Profound emotions like these are the basis of many mutual support groups among parents. Consider how this parent, a literary historian from DeKalb County, Georgia, describes her community's discovery of drug use by its adolescent children:

> We had to learn the hard way—through the shocked discovery that our own child or a friend's child or a neighbor's child was using drugs. . . . For most parents, regardless of their sophistication about drugs or their political liberalism or conservatism, such a discovery comes like a sudden kick in the stomach. It's a sickening feeling—compounded of a protective fear for their children, of a bewildered fear of an alien drug culture, and of a sorrowful fear about their own apparent helplessness and loss of control. (Schuchard, 1978)

Today millions of parents either undergo forceful experiences like these or fear that they might. Not every parent, of course, chooses advocacy and mutual help. But for those who do, self-help groups that produce social change are kindling widespread enthusiasm and hope throughout the United States (Pizzo, 1983).

THE SHARED EXPERIENCE: UNIVERSAL
GENESIS OF SELF-HELP ORGANIZATIONS

Self-help—the popular name for what is actually *mutual* provision of support, guidance, and practical services—is a burgeoning American movement. The National Self-Help Clearinghouse estimated in 1981 that there were 500,000 self-help groups in the United States, reaching 10 to 15 million members. Many of us associate self-help groups only with disability, illness, or chronic problems—for example, Alcoholics Anonymous, Make Today Count (cancer), and Overeaters Anonymous. Or we think of mutual support groups only as a response to a sudden crisis shared by the group's participants. But there are hundreds (and perhaps thousands) of distinct experiences that motivate self-help groups.

One of the characteristics of any self-help group is a unifying shared experience (Pizzo, 1983), be it difficulties with obesity, alcohol, or smoking; harsh life in an impoverished urban neighborhood; or the death of a loved one. This experience attracts members to the group and braces their common belief that the individuals within the self-help group can help one another in ways in which most "outsiders" cannot, since they have not participated in the shared experience. Group members shift their images of themselves from resourceless victims to stressed but resourceful people able to offer and use one another's strengths to build confidence and competence.

To a large degree, members of very different self-help groups have all shared a deeper, unifying experience: impairment of their sense of self-worth. Disability, injuries, illnesses, stressful life transitions—these experiences sometimes threaten an established, reassuring sense of self. A large part of the value of mutual help lies in revealing to participants that their diminished sense of self-worth is shared by others. With this discovery, members of self-help groups can combat the feelings of shame that isolate stressed individuals from one another and quench their resolve to respond to stressful social conditions with advocacy for social change. Further, the very activities of mutual support organizations reinforce the bonds of the group by establishing another, special shared experience—that of conscious (and often successful) endeavor to help one another.

CULTURAL ORIGINS OF PARENT SUPPORT GROUPS

In this post-Freudian era we know of the influence that family environment has on self-image, but we are less aware of the cultural images—that is, societal conceptions about a group, used to describe or suggest characteristics of that group, in language or literature. Cultural images influence, and sometimes warp, developing self-images. Over the past two decades scholars have begun to analyze the power that negative cultural images exert on the self-images of minorities and women. Similarly, negative cultural images can powerfully distort how parents think of themselves.

Since self-image is a source of psychic energy for human caring, self-help and advocacy groups often concentrate on helping parents reshape or develop a positive view of themselves. Fundamental and sometimes unconscious negative beliefs about the relationship between parents and experts often emerge in the language and writing of policymakers, professionals, and scholars who concern themselves with children and families. In particular, three images—the Incompetent Parent, the Victimized Parent, and the Resourceful Parent—reflect sentiments that guide the assumptions upon which services to children have been and continue to be built (Pizzo, 1983). These images reveal conscious and unconscious beliefs and attitudes that have influenced the perspectives that professionals are taught to have about parents. Parent groups are particularly concerned with reversing the belittling impact of negative cultural images so as to restore and strengthen feelings of self-worth, optimism, and the courage to initiate improvements in conditions.

The image of the Incompetent Parent portrays a person who is incapable of meeting essential needs of child rearing. In this imagery, moral defects, ignorance, emotional inadequacies, and deficient skills cause incompetence. Parental incompetence in turn causes misfortune and harm to children or blocks some basic right of the child, such as the right to equal opportunity. Typically, the Incompetent Parent image appears in discussions about why professionals, programs, public and private services, and government in general should do more to help children.

The victimized parent image portrays a person who is well-meaning but swamped by events he or she is unable to influence or control. Parents fail to raise children well because external pressures prevent them from doing so, not because of personal incapacity, immorality, or character defects. Traditionally, the Victimized Parent is seen as a sympathetic figure, struggling with oppressive economic and social conditions that thwart good child development—conditions that can be countered only by professionals, programs, and government. More recently, however, in scholarly works, legislative testimony, public statements, and advocacy brochures, parents are described as victims of the very forces that are supposed to aid them: professionals, experts, helping institutions, and government.

Parent support groups have constructed a third image: the Resourceful Parent. The Resourceful Parent is first of all a decision-maker who works hard to discover what resources are available for rearing children well even in the face of strong negative social forces. When options for children are sparse, the Resourceful Parent generates new choices by collaborating with other parents to establish halfway houses, peer counseling, support groups, and preschool programs. Parents also generate alternatives through advocacy for institutional change or for a law that provides fairer, more effective services and protections for children. Resourceful Parents want help that is more accessible, more responsive, and more humane.

The most central shared characteristic of the Incompetent Parent image and the Victimized Parent image is passivity. In contrast, Resourceful Parents are contributors to public policy, not just recipients; they are partners of professionals in the delivery of public services to children; they are mediators, protective buffers between vulnerable children and powerful institutions; and they are the final arbiters (or at least the party with the most rights to that position) of all decisions about the child.

HISTORY OF PARENT SUPPORT GROUPS

Parent self-help and advocacy groups, a remarkable and little-reported phenomenon in today's society, were active in nineteenth-century America. When black children were barred from public education, parents established mutual-aid societies and financed their own schools, despite severe economic hardships. In 1807, for example, the first school for the education of blacks in the District of Columbia was founded by three illiterate ex-slaves, who built the school with their own hands. By 1898 at least twenty such schools had been founded under the sponsorship of the African Methodist Episcopal Church alone, with an annual income of $150,000 contributed by 300,000 people (Billingsley & Giovannoni, 1972; Lightfoot, 1978).[2]

During the Progressive era, roughly from the end of the nineteenth century through about 1920, mothers banded together under the aegis of "Organized Motherhood" to lobby for pure food and drug laws, equal rights for mothers in custody decisions affecting children,[3] foster care homes, Mother's Aid for widowed or abandoned mothers, kindergartens and preventive child health services. In 1897, a group of several thousand mothers, headed by Alice Birney and Phoebe Hearst, founded the National Congress of Mothers. The Parent Teachers Association (PTA) evolved in the first two decades of this century out of this national network of Mothers' Clubs.[4]

Despite these early examples of parent self-help and advocacy, *widespread* parent activism seems to be primarily a post-World War II and even perhaps a post-1960s occurrence. Some of the best-known parent self-help organizations, however, were thirty or forty years in formation before their efforts became known to the general public. The self-help movement for parents of retarded children, for example, is often associated with the Kennedy administration, when an attractive young president and his family threw a sudden bright light behind the courageous efforts of the parents of the retarded. But organized parent advocacy for retarded children had originated thirty years earlier as a response to changing historical trends. In the nineteenth century, retarded children had usually been cared for at home. But as the twentieth century unfolded, retarded children were institutionalized in state hospitals and schools set up for that purpose. This relieved parents of the tremendous burden of daily care for severely retarded children; however, parents took up the burden of worry and concern about the competence and caring available in state hospitals and schools. Separated from their children by institutional walls, parents felt powerless to protect their offspring from abuse or negligence.

In the 1930s and 1940s, parents of retarded children began forming local grassroots organizations, either to demand changes in public education and residential institutions for the retarded or to set up alternative, more responsive services for their children. These local groups slowly became known to one another, and in 1950 they joined in forming the National Association for Retarded Citizens (NARC) to lobby for federal involvement in mental retardation (Adams, 1972).[5]

Parents of the retarded were not the only visible movement before the mid-1960s. Beginning in the 1940s and 1950s, parents of black children also courageously and quietly organized in small rural communities, mostly in the South, to bring lawsuits for desegregation—sometimes risking life-threatening reprisals from the Ku Klux Klan and other white supremacist organizations.

Partly as a result of desegregation efforts, during the 1960s schools increasingly became the focal point for parent activism. Some parent activists fought hard for racial integration of schools; others just as forcefully opposed desegregation, especially if it involved the busing of school children. Heightening parent demands to have more say in the running of the schools may not have been an anticipated consequence of the movement for racial integration, but it did have this effect.

Parent activism for retarded children and advocacy by black parents also seeking fundamental civil rights for their children became the prototypes for a surge of parent self-help activity in the 1970s and 1980s. During the 1970s parents of handicapped children—representing many types of handicapping conditions, not just mental retardation—refined their skills in legislative and other kinds of advocacy for their children and added a new activity to their efforts: precedent-setting, class-action lawsuits. These included the 1971 PARC case (*Pennsylvania Association for Retarded Children v. the Commonwealth of Pennsylvania*) and the 1972 *Mills v. Board of Education for the District of Columbia*, both of which established the right of handicapped children to a free public school education.

Parents in the 1970s could look to established movements as examples of the successful use of self-help to overcome difficulties. During that decade an increasing number of self-help groups were active in helping women master a fundamental parental experience, that of giving birth.[6] So too, parents of adopted children worked hard in their local communities and states to make adoption possible for all kinds of parents (poor and rich, married and single) and for all kinds of children (babies and adolescents, healthy and ailing). The easy access of 1980s' parents to choices about adoption and about where and how their babies will be born owes much to this movement.

THE SCHOOLS

In the first five decades of this century, the prevailing parental attitude toward schools appears to have been at least respectful and almost reverential. During the late 1960s and 1970s, however, some cracks began to appear in the public trust heretofore so widely conferred on universal public education. Declining achievement by public school graduates on Scholastic Aptitude Tests (SAT) and outright failure to demonstrate even functional literacy by significant percentages of seventeen-year-olds provoked parent distrust of the schools (Pizzo, 1983). This poor student performance coincided with skyrocketing educational costs, teacher strikes, and the consolidation of school districts into larger, more bureaucratic systems. Some parents expressed their concern by forming organizations to give themselves the confidence and the clout to challenge the school system. Organizations with names such as the Parents' Union, Parents United for Full Funding, Parent Representatives on Better Education, and Parents' Action Network began to emerge in different parts of the country.

Three national organizations developed to offer support, publications, and information in the cause of increased parent and citizen participation in the schools. One was the National Committee for Citizens in Education (NCCE), founded in 1973 by several school administrators who believe deeply in parent involvement in public school policymaking. A special project of NCCE, called the Parents' Network, was developed shortly thereafter. The network links several hundred local parent-citizen groups in cities, small towns, and states into a national, loosely federated group.

Also in 1973, the Institute for Responsive Education (IRE), a Boston-based national organization, was formed to "advocate and assist citizen participation in education decision-making" (Davies, 1976). IRE also encompasses parents' groups working for basic change in the school system. Finally, the National Coalition of Elementary and Secondary Education Act Title I Parents, described earlier in this chapter, was also founded in the early 1970s. This national organization links parent groups working in low-income communities to make educational programs for economically disadvantaged children more effective.

The movement to upgrade public schools cannot yet be said to have produced large-scale national change. Some changes can be noted: better parental access to children's school records, greater emphasis on performance measures and on minimum competency for students. However, public junior and senior high schools have become a point around which many parent groups in the late 1970s and 1980s rallied to offer one another support and strategies in a grassroots parental movement against drug abuse. Perhaps parent self-help groups should refrain from exhaustive efforts to secure global change in public education and instead seek highly specific changes (for example, tighter enforcement of a ban on drugs in school or the elimination of school violence). When advocating change in the public schools—an institution that changes very slowly—specificity and success seem to go together.

ACCOMPLISHMENTS

What are the accomplishments of parent self-help and support groups? In the 1970s, acting in concert with sympathetic professionals, parent groups revolutionized childbirth practices in hospitals, special education opportunities for handicapped children, hospital policies regarding parental presence during a child's hospital stay, and opportunities for the adoption of older, minority, and handicapped children. Parents were not the only advocates for change in these settings, nor was parent advocacy the sole reason for success. It takes committed citizens and dedicated professionals, too. However, the intensity that parents brought to these struggles greatly contributed to their success (Pizzo, 1983). Consider these points.

- In 1973 more than one-third of all hospitals in a national Childbirth Education Association survey flatly prohibited father presence in delivery rooms. The remaining two-thirds conditionally permitted father presence (International Childbirth Education Association, 1975). By 1980, four out of five hospitals permitted—and many encouraged—father participation in childbirth.[7] A 1982 *Parents Magazine* poll to which more than 64,000 parents responded found that almost 93 percent of the husbands were with their wives during labor, with 85 percent present at delivery (Yarrow, 1982).
- In 1970 nearly all 50 states had laws exempting (some would say excluding) handicapped children from public education (Children's Defense Fund, 1974). By 1977, almost all those policies had been reversed: 49 states had laws *mandating* publicly provided education for at least most handicapped children (Gliedman & Roth, 1980). In 1966, between 1.2 and 1.8 million handicapped children were receiving appropriate public education; by 1979, this number had risen to 3.9 million (Select Panel for the Promotion of Child Health, 1981). These gains for handicapped children are attributed to both changes in state law and passage of the 1975 Education for All Handicapped Children Act, which was strongly advocated by parents, who have since occupied a critical place in translating this new federal law into real local and state change. Persistent exemption of some children and inadequate state resources to carry out the new laws are still problems. But without a doubt, parent groups have won major new opportunities for their handicapped children.
- In 1969, only three states provided financial assistance in the adoption of troubled or handicapped children despite the extraordinary medical and mental health services most of the children required (CSR-Creative Associates, 1982). Thousands of children were trapped in expensive institutional care or in transfers through a long string of foster care homes. These homeless children were free, under the law, for adoption, and many spent their entire childhoods hoping to be adopted. Throughout the 1970s, parent advocacy for homeless children grew; by 1979, parents had helped enact laws in 46 states man-

dating at least some type of state adoption assistance, and in 1980, parents helped pass a historic first: a federal law authorizing national adoption assistance (CSR-Creative Associates, 1982). Here, too, problems still remain, but again, parents have helped make once unresponsive governments sensitive to the needs of special children and their families.

* In the 1950s and 1960s, most parents were expected simply to leave their sick child off at the hospital and visit only at rigidly prescribed times. Even as late as 1973, more than half the hospitals in the metropolitan Boston area did not permit parents to stay overnight, or "room-in," with a hospitalized child (Children in Hospitals, 1978). By 1981, however, a national survey of hospitals in the United States and Canada showed that 97 percent permitted parental rooming-in with sick children (O'Leary, 1982). Parent advocates and concerned professionals are responsible for this remarkable turnaround in hospital policy—a profound change achieved in less than two decades.

Other efforts are reaping improvements in the 1980s. Parents active in the antidrug movement are credited by experts with helping to reduce daily use of marijuana by high school seniors from 11 percent in 1978 (when the first parent groups formed) to 7 percent in 1981 (National Institute on Drug Abuse, 1981). Mothers Against Drunk Drivers are credited with helping to reduce alcohol-related, fatal auto accidents in many states (The war against drunk drivers, 1982).

IMPLICATIONS OF THE PARENT-TO-PARENT SUPPORT MOVEMENT

Parent advocacy groups have also effected more overarching changes than are indicated by these separate accomplishments. The relationship between parents and professionals, parents and institutions, parents and government is unalterably changed by the past several decades of activity by parent support groups. Yet continuing change is needed to realize the promise of this phenomenon. In my judgment, the following adaptations will yield the most progress toward that realization.

1. *Schools, hospitals, and social agencies should be more responsive to parents:* Services to help children must be designed and organized to be open to parents on a large scale. Flexibility, easy-going sharing, and humor are features of self-help at its best. These are characteristics that professionally organized services would do well to adopt. Responsiveness requires parent access to information, explanations, data, and real opportunities to influence the policies and standard operating practices of services to children and families. It also requires that parental needs for both physical and psychological proximity to their children be respected.

2. *Relationships between parents and professionals should be reestablished*

around fundamental assumptions of equality and tolerance: Parents need to continue depending on themselves, expecting the "system" to change, fighting for their children. When this occurs, parents feel more equal to professionals and more confident. Eventually parents begin behaving as if they are equal partners, whether the professional dealing with them thinks so or not (eventually many do). Parents should avoid the pitfall of blaming individual professionals for what really is a system-wide problem.

Professionals, for their part, ought to listen to what parents are expressing when they denounce a program's failures, confront professionals, and bring lawsuits. What motivates their anger is the extraordinarily powerful responsibility parents feel for their children. It makes no sense for professionals to bemoan the diminishing sense of responsibility among parents and then to upbraid those parents whose sense of responsibility has propelled them into what the professionals may see as "neurotic pushiness." If professionals really want to encourage strong bonding between parent and child, as they often claim, they need to tolerate and even encourage parents' "neurotic pushiness."

To this end, better training for professionals is crucial. Teachers and health professionals are trained to be sensitive to children's needs. But very few teacher-training or pediatric training programs convey that parents also have needs and that fundamental to all constructive human interaction is the need to sustain feelings of self-worth. It is critical that professionals learn patterns of communication that respect and enhance—not diminish—parents' confidence and sense of competence. Parent self-help and advocacy groups provide a resource for the planners of this kind of training. Beyond that, both parents and professionals need training to understand the new partnership roles that are emerging for parents in the human service professions: coevaluator; consultant to medical and psychosocial treatment teams; educational and foster care contract cosigner; member of parent policy or advisory councils; coleaders of parent education courses; cotherapists in groups of parents struggling with severe stress.

3. *The relationship between parents and government should be seen as complex and sensitive—but also quite positive:* Parent self-help and advocacy are a rejection and an affirmation of government. Most members of parent support groups feel strongly that government should function for the well-being of the people and that parents can make government function for them. At the same time, parent activists are refusing to accept government that does not work well either for children or for themselves.

Government—particularly legislators and administrators—can support a positive relationship with parents. First, government policy makers can *listen* in many ways: by consulting with organized groups of parents; sponsoring surveys to ask individual parents their views on policy issues; and incorporating the results of those studies into policy formulation.

Second, government policymakers, working within the context of respect for the constitutional rights of both parents and children, can structure laws and regulations so that they strengthen the rights of parents in services delivered to children. When those rights are in conflict, the relationship between parents and government becomes sensitive, sometimes painful. At this intersection, policy advice from parent self-help and advocacy groups can profitably be sought. Effective reconciliation of child rights with parent rights is after all a daily task of parenting.

4. *Parent activists ought to consider greater coalescence in advocating public policies that benefit children:* For the diverse parent groups working to make government more responsive to them, concerted action matters tremendously. Coalitions among different groups of parents of handicapped children have proved their worth. Parents might coalesce around such policy issues as effective and accessible preventive child health services, child welfare services reform, better day care, and improved tax policies affecting families. The possibilities are inviting, and common goals can be realized in the 1980s if parents choose to do so.

5. *Individual parents ought to make themselves aware of the very real alternatives offered by parent self-help and advocacy organizations:* Parents should not see organized self-help or advocacy as another mandatory responsibility of parenting. Many parents now mobilize personal or family resources in order to protect and nurture their children and find that this suffices. But some parents need more or different resources to help their children and in the search for such help become discouraged at the apparent indifference or injustice of institutions established to serve children.

To those parents who are discouraged, the clearest message of the promising phenomenon of parent-to-parent support is one of stubborn and successful optimism: when we need help and it is not there, we can organize our own.

NOTES

1. A fuller explanation of these objectives can be found in Peggy Pizzo, *Parent to Parent* (Boston: Beacon Press, 1983).
2. See also Herbert Aptheker, *A Documentary History of the Negro People in the United States* (Secaucus, NJ: Citadel Press, 1973), for numerous examples of black parents' efforts to secure education for their children before the Civil War. Robert Bremner, *Children and Youth in America: A Documentary History* (Cambridge: Harvard University Press,

1970–74), also offers examples of black-established schools as early as the beginning of the nineteenth century.

3. Until the twentieth century, fathers were presumed to have the primary right to custody.

4. See Sheila Rothman, *Woman's Proper Place* (New York: Basic Books, 1978), chaps. 3 and 4, as well as Steven Schlossman, "Before Home Start: Notes Toward a History of Parent Education in America, 1897–1929," *Harvard Educational Review, 46*, no. 3, August 1976.

5. I am also grateful here to Elizabeth Boggs, one of the founders of the National Association for Retarded Citizens, who gave me hours of personal interviews and much literature helpful to understanding the history of organizing by parents of retarded children.

6. See, e.g., Marjorie Karmel, *Thank You, Dr. Lamaze* (New York: Doubleday, 1965). Also see Shonkoff's chapter (5) elsewhere in this text for a fuller description of the self-help movement that centered on childbirth.

7. Personal conversation with James Levine, codirector, the Fatherhood Project, Bank Street College of Education, New York, NY, December 1981.

REFERENCES

Adams, M. (1972). Mental retardation, the historical background to services. In J. Wortis, *Mental retardation,* Vols. 1–4, New York: Grune & Stratton.

Anonymous. (1975, Winter). From Colorado. *Frontiers* (newsletter of Parents Anonymous).

Billingsley, A., & Giovannoni, J. (1972). *Children of the storm.* New York: Harcourt, Brace Jovanovich.

Children in Hospitals. (1978, Spring). *Children in hospitals* newsletter. Needham, MA.

Children's Defense Fund. (1974). *Children out of school in America.* Washington, DC: Children's Defense Fund.

CSR-Creative Associates. (1982, January). Characteristics of state adoption assistance programs. Unpublished data.

Davies, D. (1976). *Schools where parents make a diference.* Boston: Institute for Responsive Education.

Gliedman, J., & Roth, W. (1980). *The unexpected minority: Handicapped children in America.* New York: Harcourt, Brace Jovanovich.

International Childbirth Education Association. (1975). *Father participation guide.* Milwaukee, WI: ICEA.

Lightfoot, S. L. (1978). Worlds apart: *The relationships between families and schools.* New York: Basic Books.

National Institute on Drug Abuse. (1981). Highlights for student drug use in America, 1974–1981. Washington, DC: National Institute on Child Abuse.

O'Leary, E. (1982). Survey of psychosocial policies and programs in hospitals. Association for the Care of Children's Health. Unpublished survey.

Pizzo, P. (1983). *Parent to parent: Working together for ourselves and our children.* Boston, MA: Beacon Press.

Schuchard, M. K. (1978, May 25). The family versus the drug culture. Presentation given to the Southeast Drug Conference, Atlanta, GA.

Select Panel for the Promotion of Child Health, (1981). *Better health for our children: A national strategy,* report Vol. 2. Washington, DC: Department of Health and Human Services.

The war against drunk drivers. (1982, September 13). *Newsweek,* pp. 34–39.

Yarrow, L. (1982). When my baby was born. *Parents, 57* (8).

PART IV/PROGRAM DEVELOPMENT AND IMPLEMENTATION

13 DESIGN, STAFFING, AND FUNDING OF FAMILY SUPPORT PROGRAMS

Bernice Weissbourd

The advent of family support marks significant changes in the way in which our society views families and in the way in which services are designed and delivered to meet their needs. The design, staffing, and funding of family support programs consistently reflect ideas that distinguish them from traditional social services for families and from earlier educational programs for parents.

Basic to the philosophy of family support and in conflict with the traditional view of families is the assumption that ALL families need support and should have access to it (Florin & Dokecki, 1983). Although this is an accepted premise in other Western democracies (Kamerman & Kahn, 1976), in our society, with its emphasis on individualism, family support is presumed necessary only for "deficient" families—that is, those unable to make it on their own. The fact is that industrialization, urbanization, and the resultant mobility have made families of every economic status dependent upon such community institutions as schools, hospitals, and social services to help rear their children (Keniston & the Carnegie Council on Children, 1977). Yet the American approach to families is that they are responsible for themselves, and government policy for families has reflected that view.

Family support programs start from the belief that all families must be able to provide a good environment for their children. The kinds of support needed to fulfill this basic requirement may vary, but the requirement remains the same. In addition to shelter, clothing, and food, a network of relationships with others that provides emotional and material support as well as access to information and resources is essential to every family's well-being.

The range of support services recognized as necessary to provide adequate help for families is very large in family support programs, unlike traditional social service agencies, which focus on specific problem areas. Consequently, program planners are challenged to find the particular kind of support from which a family can benefit (Powell, 1976), and parents are often involved in designing programs to meet their own needs (Pizzo, 1983).

Family support programs provide assistance of varying degrees, ranging from affording an opportunity to establish friendship networks to being available for help in times of crisis. A singular feature of programs is the capacity to expand or substitute services in response to expressed and changing needs of parents, limited only by funding capacity or the time and energy of the people involved.

Family support programs are marked by a new configuration of relationships through which services are provided and by which program decisions are made. Parents interact with other parents to define program directions and/or function as volunteer staff. Professionals and parents seek an alliance or partnership rather than fall into the hierarchical relationship typical of traditional services. Program design decisions are based on an exchange of information and experiences among all the people concerned rather than on a professional solution alone. Garbarino (Whittaker, Garbarino, & Associates 1983) suggests that "the key implication of this increasing trend toward partnership with parents is that the field . . . will quite literally never be the same again."

The grassroots nature of family support programs also distinguishes them from more traditional social service programs. Before opening their doors, the founders of a family support program know the community on two levels: they have formal data on the economic mixture, racial composition, ethnic character, and educational background of families living there and on the services and resources available; and they have knowledge of how people interact with one another, who the unofficial leaders are, and where people seek advice. Program designers work closely with community representatives, agency directors, parents, and church and school administrators to assure that the center opens in an atmosphere of acceptance and enthusiasm (Wallach & Weissbourd, 1979). It is not unlikely that those concerned with community development issues will become involved with those working with family support programs and that they will jointly evolve a better understanding of community-based family support.

Whereas traditional social service programs have emphasized behavioral or educational goals for participants, the community-organization background of many family support program personnel has made them sensitive to the issues of maintaining family and cultural integrity. Acceptance of differences often takes priority over striving for change as programs encourage the relationships necessary for support. Program designers are concerned with providing services that recognize the underlying cultural differences among families as well as the individual families' interpretation of them.

Today's family support programs represent a new form of service based on new approaches and new patterns of decision-making. It could be said that family support programs are as diverse as the needs of families. The programs come in every shape and size; they exist in almost every kind of community and under every auspice (see table 13.1). They appear with an array of services and support that earlier generations of parents could not have imagined. This chapter describes the effects of program philosophy and goals on the style and delivery of service. It is based primarily on the experience of practitioners who are defining and developing programs today.

DESIGN

Program design accrues through a series of conscious decisions about what services a program will provide and how it will provide them. These decisions are based on four essential factors: (1) the basic beliefs of program originators, including their view of parents' needs; (2) the program's stated goals and objectives; (3) the characteristics of the population to be served; and (4) available resources. The program's structure emerges as program decisions are made on the basis of these factors.

Basic Beliefs of Program Originators

A program first reflects its originators' assumptions about what parents need. These assumptions are a particular program architect's answer to questions central to program development: "Why is this program important and necessary?" "What needs of parents generate this program?" "What research and new knowledge is stimulating professionals to plan this program?"

The scope and specificity of perceived need can vary greatly among programs. The initial impetus for a program can be very specific in pointing to a way of meeting the need. An example is the Santa Barbara Birth Resource Center. Designed to be a support during the pregnancy and postpartum periods, the center includes childbirth preparation, breast-feeding information, nutrition classes, a lending library of books on pregnancy and childbirth, and information on obstetricians, gynecologists, pediatricians, and midwives.

Other programs may have a broader mission to provide wide-ranging solutions, such as alleviating feelings of loneliness and lack of connection

TABLE 13.1
Program Types

Program	Services	Staffing	Budget/funding sources
Comprehensive Community-Based Programs	Advocacy Child care Crisis intervention Drop-in Health care education Home visitors Information and referral Liaison to community services Library/toy lending Newsletter Parent/child activities Parent/child development education Parent support groups	Professionals Nonprofessional community members Volunteers: professionals, nonprofessionals Parents	$20,000–300,000 Institution/agency Private community funds Public funds Corporation/foundation Parents fund-raising Fees for service
Parent Education Classes and Groups	Parent/child activities Parent/child development education Child care during meetings	Professionals Facilitators/trainers Trained volunteers	$30,000–300,000 Institution/agency Private community funds Corporation/foundation Fees for service Parent fund-raising Public funds

TABLE 13.1 (Continued)

Program	Services	Staffing	Budget/funding sources
Self-Help Networks and Groups	Advocacy Child care during meetings Newsletter Parent/child activities Parent/child development education Parent support Special concern groups	Parents Professional consultants Paid coordinator	$2,000–20,000 Parent fund-raising Private community funds Corporation/foundation
Warm-Lines	Child development information Information and referral	Professional consultants and trainers Trained volunteers Professionals and/or parents	$10,000–50,000 Institution/agency Private community funds Corporation/foundation
Home Visitors	Child development information Concrete services Crisis intervention Health care and education Liaison to community services Parent support	Professional consultants and trainers Trained community mothers Trained volunteers	$10,000–50,000 Institution/agency Corporation/foundation Public funds Private community funds

among parents in a community. At Family Focus, a drop-in center offering comprehensive programming, parents will frequently say, "After the baby was born I called my mother first. Then I called Family Focus." In centers where there are extensive services, the center staff and *peer friendships* or *other parents* often provide a sense of support that becomes a significant personal network.

A program's designers may perceive a need to extend its services beyond providing group support for members to enlisting support from "natural helpers" in the community. The Westchester Self-Help Clearinghouse trains bartenders and barbers in sensitive listening and the provision of information and referral. Or program initiators may determine that coordination of services will be of greater benefit to parents and children in the community than a new service, as is the case in the YWCA–Clark County Abuse Project in the State of Washington, founded and run by representatives of state human service agencies, the justice system, the churches, and the medical community.

Every program answers certain basic questions even if they are not intentionally stated: "What determines child-rearing practices?" "What influences parents to change them?" and "What relationship does the family have with the society at large?" Their answers to these questions arrange programs along a continuum that moves toward a comprehensive ecological approach to family resources (Bronfenbrener, 1979) from a more traditional, targeted, information-based approach. Family support programs fall at many points along this continuum, from parent education programs based primarily on imparting a specific body of knowledge to ecologically oriented programs offering wide-ranging, comprehensive support.

In information-centered programs, education is generally a primary focus of efforts to reduce family stress and enhance family life. Parents are seen as individuals who can be educated to provide the kinds of experience their children need to grow to their maximum potential. These parent education programs are usually designed around a defined curriculum presented by a trained person, as in Parent Effectiveness Training and Systematic Training for Effective Parenting.

Some parent education programs, such as the Minnesota Early Learning Design, are based on a child development curriculum in which volunteer parents are trained by professionals to lead discussions on topics such as parent-child interaction, family relations, nutrition and health, building self-esteem, and communications. Some educational programs for new parents, such as the Evanston (Illinois) Hospital Infant Care Program, begin by having parents observe the Brazelton assessment done on their child soon after birth so that they can begin to appreciate the infant's unique character. Warm-lines, which provide information and are designed to deal with the everyday worries of parents through telephone linkages between parents and trained staff, are a common extension of information-based programs though they are often also included in comprehensive programs such as the Bright Beginnings warm-line operating out of Magee Women's Hospital in Pittsburgh, Pennsylvania.

The current parent education model, as suggested by Lois Wandersman in this volume, moves beyond the dissemination of information toward an integrated and comprehensive approach to families. There is evidence that the specific curriculum used in programs that focus on information is less important to overall parent development than the fact that parents come together in groups and share common concerns (Florian & Dokecki, 1983).

An ecological approach to family support implies that the parent is a developing adult to be viewed in relationship to the other members of the family and in the context of the social and economic forces that determine the family's environment. Ecologically based programs by definition respond appropriately to social and economic stresses, to the cultural factors that play such a large role in family life and learning styles, to child-rearing practices, and to traditional family roles within the community. Parents in a Hispanic community, for example, may feel uncomfortable in a class on child development, but might willingly share their concerns about their children in a more natural community setting. In communities where unemployment is high or poverty cuts a wide path, material assistance may take a primary place in program plans. This approach places primary importance on the self-confidence and self-esteem of parents because it believes that parents' sense of themselves is crucial to their child-rearing abilities and that those unable to cope are hard-pressed to transmit self-confidence to their children.

Comprehensive family support programs offer a wide range of core services (see table 13.2). For example, Parents Place, Inc., in White Plains, New York (*Programs to strengthen families*, 1983), includes a drop-in center, discussion groups, parent education, outreach activities, and support groups. Special programs are available for mothers of newborns and toddlers, for working parents at times convenient to them, for teenage parents, and for fathers. Services include a lending library, a newspaper, and information and referral to other resources. The Webster Avenue Family Resource Center of Rochester, New York, initially focused on parent education classes and now provides a range of services, including expanded informal support groups. In addition to parent education classes it offers respite child care for children under five, problem-solving counseling, and home visits to high-risk families. Mutual aid and self-help projects evolve in comprehensive centers such as

TABLE 13.2
Basic Beliefs that Influence Program Design

Parent education moving toward →

	Traditional approach	Ecological approach
Concept of parenthood	Parents seen primarily in role of child rearers and providers Parenthood seen as synonomous with adulthood, the culminating stage of human development Families viewed as independent units	Parents seen as multidimensional people Development continues throughout life and parenthood is a developmental stage Families viewed in the context of their environment
Major determinants of child-rearing behavior	Information on child development Attitudes about and toward children Knowledge of parent/child interaction	Parental self-esteem Cultural and family background Socioeconomic and environmental factors
Relationship of family to society	Family strength comes primarily from within the family Social change occurs primarily when individuals are able to function well	Family's interaction with larger community is a significant influence on family's strengths Social change occurs through community action as well as from well-functioning individuals
Method of influencing parental behavior	Content of program is most important Intellectual development is emphasized Curriculum approach is utilized Individual growth is most important Teacher-learner format is used	Process is as important as content Total personal development is emphasized Social interaction is encouraged Social support systems are essential A broad format for learning is used: teacher-learner, peer interaction, modeling

these as parents organize babysitting coops or clothing and equipment exchanges.

Program Goals

Goal setting takes the design process from the "why" stage to the "what" stage. After needs have been defined, goals establish exactly what will be part of the program and, implicitly, what will not. For example, if a program goal is to improve parents' knowledge of child development, it is likely that program services will revolve around education. A program whose goals include building a constituency of parents to act as advocates, such as the Mothers' Center Development Project, in Hempstead, New York, is likely to include groups that discuss social policy issues, determine areas in which they want to effect change, and mobilize to do so. A major target of the Mothers' Center's efforts has been the health care system, particularly as it relates to birth practices and to communications between pediatricians and parents. It is unlikely that the program of such a group would include counseling and therapy, as would a program whose goal is preventing child abuse, such as the Family Growth Center in Lansing, Michigan, and the Center for Children and Parents in Anchorage, Alaska. The latter may require a variety of program components, including counseling, concrete assistance to parents in the form of child care, managing family finances, and networking with other community resources.

Although a program's goals will influence the choice of services it provides, program planners recognize that several different goals may be met by a single program component. The formation of small groups of parents, for example, may help in alleviating loneliness and establishing a support network for parents as well as allowing the exchange of information about child-related policies that should be changed.

Population Served

Characteristics of the particular parents to be served by a family support program are decisive factors in the design of effective programs. Programs with similar goals may take different forms if they are to serve different populations. The goals of improving parent-child interaction by enhancing the self-esteem of parents and increasing their understanding of child development may lead a flexible, informal program when the population served is composed of educated, middle-class parents. An example of such a program is the Port Washington Parent Resource Center, which is run by a parent board. Other programs, such as the New Futures School for adolescent parents in Albuquerque, New Mexico, achieve this goal through a more structured, individually goal-oriented approach. Similarly, a drop-in center, successful in many communities, may not work well in a community whose culture perceives drop-in to be a distraction from daily responsibilities and where only attendance at a structured program is acceptable. The particular population served may also determine staffing patterns and requirements. Programs designed for teenage parents usually include a strong professional staff (Nickel & Delany, 1985), whereas those for older women having their first child may be more informal and may rely on self-help as a primary means of serving these parents. An identified high-risk population is often served by a home visitor, who may be from the community and is therefore less distant or threatening, and who provides concrete services, information, and emotional support through personal visits.

Existing Resources

Existing resources in the community also determine the form a family support program will take. Most programs emerge from a lack of services, and the accomplishment of goals can be strongly influenced by the role that community resources play. Sometimes building a network of available resources becomes a primary task. Community-service providers, such as school administrators and public health officials, provide space or funding; thus their cooperation may be a factor in shaping the program. In communities where resources are limited, accurate assessment of the need for services, knowledge of potential resources, and a strong parent constituency capable of speaking forcefully for necessary services may be the most important facets of program design.

The setting of a program, which not only defines its physical boundaries but contributes to its overall ambience, is also determined by available resources. Program settings range from a small group of parents meeting in one another's homes to a family drop-in center in a church, to a program for parents of high-risk children in a hospital, to a parent-child program in a storefront. Physical space limitations influence how many families can be served, scheduling, and the content of program activities. Sharing space with another program, such as a nursery school, limits the times when program activities can be scheduled. Programs based in a larger institution may be obliged to follow the policies of their hosts; for instance, they may have to adhere to hospital rules and regulations or the teachings of a church. The limitations imposed by the setting are important factors that planners accommodate as they envision the form their programs will take.

STAFFING

Those concerned with the delivery of human services generally acknowledge the primary importance of the "people factor" in creating and maintaining a successful program. The school matters less than the quality of the child's teacher; the physical setting of day care affects the child less than the characteristics of the caregiver. The quality of staff appears to be more closely related to program success than any particular type of training or staff roles (Florian & Dokecki, 1983). The best-laid plans of any programs inevitably falter when those carrying them out lack the qualities and abilities appropriate to the program. It is fair to say that there can be no substitute for a good staff.

Staff members in family support programs consist of professional and nonprofessional paid staff, professional and nonprofessional volunteer staff, and parents who may simultaneously be participants. This complex array raises dilemmas that have yet to be examined but that have come to the forefront as programs have developed. The role of the professional in community-based programs requires attitudes, skills, and training that differ from those of the professional working in traditional settings. The emerging role of the volunteer in organizing and leading grassroots programs requires attention. In this section, we will look at these concerns as well as the issues surrounding the involvement of nonprofessional community members in family support programs.

Staffing Patterns

An overview of family support programs reveals a range of staffing patterns that matches the range of service designs. Parent-education aspects of programs rely heavily on professional staff, both as teachers and as trainers for nonprofessionals and volunteers. Mutual aid/self-help programs may not have staff since they are run by parents, with speakers or discussion leaders recruited occasionally for particular events. Comprehensive family support programs increasingly rely on a team of people from varied backgrounds, including professionals, community members who are paid staff, volunteers, and program participants themselves.

Characteristics of the population to be served also dictate the appropriate staffing pattern. It is important to recognize the limitations as well as the strengths of particular staffing patterns for meeting the needs of certain parents. For example, families requiring special assistance to handle financial or emotional crises tend to drop out of groups based on volunteers and peer support, which do not meet their desire for professional help. At the same time, parents are often overwhelmed by the problems requiring professional help. Targeted high-risk families are often unable or unwilling to seek professional help without a reassuring link provided by a more familiar community member who serves as a home visitor or outreach worker. Parents whose primary needs are for companionship and connection with other parents may be reluctant to participate in a group or program with a heavy concentration of professional staff. The match of staffing pattern to target population in family support programs is an area that remains to be fully explored as programs are more effectively evaluated.

What can be observed in current programs is that although staffing patterns may vary considerably from program to program, the family support concept has added significantly different dimensions to the traditional roles of professionals, community staff members, and volunteers.

Role of the Professionals

The assumptions upon which family support are built have dramatically altered the traditional professional's role. As parents come to be seen less as vehicles for child rearing and more as developing adults, and when programs arise out of parents' desire for a community of others or a belief in preventive services by professionals, a reorientation of typical roles is in order, away from the explicit relationship of teacher to learner. Although informed parenting remains a primary goal, successful family support professionals are able not only to communicate information clearly but also to listen to parents' concerns attentively and to respond in ways that substantially increase understanding and therefore alter behavior. These professionals are able to be authoritative without being authoritarian and judgmental, to give advice and suggestions without making parents feel guilty for behavior that they themselves begin to perceive as incorrect.

The redefined relationship is frequently described as a "partnership," a rather facile statement of a goal difficult to achieve. In the area of child rearing, parents are experts about their own particular child, bringing to the partnership their goals for the child and a commitment to the cultural traditions that distinguish the child's environment. The professional contributes broad expertise in and knowledge of child development. A different formulation of the professional-to-parent relationship may be that of generalist and specialist, the professional being the source of information based on educational background, the parent being the specialist about her own child. A "partnership" evolves as both parties are able to share their knowledge and experience for the benefit of the child. One professional put the partnership imperative this way: "If we're going to be successful with families, we're going to need to look to parents as leaders, parents as the experts, parents as the bosses. We're going to need to ask them to join us cooperatively as equals in this partnership so that we create a reality out there that matches what all of us want to see" (Vincent, 1984).

Professional staff tend to be child development specialists, psychologists, social workers, or teachers, though the fields of home economics and nursing, among others, are also represented. Working as partners in the family support setting does not mean that they abdicate the professional role. Professionals do have special training and education, and parents often are motivated to enter family support programs by the desire for professional direction and assistance in rearing their children. There is evidence of the need for a professional helper for some problems, particularly at times of severe stress (Collins & Pancoast, 1976; Unger & Powell, 1980). The changing role of professionals requires that, having been well-schooled to monitor tendencies to be judgmental, controlling, or overly didactic, they must now also monitor tendencies to be too laissez-faire or value free. This latter attitude denies families the full benefit of skills and knowledge the professional has so painstakingly acquired.

A partnership of professionals and parents implies that the roles of both are changing. As professionals view parents as partners, parents come to see professionals in a different light. Professionals are often regarded by parents as friends in addition to resources for information and advice. However, the boundaries of that friendship, if they are not carefully thought out, may become problematic. The complexities of this partnership are at the forefront of issues in family support, since the partnership relationship is a key component in the departure from traditional forms of social services.

Role of the Community Member

Community members on staff play an important role in many programs because they share the culture of program participants and can bridge the gap that often exists between parents and a professional whose background is alien to them. When chosen because of success in their own parenting experiences, they serve as models of people who have "made it," often against great odds. Anchored in the community, these staff members are invaluable in extending their networks to others and serving as liaisons with other resources, as well as in acting as outreach workers to families in stress. Home visitor and other programs designed to reach families in difficulty are often staffed by community members, who rely on their identification with the community to make the connections with isolated high-risk families in the most nonthreatening, effective way possible. Community mothers on staff can be the key link between high-risk families and the professional assistance they need.

In the commitment to recognize and respect cultural traditions and values of the community, family support programs are challenged to examine the place of community members in the team of program staff and to understand the processes that contribute to the community member's effectiveness. In practice, tension between community members and professional staff sometimes results from a community member's dedication to beliefs that conflict with those of the professional. This becomes especially apparent in the area of child rearing, when the community member reinforces parenting behavior that the professional staff is attempting to moderate or handles children in a way inconsistent with the professional's concepts of children's developmental needs. Some program developers have dealt with this by accepting the community member's connection with the community as a priority and anticipating gradual change through the nonpressured influence of other staff and through training programs where specific attitudes are explored. When changes do occur, they are usually based on relationships of trust established between community members and professionals.

The use of community staff members, often referred to as paraprofessionals, began during the 1960s and 1970s, when expanded social programs widely extended the use of nonprofessionals as staff members. Studies suggest that paraprofessionals may function as effectively as professionals in numerous areas (Carkhuff & Truax, 1965; Durlak, 1979; Reiff & Riessman, 1965) but do not detail the processes by which they do so. Thus, the employment of community members on staff is not so much a new direction as one that requires further examination if family support programs are to become embedded in their communities.

Role of the Parent Volunteer

One type of community member intimately involved in family support programs is the parent volunteer. The nature of family support programs inevitably makes the parent volunteer role significant, and some programs depend entirely upon such parents. The word *volunteer* in fact does not accurately describe parents who participate in family support programs for their own sake and that of their children and who often are *owners* of the program. The discussion of volunteers in this section will include only those parents who are program participants but not those who are professionals, senior citizens, or community members interested merely in donating time and energy to the family program.

Parent volunteers generally play one of three roles in a family support program: (1) They may augment a staffing of professionals and paid nonprofessionals; (2) they may be trained by professionals for leadership roles in program implementation; and (3) they may be program "owners" with direct responsibility for program design as well as function. These roles are not entirely distinct; they represent points on a continuum ranging from programs in which parents do not volunteer at all to parent cooperatives.

Programs in which parent volunteers are an addition to staff require a creative structure to accommodate and make maximum use of the variety of skills available. Typically, the activities in programs expand on the basis of the talents and expertise of volunteers. A parent volunteer may fill gaps in services by assisting staff in administrative duties or working in child care. A professional parent volunteer may provide services in her particular area of expertise. In turn, the programs provide incentives, often educational, for continuing volunteer involvement.

Parent volunteers trained by professional staff and integrated into the paid staff must be able to play both a participant-family role and a volunteer-staff role. Program planners should recognize that wearing two hats can be confusing; some parents may not be comfortable enough in their role as parents to take on the additional responsibilities involved in being a volunteer (Meyer, 1982). The Jewish Family Services of Cincinnati, Ohio, serving first-time, mostly middle-class parents, defines the role of the professionals who train such volunteers as a "parenting model as well as an educator. Since our mobile society has put at a distance many of the traditional support systems for young parents, the trainer becomes, in some instances, a trusted family friend as well" (Smith, 1984).

The third role of parent volunteers, that of primary staff, is best illustrated in self-help or mutual-aid programs in which the word *volunteer* becomes synonymous with *parent*. The dedication and clarity of purpose of the volunteers who found and operate programs of this type typically create a strong, effective organization. Such an organization, however, may eventually fall prey to its own success. As the population it serves grows, demanding more and more human-power, the population of volunteer providers often begins to shrink as a result of normal, though unanticipated, attrition, threatening the life of the organization, as expressed by the organizer of the group: "Our inexperience rendered us vulnerable to the sudden unexpected near calamity that crept into the back door while we were waving confidently out the front. It is the albatross of volunteer groups. It is volunteer (ours) turnover" (Mason, Jensen, & Ryzewicz, 1979). Recognizing this pitfall ahead of time and planning for it is a challenge for every program that relies solely on parents as staff.

Role of the Partnership

The carefully designed partnership that emerges among staff members as well as between staff and participants in family support programs represents a complete restructuring of staff roles and relationships with participants. The intentional overlapping of staff and participant roles and the emphasis on cooperative relationships among staff make the resulting team far greater than the sum of its parts, and a key element in programs. Perhaps the greatest contributions of family support programs to the field of social service—and the ones with the longest lasting impact—are the innovative, creative staffing patterns and roles that have been explored and used.

Although other social services have sometimes utilized a team approach to staffing, family support teams often involve a more intricate set of relationships than the familiar interdisciplinary team of professionals from various academic fields such as education, social work, and psychology. Academic or professional service-provider teams may have to struggle with differences stemming from their varied professional expertise and terminology, whereas the eclectic family-resource teams face a multitude of differences in educational background, community knowledge and experience, and cultural and social identifications. The guiding principle of these teams is the conscious decision to value the differences and acknowledge that each participant provides a unique resource as a professional, a community member, or a fellow parent.

Whatever the differences among team members, the philosophy behind family support programs requires certain consistent expectations for everyone, regardless of status or assigned role. An individual staff member may have many jobs or only one, according to the program structure and the demands of the moment, but each team member always serves as both model and facilitator and is responsible for creating an environment in which parents feel encouraged to develop their own coping skills. Such an important, but sometimes ambiguous, mission requires a high degree of flexibility to meet the many different situations that arise in the normal course of the program. Staff members are expected to understand the dynamics of a group that may have come together only by happenstance and to be able to respond positively and productively to the concerns raised in informal interactions. They are required to recognize the needs of individual parents, find ways to alleviate discomfort, or steer discussions away from a potentially destructive direction without interfering heavy-handedly in what may be a casual group process. The sensitivity and flexibility needed to carry out these mandates are encouraged and enhanced by the cooperative atmosphere that programs work to achieve, but the significance of carefully selecting people who possess appropriate qualities in the first place cannot be overestimated.

Qualities of Staff Members

Since the ability to build relationships is essential in family support program staff, the personal characteristics of staff members assume major importance. The phrase *liking people*, when it describes genuine feelings, implies concern and caring for others and serves as an overall description of a characteristic necessary for all staff. An extension of "liking people" is empathy, a capacity integral to creating the relationship of trust through which changes in parents' attitudes and feelings can occur. A critical product of empathy is the ability to communicate caring to the parent, regardless of any possible disagreement on child rearing. This ability is the "art" required of family support staff. "In the field of human relationships, especially when the motive is to reshape or rechannel feelings, thoughts, and behaviors, the artist must start with the special gift of a sensitive capacity for empathy" (Perlman, 1985). The feeling of being cared about by staff, whether they are professionals, volunteers, or peers, often cuts through the isolation and anxiety that many parents feel and most directly affects their attitudes and behavior.

Side by side with the capacity for empathy is the ability to imbue others with a sense of their own value, special qualities, and skills. This enabling quality exists quite apart from that of being warm and welcoming. It requires the staff person to identify parents' strong characteristics and use them as a base for further development in order to help the parents gain the confidence and capacity to solve problems on their own. It means being encouraging without being patronizing. Creating an environment in which parents can appreciate themselves requires a sensitive sense of timing, a knowledge of when a parent needs a hand to hold or a hand to let go. As discussed in Wandersman's chapter in this volume, a program that helps parents believe they are valued and able to affect their children's lives may continue to influence family functioning long after the program ends.

In family support settings where the assumption is that increasing a parent's confidence and sense of competence will affect his or her attitude toward the child, the intensity of the relationship between staff member and parent is another vital factor. In her discussion of teachers, Katz (1977) defines "intensity of relationship" as that quality in the adult which instills in a child the feeling that "what he does or does not, what he is or is not, really matters to specific others." Likewise, for parents in family support programs, it makes a difference when what the parent says or does really matters to staff. Building ties with staff further requires that the staff member "manifest her own personality in an authentic way" (Spodek, 1972). This assumes the staff member's capacity to know herself, be herself, and reveal herself with honesty and integrity.

Beyond the personal attributes inherent in the capacity to build sound relationships with other people are qualities specifically necessary for the unique setting of family support. Staff in family support programs work not only with children, as teachers in early childhood education generally do, and not only with adults, as social workers generally do. They work with children, parents, and the parent-child dyad. Therefore, they must be comfortable with both adults and children and able to respond appropriately to their interaction with each other. Even programs designed to reach parents only are implicitly dealing with the parent's feelings about the child. Often the sensitive abstract thinking required of staff to conceptualize that which is not observable becomes a key component in a staff member's effectiveness. For example, as a staff member listens to a parent regretfully report on an incident in which the parent lost his temper with his child, the staff member must simultaneously think about what feelings the incident evoked in the parent, what possible message the child was conveying by his behavior, and how the incident is illustrative of patterns in the parent-child relationship.

The ability to think beyond the concrete comes into play particularly in working with parents of other cultures. Dealing with a specific technique of child rearing, such as physical punishment, demands an understanding of the cultural values that condone and support such practices. What is necessary is a reflective ability, a state of mind that can absorb dissonances, sort them out, and determine a point of departure for ongoing communication. Staff must also be able to relate what the parent is saying to that parent's own upbringing and then make a sensitive determination of the best route to take in expanding communication on the subject (Almy, 1975).

Emphasizing the personal qualities of staff members is not intended to minimize the importance of educational background, obviously integral to functioning well. Furthermore, on-going education through on-site staff training is essential to increasing the understanding of staff and enlarging the information base from which staff function. Without the personal qualities, however, education cannot help staff build the relationships with parents that define family support programs.

TRAINING

Because family support programs are a fairly recent development on the social service scene, there are not yet formalized training programs specifically designed to impart the information and skills necessary for working in these settings. The educational background of social workers and child development specialists—those most likely to choose family support as a professional field—generally does not include the specialized knowledge needed to interact with families in a nontraditional mode. The assumption that the parent is of primary importance in the life of children challenges longstanding concepts of working with children and parents. Whereas schools of eduction heretofore trained students to work directly with children and considered parents primarily as they helped or hindered the child's development, today there is increased emphasis on training students to understand the parent, his or her strengths, problems, and ways of interacting.

The current state of training relevant to the family support field includes 66 graduate programs for family studies in the United States (Family Resource Coalition, 1986). General course offerings in family studies departments include family theory and research, child development, aging/life span, marriage and family therapy, family life education, and cross-cultural studies. A few universities, such as Metropolitan State in Denver, offer undergraduate degrees in parent education, and others, such as Fordham University in New York, offer a masters degree in adult education and human resource development with a specialization in parent education. Graduates of these programs are called family life educators, and although the courses do not represent the full range of education and training called for by the field of family support, they form a basis for development of more pertinent curricula.

In addition to university degree programs, a number of nondegree programs for training family support staff are emerging, generally offering courses focused on parent education. For example, B. Annye Rothenberg offers a practical workshop for early parenting educators through the Child-Rearing Education and Counseling Program at the Children's Health Council in Palo Alto, California; Earladeen Badger trains leaders for an Infant/Toddler Learning Program through the Department of Pediatrics, University of Cincinnati College of Medicine in Ohio; the Center for Parenting Education, in Newton, Massachusetts, whose director is Burton White, offers assistance to professionals concerned with the education of children in the first three years of life through seminars, a newsletter, and program consultation.

These programs are indicative of emerging training efforts related to the family support movement, but training programs lag behind the demands of current practice (Whittaker, Gabarino, & Associates, 1983). Professional education continues to focus on the diagnosis and treatment of the individual; but this emphasis, Wiltse (1981) has suggested, may actually impede understanding and assessment of the family in relation to its environmental supports. As models of family support programs continue to flourish, training needs will become more defined and will include education in such areas as the developmental stage of parenthood, ethnic and cultural child-rearing patterns, community process and organization, and a nondeficit approach to families. This training will enable staff to function better in programs where participants are viewed, not as passive recipients, but as people affected by their environment and capable of changing it.

FUNDING

A major challenge to family support programs is the assurance of an ongoing funding base since there is not yet a tradition of funding from either public or private sources. Instead, programs exist by virtue of a combination of funding sources, and their existence is often a constant struggle. Continuing exploration of possible sources of stable, dependable funding is necessary. It is a difficult pursuit and a primary concern.

Today, the possibility of raising funds for programs still rests on a deficit model rather than on the concept of universal need. Many programs in depressed, low-income communities can garner some federal and state funding, especially if their focus is on teenage parents, a current national concern. There has been limited public funding for such programs through the Office of Adolescent Pregnancy Programs, the Administration for Developmental Disabilities, and the Division of Maternal-Child Health. Programs in high-income areas often can be self-sufficient and need not rely on federal and state funding, which they are unlikely to receive. Programs serving the middle class, meanwhile, must continually attempt to overcome the problem of an unstable funding base.

The requirements for funding are as varied as program designs, with budgets ranging from $2,000 to $350,000 annually. Funding for low-budget programs depends on resources at the local level, and planners tailor their program designs to fit the availability of financial support. Obviously, parent cooperatives and other programs that rely heavily on volunteers fall at the low-cost end of the scale while programs staffed primarily with professionals have considerably higher costs. It is also reasonable to assume that programs for high-risk families, where specialized expertise is required, will inevitably be more expensive, though their focus on prevention through early intervention has already proved to be a very cost-effective investment. When schools, hospitals, churches, and social service agencies initiate programs as an expansion of the services they already offer, these institutions generally ensure basic support and take responsibility for on-going funding. When they cannot do so, the programs are in financial jeopardy.

The grassroots nature of many programs is exemplified by their fund-raising methods, which may include bake sales, arts and crafts shows, raffles, and tag sales. The problem with such funding is that these projects typically require high effort for low return. Membership fees become another source of funding, particularly in middle-class communities. Fees fall into two categories: a yearly membership fee that includes all services, or fees charged for special classes or services while the drop-in component or resource center remains available without charge. Whereas membership fees can be a base for financing programs in some middle-class communities, in low-income communities this is not a viable option.

In the private sphere, corporations, foundations, and individual donors, as well as local funding agencies such as United Way, have given financial assistance. A funding dilemma for family support programs is associated with one of the original funding sources, foundations. At the outset, because family support programs were a new and unique development, foundations generously supported a variety of models. On a national level, the Bush Foundation, the Carnegie Corporation, the Ford Foundation, the Mott Foundation, and on a local level, community trusts such as the Chicago Community Trust, the New York Community Trust, and the Cleveland Trust gave the primary assistance that enabled programs to develop. Since such assistance is typically time-limited, most of the programs do not enjoy the continuing aid of foundations and are now in the difficult position of finding sources to replace foundation funding.

In the public sphere, in addition to federal support, there are a growing number of initiatives on the state level, with funds being allocated to family support programs through a variety of sources including child-abuse prevention funds and state education monies. In Minnesota, for instance, the State Department of Education, through the Minnesota Council for Quality Education, is supporting family support programs and early education in ten school districts. The State of Missouri is also funding programs in the schools for parents, starting at the birth of their children, and the State of Maryland has recently allocated funds for demonstration family support programs. As Muenchow discusses in more detail in the chapter on funding partnerships (14), the Illinois Ounce of Prevention Fund, a public/private partnership, is funding family support programs in 44 communities throughout the state.

Local government support is beginning to be a possible source of funding as realization of the value of a family support program to the community as a whole increases. In some instances, municipalities and townships are providing financial assistance to programs, and in others, the local business communities, led by real estate agencies, are contributing funds. These communities are at the forefront of recognizing family support programs as community assets that encourage families to live and raise children there.

The grassroots nature of family support is more indicative of the desire and demand for support programs than of the ability to financially maintain them. Furthermore, grassroots programs are least likely to emerge in communities where the need is greatest. Public-private partnerships, state and local public funds, and business and agency aid could become forerunners of a coherent plan that would include federal assistance for those communities where resources and funds are most limited. Key elements in an effective nationwide network of programs would be the public acceptance of diversity among programs and among communities, the tailoring of a funding plan to varied circumstances, and the assurance that every family has access to support.

What is required is a national commitment to programs. This would involve providing programs in every community, with funding determined on the basis of the community's available financial resources, so that family support programs can exist side by side with schools and parks as necessary to a healthy environment for parents and children. To quote a parent, "There should be a family support center on every corner." The building of a constituency that sees family support programs as a community and public issue of highest priority will be essential to ensuring long-range plans and adequate funding.

PROGRAMS CITED

Advance
1226 Northwest 18th Street
San Antonio, TX 78207

Bright Beginnings
Magee Women's Hospital
Forbes & Halket Streets
Pittsburgh, PA 15213

Center for Children & Parents
Anchorage Child Abuse Board
808 E Street #200
Anchorage, AL 99501

Center for Parenting Education
55 Chapel Street
Newton, MA 02160

The Children's Place & Parent Education Center
P.O.B. 576
Concord, NH 03301

Evanston Hospital Infant Care
Program
c/o Evaluation Center
Evanston Hospital
2650 Ridge Avenue
Evanston, IL 60201

Family Focus, Inc.
2300 Green Bay Road
Evanston, IL 60201

Family Growth Center
Child Abuse Prevention Services
300 N. Washington #51
Lansing, MI 48933

Family Support Center
2 Bailey Road
Yeadon, PA 19050

Family Tree Parenting Center
P.O. Box 51394
Lafayette, LA 70505

Infant/Toddler Learning Program
Department of Pediatrics
University of Cincinnati
College of Medicine
231 Bethesda Avenue
Cincinnati, OH 45267-0547

Minnesota Early Learning Design
(MELD)
123 East Grant Street
Minneapolis, MN 55403

The Mother's Center Development
Project
129 Jackson Street
Hempstead, NY 11550

Parent & Child Education Program
PACE Family Treatment Center
1500 Waters Place
Ginsburg Building 13
Bronx, NY 10461

Preschool & Infant Parenting Service
(PIPS)
PIPS E 105
Thalians Mental Health Center
Cedars-Sinai Medical Center
8730 Alden Drive
Los Angeles, CA 90048

Parent Effectiveness Training
 Curriculum
American Guidance Service
Publishers Building
Circle Pines, MN 55014

Parents Place
Jewish Family and Children's Services
3272 California Street
San Francisco, CA 94118

Parents Place, Inc.
3 Carhart Avenue
White Plains, NY 10605

Parents Resource Center
42 E. Jackson Street
Orlando, FL 32801

Parents of Prematures
3311 Richmond
Suite 330
Houston, TX 77098

Port Washington Parent Resource
 Center
Flower Hill School

99 Campus Drive
Port Washington, NY 11050

Santa Barbara Birth Resource Center
2255 Modoc Road
Santa Barbara, CA 93101

Systematic Training for Effective Par-
 enting Curriculum (STEP)
American Guidance Service
Publishers Building
Circle Pines, MN 55014

Webster Avenue Family Resource
 Center
148 Webster Avenue
Rochester, NY 14609

Westchester Self-Help Clearinghouse
Westchester Community College
75 Grasslands Road
Valhalla, NY 10598

YWCA Clark County Child Abuse
 Project
1115 Esther Street
Vancouver, WA 98660

REFERENCES

Almy, M. (1975). *The early childhood educator at work.* New York: McGraw-Hill.

Bronfenbrenner, U. (1974). *Is early intervention effective? A report on longitudinal evaluations of preschool programs.* Washington, DC: Department of Health, Education and Welfare, U.S. Children's Bureau.

Bronfenbrenner, U. (1979). *Ecology of human development.* Cambridge, MA: Harvard University Press.

Carkhuff, R., & Truax, C. (1965). Lay mental health counseling: The effects of lay group counseling. *Journal of Consulting Psychology, 39* (5), 426–431.

Collins, A. H., & Panconst, D. L. (1976). *Natural helping networks.* Washington, DC: National Association of Social Workers.

Durlak, J. (1979). Comparative effectiveness of professional and paraprofessional helpers. *Psychological Bulletin, 86,* 80–92.

Family Resource Coalition. (1986). 230 N. Michigan Avenue, Suite 1625, Chicago, IL.

Florian, P. R. & Dokecki, P. (1983). Changing families through parent and family education. In I. Sigel & L. Laosa (Eds.), *Changing families: Review and analysis* (pp. 23–63). New York: Plenum Press.

Kamerman, S., & Kahn, A. J. (1976). *Child care programs in nine countries* (DHEW

Publication No. OHD 76-30080). Washington, DC: U.S. Department of Health, Education and Welfare.

Katz, L. G. (1977). *Talking with teachers.* Washington, DC: National Association for the Education of Young Children.

Keniston, K., & the Carnegie Council on Children. (1977). *All our children.* New York: Harcourt, Brace Jovanovich.

Mason, D., Jensen, G., & Ryzewicz, C. (1979). *How to grow a parents group.* Milwaukee, WI: International Childbirth Association.

Meyer, N. (1982). Family resource programs: The volunteer model. Unpublished manuscript. Evanston, IL: Family Focus.

Nickel, P. S., & Delany, H. (1985). *Working with teen parents: A survey of promising approaches.* Chicago, IL: Family Resource Coalition.

Perlman, H. H. (1985, January/February). On the art of caring. *Child Welfare, 64* (1), 7. Washington, DC: Child Welfare League of America.

Pizzo, P. (1983). *Parent to parent.* Boston: Beacon Press.

Powell, D. R. (1976). *A social interactional approach to parent education: An overview of the child and family neighborhood program.* Detroit, MI: The Merrill-Palmer Institute.

Programs to strengthen families: A resource guide. (1983). New Haven, CT: Yale University Bush Center in Child Development and Social Policy (available from The Family Resource Coalition, 230 North Michigan Ave., Suite 1625, Chicago, IL. 60601).

Reiff, R., & Riessman, F. (1965). The indigenous paraprofessional. *Community Mental Health Journal,* Monograph No. 1.

Smith, M. O. (1984). Building self-confidence in the parent-infant relationship. *Child Welfare, 67* (6), 550. Washington, DC: Child Welfare League of America.

Spodek, B. (1972). *Teaching in the early years.* Englewood Cliffs, NJ: Prentice Hall.

Unger, D. G., & Powell, D. R. (1980). Supporting families under stress: The role of social networks. *Family Relations, 29* (4), 566–575.

Vincent, L. (1984, December 13). Family relationships. Opening address at conference on Comprehensive Approaches to Disabled and At-Risk Infants, Toddlers, and Their Families, National Center for Clinical Infant Programs, Washington, DC.

Wallach, L. B., & Weissbourd, B. (1979). *Creating drop-in centers: The family focus model.* Evanston, IL: Family Focus.

Whittaker, J. K., Garbarino, J., & Associates. (1983). *Social support networks: Informal helping in the human services.* New York: Aldine.

Wiltse, K. (1981). Education and training for child welfare services. Unpublished manuscript, University of California, Berkeley, School of Social Welfare.

14 INNOVATIVE FUNDING AND PRIVATE/PUBLIC PARTNERSHIPS

Susan Muenchow

The shortage and instability of funding for family support programs are manifestations of the general problems in financing prevention programs. Despite increasing evidence of the benefits of such strategies as prenatal care, home visiting, and respite care, the prevention of family dysfunction is more difficult to fund than the treatment of its consequences. Even in times of fiscal restraint, a crisis compels immediate action, but prevention, it seems, can be put off for a sunny day. Furthermore, whether the source of funding is public or private, it is easier to finance one pilot program than to obtain the funding to make services available on a wider scale.

Although none of the mechanisms described below fully overcomes these obstacles, they represent major innovations in funding family support programs that have arisen over the past decade. Family support will here be defined broadly to include not only counseling, peer support, parent education, and child care services but also prenatal care, educational services to prevent school dropouts, and abuse-intervention services. All of these programs help prevent the break-up of future as well as present families.

CHILDREN'S TRUST FUNDS

One of the most popular new mechanisms for raising public dollars to prevent child abuse is the Children's Trust Fund. The program was conceived in 1980 by a pediatrician nationally recognized in the field of

269

child-abuse prevention, Ray E. Helfer. Children's Trust Fund consists of money raised from special state-wide fees or contributions as opposed to general state taxes (National Center on Child Abuse and Neglect, 1984). Frustrated in their efforts to persuade legislators to appropriate general tax revenue for prevention services, advocates have had more success in enacting special fee increases and income tax provisions which allow taxpayers to donate their refunds to prevention purposes. As of March 1985, twenty-two states had established Children's Trust Funds to develop child-abuse and neglect-prevention programs (National Conference of State Legislatures, 1985).

Several methods are used to create Children's Trust Funds. Ten states designate voluntary income tax refund check-offs for their trust funds, seven states designate a surcharge on marriage licenses, and five states charge a fee for either live-birth registration or duplicate birth certificates. In addition, two states allow the use of divorce filing and divorce decree fees for their Children's Trust Funds, and one of these states also allocates $2 from each death certificate to the fund. Finally, two states use only foundation or federal grants and private gifts for their funds (National Conference of State Legislatures, 1985).

Children's Trust Fund monies are allocated to public and private non-profit community-based programs for both primary and secondary prevention (National Center on Child Abuse and Neglect, 1984). Primary prevention programs, available to all members of the community on a voluntary basis, include parent education, public awareness campaigns, support groups for new parents, and programs to teach school-age children how to protect themselves from abuse. Secondary prevention programs, targeted at parents thought to be at risk for abusing their children, include parenting classes for teenage mothers, home health visitors for families that have demonstrated difficulties in bonding with their newborns, and crisis nurseries.

Whether a Children's Trust Fund is used to finance primary or secondary prevention may depend on the extent of prevention services already available for targeted groups and on the composition of the lobby for the fund. In Illinois, which has the Ounce of Prevention Fund (discussed below) to help finance family support programs, the child abuse prevention trust fund is allocated for secondary prevention and for treatment of abuse. Funds which totaled $500,000 in 1984 are used for shelters for abused children, respite care, or local chapters of Parents Anonymous. In Iowa, by contrast, trust fund monies ($125,000 in 1984) are specifically restricted to primary prevention programs aimed at all parents; no trust fund money is allowed for intervention or treatment. The emphasis of a trust fund may also reflect pressure to show measurable results, such as a reduction in the incidence of abuse. These outcomes may be more likely to result from services targeted at a population known to be at risk than from general education campaigns directed at all parents.

Despite their success in creating new sources of revenue for prevention and other services, Children's Trust Funds are not without their critics (Streit, 1984). It is important to note that most of these funds have not generated large amounts of income. Only three Children's Trust Funds have raised more than a million dollars annually; most have raised less than $400,000 (National Conference of State Legislatures, 1985). By contrast, Florida has raised more money ($4.1 million in 1985) for community-based child-abuse-prevention programs through a general revenue appropriation authorized by the legislature in 1982 than have any of the state trust funds for child abuse prevention. Critics therefore argue that Children's Trust Funds unwisely take the pressure off legislators to provide larger and more stable forms of revenue for prevention services. As Samuel Streit (1984), former director of the Florida Governor's Constituency for Children, notes: as long as prevention is treated as a "special" effort requiring "innovative" funding, there is a possibility that "the entire prevention movement will continue to suffer from a sort of political illegitimacy that is attached to most children's issues."

Children's Trust Funds may also eventually be hindered by their own popularity. Various child and family services are increasingly competing for the same revenue sources to finance their trust funds. In Florida, for example, fee increases have been imposed on birth certificates, marriage licenses, divorce filing fees, and fees on forfeited bail bonds to finance training of child welfare professionals. Similar fees on forfeited bail bonds have also been tapped to finance training of juvenile justice workers, and new fees for "designer birth certificates" are being proposed to help supplement state revenue for child abuse and neglect services. Multiple one- or two-dollar fee increases on these items would eventually add up to substantial fee increases.

Children's Trust Funds have succeeded, however, in raising revenue for prevention in states where there was none. As the National Center on Child Abuse and Neglect (1984) points out, Children's Trust Funds have been enacted in states that span the political spectrum, including some conservative states known for their lack of generous prevention and treatment appropriations for child and family services. Children's Trust Funds may also focus public attention on prevention services and help develop new links between public and private agencies for the prevention of child abuse.

COUNTY TAX REVENUE FOR CHILDREN

One of the most innovative programs for raising public dollars for community-based services for children is not new but has only recently begun to be replicated. Since 1945, the Juvenile Welfare Board (JWB) of Pinellas County, Florida, has provided a broad range of services for children and families, financed by its power to assess a tax of up to one-half mill (50 cents per $1000 nonexempt property evaluation) solely for the purpose of providing services to children (Juvenile Welfare Board, 1984). By 1984, the JWB had provided funding of over $7.7 million to support 64 discrete programs, operated by 39 different community agencies. Only $1.3 million came from federal funding; the remainder was generated by the county tax levy.

In 1986, as a result of a county referendum, Palm Beach County became the second county in Florida to establish an independent taxing mechanism for children's services, and several other counties are considering the establishment of juvenile welfare boards. The Children's Services Council, as it is called in Palm Beach, is expected to generate $16 to $18 million for child and family services, including prevention services.

In Pinellas County, over one-third of the monies raised for the Juvenile Welfare Board in 1984 went to primary prevention services, including early screening, information and referral, latchkey services, child care licensing, Adopt-A-Grandchild, substance-abuse prevention, and family day care for children from low-income families. As a result of the county's contribution to such programs, Pinellas County leads Florida in the quality of some services for children. For example, the county has the strictest staff-child ratios for day care and the largest licensing staff to enforce day care standards.

According to the executive director of JWB, James E. Mills (personal communication, 1985), advocates need the support of at least the superintendent of schools, the juvenile court judge, and the county commissioners in order to win support for a similar county-taxing authority for children's services. Although quick to criticize federal cutbacks in funding that have hindered efforts to provide prevention services even in Pinellas, Mills adds that there are many communities that could afford to increase or rearrange their local tax efforts to aid children's services. "It comes down to what you value more, curbs and gutters or kids," he points out.

States can encourage counties to raise more revenue for children's services, according to Mills, by providing enabling legislation; by assisting county licensing boards that exceed state standards; and by creating fiscal incentives, such as administrative support, to counties that establish special taxing districts for the provision of children's services.

County efforts to collect revenue for children's services need not be limited to the property tax. Some counties might have more success enacting an extra penny sales tax, especially on a product that can be logically linked to the need for some child and family services, such as beer or alcohol.

PRIVATE/PUBLIC PARTNERSHIPS

In addition to Children's Trust Funds and other special taxing mechanisms, a variety of new public/private partnerships have been formed over the last decade to finance family support and other prevention programs. In some cases, state agencies pool funds with corporations to finance these programs. In others, public agencies form partnerships with parents or other volunteers. Public agencies are also working with private agencies or with other public agencies to offer family support programs. Particularly in the area of child and family health care, some counties are contracting with private professionals to serve low-income families.

Partnerships Between Public Agencies and Corporations

One of the most successful private/public partnerships on behalf of family support services is Illinois' Ounce of Prevention Fund. The fund began in 1982 when Irving Harris, former chairman of the Pittway Corporation and philanthropist for over 20 years, and Bernice Weissbourd, founder of Family Focus, approached Gregory Coler, then director of Illinois' Department of Children and Family Services, to request the money to establish a Family Focus Center for Spanish-speaking families Coler not only agreed to provide the funds for one program but also offered $400,000 to establish six programs if the Pittway Corporation Charitable Foundation would match these funds. The Ounce of Prevention Fund thus began its first year with a budget of $800,000.

With a budget of over $5 million by 1985, the Ounce of Prevention Fund now finances a variety of programs at 44 sites serving over 6000 teenagers and adults in areas of the state that have a significant high-risk population for abuse and neglect. The comprehensive, community-based programs include prenatal and postpartum home visits, peer-support groups for teen parents, developmental day care for infants and toddlers, and community drop-in centers for parents and children. The Ounce of Prevention Fund also has an extensive evaluation component that makes use of research by the Center for Health Services at Northwestern University, the School of Public Health at the University of Illinois at Chicago, and the State of Illinois, as well as by the Ounce of Prevention Fund's own staff.

From the beginning, the architects of the Ounce of Prevention Fund, according to Coler (personal communication, 1985), saw the private foundation support not as an end in itself but as a springboard for institutionalizing public funding for primary prevention programs. While initially the state and private contributions to the fund were equal, the state now contributes the larger portion, with the Pittway Corporation Charitable Foundation, other foundations, and the federal government contributing about equally to make up the rest. The Ounce of Prevention Fund has also been the inspiration for a $10 million state initiative called Parents Too Soon, which is designed to reduce teen pregnancy. It was a major breakthrough to get the legislature to approve a line item for this prevention program in the Department of Public Aid's budget, says Mr. Coler, now Secretary of the Department of Health and Rehabilitative Services in Florida. The Ounce of Prevention Fund signaled to legislators that primary prevention is not just another bureaucratic social experiment but can be an important priority of the corporate establishment.

Other examples of corporate/public agency partnerships include a variety of educational programs—Adopt-A-School, Partners in Education, and Cities-in-Schools—sponsored by businesses and schools. Although these programs may not fit a strict definition of family support programs, most of them are motivated at least in part by the desire to reduce the number of students who drop out of school, a problem that certainly contributes to and may result from family dysfunction. They are also the fruits of collaboration among various community institutions, a characteristic of family support at its best.

Through Adopt-A-School programs, a business provides volunteers, materials, or in-kind services for a school project, such as fixing up a playground. One of the oldest and largest such programs, in Dallas, Texas, began in 1969 when community groups became interested in the Reading is Fundamental program, funded by both community and federal sources. Sun Oil and the National Council of Jewish Women were among the first partners (adopters) of the Dallas Independent School District (DISD); 1,500 businesses now participate in the program (Dallas Independent School District, 1984).

DISD now has a contract with the Dallas Chamber of Commerce in support of the Adopt-A-School program. School principals wishing to participate in the program are asked to submit a list of their needs over and above the school budget, and the school is then matched with a business. This year business contributions to the Adopt-A-School program amounted to $6 million, according to Bobbie J. Foster (personal communication, 1985), director of DISD's community relations department. These contributions might be characterized as extras making the difference, for example, between a school having 10 computers or three.

However, just as the Ounce of Prevention Fund has contributed to increased public funding for primary prevention services in Illinois, so, too, has the Adopt-A-School program led to increased public dollars for the Dallas school budget. Friends of Dallas, a group of business people including many Adopt-A-School partners, led a recent campaign for a $195 million school bond issue. Passage of this bond issue will make it possible for DISD to alleviate overcrowding of school classrooms, to repair roofs, and to tackle other essential school maintenance projects.

Cities-in-Schools is another private/public partnership designed to promote school-dropout-prevention programs. Based in 17 cities across the United States, according to Executive Director Maurice Weir (personal communication, 1985), Cities-in-Schools attempts to work with public and private agencies to move social, health, and recreational services to school sites. In each of the cities where Cities-in-Schools is located, two or three people are hired to coordinate these efforts. Public funds for Cities-in-Schools come from the Department of Health and Human Services, the Justice Department, and the Department of Education. At least 100 foundations and corporations, including ARCO and the William M. Keck Foundation, provide matching funds.

Finally, some corporations are forming partnerships with public agencies to meet the child care needs of their employees. The "feminizing" of the workforce, in which the number of women is expected to increase from two-fifths to half over the next 10 years (Axel, 1985), is part of the impetus for employers to adopt family supportive policies. An estimated 1800 employers across the nation currently provide some form of child care assistance, according to the Conference Board's Work and Family Information Center (Friedman, 1985).

Recognizing that the inability to afford reliable quality child care may be a cause of absenteeism and poor work performance, a majority of employers who provide assistance with child care offer some form of financial assistance (Friedman, 1985). Of the 120 corporations and 400 hospitals that currently sponsor on-site day care, nearly all provide the necessary start-up costs and some also subsidize fees. Other methods of assisting employees with child care expenses include offering discounts for a specific child care center or providing vouchers that can be used for any licensed child care facility of the employee's choice. The federal government is in effect forming a partnership with employers who offer these child care benefits since federal tax laws, such as the 1981 Economic Recovery Act, make child care a nontaxable benefit and hence a convenient option to include in flexible benefit and salary reduction plans (Friedman, 1985).

One of the most innovative private employer–public agency partnerships on behalf of child care is in Orlando, Florida. Community Coordinated Child Care (4-C) of Central Florida, the agency that administers

Title XX-subsidized day care in that region, has voucher plans with six employers, such as McKinnon Corporation, a major citrus grower. These employers agree to cover 50 percent of the cost of care for low- to middle-income employees that 4-C cannot help with Title XX funds (Friedman, 1985); 4-C connects these employees with a range of child care facilities. This form of employer subsidy helps increase the number of families able to afford quality care without a two-tier system: employer-sponsored care for middle-income workers, and Title XX-sponsored care for employees earning marginally low or low incomes.

The major limitation on employer assistance with child care is that not all employers are well-suited to provide it. Far less than 1 percent of the nation's six million employers currently provide any assistance with child care (Friedman, 1985). Most of the companies adopting family supportive policies fit several of the following criteria: (1) companies that are in high-tech or scientific industries and see child care as a competitive edge in attracting skilled workers; (2) companies that have a relatively young work force; (3) companies that have a high proportion of female employees; (4) companies located in progressive communities; (5) companies that are nonunion; (6) companies with paternalistic leaders; and (7) companies that make products for a consumer market (Axel, 1985). There will always be some employers who do not meet these criteria and who therefore cannot justify assisting employees with their child care costs on business grounds. In addition, few companies are currently assisting employees enough with their ongoing child care expenses to make quality care truly affordable to low-income employees. Thus, while employers are providing much valuable assistance with child care, there is no evidence that they have reduced the number of families who need publicly subsidized care.

Partnerships between Public Agencies and Volunteers

Numerous partnerships have also sprung up between public agencies and volunteers. Arkansas' SCAN Volunteer Service, Inc. and Florida's Guardian Ad Litem program, for example, are designed to reduce child abuse and neglect by working primarily with families where abuse is suspected or has already occurred.

Founded in 1972 in Little Rock, Arkansas, as an alternative to traditional child-protection services, SCAN contracts with the State Department of Human Services to deliver services to families suspected of child abuse and neglect (*Programs to Strengthen Families*, 1983). SCAN now serves families in eleven counties, according to Executive Director Sharon Pallone (personal communication, 1985).

Under the SCAN model, professional staff investigate each reported case of suspected abuse. A trained volunteer then visits the family's home two or three times a week to assist in problem-solving and offer information on parenting. SCAN has 45 professional staff members who train and supervise 250 to 300 volunteers. The volunteers carry from one to three cases at any time. When the situation demands at least a temporary out-of-home placement of a child, a SCAN volunteer continues to provide intensive services in an effort to reunite the family as soon as possible. The average stay of a child in foster care in the SCAN treatment model is six months, whereas the national average has been three to four years.

Despite the SCAN program's success, its history also illustrates some of the funding problems in a private/public partnership. SCAN, which until recently served fifteen counties, now serves only eleven because funds have not kept pace with the increasing need for services. Half of SCAN's $1.4 million budget comes from federal Social Services Block Grant funds, 25 percent from state funds, and the remainder from United Way and other local funds. Although community support has increased 300 percent from $90,000 to $300,000, over a four-year period, federal and state funds have risen by only 5 to 10 percent (M. Vogler, personal communication, 1985). During a similar period, abuse reports have risen by 25 percent. As a result, SCAN has had to eliminate services in four rural counties in order to maintain the program in urban areas with more reports of abuse.

A somewhat similar partnership between the state and volunteers has existed under the auspices of the Florida Guardian Ad Litem program since 1980. In each court proceeding involving child abuse and/or neglect, Florida courts appoint a trained volunteer guardian ad litem to investigate the case thoroughly and assist the court in determining the child's needs.

The Guardian Ad Litem program now has 1800 trained volunteers and has represented over 5000 children. Their $1 million budget is administered by a state office and at least one salaried staff member in each judicial circuit. Guardian Ad Litem volunteers also represent the child and family outside of the courtroom by helping to assure that families receive necessary services from community agencies in efforts to prevent unnecessary removal of children from their families. In cases where children must be at least temporarily placed out-of-home, Guardian Ad Litem volunteers have been found by an independent evaluation to unite children frequently with relatives who were unknown to local social service agencies, thereby increasing the chances for eventual family reunification (Florida Court Services, 1983). Finally, Guardian Ad Litem volunteers represent informed, articulate advocates for increased public funding for abuse-prevention services. They were instrumental in the passage of the previously mentioned state legislation in 1982, which now provides over $4.1 million for community-based abuse and neglect prevention services.

Partnerships between Public Agencies and Parents

Partnerships between public agencies and parents are based partly on the need to supplement limited public dollars with volunteer services. But parent involvement is even more strongly based on parents' impatience with the insensitivity of many public agencies to their needs, and on the opinion that mutual self-help is more effective than professional services alone in dealing with certain kinds of family problems.

The Parent-to-Parent family support model, developed by High/Scope Educational Research Foundation, is designed to provide a low-cost, self-sustaining community support system for parents of young children (*Programs To Strengthen Families*, 1983). The Parent-to-Parent program trains parent volunteers as home visitors to help families strengthen their parenting skills and connect them with other community services. Some Parent-to-Parent programs focus on teen parents, others on families at risk for child abuse, and still others on handicapped children and their families. With funding to support training from the Bernard van Leer Foundation and salary support from local communities, the Parent-to-Parent model has now been established in twenty-five communities in the Midwest and Northeast (J. Evans, personal communication, 1985). Public agencies such as schools, community health centers, and social service agencies help connect parents with the program and provide space for meetings.

The State of Florida in September 1985 awarded $50,000 to United Cerebral Palsy to establish Parent-to-Parent support programs throughout the state for families with developmentally disabled children. Volunteers who are parents of children with disabilities not only visit families with children recently diagnosed as developmentally disabled but also follow families who have lived with such children for some years. Project staff provide training, create a statewide network of programs, and serve as a referral system for parents of children with disabilities.

Partnerships among Public Agencies

Creative partnerships are also growing among public agencies at the local level. In St. Paul, Minnesota, the public schools, the Maternal and Infant Care Project of the St. Paul Division of Public Health, and the departments of pediatrics, obstetrics, and gynecology at St. Paul-Ramsey Hospital joined forces to sponsor school-based health clinics (Porter & Butler, 1984). In an effort to reduce teen pregnancy, the clinics offer family planning information to students within the context of other health services, such as job and college physicals, immunizations, weight-control programs, and treatment of drug and alcohol abuse. The clinics are credited with reducing the fertility rate in the schools where they are located from 79 to 35 per 1000 students (Edwards, 1980); the repeat pregnancy rate has been reduced to 1.4 percent. (Nationally, 33 percent of those who become pregnant under the age of 18 will have a second pregnancy within 24 months [Porter & Butler, 1984].) Because the program also includes day care for the children of those teenagers who do become pregnant, over 85 percent of the young mothers now graduate from high school and also learn to care for their babies.

Although the St. Paul school-based health clinics are sponsored by the above-mentioned schools, public health department, and hospital departments, they also depend on federal funds from Title V (Maternal and Child Health) and Title XX (Social Services Block Grant) as well as foundation funds (Minnesota Family Planning Special Project and Northwest Area Foundation). Given the controversial nature of any program offering family planning information, however, it is doubtful that any amount of federal or foundation funding could have been obtained without the strong support of key school, hospital, and health department officials in the community.

Partnerships between Public Agencies and Private Professionals

Public agencies are also increasingly forming partnerships with private-sector professionals. In Sarasota, Florida, after realizing that existing public health services were not reaching the many children from low-income families who needed them, the county contracted with private physicians to provide complete pediatric care to these children. During health clinic hours in the morning, families go to the clinic; after hours, they go to the participating pediatricians' offices.

Tailoring services to meet the needs of families and establishing an ongoing relationship between a specific pediatrician and a family, has resulted in increased utilization of the preventive services and a sharp decline in more expensive pediatric visits to the emergency ward of Sarasota Hospital (Porter & Butler, 1984). A similar contract has now been developed between the county and obstetricians for the delivery of prenatal services to low-income pregnant women. One-third of the cost is covered through third-party billing, one-third by the county, and one-third by the state.

Reviewing the private/public partnerships described above, it is clear that they have many benefits. Private dollars and volunteers can in some circumstances provide everything from icing on the cake to essential human services. Volunteers generally have far fewer cases to serve than do publicly employed professionals and may also be less hindered by public agency regulations. Consequently, the use of volunteers may result in services more sensitive to the needs of families than those provided solely by publicly employed professionals. In addition, private/public partnerships may foster the natural alliances that have long been needed to make the most efficient use of limited resources. The very investment of private time and money raises the consciousness of the private-sector participants about the needs of families and helps build a more articulate lobby of advocates for increased public funding for child and family services.

The chief difficulty with private/public partnerships is that the level of private support available in a community varies, so that the least private money and the fewest number of volunteers may be available in the very communities where the need for family support services is greatest. Family support services must still be institutionalized if all those who need them are to be served. In the interests of equity, the public sector should not view its commitment as temporary and must help compensate for lower levels of private support in some communities.

A review of state trust funds for children, county tax revenue mechanisms, and private/public partnerships shows a great diversity in the way communities are funding family support programs. The increasing involvement and innovative partnerships of private citizens, business leaders, and community agencies in the provision of family support services are a healthy sign. Instead of duplicating or competing with each other's efforts, public and private agencies have more incentives to work together. Instead of the federal government's initiating family support programs from the top down, these programs are originating only in areas where there is strong grass roots support. Unfortunately, programs funded by private/public partnerships are not necessarily available to all who need them—they depend not only on the availability of private donors but also on the tax base of the state and/or locality. Private/public partnerships are thus no real substitute for entitlement programs, which, at least in theory, make benefits available to all citizens who fit the eligibility criteria. If new private/public partnerships can succeed not only in maintaining local citizen and private-sector involvement but also in using such involvement as leverage for more stable public funding, these new funding mechansims will indeed be worthy of the label innovative.

REFERENCES

Axel, H. (1985). *Corporations and families: Changing practices and perspectives.* New York: Conference Board.

Dallas Independent School District. (1984). Partnerships at a glance. *Volunteer News, 10* (1), 7.

Edwards, L. E. (1980). Adolescent pregnancy prevention services in high school clinics. *Family Planning Perspectives, 12* (1), 6–14.

Florida Court Services (1983, July 25–28). State of Florida Court Guardian Ad Litem Program. Paper presented at annual meeting of Conference of State Court Administrators, Savannah, GA.

Friedman, D. (1985). Corporate financial assistance for child care. *The Conference Board Research Bulletin* (No. 177), New York.

Juvenile Welfare Board of Pinellas County. (1984). *Annual Report.*

National Center on Child Abuse and Neglect. (1984). *A forum on children's trust funds.* Washington, DC: U.S. Department of Health and Human Services, Administration for Children, Youth and Families, Office of Human Services Development.

National Conference of State Legislatures. (1985). Children and youth program staff. Unpublished packet, Denver, CO.

Porter, P. J., & Butler, J. C. (1984). *Healthy children: A casebook for community action.* Boston: Harvard University, Division of Health Policy Research and Education.

Programs to Strengthen Families: A resource guide. (1983). New Haven, CT: Yale University Bush Center in Child Development and Social Policy (available from The Family Resource Coalition, 230 North Michigan Ave., Suite 1625, Chicago. IL 60601).

Streit, S. M. (1984). Legislative innovation in funding children's programs: The children's trust fund concept. Unpublished manuscript.

15 ETHNICITY AND FAMILY SUPPORT

Shirley Jenkins

Is it preferable for a homemaker helping a black family from the Caribbean to be English- , French- , or Spanish-speaking? Should a meeting of young couples to discuss parenting problems be held on Friday nights? Should newcomers to a community be welcomed at an outdoor beer-and-beef barbecue? The answer to the first question depends on whether the family is Jamaican, Haitian, or Hispanic. The answer to the second depends on whether the parents are observant Jews. As to the third, if the newcomers were Hindus from India, they might shun both alcohol and meat. The need for family support is almost universal, but custom, language, religion, and sense of group identity constitute the context of support, which should in turn determine its form.

Consciousness of culture is an even more complex issue than language in developing programs for ethnic families. By culture, we are referring here not only to customs and traditional living styles but to the deeply felt meanings of relationships and values. Prevailing concepts of mental health support in the United States are essentially western ideas, often presumed to be universal but actually relevant primarily to the social context in which they were developed. For societies that hold the family to be more important than the individual and the extended intergenerational family more significant than the nuclear family, different assumptions may be needed in developing support programs. These assumptions may affect services for teenagers who seek independence from parents, for marital and divorce counseling, and for attitudes on care of the elderly.

This chapter suggests that ethnicity is an important variable in family support programs and examines the nature of the concept. Two studies are reported; one explored how, when, and where ethnic factors are relevant to service delivery, and another analyzed ethnic associations and services to new immigrants. In addition, the 72 family support programs reported in *Programs to Strengthen Families: A Resource Guide* (1983) are reviewed for references to ethnic factors.

ETHNICITY — DEFINITIONS OF THE VARIABLE

Ethnicity as a variable has particular relevance for work with families. It is a concept that incorporates an interest factor with an affective tie (Bell, 1975). This means that ethnic group associations can be useful when seeking concrete services, such as jobs and housing, and can also bring people together on the basis of feelings and relationships. Family supports likewise offer needed help within an emotional caring context. Ethnicity has been described as a variable that can mediate between the primary group and the large bureaucratic organization (Litwak & Dono, 1976), and such bridging is also a function characteristic of family support programs.

Because it is a concept that includes many variables, ethnicity is difficult to define precisely. It may be useful to refer to a few imprecise definitions so that the terms of reference of this discussion will be more explicit. Schermerhorn (1970) defines ethnicity as "a collectivity within a larger society having real or putative common ancestry, memories of a shared historical past, and a cultural focus on one or more symbolic elements. . . . A necessary accompaniment is some consciousness of kind among members of the group (p. 12)." Among these symbolic elements, Schermerhorn includes physical contiguity, language or dialect, religion, phenotypical features, kinship patterns, and nationality, or any combination of these.

In planning for service delivery, as well as in making psycho-social assessments, ethnicity becomes one more factor to be considered, along with age, sex, interests, diagnoses, and social and class variables. Ethnicity is distinguished from some of the more traditional variables, however, in that it is not an individual characteristic, like height or weight, but must have group referents. One's ethnicity is derived from group membership, but it is tempered by the extent to which each individual identifies with his or her group. Furthermore, such identification may vary depending on the time and situation. Parkin (1974), for example, has described ethnicity as "the articulation of cultural distinctiveness in situations of political conflict or competition." This is not a criterion which can be applied in all situations, however, since it denies on-going differences. The examples given in the introduction to this chapter, child care at home, parental discussions, and social welcome, are not couched in terms of political conflict, but ethnicity is nevertheless involved in each, subsuming language, religion, and custom. In providing services to diverse families, ethnicity tends to take on an accordian-like form—it has wide potential but may be kept narrow; it can have a small sound or be fully extended and override other noises in volume.

Distinction should be made between ethnicity and race. Ethnicity is an umbrella concept and includes a variety of cultural characteristics as well as social and racial distinctiveness in various combinations. Race is primarily a biological concept, once thought to be fixed but now recognized to have many variants. Racism is considered to be the institutional form of discrimination against people based on the biological factors of race.

The focus on ethnicity in this chapter is not intended to obscure the issue of racism and its negative impact on service delivery. To begin the discussion with issues of racism, however, would be to assume a reactive approach to perceived discrimination. To begin with ethnicity, which incorporates racial factors, is to make a positive statement about the universality of ethnic factors and the need to plan services appropriately. Where racism can be identified, however, it needs to be dealt with as such, without obfuscation.

HISTORICAL FACTORS

In an earlier period, support services for people with needs were supplied by family, friends, religious groups, and immigrants of the same background. As a matter of course, the language, custom, and culture of the helpers corresponded to those of the people in need of support. The introduction of the income-maintenance programs and the involvement of the state in the delivery of social services—much-needed advances in our social system—introduced the egalitarian concept of the welfare state. A corollary to this was the professionalization and bureaucratization of help. Since the system did not operate in a cultural vacuum, it reflected the norms of the majority, concomitantly ignoring ethnic differences.

In the past decade it has become apparent that entitlements cannot be fully available unless there is recognition of special needs arising from ethnic concerns. The sense of ethnic identity has sharpened, and this has affected program directions even in the formerly "color blind" public sector. Four examples illustrate this change. As part of its services a New York City hospital has two special clinics: an Asian Clinic and a Hispanic Clinic. Each is designed to serve its particular patient group, with medical and other health personnel knowledgeable of the corresponding language, customs, and culture. A Social Security office has a Chinese interpreter whose employment caused a substantial rise in applications from elderly Chinese. A Child Welfare Department in Los Angeles has a special unit for Hispanic adoptions staffed by Spanish-speaking social workers. A Human Resources Department has outreach workers who accept applications for public welfare in the headquarters of refugee ethnic associations. These efforts are examples of new public responses to ethnic issues. In *An American Dilemma* (1944), Myrdal called attention to the gap between our professed commitment to equality and our actual practices of discrimination, particularly against blacks. There have been confrontation and change since that time, and, in spite of political setbacks, it is likely that a generation reared on ethnic power, pride, and identity will continue to press for equity. Given this context and the efforts at social and institutional reform, it is timely to ask how the more informal family support programs are recognizing and integrating ethnic components.

A FIELD STUDY ON THE ETHNIC DILEMMA

In the field of social services and family support, the dilemma is not whether to recognize the importance of ethnicity in working with people but rather how, when, and where ethnic factors enter the delivery system. To explore this question, the author undertook a field study of fifty-four "ethnic agencies" in the United States, with comparative work in England and Israel (Jenkins, 1981). Ethnic agencies were defined as those with a clear commitment to a specific group and a program incorporating both social service and ethnic goals in a single delivery system. Included were programs serving Asian, black, Chicano, Native American, and Puerto Rican children and families. In all groups support for families was a primary goal, even where there were categorical programs for a specific group, such as day care or foster care, issues of family life were of major concern.

Three issues emerged from the analysis as relevant to the study of the ethnic agency: issues of culture, consciousness, and "mixing or matching" on ethnic lines. Cultural content was found in all aspects of programming in ethnic agencies, from the use of traditional foods and holiday celebrations to treatment and child care. Family therapy, for example, was modified in one treatment center in San Francisco to conform to traditional Asian family patterns, which limited intergenerational discussion of certain subjects, such as sexual behavior. In a Native American day-care center in Arizona, the Indian director stressed the importance of knowing tribal patterns before disciplining young children. Her center served pre-school children from ten Indian tribes, which differed in significant ways. Some tribes were strict, some permissive, and some practiced avoidance of conflict in child rearing. The director had to balance practices at home with practices at school and try to help children understand their divergence.

In discussing what worked and what didn't work in programs with ethnic clients, agencies reported several areas of success and failure (Jenkins, 1981, p. 61). Agencies expressed most satisfaction with the following:

1. Bilingual-bicultural programs
2. Career development for parents and leadership development for youth
3. Supports to families to help them care for their own children
4. Recruitment of minority parents for foster care and adoption
5. Utilizing traditional cultural and/or tribal patterns to effect change.

On the other hand, the following didn't work or were problems:

1. Use of groups for therapy or treatment, especially for teenagers
2. Efforts to persuade the community to accept group homes and/or de-institutionalization
3. Handling of interethnic relations between groups
4. Conflicts between new and old arrivals, or between more and less acculturated members of the group
5. Persistence of some dysfunctional cultural patterns, particularly of bilingual programs. (p. 61)

Thus the most positive reactions were to programs related to culture, language, and family closeness, and to those that opened opportunities for advancement. Least popular were programs that were intrusive, revealing of differences, or concerned with inter- or intragroup conflict. Cultural patterns found to be dysfunctional included excessive rigidity in child rearing.

Ethnic consciousness, a second component of ethnic agency programs, was defined as the extent to which agencies were aware of involvement with larger issues affecting the group. These issues could be social, political, or cultural, and the attention given to the broader ethnic concerns varied by agency.

Among the most controversial issues in ethnic programming is mixing or matching along ethnic lines. This arises at every level of activity, between worker and client, foster parent and foster child, staff and supervisor; it is also important in the composition of groups and the selection of leaders. Perhaps the most telling example of this concern was the opposition of the Association of Black Social Workers to interracial adoptions. Their concern was that black children could not develop an appropriate sense of identity in a white home, even with caring parents.

In discussing the issue of mixing or matching it is important to distinguish between a separatist and a segregationist stance. The difference is whether the decision to be with one's own group is made by the ethnic minority itself or is imposed by the white majority. In the survey of child welfare workers, reported in *The Ethnic Dilemma in Social Services* (Jenkins, 1981), a majority of respondents opted for a mixing alternative in most situations, but significantly more ethnic workers in ethnic agencies chose matching by ethnic group than did workers in traditional settings.

To supplement the survey of worker attitudes on ethnicity in the study noted above, group interviews with parents were conducted in the child care settings to obtain parent reactions to ethnic issues in support programs. There were two group interviews in each of five field sites, involving 54 Asian, black, Chicano, Indian, and Puerto Rican parents. Parents were asked whether, if they had to choose, they would prefer help from a nonprofessional person of their own ethnic group or from someone with a social work degree. Only three of the 54 parents interviewed said they would prefer a trained worker. The other 51 were divided between those who said the choice depended on the individual and those who opted for a member of their own group. The parents placed more importance on matching than did the ethnic social workers in the larger survey. The main reasons parents gave for wanting the ethnic match were language, avoidance of prejudice, and cultural awareness.

From the field survey and the parent interviews in the *Ethnic Dilemma* study, a typology was developed suggesting ways to consider how, when, and where ethnicity needs to be activated in the areas of human service delivery. Three levels are considered, traditionally described as micro, mezzo, and macro, and referring, respectively, to individuals, groups, and societies.

At the micro level of interpersonal interactions, attention needs to be paid to both the situation giving rise to the problem and the alternatives for solution. For a person with a toothache, the ethnicity of the dentist is less important than his or her competence, and the patient can point to where it hurts. But for a family needing a homemaker to care for children, having someone of the same group may be more crucial than the homemaker's level of training, since "same group" subsumes many of the relevant variables of culture, and good mothering is not necessarily related to educational level. However, these criteria do not apply across the board; the study reports that "there was at least one parent in each of the ten groups who spontaneously commented that there are people in all races and groups who do not like children. . . ." (Jenkins, 1981, p. 113). Ethnicity is only one variable among many others, and its relative importance depends on an individual assessment.

The intermediate or mezzo level refers to group characteristics in a national setting. Affecting the significance of ethnic issues will be four relevant variables about the ethnic groups: recency of migration, geographic locale, class and caste, and homogeneity of the members. Thus culture, language, and custom may have different significance for new immigrants and for the third generation; for city dwellers and farm people; for the wealthy and the dependent; and for heterogeneous and homogeneous groups. The Native American family on the reservation, for example, lives differently from the Native American in the city. Thus there is no simple formula, only a framework of how to evaluate ethnicity as one among other group characteristics.

Beyond the group factors, there are situations in which ethnicity is relevant at the macro or societal level, which includes issues of national and international politics. Refugee policy, for example, may be affected by the ethnicity of those seeking entry. The national debate on the immigration legislation of 1986 often had overtones reflecting attitudes to a specific ethnic group.

This discussion of ethnic factors has been mainly limited to the five minority groups included in affirmative action legislation, since they are the focus of most programmatic attention. But this is too narrow an interpretation—ethnic factors are involved for all groups in the host society who have memories of a shared past and a consciousness of kind. Native Americans and blacks, for example, may have ancestors who were here many generations ago. For others, such as newcomers to the United States, family support programs must deal with factors of strangeness and adaptation as well as ethnic differences.

NEW IMMIGRANTS AND REFUGEES

There is a new wave of immigration to the United States, different from earlier waves in that the largest numbers coming are Asians and Hispanics rather than Europeans. These newcomers have the same needs for family supports as do long-time residents, but to an even greater degree. The dislocations and separations experienced, the lack of accumulated resources and family capital, and the dual struggle both to preserve identity and to accomplish acculturation often put intolerable strains on family members.

The need for family support for newcomers has been documented in numerous research studies. One study of refugee camps, for example, found that unaccompanied children from Vietnam were significantly more depressed and had many more problems than children who came with families, especially multigenerational families (Harding & Looney, 1977). Chu (1979), who studied Southeast Asian refugees as they began their resettlement in Los Angeles, concluded, "The single most influential factor in determining refugee trauma was the extent of physical family separation, a factor that was highly correlated with survivor guilt" (p. 21).

Although family disruptions and their effects on individuals or groups have been studied at the time of entry, there has been little systematic work on what has happened to families of newcomers in the acculturation process. A paradigm for the study of immigrant families, focusing on decision-making in three critical areas—quality of life, social relationships, and self-actualization and identity—is suggested by Wiseman (1985). These decisions are made following arrival in relation to survival, normative selection, and intergenerational conflict. By tracking how family decisions change over the "career" of acculturation, the impact of the new environment on family relationships may be better understood, and areas in which family support may be needed identified.

One widespread movement to deal with the needs of families of newcomers has been the organization of Mutual Assistance Associations (MAAs) among refugees of many groups. In the six years from 1975 to 1981, for example, over 500 of such associations were created by the Indochinese community alone. Although diversified in purpose, many provide educational, support, and training programs as well as serve cultural functions (Bui, 1981). Many of these groups undertake a range of activities. Many receive public funds from the Federal Refugee Assistance programs, some via established voluntary social service agencies and some directly in response to state program initiatives. These are groups in closest touch with refugee/entrant families, including Vietnamese, Cambodian, Afghan, Ethiopian, Polish, Russian, and Rumanian.

In addition to the refugee self-help groups, there are literally thousands of ethnic associations helping new immigrant families in the process of coping and adapting.[1] These ethnic groupings range all the way from fully professionalized ethnic agencies, to neighborhood centers with substantial programming, to informal groups which aid in family functioning, perhaps focusing on youth or the elderly. Both old and new immigrants are involved, and in many cases help is extended to undocumented aliens with unmet needs. In 1975, Fisher (1980), for example, found a published list of 44 Indian associations in New York City alone, many based on common home-state/language identities. The memberships ranged from 75 to 1500 families in each. The members were mostly young Indian couples with children. Although primarily social and cultural in purpose, these associations also comprise a network of families engaged in mutual self-help.

A study of ethnic associations and services to new immigrants was undertaken in New York City (Jenkins, Sauber, & Friedlander, 1985). One major purpose was to see if linkages could be established between the associations and formal public and voluntary social agencies, so that service delivery could be facilitated. The researchers interviewed leaders of 30 associations, who comprised 17 ethnic groups: Cambodians, Chinese, Colombians, Cubans, Dominicans, Ethiopians, Greeks, Haitians, Indians, Israelis, Italians, Jamaicans, Koreans, Palestinians and other Arabic-speaking people, Poles, Russian Jews, and Vietnamese. Interviews were conducted in English, Spanish, Korean, and Chinese.

The study questionnaire sought information on the history and characteristics of the associations, identity and acculturation issues, perceptions of members' needs and problems, and service activities. Ethnic associations were found to be more active in providing some form of help to families than in any other area. Of the 30 associations whose leaders were interviewed, 22 offer family support services, counseling, and special programs for youth, women, and the elderly. Some examples will illustrate the levels and types of help.

Three Haitian groups provide family counseling and escort services as well as job training and information on how to use the subway and how to cope with American society. A Korean association gives counseling to parents and youths on problems of runaways and on school supervision. The Greek agency, as part of a comprehensive program, offers child- and spouse-abuse counseling. An Ethiopian association makes referrals for youth in trouble to the elders among their group, who intervene and mediate.

Ethnic associations can reach families not accessible to other forms of intervention, for three main reasons: they are voluntary mutual aid associations—group identity is built into the structure, they provide the bond of a common language, and offer cultural cohesion.

Language may be the most significant impediment to intergroup services. Translation, an obvious tactic, has serious limitations in the field of human services. There are few truly bilingual interpreters who are not somehow deficient in one or both languages. Unless the translator has the training to identify what is meaningful in the communication of family and interpersonal problems, significant material may be omitted. The presence of a third party of the client's own group may deter frankness on the part of the client. Finally, translators have been known to suppress material they think would show the client, and therefore his ethnic reference group, in a negative light. Trained bilingual professionals of the ethnic group are the best answer. Although such people are not numerous, some are to be found among the members of the ethnic associations.

RELEVANCE OF ETHNIC CONCEPTS OF FAMILY SUPPORTS

This chapter has taken a different tack in exploring family supports than has been followed elsewhere in this volume by looking primarily at the ethnic concepts that may be involved. How relevant are these concepts to the broad national needs of families at all economic levels and in all geographic locales? How relevant are they to the current picture of family support programs? As one way of answering these questions, the author used a sample of 72 programs as reported in *Programs to Strengthen Families: A Resource Guide* (1983) and analyzed them in terms of ethnic issues. This volume, the result of a national survey, reports programs deemed to be functioning well and worthy of national attention. Many of these programs and the rubrics they fall under are mentioned in other contexts in this volume. The material for the present analysis is drawn from the self-reports of the programs' leaders contained in the Resource Guide, including brief statements about goals, history, community, services, participants, and staff.

The most frequent references to ethnicity were in the descriptions of the population composition of the communities served, specified by 59 of the 72 programs. Of the 59 responses, 18 reported communities composed of 90 percent or more whites. At the other extreme, there were 11 communities described as having over half their population of minority status. Thus family support programs were operative in a broad range of settings in terms of ethnic population composition. A smaller number of programs, only 40, gave information on the ethnic composition of the clients they served, as distinct from the community populations. Of these, nine reported participants to be primarily white; 20 said they were mixed ethnically, somewhat proportional to the community demographics; and 11 said participants were primarily minority. There were only five programs in which both the community and the participants were described as exclusively or primarily minority. These included programs for Native Americans and Hispanics, mainly Mexican Americans.

References to ethnic staff were made in very few of the program summaries, appearing only for the few Native American programs and for programs staffed by Hispanics whose bilingual capacity was noted. Cultural sensitivity was a goal implied for programs involving both of these groups. The biggest gap in reporting appears to be the lack of references to staff ethnic diversity in the large numbers of programs involving black families. This is not to imply that black staff is not involved in these efforts; the assumption is that they probably are. But the use of ethnic staff for ethnic clients tends not to be reported when the group is black. Staff ethnicity is more likely to be noted for Native Americans because of cultural differences, and for Hispanics because of language. One program reported involvement with placing Jewish foster children in Jewish foster homes or, if these are not available, instructing the non-Jewish foster parents in Jewish religious practices. Here religion, not ethnicity, is the focus.

There is only one specific reference to the matching phenomenon discussed earlier as it refers to blacks. In describing a program for teenage pregnant girls, the plan is to train volunteer mothers to participate in a mother-to-mother program: "Each volunteer mother is matched, according to race and geographic proximity, with a teenage mother who has dropped out of school" (*Programs to Strengthen Families*, 1983, p. 13). The significance of the matching concept involving identity and role models at the micro level recalls the typology already discussed, as presented in *The Ethnic Dilemma* (Jenkins, 1981). Other programs may also be involved in matching but do not make it explicit in their program reports. Avoidance of such references tends to sidestep the issue of how the significance of the black experience can be integrated into family support programs. The need to incorporate the target group's culture and ethos in program planning should be recognized. Such a goal may already be implicit in family support activities; if it is made explicit, the way may be opened for a variety of innovative approaches that will reach diverse populations.

In conclusion, ethnicity, a variable descriptive of family history and identity, is inevitably involved in support programs—explicitly where cultural and language differences are obvious, implicitly where the families reflect majority norms. Support programs need to be open to ethnic variables and to recognize their relevance not only for participation of members but for staff, program content, goals, and evaluation.

No general prescription can be offered except for sensitivity to family needs. Creativity is important, and family support can be preventive as well as remedial. An example was encountered some years ago in a refugee camp in Hong Kong, where hundreds of families crowded into makeshift structures waiting their turn for transport. Each family had a bunk bed—parents on one level, children on the other—and each bed was about three feet from the next, occupied by another family. The main possession of each family was a cook-pot, a clay vessel or crock in which the family meal was prepared each day. At dinner time, dozens of family groups could be seen, each group crouched in a small circle around its own cook-pot. With my narrow western perspective, I asked the camp director if communal feeding, cafeteria style, would not be more efficient and economical. He agreed that it probably would be, but efficiency and economy were not his primary goals. The cook-pot, he explained, is the one family possession, the task of providing the meal the one surviving remnant of family roles, and the experience of eating together each night the only social tie that binds the family group. These people will be relocated as families, he explained, and whatever can be preserved of family life will help them in their relocation tasks. The cook-pot is only a symbol, but it carries with it the ethnic tradition, and its preservation is preventive family support.

NOTE

1. "Immigrants" as used here refers to persons entering the United States as resident aliens for permanent residence, most recently under the Immigration and Nationality Law of 1965. Refugees, who are also immigrants in a generic sense, are persons covered under the Refugee Law of 1980; most come from places of earlier asylum, such as refugee camps. "Entrants" (Cubans and Haitians) had special status and came directly from their home countries.

REFERENCES

Bell, D. (1975). Ethnicity and social change. In N. Glazer & D. P. Moynihan (Eds.), *Ethnicity, theory and experience* (p. 169). Cambridge, MA: Harvard University Press.

Bui, D. (1981, June). The Indochinese mutual assistance associations. In Asian/Pacific Social Work Curriculum Development Project, *Bridging cultures, Southeast Asian Refugees in America* (pp. 167–180). Los Angeles, CA: Asian American Community Mental Health Training Center.

Chu, J. M. (1979). The psychological adjustment process of the Vietnamese refugees. Unpublished Ph.D. dissertation, California School of Professional Psychology, Los Angeles.

Fisher, M. P. (1980). *The Indians of New York City, a study of immigrants from India.* Columbia, MO: South Asia Books.

Harding, R. K., & Looney, J. G. (1977, April). Problems of Southeast Asian children in a refugee camp. *American Journal of Psychiatry, 134,* 407–411.

Jenkins, S. (1981). *The ethnic dilemma in social services.* New York: Free Press.

Jenkins, S., Sauber, M., & Friedlander, E. (1985). *Ethnic associations and services to new immigrants in New York City.* New York: Community Council of Greater New York.

Litwak, E., & Dono, J. (1976, December 21). Forms of ethnic relations, organizational theory and social policy in modern industrial society. Paper presented at Columbia University.

Myrdal, G. (1944). *An American dilemma.* New York: Harper & Row.

Parkin, D. (1974). In A. Cohen (Ed.), *Urban ethnicity, U.S.A. monograph* 12. London: Tavistock.

Programs to strengthen families: A resource guide. (1983). New Haven, CT: Yale University Bush Center in Child Development and Social Policy (available from The Family Resource Coalition, 230 North Michigan Ave., Suite 1625, Chicago, Il 60601).

Schermerhorn, R. A. (1970). *Comparative ethnic relations: A framework for theory and research*. New York: Random House.

Wiseman, J. P. (1985, September). Individual adjustments and kin relationships in the "new immigration," an approach to research. *International migration, 23* (3), 349–367.

16 CULTURAL DIVERSITY IN FAMILY SUPPORT: BLACK FAMILIES

Kenton Williams

The recognition of cultural diversity in providing services to families is a concept whose time not only has come but is overdue. Within family support programs, there are many positive practices that contribute to cultural sensitivity, such as the use of paraprofessionals from the community, bilingual staffing, and parental participation in policy and decision making. It is important for program boards, staff, and volunteers, as well as for academics and researchers, to become sensitive to cultural considerations as family support programs continue to develop. However, the innovation that would benefit minority families most would be adoption of the family support concept by public social service agencies. In this context, a family support philosophy sensitive to the needs of minorities could improve delivery systems and programs.

In the past, there has been public/private cooperation in providing services to families, with increasing dependence on public funds by private agencies. Overwhelming demands are currently being made on public agencies, especially considering today's climate of fiscal austerity. It seems natural that public agencies should turn to the concept of family support as a way of assisting parents in need. Prevention of family breakdown, one of the goals of family support, could be a very cost-effective way of serving families. Once a state makes a commitment to this concept, financial and staff resources are provided either directly or through the purchase of services from private family-support agencies rather than paying for foster or institutional care.

The views expressed herein are those of the author exclusively and do not necessarily reflect those of the Department of Health & Human Services.

Financial considerations are not the only reason for urging social service agencies to adopt a family support orientation. Insensitivity to the style, needs, and strengths of minority families characterizes many branches of the social service bureaucracy. This chapter will look at the authoritarian mode of traditional social service delivery and strategies to change it. One strategy would be recognition of the strengths that minority families derive from their culture. An important modification in the system would be a more ecological approach to serving families in their communities. A much needed revision in the service bureaucracy can be classified broadly as flexibility. And a fourth development that is called for is a shift in the research from a child outcome orientation to a family one.

Throughout the chapter references will be made to the general attitudes of social service providers, the specific flaws of the public social service bureaucracy, and some solutions offered by the more informal family-support programs that exist outside of government agencies. There are many exemplary programs that display cultural sensitivity, such as the Head Start program and such variations as Home Start and the Child and Family Resource Program. Some of these model programs will be discussed as responses to cultural diversity are explored.

CASE STUDY: THE FOSTER CARE SYSTEM

An example of a public social service that could greatly benefit from a family support approach is the foster care system. In fact, federal mandate has been given to the strengthening of families in this respect. The passage of Public Law 96–272, the Adoption Assistance and Child Welfare Act of 1980, signaled the beginning of a renaissance for child-welfare services. Among the provisions of this law is a case plan for each child *and family* and preventive services to keep children out of the foster care system. The law also calls for reunification services, with judicial determination at the end of 18 months to decide if there is a continuing need for foster care and whether adequate services have been provided to the child's biological family. Implementation of this legislation holds the promise of families being supported and strengthened.

Currently, most family support programs are inadequately funded by public social service agencies which are resisting the adoption of a family support philosophy as a way of providing preventive and reunification services. There are numerous examples in the child welfare system of black children having been removed from their natural parents and placed in foster homes. Often, little or no service is given to the biological family, and continued parental contact with the child is discouraged. There is no attempt to provide the child with any sense of permanency, and the child drifts along in foster care. After a while, contact is usually made with the biological mother to see if there has been a change in the situation that precipitated the initial placement. If there is not, an appointment is made with a social worker. If the parents do not appear at the designated time, this is generally interpreted as a lack of interest in receiving services, and attempts are initiated to terminate parental rights and place the child for adoption. This example, though oversimplified, shows the insensitivity of the social service system in that it gives parents a feeling of social impotence and does nothing to reunite the family.

Child welfare services are now at a crossroads. One road leads to improvement of the foster care system by attempting to free as many children as possible for adoptive placement and focusing on the needs of each individual child. The other road leads to serious efforts to provide intensive family support to parents, particularly minority parents, as a way to strengthen the family and keep children out of the foster care system. Much will have to change in the current social service bureaucracy before progress is made down this second road. A strong family support program administered by public social service agencies would reduce the number of children, particularly minority children, coming into foster care. As this discussion of ways to modify the social service system develops, it will be helpful to bear in mind some of these characteristics of the foster care system since they are common to much of the social service bureaucracy.

ROADS LEADING TO IMPROVEMENT

Building on the Strengths of Minority Families

One of the most crucial problems in the social service bureaucracy is its authoritarian attitude toward minorities. Most social services provided by state and local agencies call for almost complete family breakdown before intervening. When intervention does occur, in most cases parents are provided with family-strengthening services based on white middle-class norms. Poor minority and other vulnerable families are expected to assume these values and behavior patterns. The degree to which a family can adjust its behavior and living patterns determines the service providers' attitude toward them and the quality of assistance given.

Historically, sociologists have contended that minority and ethnic groups go through periods of conflict, acceptance, and assimilation. However, it is doubtful that some people of color will ever be truly assimilated into the American mainstream. Most feel the best they can expect is grudging acceptance or mere tolerance by the dominant society. Minority groups have different mores, norms, and cultures and might well have no interest in adopting other values only to be excluded from the mainstream. It is, therefore, necessary for people concerned with helping especially poor, minority families to accept their diversities. The strategy that minorities use to cope with the dominant culture must be recognized as a strength.

One of the roots of the "colonial" attitude of service providers is what Baratz and Baratz (1970) characterize as a "deficit model." This model negates legitimate black values and lifestyles. It assumes that to be different is to be inferior, and that there is no such thing as Negro culture (p. 32). An early expression of the deficit model was made by then-Assistant Secretary of Labor Daniel Patrick Moynihan. In his 1965 report *The Negro Family: A Case for National Action*, Moynihan stated:

> A national effort is required that will give a unity of purpose to the many activities of the Federal government . . . directed to a new kind of national goal: the establishment of a stable Negro family structure. The Negro community has been forced into a matriarchal structure which, because it is so out of line with the rest of the American society, seriously retards the progress of the group as a whole and imposes a crushing burden on the Negro male and, in consequence, on a great many women as well. (p. 219)

Rather than positing a deficit model, the primary goal in service delivery should be the use of the natural strengths of the family's existing values and culture. Family support offers different perspectives for serving minority families victimized by economic hardship, racism, discrimination, and disregard for the sanctity of their culture, particularly when it conflicts with establishment values. The success of such programs will depend on whether the policymakers, funders, staff, and volunteers who deliver services become more sensitized to the needs of minority families. Whether paid staff, volunteers, paraprofessionals, or professionals are used as parent aides or advocates, each must possess a positive, nonjudgmental attitude, accepting the value system and culture of the families they serve.

Working with the family's strengths, one of the hallmarks of the family support movement, is especially important in serving minorities such as blacks because, historically, black families have high expectations for their children. Some white middle-class educators, social workers, and mental health professionals have told them that these expectations are unrealistic. It is important for any family support program to provide positive reinforcement for children and parents because relationships and progress can be affected by constant reference on the part of staff to perceived negatives in the black family.

Those who intervene in the family—often social workers—must also be sensitive to the parents' need to experience some control over their environment. This need has special meaning for blacks primarily because of the peculiar position they occupy in American society. Many blacks are convinced that even if they are assertive and responsible it will do no good. There is a contradiction between the establishment's emphasis on the need for and importance of power and the actual powerlessness of black America. Low-income minority group members often feel incompetent, inferior, trapped, hopeless, and choiceless. Family support programs should seek to empower parents, help family members feel better about themselves, and look for strengths within families to help them gain some control over their environment.

This is not to imply that all low-income minority families feel powerless. In fact, many have developed effective ways of navigating the system and remaining stable even while living in great economic uncertainty. However, the concept of empowering families takes on an added meaning when applied to social services for minorities. Non-white families in this country must balance two worlds: the white economic system and their own culture. The discrepancy between these worlds is especially large for low-income families. Therefore an important element of empowering black families is helping them adjust in the dominant culture while at the same time fostering their own ethnic identity.

Social service bureaucracies with a paternalistic attitude toward their clients can neither accept the family's unique culture nor recognize their existing strengths. One way to foster sensitivity is to use staff who see themselves as the parents' peers. In many cases this means employing staff of the same ethnic or racial background as the clients served (discussed in more detail later). The concept of relating on a peer-to-peer basis is important for establishing a sense of trust. Blacks may convey a sense of trust in whites, while planning and relying on their own resources, which may be inadequate or contrary to the advice given. When perceived authority is involved, when there is a professional/client relationship, this behavior is more apt to occur. Whites often interpret it as resistance, ignorance, laziness, or lack of initiative. This misunderstanding interferes with the helping process.

If a social worker, home visitor, or other staff person is able to relate to parents as peers, then that staff person can also fill important social needs. Many low-income families have mastered budgeting and household management well enough to obtain the necessities of life. People adjust to level of income—whether it is obtained from a low-paying job or welfare—the family adjusts. However, a disruption of income creates a crisis in the low-income family. Unlike a middle-class family, which often has other resources to draw on in times of financial crisis, the poor family is living on the edge. Mere financial survival requires energy and time, leaving very little of either for family functions. A role for a family support worker may be to provide a social outlet for the breadwinner in the family. This may include an outing, window shopping, movies, or just someone to talk with. While not every problem can be solved through a family support program, there are approaches that can be used to assist a family's problem solving with hands-on assistance.

Another important consideration toward making both the public social service system and private family support programs less authoritarian and more culturally sensitive is to involve staff members from the same racial or ethnic group as the families served. Ideally, family support programs in private settings should be developed, implemented, staffed, and controlled by the minority group being served, but not exclusively. Where this is not possible, cultural sensitivity is even more critical to the success of family support programs. It is important that a sufficient number of minority people be employed at all levels of a service organization to maximize understanding of the culture, values, roles, needs, conditions, and response patterns of the minority family and community. In predominantly white agencies, minorities on the staff are often expected to adopt the values and attitudes of their Caucasian peers and to impose these same values and attitudes on minority families. As a result, they experience the same failure as the non-sensitized white workers.

Some black families have a complete distrust of whites and social institutions. Social workers and parent aides are seen by some as an extension of the attempt to control, manipulate, or denigrate blacks by use of authority. A parent aide assigned to a family should therefore be the parents' peer and, if possible, indigenous to the community, race, culture and values of the family being helped. This is crucial in assisting minority families, particularly black families.

The employment of minority members with in-service training is also crucial. They should be utilized as consultants in helping agencies work with minority families. Traditional approaches to orientation and training often overlook blacks and other minorities as valuable resources, both as staff members and as teachers. Training in race relations, prejudice, discrimination, and cultural differences is critical for a staff that hopes to develop a meaningful helping relationship. Workers and staff who feel threatened by minorities should not be working with such families.

Establishing a more egalitarian and culturally sensitive social service system means also involving family members in program decision-making. This gives minority parents a sense of control over their own and their children's lives. A model program in this respect, Head Start, has demonstrated genuine concern for the parent as well as the child through parent involvement. Parents are provided with an opportunity for leadership development, participation on policy councils, volunteering in the classroom, and social interaction. Through the social service components, parents are assisted with day-to-day child rearing by concrete services other than the more impersonal provision of information and referrals alone. Minorities participate in all aspects of the program as planners, staff, volunteers, executive directors, and board members. It is through parent involvement and minority participation that the Head Start program has become a model of family support.

Employing an Ecological Approach

The imposition of inappropriate norms on minority families is only one way a family support effort can be ineffective. A second problem with traditional social service delivery is the tendency to work with the family as if it were an isolated body. Family support programs have an ecological orientation when they recognize the interdependency of family members and the connections among the family as a whole, the community, and other institutions. This orientation is particularly important in serving minority families. Andrew Billingsley (1968), in the preface to his book *Black Families in White America*, states:

> The Negro family cannot be understood in isolation or by concentration on its fragments, or particular forms of family life, or by concentration on its negative functions. The Negro family can best be understood when viewed as a varied and complex institution within the Negro community which, in turn, is highly dependent on other institutions within the white society. These institutions are, for the most part, insensitive to the Negro experience, imbedded as they are within the Anglo-conformity doctrine. (p. 186)

An ecological approach to service delivery means, first of all, identifying and working with all members of the family (whether they are technically part of the family or not). There is a tendency to define all, single-parent-headed households, which now outnumber two-parent families among blacks, as matriarchal. More and more children are growing up in households headed by women. But this phenomenon cannot be understood by looking at nuclear family structure alone. The black male is often very influential in the life of the black woman, whether in a two-parent or a single-parent family. Therefore, any family support program should identify the significant male figure in the household, whether or not he is physically present, and involve him in the process of strengthening the family.

Equally important is the need to identify the natural support system the family has used and learn why it has broken down. Sometimes this is caused by the death of one of the strongest members. In an ostensibly single-parent family, there is often a kinship system that transcends a single household and crosses geographical boundaries.

Staff members can work with the family in its natural context by visiting the home or locating program offices within the neighborhood where most of the clients live. Home visits are important. This is the family's environment—its turf. Minorities, particularly blacks, feel isolated from the mainstream of society, and to venture from their homes and neighborhoods is to enter a strange and hostile world. When a family support program is located in the neighborhood or black community, the agency becomes a part of the community and relieves the disquiet some family members feel when they leave their familiar surroundings.

A third requirement of an ecological approach to family support is to identify and collaborate with neighborhood organizations that already have a big influence on the family. Institutions in the black community, such as the church, fraternal orders, civil rights organizations, and social clubs, play an important role in family life and are critical to any family support effort. These organizations are paying increased attention to the plight of the black family and the undermining forces of drugs, crime, unemployment, poor health, and teenage pregnancy. Family support programs should involve these organizations because of their powerful and influential role in the community.

An example of such collaboration is Project Alpha, a weekend retreat for young black men and their individual role models, sponsored by the National March of Dimes and the Chicago chapter of the black fraternity Alpha Phi Alpha. The impetus for this project was concern about the increasing incidence of high-risk births to unmarried teenage mothers. The program consists of workshops on knowledge building, values clarification, and community action planning. The project has operated in a number of cities to date, with other cities planning to implement similar projects.

Maintaining Flexibility

A tenet of family support that should be incorporated into any social service for minorities is flexibility—responsiveness to the families in terms of both scheduling and the types of service provided. In times of crisis, there should be no specific rules for how long a visit or interview will be; a parent aide should be prepared to spend as much time as needed. In some family support programs, workers have spent as many as 20 hours a week with one family, but visits are usually twice weekly. The length of such intensive intervention seldom extends beyond 90 days.

During the early stages of building a relationship with a family, accessibility to the parent aide or worker is critical. The parent aide must be available 24 hours a day, seven days a week. However, the experience of some family support programs has been that the family is comforted just by knowing they can phone for assistance at any time. Many parent aides do not consider this a burdensome chore but accept it as a challenge and opportunity for mutual growth.

Another reason for flexible scheduling has to do specifically with serving a low-income minority population. Progress toward accepting white value standards is often measured by the punctuality and regularity of a black family's appearance at scheduled interviews. In the black community there is a colloquial expression, "CP" time, meaning "colored people's time," and specific time references are made in general terms. Many low-income blacks always find themselves in the position of waiting—for medical care in clinics, for buses, for food stamps, and for the arrival of the postman with the welfare check. Therefore, it makes little difference what time an appointment is, since they feel they will have to wait anyway. Hall and King (1982), in "Working with the Strengths of Black Families," state that "they have little control over their lives and must wait for their very sustenance." It is critical for family support agencies to understand this element of black culture and not jump to the conclusion that tardiness means resistance or lack of interest.

Private family-support programs, often small and community-based, are able to contour their services to the needs of each client. The public social service system, however, often sets out to provide a specific kind of aid without regard for the unique needs of each family. What is most important is assessing the family's immediate needs. For example, if the family has no food or needs adequate housing, it is important for a parent aide to offer the family concrete assistance in obtaining these requirements. Early in the relationship, this will lay the groundwork for establishing trust and convey a sincere desire to help.

There is a tendency on the part of the helping professions to discard the family's stated priority. Sometimes services are offered and provided only because they are available and not because they are related to the real need. An example would be a homeless family with young children. Traditional child welfare practice is to place the children in foster care until the family finds suitable living arrangements. However, the family needs housing assistance, not foster-care services. It is important for family support programs to have the capacity to assist the family with its most immediate needs; any other offer to help may be perceived as superficial.

Studies have shown that family support services *can* be effective in assisting families with their concrete concerns. As early as 1962, for example, a study was done in a local housing authority in Syracuse, New York, comparing two groups (Willie, 1983). In the experimental group, a family advocate intervened with the housing authority when families were threatened with eviction. The control group received no intervention.

Few of the families with an advocate were evicted as compared with the non-intervention group.

Also attesting to the success of flexible service provision is the model program Home Start. The Home Start program was one of the first programs considered by some Head Start parents to be culturally sensitive to the needs of minorities and low-income people. The thrust of Home Start is to assist parents in educating their children and providing educational stimulation. However, in many situations the family's basic needs must be met before any attempt can be made to educate. Home Start parent aides often have visited homes and found the family without food, a child needing emergency medical care, or other domestic crises. These situations take precedence over long-term goals of cognitive development—at least temporarily.

Flexibility also necessitates recognizing the sometimes different concerns of various minority groups as well as of various families within a particular minority group. While this discussion is restricted to the experience of the black community as representative of the minority experience with social services, it is important to stress that the experiences of other minority groups may be equally complex, although for different reasons. This complexity necessitates not only flexible programming, but also new research orientations to increase understanding of family needs and effectiveness of social services.

Shifting the Research Base

Social work researchers have generally ignored the family as a field of study. Child development has focused on the parents' influence on the child's cognitive development. Child development researchers are now beginning to evaluate family support programs. However, they often use existing research designs that assess improvement in family functioning in terms of improved child outcome. This amounts to viewing just one aspect of family functioning, namely socialization of children. It also negates the impact of poverty, racism, and culture on the total family functioning of minority families. Greater efforts must be made to improve research designs that measure total family functioning.

What is needed is a shift to a broader research base for today's social programs. White liberal researchers attempt to explain differences between black and white cultures using the effect of slavery, poverty, and discrimination. Conservative researchers try to explain the supposed intellectual and cognitive differences between blacks and whites using genetics as their basis. Researchers who believe in social or genetic pathology view poverty, ill health, lack of education, unemployment, and poor housing of minorities as brought on by the individuals themselves and/or their families. Too many are not interested in exploring what negative effects education, social policies, and delivery systems may have had on minority families. It must be understood that racism and prejudice toward minorities affect their functioning and behavior. As a result, members of low-income minority families have great difficulty fulfilling their responsibilities.

Leon Chestang (1978), in "The Delivery of Child Welfare Services to Minority Group Children and Their Families," outlines a conceptual framework for understanding how racism manifests itself in society that can be applied to all aspects of life as minorities, particularly blacks, interact with the dominant society. He says:

> *Social injustice* has limited the access of minorities to opportunities for employment, health care, education, the provision of social services and legal rights. *Societal inconsistency* is a more destructive force in society which denotes a sense of personal rejection of black persons through the manners, morals and traditions of society, and expresses the rejection of blacks through informal means in person to person interactions. *Personal impotence* is the consequence of exposure of social injustice and societal inconsistency, which further diminishes feelings of autonomy and self-worth and generates feelings of fear, inadequacy and insecurity in blacks regardless of social class, although these feelings are behaviorally more apparent among the poor. (p. 176)

Thus the forces of social injustice and social inconsistency must be taken into account if family support evaluations are to be as ecologically oriented as family support programs.

Finally, many of the problems with research concerning minority families stem from the same deficit image that skews social service provision. Researchers have postulated an idealized notion of American behavior against which all behavior is measured. Thus Baratz and Baratz (1970), in "Early Childhood Intervention: The Social Science Base of Institutional Racism," state that "The normative view wrongly equates equality with sameness, which leaves the researcher with the unwelcome task of describing Negro behavior not as it is, but rather, as it deviates from the normative system defined by the white middle-class" (pp. 31–32).

The modifications recommended above are not merely theories. Many of them are already realities. Further, black America, through some of its national social institutions, such as the National Association of Black Social Workers, the Urban League, and the NAACP, is beginning to challenge existing social welfare practices. A summit meeting of some of these organizations was held in Memphis, Tennessee, in 1984, to examine the black family from the black perspective. Ripple effects have emerged throughout the country with local black organizations and institutions reviewing child welfare practices as they influence the black family.

Returning to the example of the foster care system, in 1985, a bill was passed in the Massachusetts legislature that would allow foster care payments to relatives and would mandate placement planning when the need arises. It was strongly supported by the Greater Boston Association of Black Social Workers. The Massachusetts Department of Social Services has modified its child placement policy to make placement of children with relatives the first option.

Although progress is being made, current child welfare practitioners are threatened by the concept of family support.

Family support programs and approaches are the wave of the future. As they continue to develop and become more institutionalized, attention should be paid to the cultural differences of the families they intend to support. These differences are often viewed as pathological when not modified according to white society's middle-class norms, and individual family members are considered resistant, lazy, or lacking initiative. These attitudes interfere with the helping process and doom any program to failure.

Family support programs will continue to be successful in working with minority families if it is understood and accepted that racism, prejudice, and discrimination contribute to the poor economic conditions in which most minorities live; that minority families have a distinct culture which is often overlooked, ignored, or used so as to label the family deviant; and that minority families have unique strengths. These programs must allow for blacks and other minorities to participate at every level of the delivery system—in policy development, administration, training, and services. At the same time, family support must work toward, and help minority families advocate the elimination of institutionalized racism, prejudice, and discrimination. The family must be allowed to regain its self-sufficiency. Employed black men and women will have the financial resources to care for black families, and much of the family dysfunction will cease.

Moynihan, in a series of speeches at Harvard University in April, 1985, once again called for a National Policy for Families. However, instead of directing his remarks solely at minority families, he now feels that all American families are at risk. Perhaps, just by calling attention to the pressures on the family, communication can be opened among sectors of society that impact directly on families. As dialogues, debates, meetings, and conferences are held, minority participation is of the utmost importance to insure that solutions are directed at the actual needs of minority groups and not at what society deems them to be.

REFERENCES

Baratz, S. S., & Baratz, J. (1970). Early childhood intervention: The social science base of institutional racism. *Harvard Educational Review, 40* (1), 29–50.

Billingsley, A. (1968). *Black families in white America.* Englewood Cliffs, NJ: Prentice-Hall.

Billingsley, A. (1972). *Children of the storm: Black children and American child welfare.* New York: Harcourt, Brace Jovanovich.

Billingsley, A. (1974). *Black families and the struggle for survival.* New York: Friendship Press.

Chestang, L. W. (1978). *The delivery of child welfare services to minority group children and their families* (DHEW Publication No. 78-30158). Washington, DC: U.S. Department of Health, Education and Welfare, Children's Bureau.

Family Resource Coalition Program Directory (1982, August). Chicago: Family Resource Coalition.

Hall, E., & King, G. (1982, November/December). Working with the strengths of black families. *Child Welfare, 61* (8), 536–544.

Moynihan, D. P. (1965, March). *The Negro family: A case for national action.* Washington, DC: U.S. Department of Labor, Office of Policy, Planning and Research.

Moynihan, D. P. (1985, April). Family and nation. Speech presented at Harvard University, Godkin Lectures, Cambridge, MA.

Programs to strengthen families: A resource guide (1983). New Haven, CT: Yale University Bush Center in Child Development and Social Policy (available from The Family Resource Coalition, 230 North Michigan Ave., Suite 1625, Chicago, IL 60601).

Willie, C. V. (1983). *Race, ethnicity and socioeconomic status: A theoretical analysis of their interrelationships.* Bayside, NY: General Hall.

PART V/RESEARCH AND EVALUATION

17 METHODOLOGICAL AND CONCEPTUAL ISSUES IN RESEARCH

Douglas R. Powell

Using conventional research practices with community-based family support programs is akin to putting a square peg in a round hole. Major modifications are needed before there is a good fit. The stark realities of providing services to families conflict with the ideals of experimental methodology. Research designs and procedures for controlled laboratory settings will not work in the fluid world of a family support program. The lack of control over important family variables, differences between the delivery and receipt of services, and insensitive outcome measures weaken the power and precision of the data, allowing only equivocal statements about program effects. This is not a clean brand of research.

But the potential usefulness of research on family support programs outweighs its problematic character. Program development activity has far surpassed the level of evaluation effort and, moreover, has proceeded largely without the guidance of basic and evaluation research data on social support. There is a need for careful studies of program effects. But research on family programs can and should do more than assess whether a program is effective. Evaluation research data can contribute to the development of theories of practice. A family support program provides a rich arena for examining critical questions about the ways in which services are conceived, implemented, and used. We need to determine what strategies are effective with what types of families. Research on support programs can strengthen our basic understanding of social support, family functioning, and parental behavior. It is an opportunity to learn about differences in how families carry out their child-rearing functions. Theories of parent-child relations and family-environment interaction can be generated and tested. The challenge to the evaluator of a family support program is to adopt a research strategy that adheres to scientific integrity while responding to the demands of the field setting and potential users of the data.

REALITIES OF PROGRAM LIFE

When researchers move from the laboratory to the field setting, both simplicity and control are weakened, and elegance in research design is forfeited to the pursuit of relevance (Clarke-Stewart & Fein, 1983). As is true of all human service programs, there are characteristics of family support services that limit the freedom available to a researcher. Clearly they need to be addressed in designing an evaluation.

One characteristic of family support programs that has far-reaching implications for evaluation is how the services offered and utilized in a given program vary with the characteristics of the participants. Many family support programs individualize services offered in an effort to meet each family's particular needs. Consider Head Start's Child and Family Resource Program, a demonstration project in which a home-based worker collaborates with individual families in developing and carrying out an action plan responsive to family needs and goals. The focus of the action plans varies (for example, better housing, employment training) as do the frequency and intensity of contact with staff. Some families might receive a home visit once a week while others receive a visit once a month or less (Travers, Nauta, & Irwin, 1982). A variant of the individualized approach is to provide relatively constant program structures with considerable latitude to parents in what they do within each program. For example, at Family Focus, a set of drop-in centers based in the Chicago area, parents are encouraged to visit the center at any time and for as long as they wish. Parental involvement in discussion groups, classes, and one-to-one exchanges with staff varies considerably.

Program variation also can result from changes over time in the content and structure of services offered to parents. Sometimes program services are modified to meet the interests of current and prospective participants. For instance, the Family Matters program in Syraucse, New York, initially offered two different program strategies: a home visit program and a neighborhood "linking strategy" in which families were to meet at the neighborhood level to reduce feelings of isolation, share resources and information, and possibly take action toward desired changes in the neighborhood regarding child-rearing matters. The linking strategy was well received in some neighborhoods but not in others. Insufficient numbers of parents showed an interest in participating in this program activity, and eventually it was combined with the home visit program to form one program approach (Cochran & Woolever, 1983).

The families' responses to the program service are another source of variation. Even when an effort has been made to keep program services constant across families, there may be differences in how offerings are consumed by participants. Such factors as the relationship between parents and program staff (Powell, 1985) and the mesh of parents' child-rearing values with program values (Lambie, Bond, & Weikart, 1974) may lead participants to have diverse program experiences within a uniform program.

A second characteristic of family support programs that has implications for evaluation is the lack of clearly specified means to the program goals. The pathways of intended influence generally are not well-defined. For instance, one could hypothesize that (a) interaction with peers in a program setting leads to (b) a broader personal social network and (c) a corresponding increase in the number of available informal resources, which (d) enables the parent to feel supported and, as a consequence, (e) engages the child in a more positive manner, which in turn leads to (f) improved child functioning. But an equally plausible sequence is that (a) interaction with peers in a program setting leads to (b) reduced concerns about parenthood and child-rearing practices, which is associated with (c) more positive interactions with the child and, as a consequence, (d) improved child functioning. It is unlikely that a researcher interested in examining the ways in which a program might influence participants will find an existing, precise specification of assumptions about the chains of influence operating within a program.

At least two factors seem to contribute to the vagueness in specifying desired program processes. First, there is the conceptual problem of defining support. Does support mean the provision of material and/or emotional aid? Does authentic listening to a parent constitute support? How about a parent hearing a peer describe a life experience similar to hers? Is support a means to an end or an end in itself? Researchers have been imprecise in defining and operationalizing the construct (Thoits, 1982), and program designers typically offer a variety of orientations to the idea (see "What do we mean by support?" in the Family Resource Coalition *Report*, 1982).

Second, the practitioner culture emphasizes a pragmatic orientation that values a subjective belief that "this program is working well for this family" more than the scientific culture's emphasis on theoretically driven and systematically derived explanations of behavior. Moreover, events in the real world may be seen as far too complex to accommodate the scientific model of discovering underlying principles that lead to explanation and prediction (Freidson, 1972; Katz, 1984). In the human services, it is traditional for staff discussion of program content to focus on the unique details of individual participants (for example, case review) more than on the generation of assumptions about the reasons a program works for the majority of families involved. These facts of the practitioner culture support an individualized approach to service delivery; a good deal of staff discretion is needed in responding to a range of particularistic family characteristics and circumstances.

A third program characteristic pertinent to evaluation is that it cannot be assumed that a program's guiding philosophy and stated goals are pursued consistently in the delivery of services. There are no data to indicate widespread discontinuity between program goals and actual services in family support programs. Little process research has been done on the implementation of services. However, the roles, supervision, and characteristics of staff in many programs described in the literature prompt questions about the extent to which a program's philosophical stance is carried out by program workers.

Staff autonomy inherent in the individualized approach to service delivery increases the risk that a program's goals and guiding framework will not be realized fully in staff behaviors. In the Child and Family Resource Program, for instance, researchers discovered that the program goal of optimizing the child's development was not a focus of home visits in a larger number of instances (Travers et al., 1982).

Limited supervision of staff also may contribute to weakened or misrepresented program goals. It is not uncommon to find programs where volunteers receive heavy front-end training but little or no supervision once they are on the job. The situation with paid staff may not be much different, though. In most of the sites studied in the Child and Family Resource Program evaluation, investigators found a laissez-faire attitude toward supervision of staff who had contact with families. Program administrators apparently did not wish to encroach on the one-to-one relationship between family workers and parents that was universally recognized as essential to program success (Travers, Irwin, & Nauta, 1981). Also, in community-based programs staff may be selected more on the basis of their linkages with and reputation in the community than their adherence to a program's guiding framework. This may be the case especially in programs that use paraprofessionals and indigenous workers who understand a particular community's values and lifestyles.

Staff autonomy, laissez-faire supervision, and community-based staff may be key ingredients of an effective family support program. However, in some family support programs these factors may increase the risk that program reality will be a diluted or altered form of stated program intentions.

It is important to note the distinction between ongoing community-based programs and experimental programs that are also field based. While the shift from laboratory to field settings presents a new set of demands for researchers, the use of *existing* community-based programs imposes more constraints than experimental programs in the field. With an ongoing program, it is difficult if not impossible to control such matters as age of the child at the time of family entry into the program. Important variables can be controlled in an experimental field-based program that has research as a primary reason for existence (for example, Parent and Child Development Centers; see Andrews et al., 1982). The texture of an existing program, where the provision of services is a major goal, does not easily permit an alteration of ongoing procedures.

CONCEPTUALIZING RESEARCH DIRECTIONS

At the most global level, policymakers and program advocates want an empirical yes or no answer to the question, Do family support programs work? The vast amount of research activity regarding family support programs has been in the form of outcome studies of particular types of parent- and family-oriented programs. Important information has been obtained from these investigations, as noted elsewhere in this volume. The next wave of research needs to build upon these investigations by using designs and measures that are sensitive to interactions between programs and the families they serve. To say that a family support program is effective prompts the obvious question, What was effective with what types of families? The typical evaluation approach has been to conceptualize a program as a single static variable, not as a set of variables; the program has been considered to be present or absent, with no concern for the nature, correlates, and consequences of variations in program participation (Powell, 1983). A focus on interactions between families and program in relation to corresponding program effects may help researchers assess program effectiveness with greater power and precision than past efforts have permitted. It also may help program designers improve the efficacy of programs in terms of the timing, structure, and content of services provided to particular types of families.

Needed is a research paradigm in which researchers ask, In what ways do what types of families interact with the program? This approach differs from a conceptualization of the program as a uniform entity that acts on a passive, homogeneous set of families. A limited body of existing research suggests that this may be a productive strategy for understanding how family variables interact with program participation and program effects. For instance, differences in program participation have been found to be related to such variables as life stress and dispositional tendencies (Eisenstadt & Powell, 1987), and program effects have been found to be modified by family social networks (Kessen et al., 1975), family structure and race (Cochran & Henderson, 1985), and locus of control (Travers et al., 1982).

Many critical questions can be addressed with a research paradigm that considers program-family interactions. In particular, more needs to be known about the processes of grafting social support onto families through a formal program. Studies that suggest the benefits of naturally occurring social support generally are used to justify the existence of family support programs. However, there are important differences between naturally occurring support from one's social network members and the social support offered by professionals (Gottlieb, 1981). Further, it is not clear that social support from peers in a program is similar in quality and efficacy to support from existing social network members.

Under what conditions can support derived through informal means be intentionally replicated? What types of families are the most and least receptive to naturally occurring support found in a program? When is it sufficient for a program to provide parents with the environmental opportunity to form ties with people of similar circumstances, and when might it be appropriate for a program to focus on personal characteristics (for example, locus of control, Eckenrode, 1983) that seem to influence an individual's ability to mobilize social support? Research also is needed on the factors surrounding the negative effects of social support. Not all social support is experienced positively (Belle, 1982; Unger & Wandersman, 1985), yet we know little about the circumstances that lead to negative effects.

Answers to these questions would contribute significantly to our basic understanding of how social support functions with families. Research on program-family interactions is likely to foster closer ties between basic or analytic and evaluation research traditions (Rook & Dooley, 1985). The data also could be used to guide the design of programs that attempt to provide support to families.

An initial step toward understanding program-family interactions is process research, which illuminates the ways in which support is provided and utilized within a program context. We need descriptive data on service utilization in a variety of programs: What services are provided by whom to what types of families? Large research budgets are not essential for this type of work, and family support programs may find that the collection of these data through staff records, questionnaires, and interviews helps strengthen program appeals to funding agencies. The Harvard Family Research Project has suggested that accurate data on service utilization help to clarify program purposes and justify current or proposed expenditures (Weiss & Jacobs, 1984).

In addition to research on program operations and effects, data are needed on the process by which community-based programs are implemented. Multiple-site studies have pointed to setting differences in the design and implementation of services. An ethnographic study of the Child and Family Resource Program found that individual programs reflected their special environments. The salient community characteristics varied across sites. Thus the multiethnic population was significant to the Las Vegas program; the recently unemployed ("new poor") factory workers formed a ready clientele for the Jackson, Michigan, program; in St. Petersburg, Florida, there was an enclave of black poverty in the midst of white affluence; the Salem, Oregon, program made use of a rich network of social service agencies; and the Oklahoma City program seemed to be influenced by the program's close ties to a Community Action Agency that emphasized self-help and community action goals (Travers et al., 1981). We need a better understanding of how the design and content of a program evolve in relation to community needs and network structures. Similarly, since family support programs often are ventures of such existing institutions as hospitals and schools, research is needed on the adoption of innovative service delivery within a well-established institutional setting.

RESEARCH DESIGN

Many studies of parent programs have employed a pre-post design with no control or comparison group (for a critical review, see Clarke-Stewart & Apfel, 1978). Although prevalent, studies with this weak design contribute little to the development of a solid empirical data base regarding the effects of parent programs. What we know empirically about family support programs largely comes from a small but impressive group of field-based studies of parent interventions using a true experimental design (for example, Andrews et al., 1982; Cochran & Henderson, 1985; Dickie & Gerber, 1980; Gray & Ruttle, 1980; Kessen et al., 1975; Klaus & Gray, 1968; Lambie et al., 1974; Travers et al., 1982) or quasi-experimental design (for example, Seitz, Apfel, & Rosenbaum, 1985; Slaughter, 1983).

Reicken and Boruch (1974) strongly recommend a true experimental design for outcome evaluation research. However, random assignment of participants to treatment and control groups typically is not feasible in ongoing family support programs. Ethical, political, and/or logistical problems may preclude the withholding of services from a randomly selected sample. While random assignment has been carried out effectively in studies of parent programs, a primary goal of the service enterprise has been research; indeed, usually the program under investigation exists primarily for research purposes. Of greater use to most studies of family support programs are quasi-experimental designs (Campbell & Stanley, 1966; Cook & Campbell, 1979). Seitz (chap. 18) offers a cogent examination of alternatives to true experimental design, with in-depth attention to treatment partitioning and time-lag designs.

Control or comparison groups are an essential element of a research design aimed at determining program effects. Even when they are de-rived through random procedures, control groups do not guarantee that other forms of bias will not occur. One potential problem is partici-pant attrition in both program and control groups. Studies of family support programs do not operate with captive audiences. Participation is voluntary, and attrition is generally quite high. For instance, the Parent and Child Development Center investigation lost nearly 50 percent of its sample during a three-year period (Andrews et al., 1982), and a short-term (9-week) parent education program involving a middle-class white population lost nearly 40 percent of its participants by the end of the program (Lochman & Brown, 1980). Attrition often causes control and treatment groups to be nonequivalent by the end of the study, when out-come variables are measured. The investigation of the Child and Family Resource Program illustrates this problem. Random assignment to treat-ment and control conditions yielded equivalent groups at the beginning of the study, but different types of families dropped out of the groups during the investigation, so that treatment and control groups were no longer equivalent on important pretest measures at the end, when out-come assessments were conducted. Statistical adjustments were made to compensate for the nonequivalence of the two groups (Travers et al., 1982), but this is a problematic procedure when sample sizes are small.

A second potential problem is that periodic assessments (for example, interviews, child testing) related to the content of the intervention may constitute a minimal intervention for the control group. For instance, in an experimental study of a home visiting program, control group moth-ers considered themselves participants in an educational program and felt that they and their infants had benefited from the experience. The investigators speculated that two recurring measurement situations may have contributed to changes in mothers' awareness of their infants' development and developmental needs. In one situation mothers de-scribed "what was going on" in a series of drawings of infants engaging in activities; the second situation involved observing the Bayley test with their infant (Lambie et al., 1974).

Third, control group families may be influenced indirectly by the in-tervention through direct contact with intervention families. A classic example of this occurred in the Klaus and Gray (1968) study of a home-based intervention with parents. Some control group parents talked with treatment group parents (some of whom were neighbors) about the home visit, and some attempted to carry out the treatment group experiences (for example, one week there was a brisk sale of a magazine distributed to treatment group mothers). Klaus and Gray termed this phenomenon "horizontal diffusion" of the intervention. In an experimental paradigm, it represents contamination of a "no touch" control group.

Regardless of the type of research design used, investigators need to consider carefully the feasibility of implementing a particular design, especially if an ongoing program is involved. For instance, treatment partitioning (see Seitz [chap. 18]) is an especially useful strategy for determining the effects of different types of program services. However, this design involves the potential problem of program-staff resistance to the idea of randomly assigning families to different treatments independent of severity of need; a well-ingrained notion in the human service field is that the neediest require the most comprehensive intervention. For example, in a study of a home visiting program for teenage mothers, it was found that the home visitors occasionally decided to provide services to a particularly needy mother in the comparison group even though the design called for contact only once every three months to note the progress of the mother and baby and to provide referral (not services) when needed. The investigators speculated that this may have weakened the findings about the effect of the intervention (Unger & Wandersman, 1985).

Researchers also need to be diligent in measuring important characteristics of control and treatment groups. Detailed comparative data on participant characteristics at baseline (preprogram) and subsequent assessment points are essential to determine the degree of equivalence across participant groups. Measured characteristics should transcend global indicators such as socioeconomic status and race to include variables that may influence program utilization and effects (for example, social network ties).

Earlier in this chapter it was argued that future research should examine interactions between family charcteristics and program properties. A basic design decision here pertains to the extent to which the family support program controls the nature of the service provided. If a high degree of control over service provision and utilization is possible within the family support program, then a design such as treatment partitioning may prove to be most beneficial (see Seitz [chap. 18]). Within each treatment, family characteristics and differences in the rate of "consumption" or utilization of a particular treatment could be investigated. If a family support program does not lend itself to controlling the services provided (for example, because of individualization of services, discussed earlier), the researcher faces a greater challenge: meaningful clusters or subgroups of participants need to be organized post hoc on the basis of indicators of service utilization. This is a less desirable strategy because of the difficulty of isolating the relevant dimensions of the intervention. Program participation variables can be used to partition the sample (post hoc) and investigate antecedents (for example, participant characteristics) and effects (for example, parent behavior) of each type of service utilization. For instance, the evaluation study of the Child and Family Resource Program partitioned the sample by attendance rates and by participants' locus of control to examine the possibility of differential program effects (Travers et al., 1982).

Experimental and quasi-experimental designs are unnecessary for descriptive studies of service delivery and utilization and for examinations of program interactions with the host community. Qualitative research methods, discussed in the following section, can be particularly illuminating in these instances.

MEASUREMENT OF OUTCOME AND PROGRAM VARIABLES

Selection and measurement of outcome and program treatment variables are problematic aspects of evaluating a family support program. A major cause of failure to detect effects of a parent- or family-oriented program is poor measurement. This typically involves two problems: partial irrelevance of the response or outcome variables and, as discussed earlier, lack of careful measurement of the treatment variables (Boruch & Gomez, 1977).

Problems in selecting outcome variables for family support programs stem from several sources. First, there is no set of outcome variables that is commonly recognized as appropriate within the field of family programs, and it is questionable that there could be such a set in the future. The heterogeneity of family-oriented programs in terms of goals, methods, settings, and population groups makes it difficult to specify outcomes that would be relevant to a large number of programs.

A critical issue here is the extent to which child variables should be used to assess the effects of a family-oriented program. An argument in support of the heavy use of child measures is that family support programs promise improved conditions for child development; therefore, a good test of a program's efficacy is its impact on the child. An alternative position is that parenthood is a unique stage and developmental process, and family support programs exist to help parents deal with the stresses of child rearing (see Weissbourd [chap. 13]). This line of thinking places emphasis on the parent's behaviors and development as important in their own right. With this latter program rationale, parent and family functioning is a more relevant outcome area than child functioning. The so far unproved assumption is that interventions cause an improvement in family life that leads to a more competent child.

Second, not unlike the across-program heterogeneity discussed above, within-program variations can make the selection of measurable outcome areas very difficult. This is especially the case with comprehensive and/or individualized service programs. When parents or staff exert influence in determining the substance of the intervention, the goals and expected outcomes of the program cannot be predefined with great precision (Travers & Light, 1982). A great many domains of family life may be affected by a program, and not all families are likely to be influenced in the same way.

Third, in some settings there may be a tendency to select outcome variables that reflect the political and social context of a program but are largely irrelevant to the program's operations. For instance, a community's concern about child abuse may give credence to the existence of a family support program, but the incidence of child abuse may be an inappropriate measure of a particular program's effectiveness. In an effort to mobilize financial resources during difficult times for social programs, advocates may speak to societal concerns that in reality are only peripherally addressed by family support programs. It is a mistake to naively translate political and funding rhetoric into outcome measures.

Last but certainly not least, there is a limited number of reliable and valid measures of child and family functioning that are relevant to anticipated program outcomes. Children's social competence may be influenced by a family support program but there are few standardized measures in this area (Zigler & Trickett, 1979). Social support is another domain where good measures are lacking (Rook & Dooley, 1985).

These factors have contributed to the use of a wide range of outcome measures in studies of parent-oriented programs, and occasionally to an atheoretical shotgun approach, in which numerous outcome measures are employed in a single study. Standardized IQ tests have been used extensively to measure child outcome. There also has been measurement of maternal personality and parents' child-rearing attitudes and beliefs, interaction with the child, personal well-being, locus of control, use of community services, and pursuit of further education, job training, and employment. Parent outcomes generally have been measured with self-report questionnaires and/or interview procedures.

Systematic observation of parental behavior or parent-child interaction is generally regarded as superior to self-report measures which assume a relationship between child-rearing attitudes and practices. Some studies of parent-oriented programs have used time-sampling observational methods successfully to assess parental behavior (for example, Andrews et al., 1982; Kessen et al., 1975; Lambie et al., 1974; Slaughter,

1983), but this approach is not without practical and methodological problems. To ensure the objectivity of observational measures requires well-trained observers and costly data collection that most evaluation projects cannot afford. Methodological issues include questions about the utility of the relatively fine-grained behaviors often coded in observational work. Do they have psychological significance? Can they be generalized to other situations? Do they reflect short-term developmental change or long-term stability (Travers & Light, 1982)? There also are issues regarding observational work in a controlled laboratory setting versus naturalistic settings (home), and the consideration of child effects on parental behavior in the coding scheme and data analyses. These matters are not unique to evaluation research; they cut across basic and applied research fields.

Regardless of whether self-report or observational outcome measures are used, the timing of outcome assessment can pose a problem in evaluating support programs intended to ameliorate a family's response to a stressful event. Most studies of long-term intervention programs measure outcome variables at intervals determined by program duration (for example, assessments after one and two years of participation) rather than key stresses in family life. If the goal of a family support program is to reduce stress surrounding a critical family event, the best time to evaluate program effectiveness is at the time of the stressful event. Assessment at predetermined intervals may not correspond to the stressful event, and retrospective data may not provide an accurate or sensitive indication of a program's usefulness to a family in time of high need. However, outcome assessment schedules organized around family life rather than duration of program participation have undesirable features. The lack of a uniform assessment schedule makes comparison of program outcomes across participants exceedingly difficult if not impossible. There also are practical problems surrounding the identification of unpredictable stressful events and the availability of data collection staff at times not previously anticipated.

The measurement of program participation is no less difficult than the selection and measurement of program outcomes. Most research on program activities has been motivated by a desire to ascertain the integrity of the curriculum or treatment plan at the operational level. Until recently few researchers had undertaken a serious investigation of program services as a way to improve the estimate of program effects. Attendance (or level of service received) is a relatively easy variable to measure, but it does not indicate what happens when individuals do attend a program. Research on participation patterns in a comprehensive group-based program for low-income mothers found verbal behavior in group discussions and orientation to peers versus staff to be useful in discerning different types of program experience (Eisenstadt & Powell, 1987; Powell, 1985). Previous research in this area suggests that it may be productive to focus on the interpersonal structure of the program setting and to consider changes over time in the nature of program involvement (Powell, 1985).

A pilot study conducted prior to a full-fledged investigation is a helpful method of addressing many of these measurement problems. It is an opportunity to dig carefully and deeply into a program's life to generate hypotheses about relevant outcome and program variables. No less important, it is a chance to develop assumptions about how program and outcome variables are linked. Qualitative data are a well-justified beginning point. Unstructured interviews with participants and staff and informal observations of program activities serve as rich data bases for the subsequent identification and/or development of quantitative measures. It is essential at this stage to reach as broad a spectrum of participants as possible. For example, eager-to-be-interviewed parents may portray program experiences that are not representative of the experiences of those less likely to volunteer for an interview. It also is necessary to avoid total reliance on staff images of program operations and effects. What staff think is being delivered may differ from what participants claim is being received. It is far better to base the selection of study variables on unstructured interviews and observations involving a random sample of the participant pool than on the impressions of staff alone. One procedure would be to use pilot participant data to test hypotheses generated through discussions with staff; discrepancies would signal a need for further pilot work.

Although it is important to consider the participant's perspective in evaluating family-based programs, there is little value in conducting a consumer survey to determine whether parents are satisfied with program services. Generally questionnaires of this type yield high scores of satisfaction; this is not surprising since most programs are voluntary, and dissatisfied parents probably withdraw from participation. Furthermore, high levels of participant satisfaction do not necessarily mean that a program is effective according to objective outcome indicators. For instance, in an evaluation of a short-term parent group, participants indicated satisfaction with the group, but there were no outcome differences between program and comparison samples in general well-being, quality of marital interaction, and parental sense of competence, as determined by established measures (Wandersman, Wandersman, & Kahn, 1980). Examination of a program from the parents' vantage point requires the collection of detailed information about the perceptions and utilization of the program.

The use of qualitative work in program research should not be limited to defining the parameters of a quantitative study, as discussed above. Qualitative research can be carried out concurrently with quantitative investigations in an effort to give meaning to quantitative data. There are two recent examples of this approach in investigations of family support programs. In an examination of Cornell University's Family Matters program in Syracuse, New York, a process study was conducted to examine the evolution of program services, including variations in program utilization by neighborhood type and by parents representing different races, socioeconomic status, and family structures (Mindick, 1983). The qualitative work complemented the quantitative findings of differential program effects by race and family structure of program participants (Cochran & Henderson, 1985). An ethnographic study of the Child and Family Resource Program in five different sites provided poignant descriptions of individual family uses of program services (Travers et al., 1981). Among the illuminating aspects of this ethnographic work are details of how programs were shaped by the communities they served. These contextual data and the portrayals of families add depth to the quantitative findings of the program evaluation (Travers et al., 1982).

Future research needs to consider conceptual and methodological ways to combine quantitative and qualitative methods. Qualitative work offers depth generally at the sacrifice of breadth, while quantitative research typically provides little understanding of the real lives reflected in numerical values. Readers are referred to Campbell (chap. 19) for a statement of the importance of qualitative research methods in evaluating family support programs.

All research on family support programs faces the decision of whether to use existing measures and/or develop new ones. The use or adaptation of existing measures may save enormous amounts of energy and time, and it permits comparisons of findings across studies. The use of existing measures that have been examined carefully for reliability and validity also provides greater assurance of a measure's ability to discriminate across individuals than the use of new measures does. Whether the existing measure does so in a manner that is relevant to the population under study and to the essence of the program treatment is yet another matter. Herein lies the rub: existing instruments offer reliability and convenience but may not measure pertinent variables.

Boruch and Gomez (1977) recommend the construction of new measures when novel programs are tested on small and idiosyncratic populations. Standard measures are suggested for global programs aimed at the same populations that were used to develop the standardized measure. For research falling between these extremes, both tailored and standard measures are recommended. It is important to note that measurement development requires an extensive amount of work and should not be undertaken at the same time an intervention and/or evaluation is being implemented.

SUPPORT SYSTEMS FOR RESEARCH

At present the infrastructure for research on family support programs is weak. Two needs are especially pressing: adequate funding for evaluation and measurement work, and mechanisms for providing technical assistance to programs that wish to carry out evaluations.

The pattern of diminishing resources for human services in this country heightens the need for prudent expenditure of available funds. The arguments for family support programs presented elsewhere in this volume are promising from both economic and human-service perspectives. Yet there is a limited research base for making a persuasive case for the family support approach. Findings of many existing studies do not generalize easily to other populations and programs; for instance, data from evaluations of high-cost interventions of the 1970s cannot be used to justify the existence of 1980s' programs that operate with significantly fewer resources. Research funds are needed to address critical questions about the nature and effects of family support programs. Both public and private sources of funding need to establish this area of research as a high priority. Leadership from a key government agency or philanthropic foundation would be especially beneficial in setting research directions and stimulating interest among researchers and other funding agencies. This step is crucial if there is to be serious examination of the benefits and limitations of the family support approach to fostering the development of young children.

Technical assistance would help programs with small research budgets collect data on service utilization and perhaps program effects. Many family support programs operate in a grassroots context that does not provide easy access to technical-assistance sources typically available to programs funded by state or federal sources (for example, Head Start). The high level of practitioner attendance at sessions on evaluation at national professional meetings suggests that many family support programs, both small and large scale, wish to carry out evaluations. Traditional tensions between researchers and practitioners seem to be undergoing some modifications as program staff see the need for research to justify program operations and to guide the improvement of services. Efforts such as the Harvard Family Research Project (Weiss & Jacobs, 1984) are needed to provide guidance to programs in the selection of measures and the design of feasible evaluation studies.

Family support programs provide an important research opportunity. The methodological and conceptual problems that their evaluation presents are many, and no one study can find solutions or generate answers to critical questions about program processes and effects. Over time the findings from individual studies can be combined to advance our understanding of useful program approaches and, ultimately, the conditions under which programs are effective. This chapter has argued that progress toward this end depends largely on augmentation of conventional research designs, broadening of the questions addressed by researchers, careful measurement of both program and outcome variables relevant to the participant experience, and a stronger base of financial and technical support for research.

REFERENCES

Andrews, S. R., Blumenthal, J. B., Johnson, D. L., Kahn, A. J., Ferguson, C. J., Lasater, R. M., Malone, P. E., & Wallace, D. B. (1982). The skills of mothering: A study of Parent Child Development Centers. *Monographs of the Society for Research in Child Development, 47*, (6, Serial No. 198).

Belle, D. (1982). *Lives in stress: Women and depression.* Beverly Hills, CA: Sage.

Boruch, R. F., & Gomez, H. (1977). Sensitivity, bias, and theory in impact evaluations. *Professional Psychology, 8*, 411–433.

Campbell, D. T., & Stanley, J. C. (1966). *Experimental and quasi-experimental designs for research.* Chicago: Rand McNally.

Clarke-Stewart, K. A., & Apfel, N. (1978). Evaluating parental effects on child development. In L. S. Shulman (Ed.), *Review of research in education* (pp. 47–119). Itasca, IL: Peacock.

Clarke-Stewart, K. A., & Fein, G. (1983). Early childhood programs. In P. Mussen (Ed.), *Manual of child psychology.* New York: Wiley.

Cochran, M., & Henderson, C. (1985). *Family matters: Evaluation of the parental empowerment program.* Final report to the National Institute of Education. Ithaca, NY: Cornell University.

Cochran, M., & Woolever, F. (1983). Beyond the deficit model: The empowerment of parents with information and informal supports. In I. Sigel & L. Laosa (Eds.), *Changing families* (pp. 225–245). New York: Plenum Press.

Cook, T. D., & Campbell, D. T. (1979). *Quasi-experimentation: Design and analysis issues for field settings.* Chicago: Rand McNally.

Dickie, J. R., & Gerber, S. C. (1980). Training in social competence: The effect on mothers, fathers and infants. *Child Development, 51*, 1248–1251.

Eckenrode, J. (1983). The mobilization of social supports: Some individual constraints. *American Journal of Community Psychology, 11*, 509–528.

Eisenstadt, J., & Powell, D. (1987). Processes of participation in a mother-infant program as modified by stress and impulse control. *Journal of Applied Developmental Psychology, 8*, 17–37.

Friedson, E. (1972). *Profession of medicine: A study of the sociology of applied knowledge.* New York: Dodd, Mead.

Gottlieb, B. (1981). Preventive interventions involving social networks and social support. In B. Gottlieb (Ed.), *Social networks and social support* (pp. 201–232). Beverly Hills, CA: Sage.

Gray, S. W., & Ruttle, K. (1980). The family-oriented home visiting program: A longitudinal study. *Genetic Psychology Monographs, 102*, 299–316.

Katz, L. (1984). Some issues on the dissemination of child development knowledge. *Society for Research in Child Development Newsletter*, 7–9.

Kessen, W., Fein, G., Clarke-Stewart, A., & Starr, S. (1975). *Variations in home-based infant education: Language, play and social development.* Final report to the Office of Child Development, U.S. Department of Health, Education and Welfare. New Haven, CT: Yale University.

Klaus, R. A., & Gray, S. W. (1968). The Early Training Project for Disadvantaged Children: A report after five years. *Monographs of the Society for Research in Child Development, 33*, (4, Serial No. 120).

Lambie, D. Z., Bond, J. T., & Weikart, D. P. (1974). Home teaching with mothers and infants. *Monographs of the High/Scope Educational Research Foundation*, (No. 2). Ypsilanti, MI: High/Scope Press.

Lochman, J. E., & Brown, M. V. (1980). Evaluation of dropout clients and of perceived usefulness of a parent education program. *Journal of Community Psychology, 8*, 132–139.

Mindick, B. (1983, April). Intraprogram and extraprogram influences on the effectiveness of parent-child interventions. In D. Powell (Chair), *Variations in the effectiveness of parent-child support programs.* Symposium conducted at the Biennial Meeting of the Society for Research in Child Development, Detroit, MI.

Powell, D. R. (1983). Evaluating parent education programs: Problems and prospects. *Studies in Educational Evaluation, 8*, 253–259.

Powell, D. R. (1985). Stability and change in patterns of participation in a parent-child program. *Professional Psychology: Research and Practice, 16*, 172–180.

Reicken, H. W., & Boruch, R. F. (1974). *Social experimentation: A method for planning and evaluating social intervention.* New York: Academic Press.

Rook, K., & Dooley, D. (1985). Applying social support research: Theoretical problems and future directions. *Journal of Social Issues, 41*, 5–28.

Seitz, V., Rosenbaum, L., & Apfel, N. (1985). Long-term effects of family support intervention: A ten-year follow-up. *Child Development, 56*, 376–391.

Slaughter, D. T. (1983). Early intervention and its effects on maternal and child development. *Monographs of the Society for Research in Child Development, 48*, (4, Serial No. 202).

Thoits, P. A. (1982). Conceptual, methodological and theoretical problems in studying social support as a buffer against life stress. *Journal of Health and Social Behavior, 23*, 145–159.

Travers, J., Irwin, N., & Nauta, M. (1981). *The culture of a social program: An ethnographic study of the Child and Family Resource Program.* Cambridge, MA: Abt Associates.

Travers, J., & Light, R. (Eds.). (1982). *Learning from experience: Evaluating early childhood demonstration programs.* Washington, DC: National Academy Press.

Travers, J., Nauta, M. J., & Irwin, N. (1982). *The effects of a social program: Final report of the Child and Family Resource Program's Infant Toddler Component* (AAI No. 82–31). Cambridge, MA: Abt Associates (HHS-105-79-1301).

Unger, D. G., & Wandersman, L. P. (1985). Social support and adolescent mothers: Action research contributions to theory and applications. *Journal of Social Issues, 41*, 29–45.

Wandersman, L. P., Wandersman, A., & Kahn, S. (1980). Social support in the transition to parenthood. *Journal of Community Psychology, 8*, 332–342.

Weiss, H., & Jacobs, F. (1984). The effectiveness and evaluation of family support and education programs. Final report to the Charles Stewart Mott Foundation (Cambridge, MA: Harvard Family Research Project).

Weissbourd, B. (1983). The family support movement: Greater than the sum of its parts. *Zero to Three, 4*, 8–10.

Zigler, E., & Trickett, P. K. (1978). IQ, social competence, and evaluation of early childhood intervention programs. *American Psychologist, 33*, 789–799.

18 OUTCOME EVALUATION OF FAMILY SUPPORT PROGRAMS: RESEARCH DESIGN ALTERNATIVES TO TRUE EXPERIMENTS

Victoria Seitz

There are many more high-quality family support programs than there are interpretable evaluations of their effects. One of the most persistent impediments to evaluation is the ethical problem raised by the necessity of choosing to withhold services to a segment of the eligible clientele (the control group). As is well known, the strongest research procedure for determining whether a treatment is effective requires that some persons not receive the treatment and also that the choice of such persons be made in a manner totally unrelated to their probable need for the treatment. From the viewpoint of rigorous experimental design, the recommended method of deciding who will and who will not receive treatment is by random assignment to conditions.

The decision to deny services on the basis of research considerations alone is obviously a difficult one. Yet, if it is avoided, selection bias usually makes it impossible to ascertain a program's effects. Selection bias is so prevalent that it can be regarded as the patron devil of evaluation research: People who choose to attend a program, or who are referred to it, almost inevitably differ in many important ways from those who are not attending. It is difficult to distinguish such preexisting differences from the effects of differential treatment when trying to compare the groups.

Ironically, because of the ethical problem, the more likely it is that a

This chapter is adapted from a presentation at the Bush Center Conference on Family Support, New Haven, CT, May, 1984. Preparation of this chapter was supported by Grant No. HD-03008 from the National Institute of Child Health and Human Development.

329

program is needed by and helpful to its recipients, the less likely it is that the program will be evaluated. It is much easier to justify random assignment to evaluate a program that provides only a modest amount of support than one that gives extensive help to very troubled families. The effects of a brief program for expectant mothers, for example, would be much easier to determine than would those of a lengthy program designed to help families of severely handicapped newborns. Yet the effects of more intensive programs on persons whose need for them is perhaps almost desperate are likely to be much more powerful than those of only modest efforts, if only they could be assessed.

There is clearly a pressing need for more assessment. Without it, there is relatively little pooling of useful knowledge about what has been shown to be effective practice and what has not. Also disturbing is the risk, in the absence of evaluation, that exemplary programs whose effects have not been documented may disappear for lack of funding. Successful programs are probably reinvented when conditions are favorable, but in the process, errors that were made and corrected in previous incarnations may be made again. If there are coherent principles of good intervention, establishing a lasting body of useful knowledge about them requires that more evaluations of good programs be performed, published, and made part of the public domain.

Because it is unlikely that future researchers will be more eager to embrace random assignment than previous investigators have been, it is worth examining more closely the realm of slightly modified procedures called "quasi-experiments" (Cook & Campbell, 1979) as these might apply to family support programs. Quasi-experiments are not always feasible, but they are likely to be a good alternative more often than will true experiments in this area.

Several investigators have already turned to quasi-experimental designs in evaluating family support programs, with encouraging results. Where these designs have been used successfully, they illustrate the potential of certain kinds of quasi-experimentation for meeting both scientific and ethical concerns in performing outcome evaluations. In studies where the designs have not led to interpretable results, it is useful to examine why this has occurred, to determine more precisely those situations in which the method is inappropriate. Here I will focus on two particular classes of designs: treatment partitioning designs and time-lag designs.

TREATMENT PARTITIONING

Treatment partitioning is one of the most widely used alternatives to the standard experimental design. This approach involves contrasting two or more treatments, using random assignment to each. If all the treatments are desirable, people are less likely to resent being randomly assigned, and investigators can feel less concerned about the ethics of their procedures. The problem, of course, is that the absolute effectiveness of the treatments cannot be ascertained without comparison with an untreated group.

An example of the successful use of treatment partitioning is provided in a study of the Adolescent Family Clinic (AFC) at Sinai Hospital of Baltimore (Furstenberg, 1976, 1980). In this study, pregnant adolescents who were registering for prenatal care were randomly assigned to attend either the newly established AFC or the hospital's regular prenatal clinic. The adolescents received high-quality medical care in both treatments. In the special adolescent clinic, however, a team of physicians, social workers, and public health nurses provided a coordinated program designed to meet other needs of pregnant adolescents and their families. In addition to medical evaluation and nutritional advice, the teenagers received child care advice, educational and vocational guidance, family counseling, and birth-control information. Instead of terminating shortly after delivery, the AFC services continued into the early years of parenthood.

In a long-term follow-up, it was found that the two treatments led to different outcomes in at least one area—the prevention of early, repeated pregnancy. As Furstenberg (1976) notes, AFC attenders reported using contraception for a longer time than the regular-clinic attenders. Other findings confirmed their self-report of contraception: by five years postpartum, 39 percent of the AFC attenders had not become pregnant again compared with 25 percent of the regular-clinic attenders. As Hardy and her colleagues have noted in their report of a similar intervention (1981, p. 279), there is now good evidence to indicate that family support of this kind, involving "the addition of intensive psychosocial and educational services to the good routine prenatal care provided during the pregnancy, labor, and delivery" has significant benefits for pregnant adolescents.

A second example of treatment partitioning is provided in a study reported by Olds and his colleagues (Olds et al., 1985a, 1985b) of an intervention using home visits by nurses to provide family support.[1] The subjects were women living in a semirural region of New York who were pregnant with their first child and were believed to be at risk for poor life outcomes because of youth, marital status, and/or poverty. They were randomly assigned to one of three treatments, differing in the level of intervention each represented.

The first treatment consisted of providing families with free transportation to doctors or clinics for prenatal and well-child care, and providing sensory and developmental screening by an infant specialist when the children were 12 and 24 months old. In the second treatment, in addition to the services just described, a nurse visited the family's home approximately nine times during the pregnancy, for more than an hour at each visit. The third, most extensive treatment condition encompassed all the services provided in the first two but added postnatal home visits by a nurse until the children were two years old. Over thirty postpartum visits were made to each family in this condition, again with each visit lasting more than an hour.

Home visits in this study were intended to offer parent education to the mother, to help link her with other health and social services in the community, and to help strengthen her personal support networks. Parent education covered such topics as the infant's temperament, crying and its meaning, physical and emotional development of children, and how to handle common health problems. To strengthen support networks, the nurses encouraged the mothers' close friends and relatives to help with household responsibilities and child care. The nurses also reinforced the recommendations of the physicians caring for the children and urged parents to keep regular well-child appointments and to call the physician's office when a health care problem arose. When necessary, the nurses referred parents to other services such as vocational training programs, Planned Parenthood, mental health counseling, and legal aid.

The results of this study have shown a number of significant differences across treatments. For example, during pregnancy, nurse-visited women (groups 2 and 3), compared with women who were not visited, showed many behavioral changes, including more frequent attendance at childbirth classes and greater dietary improvements. They also had more help from their families and friends, as shown by their being more likely to have a supportive person accompany them to labor, and they had better health, as indexed by fewer infections (Olds et al., 1985b). In the second year of life, the children of women who received postnatal visits (treatment 3) required fewer emergency room visits and had fewer accidents and ingestions of dangerous substances than did the children of women who were not visited postnatally (Olds et al., 1985a). Prenatal nurse visits alone (treatment 2) did not lead to significantly better outcomes of this kind than did the provision of no visits at all. As was true with the Furstenberg study, the results of this study clearly demonstrate that random assignment to different treatments can, in some circumstances, yield readily interpretable data.

Minimizing Risks in Treatment Partitioning

There are risks associated with using treatment partitioning because it is so conservative a way to estimate efficacy. A true control group provides a no-treatment baseline as a standard for assessing the magnitude of treatment effects. When such a group is missing, and the baseline is instead provided by partially treated subjects, the impact of the best treatment studied can be underestimated very substantially. For this reason, treatment partitioning is not a good choice for performing a cost-benefit analysis.

A second problem is that if no significant differences are found among the various procedures studied, this outcome is not readily interpretable. It may mean either that all the treatments are ineffective or that they are beneficial, but to an equal extent. The strategy of treatment partitioning is therefore particularly risky when comparing treatments that are expected to be equally good.

A study by Kathryn Barnard and her colleagues (1982) illustrates the use of treatment partitioning with an indeterminate outcome. The investigators examined three alternative approaches to providing nursing services for newborns and their families. The first approach was the Nursing Parent and Child Environment (NPACE), an individualized program tailored to the specific strengths and needs of each family. Nurses in this program were free to use their own professional judgment in setting priorities for addressing a family's various needs and in determining how they could offer assistance. The second approach, Nursing Support for Infant Biobehavior (NSIBB), was a standardized program in which nurses used a predetermined curriculum to provide specific information about the biological and behavioral development to be expected in the first three months of life. The focus of this approach was limited to child care and parenting, with no effort directed at solving the parent's life problems. Nursing Standard Approach to Care (NSTAC), the third approach, consisted of using the established procedures for public health nurses in the area where the study was conducted. These involved an initial phone call followed by one or two home visits, if the nurse believed these advisable, to assess maternal and infant health. The nurses also provided assistance in the areas of family planning and establishing a regular source for health care of the children. In all the programs, the intervention period was from the birth of the infant to three months later.

The subjects of the study were 185 women who had been enrolled in prenatal programs for high-risk mothers-to-be during their pregnancies and who were then randomly assigned to one of the three nursing program alternatives. Because all the programs involved extensive personal contact, home visits, and provision of support in many ways, it is reasonable to believe that the recipients of any one program might have shown highly significant effects compared with a true control group. (Several true experiments comparing nurse-visited with non-nurse-visited mothers have established the basis for such an expectation [Gutelius et al., 1977; Larson, 1980; Olds et al., 1985a, 1985b].) Yet in this study, comparisons of the three treatments found no differences among them on outcomes assessed when the intervention ended and several months later.

While this study illustrates the risks of using this ethically strong but statistically weak design, a no-difference outcome may nevertheless be interpreted if there are meaningful subgroups of subjects for whom the treatments are not equivalent. For example, healthy full-term infants and premature infants might react differently to some kinds of treatments; young and older mothers might respond differently. If such treatment-by-subject interactions do exist, reanalyzing the data for each subgroup separately will reveal them.

In the Olds study described above, for example, the investigators found that a meaningful subdivision of subjects could be made on the basis of maternal age. When they analyzed their findings for young adolescents alone (under 17 years old), they found that mothers assigned to receive nurse visits during pregnancy bore children who were significantly heavier at birth than did those who had not received nurse visits. This particular benefit of nurse visitation was not seen when the treatments were compared for the entire study population.

As long as the subdivisions of subjects are made on the basis of pre-existing differences among them (for example, sex, race, and age) and as long as there are enough subjects to make the comparisons statistically meaningful, this strategy of subject partitioning as an adjunct to treatment partitioning has much to recommend it. It represents an effort to uncover subject-by-treatment interactions and is a scientist's reasonable approach to increasing the power of the treatment partitioning design. In the case of the Barnard nursing services study, the authors observed that the NSIBB model—in which a standardized parent-education curriculum was employed—appeared to work well only when neither the infant nor the mother had unusual problems. It did not, for example, seem well adapted for families who had premature infants or who were suffering from chronic stress. In contrast, the individualized NPACE model appeared best suited for families with multiple problems. Such observations could form the basis for a reanalysis of the data for multiproblem families only (many were randomly assigned to each condition), and similarly for a reanalysis for families with full-term infants and no chronic stresses. Since there are theoretical grounds for postulating that different treatments might work better with one type of family than with another, it would be highly advantageous to make such comparisons of the randomly assigned subgroups.

Importance of the Magnitude of Treatment Differences

The difference between a true experiment and treatment partitioning is sometimes not clear-cut. When the services offered in a treatment condition are minimal, the study design straddles the line between the two classifications. Clearly a minimal treatment offers greater contrast than a stronger one with procedures the investigator believes may be most powerful; whether the ethics side of the power-ethics balance is adequately addressed in such a design is not obvious and would have to be decided on a case-by-case basis.

That minimal services can offer an outcome equivalent to that of a true control condition is illustrated in the Olds study. As noted earlier, one treatment in this study involved providing free transportation to families so that they could attend clinics or take their children to physicians' offices for well-child care. The results for such families were indistinguishable from those for a true control group, for whom no services were provided.

A good illustration of the principle that the greater the differences among alternative treatments, the more likelihood there is of a difference in outcomes is provided by the Carolina Abecedarian Project (Ramey & Haskins, 1981), an intervention program designed to promote intellectual development and to prevent school failure. In this study, infants who were believed to be at risk of eventual school failure because of low maternal IQ, family income, parental education, and several other social criteria were randomly assigned to receive one of two treatments. The minimal treatment condition consisted of the provision of iron-fortified Similac to the families during the first 15 months of the infant's life, pediatric care or help in obtaining it, and referrals to social services if the families requested them. The extensive treatment condition added to these services a day care program which the infants entered at about three months of age and attended for 6 to 8 hours a day, five days a week, 50 weeks per year until they began kindergarten. The day care program provided a highly structured curriculum intended to stimulate cognitive development.

As the investigators have reported, the children in the two groups began to differ significantly on standardized developmental measures by 18 months of age, and by age four the IQ difference between the groups was substantial. In this study, although some services were provided for the minimal treatment group, they were clearly much less extensive than five years of full-time, free day care and preschool education. When differences between treatments are as large as in this example, large differences in outcome are likely to be found.

Since the major reason for employing treatment partitioning is to address ethical concerns, designing studies with very extensive differences among treatments may represent little gain from this point of view. It is therefore worth noting that this strategy will be strongest in both humanitarian and scientific ways when the treatments being compared are similar in intensity or duration but differ along some important other dimension chosen for good theoretical reasons.

As an example, consider the issue of timing in offering family support programs. There is increasing evidence that the transition to first parenthood is an important developmental event (Belsky, Spanier, & Rovine, 1983; Entwisle & Doehring, 1981; Hobbs & Cole, 1976). One implication of this fact is that people might be more open to receiving information and support at that time than they would otherwise be. Within this theoretical framework one might hypothesize that offering support services late in the first pregnancy through the early postpartum period would have quite different consequences from offering the same support services at some other time. One could investigate this hypothesis both ethically and with considerable experimental power by randomly assigning subjects to receive comparable services but at different times. As researchers attempt to develop better theories of intervention, the importance of such issues as timing and targeting is becoming increasingly evident. These areas therefore seem to provide especially rich ground for treatment partitioning designs.

TIME-LAG DESIGNS

A second group of designs with considerable potential for satisfying both ethical and scientific demands consists of those using a time-lag strategy. In this approach, the investigator recruits control subjects using the same criteria as are used to select experimental subjects, but recruits them at a different time.

A time-lag design could be appropriate where an apparently effective program must be discontinued. Faced with this regrettable situation, the researchers could continue to identify people whom they would have enrolled had the program continued, thereby creating an after-the-fact control group. If it is reasonable to assume that general environmental conditions and specific conditions in the community will not have changed appreciably over the time needed to identify such people, it is reasonable to let them serve as a control group.

A project conducted in the early 1970s by Sally Provence and her colleagues at the Yale Child Study Center illustrates the time-lag design strategy. As they describe in two books concerning the project (Provence

& Naylor, 1983; Provence, Naylor & Patterson, 1977), the investigators provided a 30-month program for impoverished families who were expecting their first-born child. The program was tailored to the specific concerns of each family and its focus was on family support; it attempted to help parents reduce the stresses in their lives and gain an increased sense of competency. There were four program components: a home visitor for the parents, pediatric care for the children, regular developmental examinations, and day care.

After the project ended, the researchers recruited a control group of people whom they would have invited to receive the treatment if the program were still in operation. Perhaps because they offered payment for participating, they had a similar acceptance rate as they had had in recruiting experimental subjects.

Seitz and her colleagues (1985) have continued to follow both experimental and control subjects, finding indication of the program's long-term effects in several areas, including the number of children the mothers subsequently chose to bear and the children's school attendance. For boys, there are also significant differences in how their teachers view them and in the number of special educational and remedial services they need. The experimental children are doing conspicuously better in these areas than the controls. The time-lag strategy clearly has its risks, but if the recruitment procedure is identical, the length of time between recruitments is not much different for the two groups, and the rate of acceptance in both groups is similar, as in the present example, this strategy can be a useful one.

A time-lag strategy can also be planned to create a control group in advance of a program's establishment. If an experimental treatment has been proposed but not yet funded or implemented, the researchers could identify the persons they would like to serve when the program is in operation, measure them, allow them to have the services when program is finally established, and use their earlier data to show what happens to such people during the time they are not receiving treatment.

For example, suppose a researcher designed a treatment for families in which the mother was clinically depressed during pregnancy, with the intention of offering a specific program of family support services from birth to three years postpartum. Prior to receipt of the funding needed to implement the services, recruitment could begin with the understanding that the subjects would be on a waiting list with priority to receive the services when available. If this group began receiving services at one year postpartum, whereas subjects recruited after the program was in operation began receiving services when their babies were born, it would be reasonable to compare the outcomes for the two groups when the babies were one year old to assess the importance of providing early services.

As this example suggests, the waiting-list design, long recommended as a strong quasi-experimental procedure (Campbell & Stanley, 1963; Cook & Campbell, 1979), belongs to the general class of time-lag designs. The only difference between the hypothetical example just described and a standard waiting-list design is that in the latter, the control subjects are waiting for a program that is already in operation instead of one that is in the planning stage.

A time-lag strategy can also be built into a study of the efficacy of different procedures without reference to program evaluation. Larson (1980) has successfully used such a strategy in studying the importance of timing in offering home visits to nonimpoverished, but low-income, mothers of newborns. In Larson's study, 115 mother-infant pairs were assigned to receive home visits beginning in late pregnancy, home visits beginning when the infant was six weeks old, or no visits (a control group). In this study, unlike the Olds and Barnard studies described earlier, the home visitors were not nurses but were women with undergraduate degrees in child psychology who had received special training in preventive child health care from a pediatrician before the study began.

The home visits were designed to provide information about general caretaking, such topics as feeding, sleep schedules, clothing, accident prevention, and the need for regular well-child care. The visitors also encouraged the mothers to talk to their infants during caregiving and to respond to their vocalizations. Child development counseling involved reviewing with the mother her child's developmental competence and suggesting types of activities she could engage in to promote the child's capabilities.

In condition A (early visiting), one visit was made in the seventh month of pregnancy, one visit was made in the hospital during the recovery period, four home visits were made in the first six weeks postpartum, and approximately five visits were made over the next year, ending when the baby was 15 months old. In condition B (late visiting), the home visitors made the same number of visits as in condition A, ending at 15 months postpartum, but the visits did not begin until the child was six weeks old. In condition C (a true control group), no visits were made.

While assignment to conditions B and C was random, Larson used a time-lag approach in choosing subjects for the condition in which visits began during pregnancy. A pilot study had shown that mothers who received a hospital visit shared their experience with other women in the same room. In order to prevent sharing and to keep the treatments separate, therefore, the investigator randomly assigned the first 80 subjects to conditions B or C, then assigned the next 35 to receive the early-visitation treatment.

The results of the study were clear-cut, and consistent with the results reported by Olds and his colleagues in indicating that the timing of home visits was an important factor affecting outcomes. The early-visited group showed a significant advantage over both other groups in several areas. The children of early-visited mothers had a lower accident rate, and the mothers scored higher on assessments of maternal behavior and providing appropriate and stimulating home environments. In group A, there was also a significantly lower prevalence of nonparticipating fathers. The only significant difference between the late-visited and the control mothers was a lower accident rate for the children of the former (although not as low as the rate for children of group A).

In using a study design such as this, the obvious concern is whether a few months' difference in the timing of birth (evidently the key difference between groups A and B) could have produced the different outcomes. Perhaps babies born in the summer months, for example, tend to have more or fewer accidents than those born in the winter. In the Larson study, however, seasonal differences would appear to be a weak explanation for the different outcomes compared to true treatment effects. The differential accident rates of groups B and C (the experimental part of the design) give strong evidence that home visits affected accident rates. This particular study appears to be an unusually good example of the successful use of a time-lag strategy.

Risks Associated with Time-Lag Designs

As noted earlier, using a time-lag approach to create a control group requires the presumption that causal factors for the outcome one is studying do not differ according to the times of recruitment. If there is an important change in the social environment or in the nature of persons living in a neighborhood or served by a program, a time-lag design is not a good choice.

An example of a situation in which societal change negated the interpretability of comparisons between two time-lagged groups is provided in an important study of teenage mothers by Klerman and Jekel (1973). (Recognizing this fact, these investigators also employed another strategy for forming a control group.) In this study, the subjects were pregnant teenagers enrolled in a special Young Mothers Program (YMP) at Yale New Haven Hospital between September 1, 1967, and June 30, 1969. The investigators established a comparison group by taking teenagers who met identical age, residence, and other entrance criteria for their study, but who had registered for prenatal care at the hospital before the special program was established—between October 1, 1963, and March 31, 1965. At 15 months postpartum, 25 percent of the YMP group had become pregnant again as compared with 47 percent of the comparison group. During the four years between the beginning of the two recruitment periods, however, a major change was made in a Connecticut law that had previously forbidden the use of contraceptives. As the investigators noted, such a change in legal codes could as plausibly be the cause of the difference in the pregnancy outcome for the intervention and comparison groups as could differences in the services they received.

As suggested earlier, when there are changes in the population served or in prevailing community attitudes or professional practices, the time-lag approach will not produce a good comparison group. Where the assumption of no significant changes associated with time is a reasonable one, however, some version of the time-lag strategy can provide an excellent choice. The strength of the design as compared to, for example, treatment partitioning arises from the fact that it can yield truly untreated comparison groups—a factor that also can make it suitable for cost-benefit analyses of programs.

OTHER APPROACHES

There are other potentially promising quasi-experimental design alternatives that will not be considered in detail here because they currently lack published examples of their successful and unsuccessful use. One of these is a modified random-assignment procedure, in which participants are first assigned randomly to treatment and control conditions. The investigator, however, distressed to discover that some of the persons who seem to be most at risk for undesirable outcomes have not been assigned to receive the treatment, decides to give them the treatment anyway. This is obviously not the usually recommended scientific procedure. In fact, the researcher is loading the deck in a conservative manner, risking the possibility that a program that is actually quite effective will be seriously underrated. If the program in question is extremely effective, however, the strategy of modified random assignment may be worth the risk.

Donald Campbell has pointed out (personal communication) that a more systematic version of this approach would be to give the treatment to all persons who are most clearly in need of it and use random assignment only for the remaining group of potential recipients. In either case, researchers should develop unambiguous measures of need so that the decision that a person is "clearly in need" is not an arbitrary one.

A final strategy cannot be recommended if the researcher's only interest is in evaluating a treatment. But under the right circumstances, this approach can yield an outcome evaluation as a useful by-product. The procedure is to define the target population appropriate to receive the intervention, then to include every member of that population in the assessment, whether or not they have received the intervention. If sufficient information can be obtained about program attenders and nonattenders alike, it may be possible to determine the direction and magnitude of whatever selection bias exists and to find a meaningful way to deal with it in interpreting the program's outcomes.

Research carried out by Seitz and her colleagues (1983) in New Haven illustrates this approach. There are a number of excellent programs in New Haven for pregnant teens and for teenage mothers. One alternative public high school offers pregnant students regular course work supplemented by courses on pre- and postnatal health care, labor and delivery, and infant care. In the hope of evaluating this school-based prenatal program and other programs serving this population, the investigators decided to identify, through hospital records, every school-aged mother in the city who bore a first-born child during a calendar year. They reasoned that if enough baseline data could be gathered about the full population eligible to attend available programs, perhaps meaningful information about the pregnant teens who were being served would emerge. In addition, it would be possible to test for selection biases confounded with such factors as the length of program attendance.

The full population data revealed that the prenatal program successfully reached 85 percent of all first-time black school-aged mothers-to-be. Half the group not reached chose to attend regular classes instead of the alternative school program; therefore, only about 7 percent of the relevant black population did not receive any school program during their pregnancy. However, less than one-third of the pregnant white and Hispanic populations was reached by the prenatal program. This finding has service implications that have influenced the prenatal program providers to recruit underserved populations more actively.

For approximately 90 percent of the population referred to the prenatal program, the investigators obtained data showing what kind of students these young mothers had been before becoming pregnant; educational, health, and social outcome data for these mothers up to two years postpartum; and information about what kinds of intervention programs and services they had received.

For the prenatal program, operating on a school calendar year (September through June), the major factor determining how much intervention a student received was found to be related to the month in which her baby was conceived. For example, girls who conceived in the spring tended to enter the special school in September and then received the maximum amount of intervention possible (four academic quarters); girls who conceived in the winter (for example, December and January) typically received only one academic quarter of intervention. A comparison of groups of students who received different amounts of intervention revealed that there was no selection bias in the students' performance in school prior to becoming pregnant or any other factor examined. Yet there was a significant outcome effect—the longer the girl attended this program, the better her educational outcome two years later.

The researchers were not as successful in trying to evaluate a postnatal school-based program. This program, located in the regular high schools, apart from the prenatal program, served some but not all of the prenatally served group. Here selection bias was found: the school having the highest percent of good educational outcomes also had the highest percent of returning good students, as assessed by prenatal school performance. In addition, more students who became pregnant at a later age (and who were therefore closer to achieving a high school diploma) received their postnatal program at this particular school. This part of the evaluation scheme had to be dropped because of the selection bias.

As this example illustrates, the principal advantage of a full population study is that it permits the identification of selection bias. If such bias is extensive, it will usually not be possible to differentiate between preexisting differences and the effects of different treatments. However, if a program's recruitment works so well that selection bias is minimal, comparisons between different kinds or lengths of treatments may be very reasonable.

There are doubtless other strategies, but these few give a flavor of some possible alternatives to the deliberate denial of services to some persons in order to evaluate the effectiveness of programs. Since research on the effects of family support will continue to raise this concern indefinitely, it would be highly advantageous for researchers to attempt to deal creatively with this problem.

NOTES

1. This study also included a true control group. Only the portion involving treatment partitioning is described here.

REFERENCES

Barnard, K. E., Booth, C. L., Mitchell, S. K., & Telzrow, R. W. (1982). *Newborn nursing models.* Final Report to the Division of Nursing, Bureau of Health

Manpower, Health Resources Administration, Department of Health and Human Services (Grant Number R01 NU-00719).

Belsky, J., Spanier, G., & Rovine, M. (1983). Stability and change in marriage across the transition to parenthood. *Journal of Marriage and the Family, 45*, 553-566.

Campbell, D. T., & Stanley, J. C. (1963). *Experimental and quasi-experimental designs for research.* Chicago: Rand McNally.

Cook, T. D., & Campbell, D. T. (1979). *Quasi-experimentation: Design and analysis issues for field settings.* Chicago: Rand McNally.

Entwisle, D., & Doehring, S. G. (1981). *The first-born: A family turning point.* Baltimore: Johns Hopkins University Press.

Furstenberg, F. F., Jr. (1976). *Unplanned parenthood.* New York, NY: The Free Press.

Furstenberg, F. F., Jr. (1980). The social consequences of teenage parenthood. In Catherine S. Chilman (Ed.), *Adolescent pregnancy and childbearing: Findings from research* (pp. 267-304). Washington, DC: U. S. Department of Health and Human Services, Public Health Service, National Institutes of Health, NIH Publication No. 81-2077.

Gutelius, M. F., Kirsch, A. D., MacDonald, S., Brooks, M. R., & McErlean, T. (1977). Controlled study of child health supervision: Behavioral results. *Pediatrics, 60*, 294–304.

Hardy, J. G., King, T. M., Shipp, D. A., & Welcher, D. W. (1981). A comprehensive approach to adolescent pregnancy. In K. G. Scott, T. Field, & E. Robertson (Eds.), *Teenage parents and their offspring* (pp. 265–282). New York: Grune & Stratton.

Hobbs, D., & Cole, S. (1976). Transition to parenthood: A decade replication. *Journal of Marriage and the Family, 38*, 723–731.

Klerman, L. V., & Jekel, J. F. (1973). *School-age mothers: Problems, programs, & policy.* Hamden, CT: Shoestring Press.

Larson, C. (1980). Efficacy of prenatal and postpartum home visits on child health and development. *Pediatrics, 66*, 191–197.

Olds, D. L., Henderson, C. R., Jr., Chamberlin, R., & Tatelbaum, R. (1985a). Preventing child abuse and neglect: A randomized trial of nurse home-visitation. Unpublished manuscript, Rochester, NY: University of Rochester.

Olds, D. L., Henderson, C. R., Jr., Tatelbaum, R., & Chamberlin, R. (1985b). Improving the delivery of prenatal care and outcomes of pregnancy: A randomized trial of nurse home-visitation. Unpublished manuscript, Rochester, NY: University of Rochester.

Provence, S., & Naylor, A. (1983). *Working with disadvantaged parents and their children: Scientific and practice issues.* New Haven: Yale University Press.

Provence, S., Naylor, A., & Patterson, J. (1977). *The challenge of daycare.* New Haven: Yale University Press.

Ramey, C. T., & Haskins, R. (1981). The causes and treatment of school failure: Insights from the Carolina Abecedarian Project. In M. J. Begab, H. C. Haywood, & H. Garber (Eds.), *Psychosocial influences in retarded performance.* Vol. 2. *Strategies for improving competence* (pp. 89–112). Baltimore, MD: University Park Press.

Seitz, V., Apfel, N. H., & Rosenbaum, L. K. (1983). Schoolaged mothers: Infant development and maternal educational outcome. Paper presented at the Biennial Meeting of the Society for Research in Child Development, Detroit, MI, April 21, 1983.

Seitz, V., Rosenbaum, L. K., & Apfel, N. H. (1985). Long-term effects of family support intervention: A ten-year followup. *Child Development, 56*, 376–391.

19 PROBLEMS FOR THE EXPERIMENTING SOCIETY IN THE INTERFACE BETWEEN EVALUATION AND SERVICE PROVIDERS

Donald T. Campbell

Much of our practice and rhetoric in program evaluation—"management by quantified goal attainment," "cost-benefit analysis," "quantified accountability measures," etc.—is harmful rather than beneficial to valid reality testing in the arena of social services. This ideology needs to be modified so as to avoid harmful side effects and pseudo-science while retaining the spirit of an experimenting society that continually tries out new service modalities, new therapies, and new organizational rearrangements, retaining those that are genuine improvements.

The explicit ideology of program evaluation as expressed by the enthusiastic young economists of the Office of Economic Opportunity during President Lyndon Johnson's great War on Poverty was that the results of program evaluation were to be immediately useful in administrative decision-making on next year's program budgets, pointing to ineffective programs to be cut out and effective ones to be expanded. This norm, to which our new profession of evaluators on the whole acquiesced, exacerbates a natural enmity between the program team and the evaluation team. Combined with the federal government's one-year budgeting cycle, it adds a destructive influence to the whole operation. It almost inevitably results in well-intentioned, honest people conspiring to deceive those enemy external evaluators who fly in with their pin-striped suits and their computer consoles. As a long-time observer of the city of Chicago under Mayor Daley, I came to the conclusion that less government money would be wasted if we built into the basic evaluation ideology the notion that if a program were found ineffective, its budget should be *raised* by 10 percent, with the same staff encouraged to continue work on the problem with revised procedures. The real budgetary threats under which program staffs live and manage their lives, such as not knowing whether one has a job for July 1st until that very date or later, create havoc and adversarial relations. These uncertainties inevitably jeopardize the accuracy of evaluation since the quantitive data used by number-crunchers are based on discretionary judgments, which are in turn dependent upon the social trust so seriously undermined by this program evaluation model.

Thus for applied social research, the most important general threat to validity is the program administrator's knowledge or belief that the results are going to be used in major financial decision-making affecting his or her own program. In "Reforms as Experiments" (1969), my first advocacy of quasi-experimentation for governmental decision-making, there is a section entitled "Advice to the Trapped Administrator." In subsequent years, I have had very mixed feelings about that section. While I hoped that the obvious contrast with the noble "experimenting administrator," also described, would move more people to take the latter role, most program administrators are caught in a setting closer to that of the "trapped administrator," and the recipes I gave, although tongue-in-cheek, remain efficacious. In most programs, the administrator and staff know that any evaluation will be very fragmentary; that many of the program's good effects cannot be measured; and that the program is going to be much better next year but that currently honest program self-criticism could be used bureaucratically to kill it. Thus a selective presentation of data designed to argue for refunding can be rationalized morally.

Another part of the official ideology of program evaluation that I want to challenge is that evaluations should be external rather than internal. Now, I know the selective self-enhancement that goes into a normal annual report in any operating agency. But I don't think that external evaluations have solved the problem. While I have argued that the quasi-experimental approach is a distillation of social science experience and not an imposition of the physical science model, I am tempted to learn from their successful experience. In most sciences, the person who designs the experiment implements it as a partisan observer, one who hopes that the data confirm his or her exciting new prediction. And how does science control for honesty in this? It doesn't—at least not 100 percent. But insofar as it does, it is not by delegating the experimental evaluation to an external specialist with no stake in the matter, but rather by a tradition of cross-validation.

For future program development efforts, I would like to see substituted for the current external evaluation ideology a *contagious* cross-validation model. Its norms would be, first of all, to evaluate no program until it is proud. We should not be in the business of selecting efficient and inefficient local staffs. We should not be in the business of finding heroic programs whose teams work 80 hours a week and of expecting the program design to be that effective when secondary borrowers (recipients of the program when disseminated) insist upon a 40-hour week. What we are interested in is disseminable programs, programs that have something different that can be transported, disseminated elsewhere. We should have no external evaluations until a program sends up a flag that says, "We've got something special that we know works and think others ought to borrow." At that time, federal evaluators should help those who borrow the program model in order to cross-validate its excellence in their own settings. We would end up with dozens of borrowings and interpretable cross-validations. This would be closer to the physical science model. But instead, premature evaluation is now the rule—devastating negative or deceptive evaluations taken on programs known by the staffs to be not yet debugged, not yet working. In the contagious cross-validation model, the evaluation would be postponed. Of the many programs funded, only those few that report notable success, that are proud programs, would be evaluated, evaluated in the dissemination process of the voluntary borrowing. We would also pare down our concept of program to that narrow aspect of it which is transportable, transmissible, and borrowable.

A related norm that I deem wrong is that the first-year evaluation be comprised of a single national study intended to be a "uniform" evaluation once and for all, consisting of lengthy questions that are irrelevant to one's particular situation. In contrast to this instrumental uniformity, the contagious cross-validation model would resemble hard science, where the cross-validation is regarded as more complete if the confirmation comes under differing instrumentation that is theoretically equally relevant. In other words, the different evaluation formats that diverse community-based family support programs naturally engender can be constructively compared.

Still another erroneous and prejudiced element of our original program-evaluation ideology is that a focal evaluation study should serve as the sole research guide to a specific administrative decision. Lindblom and Cohen (1979) have called attention to this bias. The choice is this: should we advise the government on the basis of a single study designed solely for this decision, or, should we advise from a cumulation of applied social science wisdom? I judge that the construction of a single evaluation to inform a single decision and the decision-theory on which it is based is wrong. The critical realistic approach to evaluation research is much better. A related choice is between writing an evaluation report for the benefit of the administrative decision maker and writing one for fellow applied social scientists, using their critical methodological tools. I disagree with those leading social scientists who advise the government and have said we should turn evaluation research over to nonacademic agencies that will immediately complete the work and tailor it to the uses of decision-makers, rather than give the contracts to academics who will meticulously and often inconclusively report their results with the standards and plausible rival hypotheses of their fellow applied social scientists in mind. At least in detailed appendices publicly available, the results should be available for fellow scientists. I recommend that our government foster self-disciplining communities of applied social scientists who are familiar with the problem areas of many actual and potential programs, and would advise the government on the basis of all relevant research, including the dozens of scientifically evaluated government programs of a similar nature (Campbell, 1979a, 1984).

A final disagreement I have with evaluation practices is the exclusive emphasis on quantitative measures. When, as in scientific management efforts, quantitative measures are used in regular administrative decision-making, so much pressure is placed on the fragile, judgmental, social science measures that they are distorted. (Too often they actually distort the very social processes they purport to describe.) The measures become as meaningless as the time-allocation forms academics are required to fill out. (See Ginsberg, 1984, and Campbell, 1979a, for a review of concrete examples and the relevant sociology of bureaucracy.) The continuing belief held by the scientific management field that such numbers are valid for regular bureaucratic decision-making is incredible, especially when jobs and promotions are dependent upon them. I am now opposed to the quantitative accountability movement, while still favoring quantitative methods (as well as qualitative) for evaluating those program alternatives that are genuine options for the staffs involved and do not threaten their survival.

Campbell and Stanley (1963) and Cook and Campbell (1979) have collected mutual criticisms of causal inferences about the social world outside the laboratory and compiled long lists of rival hypotheses, which are occasionally plausible. In a broader perspective, the plausible rival hypothesis concept is more basic to science than experimentation itself. Experiments become merely a formalized way of reducing the plausibility of *some* rival hypotheses, reducing the number of conclusions we can draw about a particular phenomenon. Thus, the program evaluation ideology has added powerful plausible rival hypotheses to those we already have in applied social science—so powerful that scientifically valid inference about program effectiveness is very difficult.

The pivotal role of the service provider is a thread running throughout these modifications in the dominant ideology of program evaluation. Those who provide services serve important roles in developing, trying out, debugging, and evaluating new programs. They oversee all the stages leading to the designation of a proud program ready for external evaluation. Such process evaluation cannot feasibly be undertaken by randomized experiments to test causal hypotheses. They depend upon the situation-specific knowledge and qualitative discretionary judgments of program staff who determine the goals and progress of a program. This situation-specific information is also essential to more formal impact evaluations of the debugged proud program, especially when judging the plausibility of the rival hypotheses and generating new rivals to be considered. Even Tom Cook's list of 33 or so plausible rival hypotheses (Cook & Campbell, 1979) is far from complete. Program staff, who know the situation, know "where the bodies are buried" and have a sense of the multidimensional complexity of the setting, will be the ones to generate new, relevant, plausible rival hypotheses. All quantitative research builds upon and trusts qualitative judgment (Campbell, 1978, 1979a, 1979b).

In that key phrase from Campbell and Stanley, "plausible rival hypothesis," the plausibility is a human discretionary judgment. Such judgment characterizes science not only at the level of accepting theories but also at the level of generating the basic facts used in theory choice. Thus if the formalized computer output disagrees with the qualitative judgments of well-placed observers, such as program implementors, it should be challenged, for it too is subject to optical illusions. The formalized computer output depends upon simplifying assumptions, often grossly oversimplifying assumptions. It is based upon fragmentary observations on too few dimensions of measurement, just as is our unaided judgment. The qualitative and quantitative modes of knowing will often agree on the most clearly successful programs. When they disagree, the qualitative should be allowed to override the quantitative as often as vice versa, as should have been allowed to happen in the first big Head Start evaluation (Campbell & Erlebacher, 1970; Campbell & Boruch, 1975; Magidson, 1977).

Quantitative measures and complex statistical manipulations seem typical of the successful sciences and are thus overly impressive in applied social science. Those whose expertise is in situation-specific knowledge, usually expressed in terms of qualitative judgments, need help in developing that discretionary skepticism that will provide the self-confidence necessary to speak out in public disagreement with quantitative results when these seem wrong. Concrete illustrations of deceptive quantitative findings can help stir this healthy skepticism. Producing valid applied research requires the recognition that our natural social situations are not natural laboratories—that causal inference is confounded not only by lack of experimental control but also by subjective interpretation due to political, economic, and program survival concerns.

Therapists or evaluators, we all long to play some role in an experimenting society that tries out new treatments and honestly learns what works best. Because the original ideology of program evaluation tied such exploration to budget renewal, put external evaluation first, called for premature, uniform, nationwide evaluations, neglected situation-specific knowledge and qualitative judgments based thereon, this original ideology has had unwanted side effects inimical to the experimenting society and has generated new threats to validity not found in unapplied field research.

We must seek out new models for applied social experimentation. Perhaps new slogans such as "evaluate only proud programs" or "contagious cross-validation" will help. Certainly we must increase our emphasis on situation-specific knowledge. This new emphasis will in turn engender the need to create arrangements that optimize honest reporting of the qualitative judgments of those best placed observers, the service providers.

REFERENCES

Campbell, D. T. (1969). Reforms as experiments. *American Psychologist, 24*, 409–429. (Reprinted in Struening, E. L., & Guttentag, M. [1975]. *Handbook of Evaluation Research*. Beverly Hills, CA: Sage.)

Campbell, D. T. (1978). Qualitative knowing in action research. In M. Brenner, P. Marsh, & M. Brenner (Eds.), *The social context of method* (pp. 184–209). London: Croom Helm.

Campbell, D. T. (1979a). Assessing the impact of planned social change. *Evaluation and Program Planning, 2*, 67–90.

Campbell, D. T. (1979b). "Degrees of freedom" and the case study. In T. D. Cook & C. S. Reichardt (Eds.), *Qualitative and quantitative methods in evaluation research* (pp. 49–67). Beverly Hills, CA: Sage.

Campbell, D. T. (1984). Can we be scientific in applied social science. In R. Conner, D. G. Altman, & C. Jackson (Eds.), *Evaluation studies review annual, Vol. 9*, (pp. 26–48). Beverly Hills, CA: Sage.

Campbell, D. T., & Boruch, R. F. (1975). Making the case for randomized assignment to treatments by considering the alternatives: Six ways in which quasi-experimental evaluations in compensatory education tend to underestimate effects. In C. A. Bennett & A. Lumsdaine (Eds.), *Evaluation and experiments: Some critical issues in assessing social programs* (pp. 195–296). New York: Academic Press.

Campbell, D. T., & Erlebacher, A. (1970). How regression artifacts in quasi-experimental evaluations can mistakenly make compensatory education look harmful. (Reply to the replies, 221–225.) In J. Hellmuth (Ed.), *Compensatory education: A national debate*, Vol. 3: *Disadvantaged child* (pp. 185–210). New York: Brunner/Mazel.

Campbell, D. T., & Stanley, J. C. (1963). Experimental and quasi-experimental designs for research. In N. L. Gage (Ed.), *Handbook of research on teaching* (pp. 171–246). Chicago: Rand McNally. (Most widely distributed as *Experimental and quasi-experimental designs for research*. [1966]. Chicago: Rand McNally. [Currently distributed by Houghton Mifflin.])

Cook, T. D., & Campbell, D. T. (1979). *Quasi-experimentation: Design and analysis issues for field settings*. Boston: Houghton Mifflin.

Ginsberg, P. E. (1984). The dysfunctional side-effects of quantitative indicator production: Illustrations from Mental Health Care. *Evaluation and Program Planning*, 7, 1–12.

Lindblom, C. E., & Cohen, D. K. (1979). *Usable knowledge*. New Haven: Yale University Press.

Magidson, J. (1977). Toward a causal model approach for adjusting for pre-existing differences in the nonequivalent control group situation. *Evaluation Quarterly*, *1* (3), 399–420.

20 EVALUATING FAMILY SUPPORT PROGRAMS

Edward F. Zigler and
Johanna Freedman

The survival of family support programs—that is, programs that provide "emotional, informational, and instrumental support to promote human development and prevent diverse child and family problems" (Weiss, 1983, p. 2)—is dependent in part on having accurate information about their efficacy. Unless policymakers, planners, and implementers—that is, *consumers* of evaluation research—know much more than whether some treatment produced positive results, they are unlikely to provide funding for it. Any expenditure of tax dollars raises concern among taxpayers and decision-makers over whether the programs are likely to succeed or fail. The desire for what in governmental circles is termed "accountability" necessarily takes a quantitative form, and responsible social scientists cannot turn aside from the onerous duty of providing objective research assistance in cost-benefit analyses. If funding is to continue or be increased in the future, it is vital that we address the concerns of taxpayers and policymakers about the costs and benefits of such efforts.

In addition, researchers' recognition of the need to be concerned with the scientific and policy issues inherent in social program evaluation has greatly increased our understanding of program effects and enhanced our ability to document them through a variety of evaluation methods. Policymakers and planners also need to know how or why the results (if produced) were produced. Conversely, when anticipated results are not forthcoming, they need to know why not. In particular they need to know the circumstances under which positive outcomes would be more or less likely. They also need to know something about unanticipated outcomes and the costs of producing these outcomes. All this requires careful quantitative and qualitative examination of program activities and outcomes in specific sites (Zigler, 1979). This is especially true in the cases of research domains in which practical conditions do not permit either the delivery of homogeneous programs or the random assignment of subjects to treatments, as is the case in family support programs.

Family support programs have not, as a whole, been characterized by experimentation and gradual development. Many family support programs originated in the past twenty years. Their existence was virtually unrecognized until quite recently (Weiss, 1983). In consequence, few empirical efforts have been made to substantiate their effectiveness. It is time that research efforts begin to ensure that current experiences will help shape future directions of family support efforts. While the number of programs seems to be growing at a healthy rate, we are at something of an impasse as to the course growth should take. One option is to keep the heterogeneous collection of programs we now have and hope that there is enough to offer something to everyone. The problem with this approach is that what is learned from one program is not readily generalized to allow other programs to benefit from it or to add to our knowledge base.

Another course of action is to move in a relatively new direction that capitalizes on the most successful aspects of many already implemented projects. Though it would be impossible to evaluate the multitude of family support programs now extant, this is surely the alternative of choice, ensuring informed change.

Experience in other fields, such as early childhood intervention, has taught researchers to evaluate carefully the intent as well as the outcome of intervention programs. Although the most general goal—to improve lives—has remained constant, the emphases of current family support programs reflect a greater understanding of the effects of intervention and the factors mediating these effects. Yet, despite recent progress in improving the quality of evaluations, many issues remain as to the proper role of evaluators, and appropriate components of evaluations. As Travers and Light (1982) have noted with regard to early intervention programs, "Evaluation has come under attack . . . Professionals question the technical quality of evaluations while parents, practitioners, and policy makers complain that studies fail to address their concerns or to reflect program realities" (p. 3). In his impressive critique of the dominant ideology of program evaluation, Campbell (chap. 19) has clearly identified a real and present problem, and we agree in theory with many of his conclusions. We are concerned, however, that while he has correctly identified many of the problems with "management by quantified goal attainment," "cost-benefit analysis," and "quantified accountability measures," some of the solutions he proposes will not adequately address the difficulties he has identified so accurately. Our goal is the same: the construction of an experimenting society in which "we try out new programs designed to cure social problems, in which we learn whether or not these programs are effective, and in which we retain, imitate, modify, or discard them on the basis of their apparent effectiveness on the multiple imperfect criteria available" (Campbell, 1969, p. 409). It seems, though, that Campbell may be rejecting a few procedures that in the past have served to ensure valid, reliable evaluations.

Campbell points out, and we agree, that premature program evaluation, tied to budget renewal, can lead to self-protective deception on the part of program administrators in program analyses or inappropriate dismantling of programs still in the process of development. His resistance to any form of accountability measures early in the life of a program seems unrealistic, however, in an era of increased concern with cost effectiveness and budget considerations.

His point that an adversarial relationship between program administrators and evaluators obviates the potential benefits of the action-research cycle is a good one. Unfortunately, his proposed solution of having initial internal evaluations by practitioners seems to ignore much that we have learned from both the social and hard sciences about experimenter and subject effects.

We can only agree, however, with his warning that no single, necessarily limited study can possibly function as the basis for national social policy and that nationwide evaluations that ignore the variability among local programs lack both internal and external validity—the very error that Campbell (Campbell & Erlebacher, 1970) pointed out in the Westinghouse-Ohio review of Head Start (1969).

The intent of this chapter is to consider the methodology involved in evaluating family support programs in order to guide such efforts in the future. Throughout this chapter, Head Start evaluations will be used as examples of appropriate or inappropriate strategies in evaluating family support programs.

EVALUATION OF FAMILY SUPPORT PROGRAMS

The future of many intervention programs for young children has hinged on the outcome of one evaluation or another. Most evaluations have been informed by the general question, "Do participants benefit?" This question is open to multiple interpretations and hence to multiple means of assessment. Who should be evaluated? By whom? How? When? We will address each of these questions in turn, with the forewarning that there are no universally accepted answers.

Who Should Be Evaluated?

The goal of many family support programs is unstated. Even when goals are explicit, outcome evaluations are often too limited in focus to assess the real impact of a program. As experience in early intervention programs has shown, indirect benefits can extend to the family as a whole and to the community at large. These more general gains must be measured if the value of family support programs is to be accurately gauged.

A fine example of a report on the general impact of an intervention program is a review by Kirschner Associates (1970) of the effect of Head Start on community life. Fifty-eight Head Start communities were studied and compared to seven non-Head Start communities. A total of 1,496 changes were counted in the Head Start communities, whereas few were found in the non-Head Start areas. Head Start, at once a precursor and an early exemplar of family support efforts, was found to have a demonstrable impact on the community by providing services to families and by contributing to the local economy through employment and the purchase of goods and services. In addition, staff and family members used Head Start as a stable base from which to work for change in the community. Overall, 50 percent of the changes involved greater emphasis on the educational needs of low-income and minority populations, 26 percent involved better and more sensitive health care delivery to disadvantaged populations; and 20 percent related to greater involvement with service institutions by individuals, especially in decision-making capacities. As the authors point out, the findings indicate an association between the existence of Head Start and fundamental changes in local responsiveness to the needs of low-income populations. Again, had the ground-breaking Kirschner analyses never been carried out, Head Start's wide-ranging effects, benefitting children, families, and the social institutions serving intervention families would not have been identified. The implication for present-day family support programs is clear. Evaluations should include a wide number of measures sensitive to all of a program's possible benefits to the members of families involved and to the community at large.

Gains in the familial sphere generally fall under the rubric of social competence, including physical well-being, optimal intellectual functioning, reasonable levels of achievement, and healthy emotional adjustment, as realized in the form of reasonable self-care (lowered rates of alcoholism, smoking, and drug abuse), possession of such basic cognitive skills as the ability to read and write, the capacity to hold a job, and basic satisfaction with life. Community gains could be gauged in terms of the economic health of the community or the crime rate, to name only a few possible measures.

By Whom Should Programs Be Evaluated?

Campbell (chap. 19) states: "Producing valid research requires that we recognize that our natural social situations are not natural laboratories—that out in the real world causal inference is confounded not only by lack of experimental control but also by subjective interpretation due to political, economic, and program-survival concerns." This is true. Truer, in fact, than Campbell himself seems to believe, as he offers the simple replication model used in the early years of the hard sciences as a model for social science evaluation. But since 1948, when Robert Merton first argued that social scientists' predictions concerning the outcomes of social science experiments will increase the likelihood that these outcomes will occur, the techniques of the hard sciences have been avoided. What is more, it is common knowledge that just being part of an experiment can alter the behavior of subjects (Orne, 1962). When this occurs, the results of an evaluation may not be valid for real-life events (Roethlisberger & Dickson, 1939).

The program administrators whom Campbell proposes as the appropriate initial evaluators are not trained to deal with these problems. It requires years of education and an objective relation to the experiment under examination even to begin to sort out causal factors in research outcomes (Wrightsman, 1977). Furthermore, administrators with an investment in a program's success are especially susceptible to influencing outcomes through their expectations and biases (Rosenthal, 1963). Campbell acknowledges this concern in his chapter, without offering a viable corrective.

Even in the hard sciences, which Campbell cites as his source for offering an internal evaluation model, procedures have been developed to control for experimenter bias. In medical research, the risks of expected results affecting the outcome of research are so widely recognized as to have made double-blind experiments the norm. In psychological research, we cannot use such simple means as gelatin capsules to disguise our treatments, and it is less easy to achieve the double-blind standard of objective distance from procedures. We could, however, strive to develop more creative and unobtrusive measures whenever possible. There are better models for program evaluation in the family support movement than internal evaluation and contagious replication, many of them proposed by Campbell himself in his work on quasi-experimental studies. The addition of an objective evaluator is too valuable a control to discard at any point in program evaluation. Such an evaluator is less likely to influence subject performance, and less likely to arrive at a biased evaluation. At the very least we should recognize that it is problematic for the person who designs or implements a treatment to also attempt to evaluate it.

The subjective insights of those directly involved with a project are valuable, however. We suggest, therefore, that in both process and outcome evaluation external evaluators, trained researchers in the social sciences, should work with lay program practitioners to analyze programs. In this way, the qualitative judgments and unique insights of those involved with the program can be effectively combined with the objectivity and methodological sophistication of the social scientist.

Under these circumstances evaluation would become a systematic learning from experience—both the experience of the program practitioner and that of the evaluator. This experience would then become part of public discourse and could be brought to bear on research generally.

How Should Programs Be Evaluated?

In order to arrive at a valid evaluation of any social program, its goals should be explicitly stated and widely recognized. In the case of family support programs, the goal must, of course, be determined by the nature of each program, but one principle is clear: although predetermined goals should not take precedence over sensitive adaptation of services to participants' needs, the ability to perform outcome evaluations is enhanced to the degree that the goals of a program are clear and explicit and are held constant through the life of the program (Zigler, 1979; Zigler & Berman, 1983).

The classic design for outcome evaluation studies has been, at least in attempt, the experimental model. In this model, individuals from the target population are randomly assigned to either an experimental or a control group. The relevant criterion variable is measured before the program starts and after it ends. Any differences between the two groups at the end of the program are used to determine the success or failure of the program. The experimental model has some limitations in that social programs are rarely developed or implemented in such a way as to allow its use in evaluation (Abt, 1974) without raising the ethical problem of denying help to those who might benefit. Further, it is unlikely that families can be found that are equally willing to participate in a support program and to act as a control if so assigned by the draw. If it is not possible to exclude misleading results due to improper experimental conditions, it will not be possible to assign the results to the treatment tested, whether good, bad, or indifferent. The early matched-sample evaluations (Cicirelli et al., 1969) that mistakenly found Head Start to be ineffective or even harmful made precisely this error, as Campbell has pointed out in the past (Campbell & Erlebacher, 1970). In every case where the comparability of treatment and control groups is not assured by randomized assignment, a whole host of selective-bias issues will emerge that cannot be fully eliminated by matching on quantitative or qualitative variables, by covariate adjustments, or by regression adjustments based on multiple covariates (Campbell & Erlebacher, 1970; Campbell & Boruch, 1975).

This does not mean that all nonclassically designed experiments are not viable. On the contrary, Campbell himself has outlined numerous effective quasi-experimental designs—that is, studies in which experimental and control groups are formed by means other than random assignment (Campbell & Stanley, 1963). These research designs, including the multiple-time series and partitioned treatment designs, have a very important role to play in psychological research in nonlaboratory situations.

When Should Programs Be Evaluated?

We agree with Campbell that programs should not be evaluated until they have passed through their purely evolutionary developmental stages. Yet, in his otherwise incisive critique, Campbell fails to draw a distinction between outcome and process evaluations (Zigler & Trickett, 1978), a distinction he had earlier made between "formative" and "summative" information (Cook & Campbell, 1979). As a consequence of ignoring this crucial distinction, he prematurely dismisses much that is useful about initial evaluations. Outcome evaluations inform decision-makers, among others, whether program goals are being met, and should be delayed until program practitioners feel that the program is solidly in place and has begun to achieve measurable results. Process evaluations, on the other hand, provide continuous feedback to program participants and can be useful to practitioners in the course of program development for the purpose of improving program operations. Process evaluation, then, ascertains the types of services that are being made available to program participants and, by providing information on obstacles to service, can function as part of a feedback loop that ultimately improves service. An example of process evaluation is the monitoring effort in Head Start programs to guarantee that each Head Start center delivers the services mandated by the program. If a parents' group intends to meet weekly, a process evaluation will determine whether they in fact do so, and what prevents them if not. If evaluators discover that lack of transportation or child care is lowering attendance, steps can be taken to ameliorate these problems.

Outcome evaluations are important sources of knowledge and direction, vital to the shaping of policy. They provide essential information about which programs work and which do not and why. This is especially relevant to decision-makers who are faced with the many unmet needs of America's children and limited public funds. These policymakers must decide whether to continue programs that have been given a fair chance to achieve their ends and have not done so or to allocate funds to new programs that hold the promise of achieving these specific goals.

This distinction between process and outcome evaluations gives definition to Campbell's proposed bipartate evaluation process, involving an initial internal self-evaluation by program administrators without any accountability, and a second external evaluation once the program is "proud." At the same time, preserving the distinction between process and outcome evaluations will prevent the researcher from falling victim to the demand constraints, experimenter effects, and program provider/evaluator confounds to which his proposed internal evaluation is subject.

HOW WE SHOULD PROCEED

One model for such controlled and rational knowledge transfer exists in the field of child development, where for several decades there was a central location within the executive branch where recognition of children's problems could be turned to action. The Children's Bureau, established by congressional legislation in 1912, was directed to "investigate and report upon all matters pertaining to the welfare of children and child life among all classes of people," with particular emphasis on the pressing problems of the time. A similar "Family Bureau," ideally within the venue of the Administration for Children, Youth, and Families, could serve as a focal point where the broad needs of today's family support programs could be examined and addressed with some degree of continuity. Rather than leaving information concerning programs that attack one problem or another, such as poor nutrition, disease and injury prevention, teenage pregnancy, child care and child abuse, scattered across hundreds of private, state, and federal agencies as at present, such a bureau could become the central repository for an authoritative data base on family support programs in the United States, a focus for ongoing data collection and analysis. With such a statistical base available, the proposed bureau could also promote research and demonstration programs on family support programs as a logical outgrowth of information gathering.

Finally, the bureau could serve as an interagency and interdepartmental coordinator of family support programs in the federal government. Precisely because the bureau would not be actually administering or competing for control of service programs, it would be in an excellent position to coordinate major federal efforts on behalf of families, fairly and objectively.

In conclusion, public policies and programs are the result of many forces. A variety of constituencies, many with conflicting needs, influence policy and are in turn affected by program construction. As a result, evaluations must address multiple concerns and must change focus as the programs they study evolve to adapt to participants' needs. Any single study is limited in its capacity to react to change, but as Campbell astutely points out, a single study is only a part of the larger evaluation process, and any single study has too many unique features to provide an adequate basis for far-reaching social policy.

As Campbell implies, the most valuable lesson to be learned from a program is often not whether it has achieved a specified end—which could result from the efforts of a uniquely talented staff or some other variable peculiar to a particular site at a particular time—but precisely how it functioned. Analysis of salient variables in the functioning of even an ostensibly unsuccessful program may reveal successful elements deserving replication in different contexts and other practices that should be amended or avoided. A true Family Bureau could be invaluable in achieving this end.

REFERENCES

Abt, C. (1976). The evaluation of social programs. Beverly Hills, CA: Sage.

Campbell, D. T. (1969). Reforms as experiments. *The American Psychologist, 24*, 409–429. (Reprinted in E. L. Struening & M. Guttanlag (Eds.) (1975), *Handbook of evaluation research*. Beverly Hills, CA: Sage.)

Campbell, D. T., & Boruch, R. (1975). Making the case for randomized assignment to treatments by considering the alternatives: Six ways in which quasi-experimental evaluations in compensatory education tend to underestimate effects. In C. Bennett & A. Linsdaire (Eds.), *Education and experiment* (pp. 195–296). New York: Academic Press.

Campbell, D. T., & Erlebacher, A. (1970). How regression artifacts can mistakenly make early education look harmful. In J. Helluth (Ed.), *Compensatory education: A national debate, Volume 3, Disadvantaged children* (pp. 185–200). Chicago: Rand-McNally.

Campbell, D. T., & Stanley, J. (1963). *Experimental and quasi-experimental designs for research*. Chicago: Rand-McNally.

Cicirelli, V., et al. (1969). *The impact of Head Start: An evaluation of the effects of Head Start on children's cognitive and affective development*. Vol. 1, text and appendices A–E; Vol. 2, appendices F–J. Washington, DC: National Bureau of Standards, Institute for Applied Technology.

Cook, T., & Campbell, D. T. (1979). *Quasi-experimentation: Design and analysis issues for field settings*. Chicago: Rand-McNally.

Kirschner Associates. (1970). *A national survey of the impacts of Head Start centers on community institutions*. Washington, DC: Office of Economic Opportunity (ED045195).

Merton, R. (1948). The self-fulfilling prophecy. *Antioch Review, 8*, 193–210.

Orne, M. (1962). On the social psychology of the psychological experiment: With particular reference to demand characteristics and their implications. *American Psychologist, 175,* 776–783.

Roethlisberger, F., & Dickson, W. (1939). *Management and the worker.* Cambridge, MA: Harvard University Press.

Rosenthal, R. (1963). The effect of the experimenter on the results of psychological research. In B. A. Maher (Ed.), *Progress in experimental personality research* (Vol. 1) (pp. 79–114). New York: Academic Press.

Travers, J., & Light, R. (1982). *Learning from experience: Evaluating early childhood demonstration programs* Washington, DC: National Academy Press.

Weiss, H. (1983). Strengthening families and rebuilding the social infrastructure: A review of family support and education programs. A state of the art paper prepared for the Charles Stewart Mott Foundation., Flint, MI.

Westinghouse Learning Corp. (1969, June). *The impact of Head Start: An evaluation of the effects of Head Start on children's cognitive and affective development.* Executive Summary. Ohio Univ. Report to the Office of Economic Opportunity. Washington, D.C.: Clearinghouse for Federal Scientific and Technical Information (Ed-36321).

Wrightsman, L. (1977). *Social psychology.* Monterey, CA: Brooks/Cole.

Zigler, E. (1979). Project Head Start: Success or failure? In E. Zigler & J. Valentine (Eds.), *Project Head Start: A legacy of the war on poverty* (pp. 495–509). New York: Free Press.

Zigler, E., & Berman, W. (1983). Discerning the future of early childhood intervention. *American Psychologist, 38,* 894–906.

Zigler, E., & Trickett, P. (1978). IQ, social competence and evaluation of early childhood intervention programs. *American Psychologist, 33* (9), 789–798.

PART VI/SUMMARY AND RECOMMENDATIONS

21 PAST ACCOMPLISHMENTS: FUTURE CHALLENGES

Sharon L. Kagan,
Douglas R. Powell,
Bernice Weissbourd,
and Edward F. Zigler

Family support has existed in America since the village green. Communal barn buildings, quilting bees, church meetings, and gatherings on the porch of the general store were vehicles by which talents were traded, information was exchanged, and support was lent. These informal events engendered important ties, creating a sense of identity and community for the individual. In fact, concern for neighbor and community became part and parcel of the American ethos. Although nearly all these customs have disappeared, the needs they met and the purpose they served—that of empowering individuals—persist. Today, new forms of family support have emerged similar in function but different in design. To some extent, today's efforts reconstitute networks that were taken for granted a century ago. But they do so within a strikingly different demographic, bureaucratic, and political context—a context that simultaneously contours and complicates the family support effort.

Recent demographics depict family disorganization and restructuring as general features of the American population, which accelerates widespread national concern about today's families and about the future of our nation. In the United States, in contrast to other industrialized nations, changes in the rates of maternal employment, divorce, and teenage pregnancy are occurring both more rapidly and more intensely (Bronfenbrenner, this volume). The teen parent in Detroit, the divorced mother in Manhattan, the immigrant family in Texas, the abusing parent in Iowa, and working parents in Baton Rouge are all part of a major social realignment altering the ways we define, conceptualize, anu serve families.

Family support efforts characterize this realignment, which emerges as a uniquely American response to our particular social challenges. Family support programs are simultaneously a symptom and a solution: a symptom in that their very existence signals the pervasiveness of the problem, a solution because they represent concrete efforts to ameliorate problematic conditions in which families find themselves. The programs are not always easy to understand, either individually or when we try to ascertain their collective mission. Why do some nest themselves within large bureaucracies like schools, hospitals, and social service agencies while others establish themselves as independent entities? Why do some programs strive to serve only their participants while others assume the broader mission of changing the institutions they infiltrate? What are the programs really accomplishing? What can we hope for from them in the future?

The purpose of this chapter is to look at today's family support programs in light of the current social context and to assess their impact to date. We also will posit recommendations that may help safeguard the future of family support programs.

THE NATURE OF FAMILY SUPPORT

Blending Service and Advocacy

Our review indicates that family support programs, however unique, are characterized by two major components: direct service and advocacy. By direct service, we mean the educative and supportive events and activities offered by programs that help individuals. By advocacy, we mean activities that seek to propel changes in organizational practice or in governmental or institutional policy. This volume, not unlike the field itself, has focused much attention on the service component. Reflecting an important evolutionary stage, this orientation has been helpful to the nation. Yet the editors suggest that family support is at a turning point in its development, a point where a focus on service alone is no longer sufficient. Rather, the coming decades in family support must focus on service *and* advocacy. It is our belief that quality services combined with well-orchestrated advocacy efforts represent the best chance for the programs' long-term survival. This is not a new idea. Historically, we have seen the important role of advocates in sustaining settlement houses, self-help, parenting education, and early intervention efforts. Our analysis suggests that contemporary forces, perhaps more insidious than those of Jane Addams' time, hasten the press for advocacy. Nevertheless, today, in spite of vigorous rhetoric on behalf of supporting and strengthening families, there are painfully few advocates. Who speaks on behalf of children and families? For example, what steps has the women's movement in America taken to support families?

In a recent and provocative work, Hewlett (1986) chronicles the growth of the women's movement in the United States, challenging its functional utility for American families. Hewlett points out that American feminists have sought formal equality of rights between men and women whereas European social feminists have focused on developing support systems for women that allowed them to be more effective workers, wives, and mothers.

Propelled by different goals and adopting different strategies, European and American feminists have had different impacts. European feminists, working through labor unions, political parties, and existing professional organizations, have established effective coalitions. American feminists, not aligning themselves with interest groups such as political parties and labor unions, have worked independently, sometimes generating a strident backlash that has hampered their work, as in the effort to pass the Equal Rights Amendment. In Europe, governmental policies that support family well-being are the norm; child care and maternity leaves are common. Owing to the nature of American feminists' pursuits, child care until recently was very low on the feminist agenda. Not only does NOW not support a universal maternity leave policy, but it has gone on record against it.

Hewlett's point, and ours, is not to castigate the women's movement, for it surely has brought about advances for women. It is to point out that supporting women in their roles as mother and worker has never been a top priority for American feminists. If America's prominent women's organizations are not advocating support for the family, then who is? What stance have other organized groups taken on these issues?

Trade unions, historically oriented toward supporting the male breadwinner, have generally not been strong advocates for women in their dual roles as worker and mother. In response to a lack of support for their work-place concerns, women formed their own organizations. The Women's Trade Union League, founded in 1903, was one such organization that provided the needed supports. Later, as greater numbers of women were drawn into the labor force, they were accorded adequate pay, seniority, and vacations. Despite these advances, unions have not been known for their efforts to support women and their families, perhaps because of the underrepresentation of women in unions. In 1980, for example, only 14 percent of women workers belonged to unions in comparison to 23 percent of male workers; and, of those who belonged, women made up 28 percent of union membership in spite of the fact that they constituted 45 percent of the work force (Adams, 1985).

Without strong support from the institutional infrastructure—feminists and unions, as two examples—and without a national governmental policy that supports families, the pressing need for a strong advocacy component in America's family support efforts is apparent. Unless family support programs advocate for themselves, their existence as individual efforts is jeopardized and their potential national impact is minimized. Fortunately, the advocacy role is not an unfamiliar one, conceptually or practically. Today's adults, youth of the 1960s and 1970s, absorbed advocacy lessons from civil-rights and antiwar movements. Pizzo (1983) sums it up well: "Would a young man who had been willing to defy the American selective service system accept the obstetric ward's policy of 'fathers aren't allowed?'" (p. 47). Armed with experience and a commitment to advocacy, members of today's family support programs are well qualified to assume a leadership stance in winning recognition for the family support movement. To some extent, this has been accomplished. Let us turn to an analysis of the contributions of family support to ascertain how.

Service and Advocacy Contributions of the Family Support Movement

Throughout this volume, various metaphors have been used to characterize the state of family support programs and family support research. This kaleidescopic picture is due as much to the differing perspectives of the contributors as to the incomplete and transitory state of our knowledge about family support programs. Yet, in spite of these different perceptions, all will agree that family support has had a definite impact. Changes in the kinds of services being offered, the way they are being offered, and institutional practice are apparent.

With the advent of family support efforts, many theoretical notions about service delivery were consciously put into practice. For example, the concept of prevention, although somewhat elusive theoretically, has been made concrete via family support. In social science terms, family support programs have "operationalized" the concept of prevention. Hundreds of "preventive" family support programs are now in place throughout the nation, serving children and families before problems begin. Prevention programs dealing with prenatal nutrition and child abuse abound, as do accident prevention, parent education programs, and programs that encourage links between parents and the institutions that serve their youngsters. Family support programs have also incorporated an ecological orientation in their programming, not emphasizing

solely the child or the adult as the focus of the effort but fully acknowledging the importance of the total family, neighborhood, and community. Given the primacy of these interactions in the conception, organization, and operation of most family support efforts, an ecological
perspective is a practicable approach to support.

Family support programs have contributed a great deal to our knowledge of community organization and community development. Often
established as alternatives to existing bureaucracies or as mechanisms
for their reform, family support programs have clearly demonstrated
that it is possible, and in some cases preferable, to launch and sustain
meaningful supports without heavy bureaucratic ties. In maintaining
distinctiveness and freshness, these programs provide alternatives to the
traditional service approach, alternatives that may be more responsive
to individual needs and more comfortable for participants. As such, they
are a new key element in the spectrum of available human services, and
they may also help reduce the burdens of traditional social service
organizations.

Family support efforts have also contributed to our knowledge of institutional change. As many of the chapters in this volume indicate, institutions are modifying their policies and practices to reflect the needs of
families. These changes may come about in a variety of ways. Sometimes
family support efforts begin as programmatic add-ons. Funded as pilot
or demonstration projects within an institution, these programs provide
a service that was not previously offered. Often as a precondition of
funding, the recipient agency agrees to "institutionalize" the program
when outside funds terminate, thus ensuring the continuation of the
program and the modification of services offered by the institution.
Sometimes special funds used for in-service training evoke attitudinal
changes on the part of staff or faculty that result in a changed policy. For
example, following in-service training on working families, one school
district completely revamped its intake procedures for kindergarten
children and its system of report card conferencing to accommodate the
needs of working and single-parent families. Sometimes institutional
policies are modified in response to specific client concerns. Irrespective
of impetus, the very process of establishing such reforms begins a
realignment of the relationship between the institution and the individual. So, in addition to rendering direct services, family support efforts
have successfully advocated for institutional change.

Whether family support programs are ends in themselves in that they
provide services or means in that they advocate for a broader goal, they
have also been instrumental in realigning relationships among staff and
between staff and clients. The shift has been so remarkable that the term
client is barely applicable in family support. Emerging from a commit-

ment to serve families in the most productive way possible, staffing patterns often include parents or volunteers in lead responsibilities. Professionals, taking on new roles, act as orchestrators, coordinators, and facilitators of dialogue among those who help themselves. As an approach to human service delivery, this staffing makes good sense. Ultimately, the typical treatment model, where one professional "treats" one client, will be difficult to maintain because the numbers of "clients" will surpass the number of available professionals. Additionally, this hierarchical model militates against the feelings of competence and independence that the client seeks to develop. Family support programs aim to eliminate paternalism associated with many early governmental intervention efforts. Thus, the programs have consciously tried to reduce client dependency, which has been considered an inherent liability of so many intervention efforts. New and successful staffing patterns in family support programs help remedy these problems and are potential models for human services in general.

Perhaps the greatest contribution of family support programs is the subtlest. The American orientation for support has long been predicated on a deficit model—the assumption that "healthy" families do not need support while "sick" families or families unable to care for themselves are dependent upon support. With the existence of family support programs, a new definition of support has emerged. No longer seen as the purview of the poor, family support efforts are more universal in orientation and appeal to families of all socioeconomic, racial, and geographic backgrounds. Family support programs may be designed to meet the needs of an issue-specific population (for example, divorced fathers) or broadly targeted to a wider audience (for example, parents). They may be short term, lasting only a few sessions, or provide support over a period of years. Whatever the structure, the traditional stigma associated with support has been removed. It is now widely acknowledged that given normal life stresses, everyone needs support, particularly as one faces natural life transitions. Family support has dispelled the belief that support is only for the high-risk, the dependent. It has moved human services to a mutually supportive orientation and in so doing has opened the door for many Americans to solicit and give assistance.

Although the family support movement's contributions are only beginning to be chronicled, it is clear that these programs are breaking through traditional service patterns to meet individual needs in new and promising ways. If their benefits were measured in terms of service delivery alone, the contributions would be large. Add to this their value as advocates for social change within institutions, and the contributions of family support efforts escalate in importance. Yet, the programs face serious obstacles, practically and conceptually. Indeed, they are at a critical juncture.

AT A CRITICAL JUNCTURE

It is quite tempting to be optimistic about the future of family support. All over America family support programs are springing up as parents, professionals, and institutions experiment with the concept. Further, demographic trends foretell continuing, if not escalating, need for family support. For example, as new parents are bombarded with emerging research on parenting, they will seek support, beginning in pregnancy. Parents of teenagers of all economic classes will continue to seek assistance in helping their children cope with the insidious effects of narcotics and alcohol. Teenage parents will need support for themselves, their infants, and their families.

There are other reasons for optimism about the durability of family support programs. First, they are cost effective because they save countless dollars by reducing the need for extensive remedial services later. Second, preliminary research indicates that family support programs are making a difference in the lives of children. Third, new and successful public-private sector partnerships are financing family support programs, and their evaluations are emerging. These positive trends signal the tremendous potential inherent in the family support movement. Nonetheless, conceptual and pragmatic hurdles must be addressed if family support programs are to thrive.

Conceptual Challenges

Although many family support programs are dealing successfully with difficult conceptual issues, several prominent challenges remain unsolved. The question of whom to serve, in light of limited resources, is one that plagues family support practitioners. As family support efforts have moved from a deficit orientation to more universal application, more people want, need, and are candidates for this new type of service. Consequently, the question arises as to whether services should be provided as a right to all families or made available only to families that demonstrate an inability to meet their own needs. Advocates for low-income populations question whether the emphasis on universal family support is drawing attention and resources away from the poverty population that is most in need. This tension between universal service and serving the neediest has characterized many policy debates. In fact, it has led to the policy stance this nation has taken with respect to families, one rooted in the deficit orientation, wherein the federal government provides services primarily to those whose needs are not met by family members, friends, neighbors, or church: the government has become the provider of last resort.

Two important attributes characterize family support programs and lend clarity to the question of who should be served. First, family support efforts are totally voluntary, which means that all who take advantage of them perceive themselves as needing the service. This is not to say that *all* Americans need or want family support efforts, but for those who do, family support is a viable option, based on the free choice of the participant. Second, an axiom of family policy is that as an issue impacts more of the population, it draws greater media and policy attention. When child care was an issue only for poverty families, there was little public discussion. Now that it has become a middle-class and more universal concern, the quest for child care receives front-page coverage and vociferous debate. So it is with family support. As more families, irrespective of income level, are stressed, need escalates. Moynihan (1986) verifies the growth in family stress by maintaining that the problems of minority and low-income families of the 1960s are now affecting the general population in unprecedented numbers. Because demographics help drive policy, this universalist need might actually heighten public interest in family support programs. Rather than robbing high-risk families of badly needed services, this development may lead to the generation of more programs for the entire population.

Because many family support programs are designed to serve families experiencing similar stresses (for example, pregnant teens, divorced fathers), a second challenge arises. Do programs serving only "like" families quash diversity? Do they risk subdividing families into such discrete units that we may become insensitive to problems with which we are unfamiliar?

Although these questions are not to be dismissed lightly, there are two salient facts that help assuage concern. First, although programs may serve families with like problems, the families themselves may be heterogeneous. For example, single parenting is not limited to any one class, socioeconomic group, or race. Second, the banding together of individuals from disparate groups around family support issues may be seen as a strength, rather than a weakness, of the programs. Certainly, from an advocacy perspective, individuals with like concerns have been and may continue to be mobilized into effective advocacy groups. For example, the National Council for Retarded Citizens, composed of individuals with like concerns, has been extremely effective in moving policy forward. Bonded by concern for one specific population segment, this group has been effective in shaping policy and program. Out of like concerns comes strength.

A third conceptual challenge, with a long history of traditional social service delivery, has been addressed by family support programs. It is the dependency issue. Scholars (Moroney, [chap. 2]; Pinker, 1973) have suggested that because there is no real opportunity for reciprocity between clients and professionals in traditional human services, dependency is encouraged. The question then becomes, given the changed nature of relationsips between professionals and clients in family support programs, what has been and is being done to reduce client dependency? Has this effort been successful? Can family support programs become viable models for providing care and education without creating dependency? Our analysis reveals that the dependency issue, although still a matter for concern, is being addressed in family support programs by modifications in traditional staff roles that foster interdependent relationships and second by building in procedures, such as phasing down of staff involvement, to reduce or eliminate dependency in existing programs. For example, the Family Matters Project (Cochran & Woolever, 1983) invites families into self-help groups by offering a combination of home visits and group meetings to involve them in common activities. Once the supportive networks are established, families function with decreased support from the program.

So family support programs have faced and must continue to face challenges that are the residual effects of a traditional approach to human services. Clearly, even in their infancy, these programs have provided viable and exciting alternatives to conventional strategies. Yet, the conceptual challenges confronting them are real and ongoing.

Practical Challenges

Whereas the conceptual challenges may be, in part, a legacy from past approaches to human services, practical challenges, characteristic of new endeavors, also plague family support. The linchpin of the practical challenges is garnering adequate financial support. The problem of maintaining a stable funding base, cited as the number one challenge by program directors at the Yale Family Support Conference in 1983, has been exacerbated by federal and state funding reductions. Financially frail, family support programs are often dependent on the largesse of communities and volunteers. But as funds for human services evaporate, beneficent local foundations and trusts are besieged with increasing numbers of requests. Often the grassroots family support efforts do not stand up well in competition with sophisticated agencies in the grants and funding process. Moreover, the new programs may be reluctant to compete for funds for fear that the very qualities that drove them to success (parent ownership and reliance on volunteers) may be forced to give way to more bureaucratized structures. Striking a balance between preserving funding and preserving program values remains a constant challenge.

In addition to the lack of direct financial support, the lack of opportunity to network with other programs is troublesome for practitioners who wish to share information and learn from others' work. The Family

Resource Coalition (FRC) in Chicago remains the mainstay of training and networking efforts nationally. Yet it is limited in what it can do because, in spite of its effectiveness, FRC needs difficult-to-find financial infusions.

Another grave concern for family support practitioners and researchers arises from ambiguity about the appropriate role of government in family support. Generally, the lack of a cohesive government policy regarding family support does not bode well for the effort. More specifically, the Reagan administration, despite its vigorous rhetoric, has taken only limited steps in behalf of family support programs. One of these was the sponsorship of the Yale conference and support for this volume; another involved supporting the dissemination of information about family support programs. The lack of a more vigorous and more financially sufficient commitment to family support remains surprising, particularly in light of the compatibility of family support with the Reagan administration's "new federalism." More than just a corrective to cut the deficit, limited governmental funding for family support programs seems to reflect a deeply held ideology regarding the noninvolvement of government in family policy.

Not only are programs in need of funds, but research efforts also require financial commitment. While some very worthwhile research, funded by private foundations, is being pursued, it is limited in scope. Without sufficient research to assess the actual efficacy of family support, arguments for additional funding from the public and private sectors lose their persuasiveness. Not only is more research needed on the programs themselves, but additional resources are necessary to develop and test procedures appropriate to programs that are preventive and that target the entire family, not simply one member. Just as the programs are pioneers in human-service-delivery modes, so their evaluation is also at the methodological frontier. Funding for research is especially important because it will contribute to our knowledge about family support and to advances in research methodology generally.

Perhaps the most pressing issue facing those who are concerned about family support relates to advocacy. As indicated earlier, today's family support programs hold special promise because they combine a commitment both to service and to advocacy. The challenge becomes clearer when the advocacy stances of family support programs are explored in greater detail. Programs are concerned, appropriately, about their own longevity, so that the first level of advocacy is typically motivated by a program's own financial survival. Therefore, programs advocate for their particular form of family support, typically at the local or state level. As this volume makes clear, however, there is not just one type of family support. So, in reality, advocates of family support, rather than coalescing around the broad issue of family support, may be competing against one another by lobbying for issue-specific interests (for example, child abuse, trust funds, maternity leave, afterschool care). Although this approach may be effective on an issue-by-issue basis, the lack of a unified approach to advocacy for family support generally may lead to the demise of the family support movement. An alternative to this situation, although difficult to achieve because of America's piece-meal approach to child and family policy, is to popularize the concept of family support so that practitioners will understand and perhaps become advocates for an orientation that transcends individual issues to support families generally. Without such an effort, family support will lose viability as a concept and as a funding vehicle.

As this review indicates, family support programs are at a critical juncture. The programs' past successes are certain, but their future funding is tenuous. The question now, and in fact the question that prompted this volume, is what next? What needs to be done to preserve family support and to nurture it beyond its youth?

TOWARD THE FUTURE

Our recommendations for the future of family support programs are predicated on the belief that family support is nearing the completion of an important stage of development and that the start-up tasks of the initial phases have been met. Now, we are entering a new phase, one that must look beyond individual program development to the development and financing of a field. Further, we believe that the long-term success of family support is essential in revitalizing human services in this nation. We do not believe that family support can function without support from a broadened constituency or that family support programs alone should be expected to meet America's human service needs. These programs aid, not supplant, current federal efforts on behalf of children and families. To this end we recommend that the following steps be taken.

Broaden Participation

At present, the palette of family support is dominated by practitioners. A handful of talented researchers and one major advocacy/support group, the Family Resource Coalition, are involved. Some training exists, but the person power to adequately staff, run, and evaluate family support efforts is simply not available.

We call for the establishment of a series of centers throughout the nation devoted to training individuals to work in the family support arena. These centers should be autonomous but linked so that cross-fertilization of ideas and scholarship can take place. Our goal is to seed a new generation of practitioners and scholars who will receive specific training in organizational development, community dynamics, developmental stages of parenting, and ethnic and cultural child-rearing patterns, and who will employ a nondeficit approach to families. Certainly, training should consist of units devoted to content areas (teen pregnancy, child abuse, school-age child care, parenting education), but they would be linked by a conceptualization of family support. Drawing from the disciplines of education, sociology, social work, psychology, and organizational management, the centers would produce individuals who are committed to family support generically and have an understanding of content, research, and research methodology and practice. Ultimately, this cadre of trained professionals could assume leadership roles in policy arenas, research institutes, associations, advocacy organizations, and in the field.

Enhance Public Awareness

In his preface, Urie Bronfenbrenner noted that a tone of guarded optimism runs through this volume. He conjectured that the guardedness was due in part to lack of public support and to public apathy. We concur and suggest that public apathy is rooted in a lack of information. Family support programs seem to be among our nation's best kept secrets. In recent years, the public, largely via the print and broadcast media, has become aware of serious problems facing American families. We encourage the media to complement the coverage of sensational child and family problems with coverage of family support efforts showing them as possible solutions or prevention strategies. By publicizing viable efforts on behalf of families, the media will not only report more equitably but will dispel the helplessness that reporting sensational issues engenders. We support the addition of professionals interested in and knowledgeable about families as media advisers, broadcasters, writers, and board members.

Coalesce and Expand Advocacy Efforts

At present, family support has a large but amorphous constituency. Concerned individuals need to be brought together to develop a common vision and to expand the advocacy coalition. Coalition building, while not easy, is the necessary lifeline to public policy and financial support. The Family Resource Coalition is a pivotal organization. It must continue its vital role as a clearing house of information on family support. But its staff needs to be expanded to allow its personnel to concentrate on this advocacy dimension. Although beginning this advocacy work at a national level makes good sense, we also recommend that advocacy organizations be developed on a grassroots level in municipalities and states throughout the nation, perhaps following the federated structure of the Junior League or the National Council of Jewish Women.

The focus of advocacy efforts must be broad enough to capture the attention of individuals who are not currently affiliated and to allow for linkage with existing coalitions on issues of overlapping concern. Efforts need to be targeted not solely at engendering financial support but also at creating a climate of opinion that supports interdependence, that affirms parenting as a vital responsibility, and that values the individual and family within the community. Pizzo (chap. 12), in supporting the need for advocacy, suggests that parents who are activists need to be mobilized and that all parents need to see an advocacy role in policy as part of responsible parenting. Advocacy must be acknowledged as a key component of local family support programs and as a critical strategy worthy of time, effort, and dollars at the national level.

Mobilize the Research Community

Research on family support has enormous implications for practice and policy. Yet, such research is at a fairly primitive stage. There are some notable efforts under way, but limited isolated projects do not make a research community or a research strategy. We believe that in order to maximize the nation's research capacity in family support, such a community and such a strategy must be developed. To that end, we call for the establishment of a network that would enable researchers to share their methods and findings and to conceptualize new research paradigms. Furthermore, in view of the challenges inherent in evaluating preventive, family-oriented programs, we call for a national infrastructure that supports empirical research through adequate funding. Forums must also be created for the dissemination of research findings so that research results and methods are publicized beyond the academic community.

In addition, we recommend that serious attention be paid to process evaluations and cost-benefit analyses. Process evaluations help programs document the services being delivered and help program personnel better understand processes and interactions that mediate the program's effects. Information gleaned from this internal research can then be used for program planning and improvement. Cost-benefit analyses are critically important as well. The calculation of dollars saved by society as a result of family support programs is one sound way to measure their efficacy. Participants in family support programs are using and, in all likelihood, will continue to use fewer social services, thereby saving tax dollars. Approaches to verifying such information would be particularly beneficial if they were made available to program practitioners who could then select and use the most appropriate cost-benefit-analysis model. Such an approach, developed by the Harvard Family Research Project, will make various program evaluation methods available to local programs. Support that enables the research community to prepare evaluation tools or models and then makes them available to local programs is an especially wise investment.

Finally, expenditures on research must be regarded as long-term investments that benefit the family support community, not only because the research assesses program efficacy but because it contributes to the development of theories of practice; these expenditures would also benefit the broader research community because conventional research designs and strategies will be augmented by work in family support.

Join the Funding Sources: Expand the Commitment

Many existing family support programs and their related research are supported by innovative funding partnerships (see Muenchow [chap. 14]). A review of this work clearly shows that to date foundations have been involved in financing family support efforts. States, some corporations, and the federal government have also contributed financially. We see this collaborative approach to funding as healthy because it spreads the financial burden and broadens the base of support. We hope these partnerships will expand.

Strategically, one road to expansion would be to move the generic family support concept to a higher priority when funders review options. Many funding sources, particularly corporations, identify a specific need and make heavy contributions toward alleviating that social ill. Because of its more generic nature, family support may be somewhat less concrete and more difficult to understand. Nonetheless, we encourage foundations and corporations to don a more holistic, ecologically oriented cap and envision a priority called family support. Fragile family support efforts need and merit this recognition.

Clarify the Governmental Role

Many contributors to this volume have addressed the general issue of governmental responsibility to children and families and the specific issue of supporting family well-being. The responses have run the gamut from those who feel that there should be a national commitment to family support programs—that they should sit side-by-side with schools and parks as a part of a community's natural repertoire of services (Weissbourd, this volume)—to those who feel that the government should provide incentives to see that exemplary programs are established. Garbarino (this volume) suggests that where children, particularly high-risk youngsters, are concerned, the community and the parent should share joint custody; as the parent is to the child, so must the community be to the parent. A partnership between adults and communities, and between adults and their government, is desirable.

Our vision of government's role in society extends beyond maintaining national security and expediting mail delivery. We believe that government has a definite responsibility to children and families. Since it is clear to us that a network of informal support programs, no matter how comprehensive, cannot provide the infrastructure to prevent economic dependency, we endorse a broad systems approach, one that incorporates informal supports like family support programs as well as formal social support. Moroney stated it well: "Support systems cannot now or in the future provide income supports, housing, and jobs on a continuous basis." (this volume, p. 35). So, federal funding of family support programs is not an alternative to federal funds currently allocated to social services. A policy stance that encourages and provides *both* formal and informal support must be developed. The government cannot retreat and leave informal supports to the private sector for several reasons. The private sector, as we have seen, is not in a position to support informal efforts unilaterally. In addition, in order for informal efforts to flourish to the extent that they might reduce expenditures for formal efforts, they must be widespread. Twenty family support programs may affect the lives of involved families, but they will not significantly affect social service expenditures in the United States. A wider proliferation of family support programs, because of their cost effectiveness, may well reduce formal program expenditures over time.

The best strategy for the federal government is, first, to recognize the importance of family support programs for families currently being served and acknowledge their viability in preventing families from becoming dependent on the social service system; and, second, to foster the development of such programs. We suggest that the government reinvigorate its family focus within the Administration for Children, Youth and Families and that a special office be designated and funded to examine the current status of family support programs and develop an action agenda to strengthen these efforts. Such an agenda would include developing plans to solidify the funding for family support programs—perhaps through public-private collaborations, trust funds, or other innovative partnerships. Through a series of matching funds, the government could provide incentives for public/private collaboration in the establishment of family support programs. Ideally, all communities would have resources available to fund such programs, but where private sector funds or partnerships were not forthcoming, an entitlement mechanism would be established.

The special office would also be a repository for data related to family support programs and would promote research by funding a research network along with the work of individual scholars. The office would disseminate these research results, along with the evaluation results of demonstration efforts funded by the bureau. Further, the office should take initiative in helping foundations realize their role in family support by, for example, sponsoring a national conference that would bring together representatives from our nation's local foundations. At such a conference, the value of the family support movement could be emphasized and foundations encouraged to establish family support networks in their own geographic locales. Clearly, the government must do all it can to accelerate the growth of family support. Above all, its rhetoric on the central position of the family in American life should be fortified by active policies and practices that stimulate local familly support efforts. It is our contention that government funds, well spent, can go a long way toward improving the lives of families in this country.

Family support programs today are alive and well. They have come a long way since the days of quilting bees, church meetings, and gatherings at the general store. They now serve diverse populations, meet real needs, hep prevent the growth of critical problems, and contribute to the healthy functioning of America's families. Family support programs possess potential that we are only beginning to comprehend. But in order to flourish, they must nourish and be nourished. They must provide services and develop an advocacy constituency. In short, like families themselves, they must support and be supported in order to survive and to thrive.

REFERENCES

Adams, L. T. (1985, February). Changing employment patterns of organized workers. *Monthly Labor Review, 108* (2), 25.

Cochran, M., & Woolever, F. (1983). Beyond the deficit model: The empowerment of parents with information and informal support. In I. Sigal (Ed.), *Changing families* (pp. 225–247). New York: Plenum Press.

Hewlett, S. A. (1986). *A lesser life: The myth of women's liberation in America.* New York: Morrow.

Moynihan, D. P. (1986). *Family and nation.* New York: Harcourt, Brace Jovanovich.

Pinker, R. (1973). *Social theory and social policy.* London: Heinemann.

Pizzo, P. (1983). *Parent to parent.* Boston: Beacon.

EDITORS

Sharon L. Kagan is associate director of the Yale Bush Center in Child Development and Social Policy and is assistant professor of education at the Child Study Center at Yale University. Formerly a Head Start and Project Developmental Continuity director, Dr. Kagan, currently on leave from Yale, is director of the Mayor's Office of Early Childhood Education, New York City. She has lectured and written in areas of child care, educational policy, and parent involvement. She has recently coedited with Edward Zigler and Edgar Klugman *Children, Families and Government: Perspectives on American Social Policy* and, with Edward Zigler, is coediting *Early Schooling: The National Debate.*

Douglas R. Powell is associate professor of Child Development and Family Studies at Purdue University. He has developed and directed an innovative neighborhood-based educational support program for parents of young children. Previously, Dr. Powell was a faculty member and director of Program Development at the Merrill-Palmer Institute and an associate professor of Human Development at Wayne State University, Detroit. His work on interactions between families and day care centers, on parents' social networks, and on parents' strategies for finding child care has been published in books and journals. He is at present research editor of *Young Children.*

Bernice Weissbourd is founder and president of Family Focus, a program for parents and prospective parents, and the Family Resource Coalition, a national network of family support programs. She is a contributing editor to *Parents* magazine and has coauthored *Infants: Their Social Environments* (1981) and *Creating Drop-in Centers: The Family Focus Model* (1979). She has also written numerous articles on family support and child care. Formerly vice-president of the National Association for the Education of Young Children, Mrs. Weissbourd is also a member of the Board of the National Center for Clinical Infant Programs and the Child Care Action Campaign. She has received many awards including the Chicago YWCA Outstanding Leadership Award, the Chicago UNICEF World of Children Award, and the National Forum on Women's Outstanding Leadership Award.

Edward F. Zigler is Sterling Professor of Psychology and Director of the Bush Center in Child Development and Social Policy at Yale University. He served as the first director of the U.S. Office of Child Development and was Chief of the Children's Bureau in the U.S. Department of Health, Education and Welfare. Serving on many presidential commissions and panels, Dr. Zigler was a member of the original Head Start Planning Committee and led the presidentially appointed committee on the future of Head Start. Dr. Zigler has served as a government consultant in the United States and abroad and is the author of several books and numerous articles. Dr. Zigler received the 1982 Distinguished Contributions to Psychology in the Public Interest Award from the American Psychological Association and the C. Anderson Aldrich Award in Child Development from the American Academy of Pediatrics in 1985.

CONTRIBUTORS

Urie Bronfenbrenner is Jacob Gould Schurman Professor of Human Development and Family Studies and professor of psychology at Cornell University. In 1986, the American Psychological Association awarded him the G. Stanley Hall Medal, the highest scientific award in the field of Developmental Psychology. One of the founders of Head Start, Dr. Bronfenbrenner was recently honored by The Society for Research in Child Development for his outstanding contributions to science and social policy. Professor Bronfenbrenner's book *The Ecology of Human Development: Experiments by Nature and Design* (1979) received the 1981 Anisfield-Wolf Award in Race Relations.

Donald T. Campbell is best known for his work on research methods for nonlaboratory settings, exemplified in *Experimental and Quasi-Experimental Design for Research* (1966, coauthored with Julian C. Stanley) and *Quasi-Experimentation* (1979, coauthored with Thomas D. Cook). He was president of the American Psychological Association in 1975, and has been the recipient of distinguished scientific contribution awards from that organization, the American Education Research Association, the Evaluation Research Society and the Eastern Evaluation Research Society. He is also a member of the National Academy of Sciences. At present, he is University Professor of Social Relations, Psychology, and Education at Lehigh University.

Marilee Comfort received her Ph.D. in Special Education at the University of North Carolina at Chapel Hill. Her clinical and research experience involves early intervention with families of young children with developmental handicaps. Currently, she is a postdoctoral fellow in maternal and child health at The Johns Hopkins University School of Hygiene and Public Health.

Johanna Freedman is a research assistant at the Bush Center in Child Development and Social Policy at Yale University.

James Garbarino is president of the Erikson Institute for Advanced Study in Child Development in Chicago. Formerly Associate Professor of Human Development at Pennsylvania State University and a Fellow and Director of the Maltreatment of Youth Project at the Center for the Study of Youth Development at Boys Town, Dr. Garbarino is the author of *The Psychologically Battered Child; Protecting Children from Abuse and Neglect; Creating and Maintaining Family Support Systems; Understanding Abusive Families; Children and Families in the Social Environment; Troubled Youth, Troubled Families; Adolescent Development: An Ecological Perspective;* and *Successful Schools and Competent Students.* In 1985 he received the first C. Henry Kempe Award from the National Conference on Child Abuse and Neglect for "the outstanding professional contribution to the field."

Shirley Jenkins is professor of social research at the Columbia University School of Social Work. Her interests lie in child welfare, ethnicity, and social policy. She directed the Family Welfare Research Program and was senior author of two books based on that study: *Filial Deprivation and Foster Care* (1972) and *Beyond Placement: Mothers View Foster Care* (1975). Her studies on ethnicity resulted in her latest book, *The Ethnic Dilemma in Social Services* (1981). Her forthcoming book is entitled *Ethnic Associations and the Welfare State.*

Robert Moroney, a professor of Social Policy and Planning at the School of Social Work, Arizona State University, has masters degrees in Social Work (Boston College) and Public Health (Harvard) and a doctoral degree in Social Policy (Heller School, Brandeis University). He is the author of five books on family policy, planning, and program evaluation and does extensive consultation with various state and local human service agencies.

Susan Muenchow is acting director of the Governor's Constituency for Children in Florida. She was previously a research associate in the Department of Psychology at Yale University and head of the Section in Public Education and Media of the Yale Bush Center in Child Development and Social Policy. She has also worked as a journalist specializing in social service issues for the *Christian Science Monitor, Time,* and *Parents Magazine.*

Peggy Pizzo has an extensive background in public policy affairs related to maternal and child welfare. Author of *Parent to Parent,* a book on family support systems, she is an affiliate faculty member of the Bush Center at Yale University. Ms. Pizzo has served as Associate Director for Human Resources on the White House Domestic Policy Staff and as Special Assistant to the Commissioner at the Department of Health and Human Services' Administration for Children, Youth and Families. Ms. Pizzo was listed in Outstanding Young Women of America in 1976 and 1981.

Victoria Seitz is a research scientist at the Yale University Child Study Center and the Department of Psychology. She is on the editorial board of *Child Development* and *Review of Research in Education* and has been a consultant to federal, state, and local organizations, most recently as a member of the Program Evaluation Task Group of the National Center for Clinical Infant Programs. A recipient of numerous research grants and awards, Dr. Seitz' research interests include studies of the effects of intervention programs for high-risk children and families and studies of the consequences of adolescent motherhood for the teenagers and their children.

Alexandra Shelley received her B.A. from Yale University in English literature with a concentration in psychology. She has worked with children in treatment settings, as well as Head Start programs. She was a research and editorial assistant in the Bush Center in Child Development and Social Policy at Yale and is now a reporter for the *East Hampton Star.*

Jack P. Shonkoff is associate professor of Pediatrics and director of the Child Development Service at the University of Massachusetts Medical School. He has served as a consultant and panel member for the Committee on Child Development Research and Public Policy of the National Academy of Sciences. Dr. Shonkoff is on the editorial boards of *Child Development, Infant Mental Health Journal,* and the *Journal of Child Neurology.* He is a member of the Board of Directors of the National Center for Clinical Infant Programs and is the principal investigator and project director of the *Early Intervention Collaborative Study.*

Lois Pall Wandersman is a developmental and clinical child psychologist who has developed several parent education and support programs for parents of newborns. She is currently adjunct assistant professor of psychology and research assistant professor of preventive medicine and community health at the University of South Carolina.

Heather B. Weiss is director of the Harvard Family Research Project and research associate at the Department of Human Development, Harvard Graduate School of Education. She was director and co-principal investigator for the Family Support Project at Yale University and was a research associate in psychology at the Yale Bush Center in Child Development and Social Policy. She is coeditor of *Evaluating Family Programs* (1987) and the coauthor of several articles on family support theory, policies, programs, and evaluation.

Ronald Wiegerink, professor of special education and administration at the University of North Carolina at Chapel Hill, has been conducting child-development and parent-education research since 1965 and is currently focusing on parent involvement and school improvement at the Frank Porter Graham Child Development Center and the Research Triangle Institute.

Kenton Williams is the Regional Administrator for the Office of Human Development Services in Boston. Prior to moving to this position in 1978, Dr. Williams was the Regional Administrator for the Office of Human Development Services in Kansas City, Missouri. He has served as assistant regional director in the Office of Child Development in Kansas City, executive director of the Niles Home for Children, director of the Division Social Services for the State of Nebraska, and district administrator with the Department of Children and Family Services for the State of Illinois.

INDEX